W9-ANP-804

AMERICA IN VIETNAM

AMERICA IN VIETNAM

A DOCUMENTARY HISTORY

Edited with commentaries by

William Appleman Williams
Thomas McCormick
Lloyd Gardner
and Walter LaFeber

ANCHOR BOOKS
ANCHOR PRESS / DOUBLEDAY
GARDEN CITY, NEW YORK
1985

"An Irony of History" Copyright © 1975 by Newsweek, Inc. All rights reserved. Reprinted by permission.

Library of Congress Cataloging in Publication Data
Main entry under title:

America in Vietnam.

Includes bibliographical references and index.
1. Vietnamese Conflict, 1961–1975—United States.
2. Vietnamese Conflict, 1961–1975—Sources.
I. Williams, William Appleman.
DS558.A44   1985   959.704'3   84-9321
ISBN 0-385-19752-7
     0-385-19201-0 (pbk)

Copyright © 1985 by William Appleman Williams, Thomas McCormick,
Lloyd Gardner, and Suzanne LaFeber
All Rights Reserved
Printed in the United States of America
First Edition

CONTENTS

It is time we recognized that ours, in truth, was a noble cause.

—Ronald Reagan, Republican presidential
nominee, discussing Vietnam in August 1980

The legacies of Vietnam hold hostage millions of Americans who have neither seen nor heard of that faraway land: millions whose lives are ravaged by an economy still reeling from a trillion-dollar war, millions whose faith in America has so eroded that we are as gypsies—without sense of national purpose. One day, in another faraway place, other teenage Americans may fight and die for a reason as criminal as our mere reluctance to discuss Vietnam. For if we do not speak of it, others will surely rewrite the script. Each of the body bags, all of the mass graves will be reopened and their contents abracadabra-ed into a noble cause.

—George Swiers, returned Vietnam veteran,
writing in *Vietnam Reconsidered: Lessons
From a War,* edited by Harrison E. Salisbury
(New York, 1984)

INTRODUCTION
The Tangled Lines of Cause and Consequence
William Appleman Williams

These essays, each illuminated by extensive documents, are offered to encourage and help you confront and consider the causes, character, and consequences of American intervention in the Vietnamese revolution against colonialism and the ensuing civil war.

It is a complicated and convoluted story. To begin with, it is not true that the United States was ignorant of, or indifferent to, Vietnam until near the end of World War II. But it is correct to say that our concern with Vietnam was largely defined in terms of our traditional involvement in the Pacific—particularly with China and the East Indies. In the broadest sense, therefore, our approach to Vietnam was highly influenced by the ideological and economic forces that defined our policy toward China.

Hence from the beginning we came into conflict with various other powers, most especially Russia and Japan. About a century ago, Vietnam eased its way into those complications. We were worried about the French nibbling away in the south as Russia and Japan bit off chunks in the north. Thus the confrontations over China influenced our policies in Europe, as when in 1898–1901, as well as at the end of World War II, our concern with Russia influenced our dealings with France in Vietnam. And, unhappily, we must consider the degree to which American racial prejudices, along with our trauma about socialism and communism, affected all those relationships.

In a fundamental sense, therefore, the history of American intervention in Vietnam is a story of how we shifted from viewing that tiny country as a means to another end—our position in China, the East Indies, and Europe—to defining it as an end in and of itself. Such a sea change is never wholly, perhaps not even largely, a conscious or rational process. A philosopher might classify American intervention in

Vietnam as a particularly revealing example of the general proposition of Misplaced Concreteness. We allowed a secondary issue to become a primary issue.

For all those reasons, no one book of essays and documents can untangle the snarled lines of causes and consequences. Our purpose is to help you reach your own conclusions by providing documents about the tragedy of American intervention in Vietnam. As historians, we have also written introductory essays that provide both a context for the documents and some of our own views about that tragedy—views which you can, after carefully studying the documents, either accept or replace with your own conclusions about this tragedy.

Part I

THE ROOTS OF
INTERVENTION

1776–1945

VIETNAM AND MAINLAND SOUTHEAST ASIA
1954 – 1975

C H I N A

RED R.

NORTH VIETNAM

• Mandalay

BURMA

• Dien Bien Phu

Hanoi

RED R.

• Haiphong

MEKONG R.

Luang Prabang

Thanh Hoa

GULF OF TONKIN

HAINAN (CHINA)

L A O S

• Chiang Mai

MEKONG R.

• Vientiane

17° (PARTITION LINE) 1954-1975)

• Rangoon

• Hue

• Da Nang

THAILAND

• Pleiku

• Bangkok

CAMBODIA (KAMPUCHEA)

SOUTH VIETNAM

• Cam Ranh

• Phnom Penh

MEKONG R.

ANDAMAN SEA

• Saigon

(after 1975: Ho Chi Minh City)

• Kompong Som

MEKONG DELTA

GULF OF THAILAND

SOUTH

CHINA SEA

MALAYSIA

N

W   E

S

SUMATRA (INDONESIA)

0   MILES   300

0   KM   300

palacios

INTRODUCTION
William Appleman Williams

I

No one can be certain, but it is highly probable that the first Americans to reach what we now call Vietnam were various masters and sailors who, seduced by the lure of wealth and adventure, became international pirates during King William's War (1689–97). They returned with gold and silver and other exotic wealth to flaunt their success in the streets of Boston and other ports south to Charleston. They indulged themselves in colorful and garish costumes, and made bold advances to women of all classes.

As dramatized by the daring exploits of Francis Drake and John Hawkins, piracy was one of the cutting edges of English and American capitalism and empire. The ultimate objective, however, was to create an ordered system involving the coordinated exploitation of resources, labor, and markets on a global scale. As part of that process, Americans became regularly engaged in trade with China and Southeastern Asia as a member of the British Empire.

Such imperial expansion helped strengthen the American colonies, and ultimately encouraged them to strike for independence. One of the prices of winning the Revolutionary War, however, was losing most of the economic and naval benefits of being part of the British Empire. Americans had to find new markets, raw materials, and other trading goods through their own efforts. Robert Morris of Philadelphia (supported by a group of New York merchants) was probably the first capitalist to open an American vista on the Far East. His venture capital ship, the *Empress of China,* sailed on George Washington's birthday in 1784, and, ironically enough, was guided by the French through the dangerous passages from the East Indies past Vietnam to Canton.

The voyage turned a profit ($37,727 on an investment of $120,000).

3

That was not quite enough to secure a family fortune, but it stimulated a great boom in the trade and prompted vigorous efforts to induce the government to provide various forms of public (taxpayer) assistance for private enterprise.

The Congress saluted the *Empress,* for example, in a resolution that expressed "its peculiar satisfaction in the successful issue of this first effort . . . to establish a direct trade with China." Such business was subsidized by various exemptions on import duties; and in 1800 the frigate *Essex* was dispatched to Asian seas to protect the expanding American commerce. Although the profits—and related political and ideological dreams—were disturbed by the War of 1812 between the United States and Great Britain, the naval contingent was enhanced in 1818 by the addition of the thirty-six-gun frigate *Congress* and, a bit later, by the *Vincennes* (the first naval ship to circumnavigate the globe).

Americans concentrated their attention on China. They did negotiate a treaty with Siam (now Thailand), but neglected Vietnam. The French soon exploited that oversight and thus began their penetration of China from the south. That would sooner rather than later evoke warnings from some American diplomats, but nevertheless the main thrust of American expansion was directed into China.

II

The profits of the trade with China reinforced the belief that the expansion of the marketplace would secure the prosperity and welfare of the United States. Many people also assumed that such an extension of America's exceptional capitalism would generate freedom, democracy, and cultural progress throughout the world. Others thought that it was necessary—or at least prudent—to make a concerted effort to export their ideas and ideals—even their dreams. Thus ideology was from the beginning married to economics.

Americans were not unique in their propensity to integrate religious and secular ideas with countinghouse calculations in the process of extending their influence into other cultures. If one wishes to be unique, after all, one ceases to be imperial. In our dealings with Asia, therefore, we Americans were simply part of the general Western European penetration of the rest of the world; a penetration designed to assert our particular culture over other cultures.

An early example was provided by the Reverend Peter Parker. He neatly combined religion and strategic concerns in his 1857 proposal to establish a protectorate over Formosa (now Taiwan). His views (Doc. 1) nicely reveal the marriage between commerce and Christianity, and between humanity and profit.

Secular leaders developed their own ceremony of empire. They argued that the triumph of American commerce would transform backward Asian cultures into copies of Western civilization. Consider the argument advanced by Senator Thomas Hart Benton of Missouri. His vision was focused on Asia as "a boundless field, dazzling and bewildering the imagination from its vastness and importance." (Doc. 2.)

One of Benton's more fervent acolytes was William Gilpin of Philadelphia. He was born into the upper reaches of American wealth and political power, and distinguished himself as a front-line trooper in the battles of American expansion against the First Americans and the Mexicans. Gilpin was concerned "to cause a stagnant people to be reborn" (Doc. 3), but it is not surprising that his revelation was translated into the language of profit by many businessmen.

One of those was Asa Whitney, a New Englander who became a New York merchant. Having lost one fortune, Whitney went off to Asia and returned with enough money to buy time to make more money and to think grand thoughts about imperial philosophy and strategy. "Here we stand forever," Whitney proclaimed in 1848; "we reach out one hand to all Asia, and the other to all Europe, willing for all to enjoy the great blessings we possess, claiming free intercourse and exchange of commodities with all, seeking not to subjugate any, but all . . . tributary, and at our will subject to us."

Given Whitney's intelligence, wit, and will, the irony was probably intentional. In any event, Whitney's "one hand to Asia" soon became (1853–54) Commodore Matthew Perry's Black Squadron off Tokyo. That display of force was less important because of the immediate profits it produced than for the way it incited the Japanese to mimic Western powers and intensify the competition to control China.

The ultimate Japanese thrust through China into Malaysia (1937–41) was a pivotal event in America's involvement in World War II and in Vietnam, but the French intrusion into that area set the stage for that confrontation. Many centuries earlier the regions of Tonkin and Annam were known as the Chinese province of Giao Chi. But the relationship was always tenuous and violent, and the Vietnamese struggle for autonomy continued with fluctuating fortunes until the middle years of the nineteenth century, when the French arrived with superior firepower. Though they were in many respects defeated, the determination of the Vietnamese to continue their struggle for independence is apparent in the account of those battles provided by one of their historians. (Doc. 4.)

Western capitalist powers, including the United States, were slow to comprehend the consequences of their imperial policies. Their effort to integrate the so-called backward cultures into their own system inevitably produced resistance and competitors. Japan was the first nation to begin that education of the West. Less than two generations after the arrival of Perry's Black Squadron off Tokyo the Japanese defeated China and asserted their primacy in Manchuria and Korea (1894–95). Western powers promptly recognized the need to establish a set of rules for the imperial competition. A system had to be created. Otherwise there would be chaos.

III

Most Europeans, and the Japanese, initially favored dividing China and the rest of Asia into spheres of influence that might in time become colonies. Key American leaders were far more perceptive and tough-minded. Guided (if not indeed directed) by a relatively small group of keen-minded academics, sophisticated businessmen, and responsive politicians, the United States devised a strategy to keep China and Asia—and the rest of the world—open to its superior economic power and its ideology of freedom and democracy.

That approach, perfectly described by its spokesmen as an Open Door Policy (Doc. 5), was designed to establish new rules for imperial competition. Instead of colonies and spheres of influence, there would be a free marketplace in which it was assumed that the United States would emerge triumphant.

The proposal contained some contradictions. To begin with, the United States had declared (in 1823) that the western hemisphere was its sphere of influence. And in the course of its war against Spain (April–December 1898) the United States had established a protectorate over Cuba, and had annexed Puerto Rico, Hawaii, Guam, and the Philippines. The Japanese, among others, had legitimate reason to wonder about the substance behind Washington's rhetoric about an Open Door.

The most perceptive American leaders understood the problem. Japan had somehow to be integrated into a system that kept China independent yet at the same time subject to American influence. It was all very complicated; indeed even convoluted. Having taken the lead in forcing Japan into the modern capitalist system, American leaders had to deal with the harsh truth that Japan lacked both the resources and the market to function as a capitalist political economy. The choices were stark. Either:

One. Japan would have to be guaranteed access to such resources and markets; or

Two. Japan would move to secure its own access through the threat or the use of force; or

Three. Japan would have to be stopped by the use of force in its program of Westernization in order to save China and the rest of Asia for modernization under American leadership and control.

Those choices were soon complicated by the rising opposition to the capitalist idiom of modernization. Radical revolutionaries challenged the established system in Mexico and China (1910–11), and then made an avowedly Communist revolution in Russia (1917). Such turmoil intensified the dilemma faced by American policy-makers in dealing with Japan and the rest of Asia.

They could try to work with the more moderate elements in Japanese politics to devise a way of sharing the capitalist development of China and other parts of Asia. They could provide Japan with some of its basic needs, as with steel and oil. They could acquiesce as Japan used force to acquire such resources and markets. Or they could go to war. The option of supporting alternative modes of modernization in China and elsewhere was never seriously explored. American leaders closed down their choices and suffered the consequences.

To complicate matters even further, American leaders were primarily concerned in the short run to save the center of the capitalist system in Western Europe. Thus they defined Nazi Germany as the primary enemy. The United States went to war in the North Atlantic sea lanes long before the Japanese attacked Pearl Harbor. The cross-purposes became complicated. For in order to preserve Western European capitalism, the United States had to try to save the Far Eastern colonies and spheres of influence of their allies; and yet also had to try to maintain the principle and establish the practice of the Open Door Policy, which was designed to secure American access to the resources and labor of China and Southeastern Asia.

Even then, American leaders were chasing the nightmare of a global Pax Americana. It was a mindless hunger that led first to war with Japan, second to opposition to the Chinese Revolution, third to war in Korea, and finally to intervention in Vietnam.

IV

No intelligent and responsible leaders want to fight a two-front global war. Hence American leaders sought to postpone a confrontation with Japan until the Russians had stopped the Germans, and until the United States was prepared to defeat the Japanese in a short war. It was truly an imperial nightmare because America had to support its European allies in Asia. Thus American leaders steadily increased the economic and political pressure on Japan while at the same time directing most of their aid to Europe in 1940–41.

The Japanese recognized and exploited that discrepancy and moved south through China into Vietnam. The Americans had trapped themselves. They had to draw a line in Southeastern Asia while at the same time committing their primary energies to Europe. The State Department offered a hardheaded explanation: "our general diplomatic and strategic position would be considerably weakened—by our loss of Chinese, Indian and South Seas markets (and by our loss of much of the Japanese market for our goods, as Japan would become more and more self-sufficient) as well as by insurmountable restrictions upon our access to the rubber, tin, jute, and other vital materials of the Asian and Oceanic regions."

That was straightforward imperial talk. Candid and responsible. President Roosevelt wanted the fruits of imperialism without the costs of imperialism. It is a kind of charming nightmare. Back there in January 1941 he talked about American war aims (even though he was professing not to take the country into war): freedom of religion, freedom of speech, freedom from want, and freedom from fear.

It was a speech that implicitly recognized the power of the revolutions in Mexico, China, and even Russia. Roosevelt's war aims were designed to preempt those revolutions for a Pax Americana. But it was a dangerous game. Talking about revolution without being prepared to make a revolution is a prescription for trouble. Roosevelt was quickly called on the implications of such rhetoric by Henry Robinson Luce. He asserted with considerable logic and force that such freedoms could be established only by the exercise of American power to create what Luce candidly called "The American Century." (Doc. 6.)

Perhaps the most telling comment on all such rhetoric—and fantasy —was provided by John Chamberlain, a once-upon-a-time-radical who had become a wry conservative writing for Luce's *Time, Life,* and *Fortune.* Responding explicitly to Luce's sermon, and implicitly to all such exhortations about imperial wonderlands, Chamberlain offered this bit of wisdom. Such dreams are all very well, he noted, even uplifting, so long "as we do not waste too much of our blood and substance trying to control the course of events in parts of the world that are beyond our effective reach."

There is implicit in Chamberlain's remark the proposition that impe-rialism is defensible as long as it works. That is a worthy subject for another essay, perhaps even another book, but for the moment let us reflect upon the degree to which President Roosevelt was inclined to embrace that proposition in dealing with Vietnam after the defeat of the Japanese. Roosevelt initially thought that Vietnam (Indochina in general) was within his reach, and proposed to transform that French colony into a trusteeship that would become at some unspecified time in the future an independent country. (Doc. 7.)

The Vietnamese had a different approach. (Doc. 8.) So did other Americans. The military, for example, did not want to prejudice their hunger to control various other pieces of real estate in the Pacific. And liberal as well as conservative critics argued that the greater part of imperial wisdom involved allowing the French to reestablish their power in Indochina. (Doc. 9.)

It seems doubtful that Roosevelt changed his mind about his prefer-ences, but he did reluctantly acknowledge that Vietnam was beyond his reach. (Doc. 10.) Much to his frustration, the President was caught in that corner of history when an empire confronts its limits. He did not handle it candidly. He had a way of sliding off such important matters. He should have talked straight to the American people, telling them that no one, not even Americans, could control the future of the entire world.

And so we continued with the nightmare of the American Century. It was a beguiling fantasy, a rational absurdity that we could draw lines on the map. A self-indulgent arrogance that we were preparing benighted peoples "for the duties and responsibilities of self-government."

And so to war in Vietnam.

1. PETER PARKER
TO THE STATE DEPARTMENT

This dispatch from Dr. Peter Parker to the State Department dated February 12, 1857, reveals the direct connections between missionaries and the government. The second, supplementary item, of March 10, 1857, exposes his secular appreciation of imperial politics. Later, in Doc. 5, we will see how the government was developing a more sophisticated way of establishing American power and influence in Asia. (Source: U.S. Senate, *Correspondence of the Late Commissioners to China* [Washington, 1859].)

Next, a note about sources and citations. All the government documents offered in this section come from the various manuscript archives of the United States Government. As often as possible, however, I have cited them from others who have printed them in places more easily available to teachers, students, and the general public. This convenience is wholly within the law and the doctrine of fairness. Public documents cannot by definition be copyrighted for the personal benefit of any citizen.

Finally, it is fitting in this first instance to salute Tyler Dennett. He published a book called *Americans in Eastern Asia* back in 1922 (later reprinted in 1941). One of the pleasures of doing this collection of essays and documents involved being once again reminded of how very good he was as a historian, and how his keen perceptions have survived the test of time. He cared, and our leaders should have paid more attention to his insights.

DR. PETER PARKER TO THE SECRETARY OF STATE, FEBRUARY 12, 1857.

The subject of Formosa is becoming one of great interest to a number of our enterprising fellow-citizens, and deserves more consideration from the great commercial nations of the West than it has yet received; and it is much to be hoped that the Government of the United States may not *shrink* from the *action* which the interests of humanity, civilization, navigation and commerce impose upon it in relation to Tai-Wan, particularly the southeastern portion of it, at present inhabited by savages, to whose depraved cruelties we have every reason to believe many Europeans, and among them our own friends and countrymen, have fallen victims.

DR. PETER PARKER TO THE SECRETARY OF STATE, MARCH 10, 1857.

Great Britain has her St. Helena in the Atlantic, her Gibraltar and Malta in the Mediterranean, her Aden in the Red Sea, Mauritius, Ceylon, Penang and Singapore in the Indian Ocean, and Hongkong in the China Sea. If the United States is so disposed and can arrange for the possession of Formosa, England certainly cannot object.

2. SPEECH BY THOMAS HART BENTON: TAKE THE ROAD TO INDIA

Speech by Senator Thomas Hart Benton on February 7, 1849. The basic document is from the *Congressional Globe*. The context and significance were first revealed by Henry Nash Smith in his book *Virgin Land*. (Source: Henry Nash Smith, *Virgin Land* [Cambridge, Mass., 1970], pp. 30–31.)

The trade of the Pacific Ocean, of the western coast of North America, and of Eastern Asia, will all take its track; and not only for ourselves, but for posterity. That trade of India which has been shifting its channels from the time of the Phoenicians to the present, is destined to shift once more, and to realize the grand idea of Columbus. The American road to India will also become the European track to that region. The European merchant, as well as the American, will fly across our continent on a straight line to China. The rich commerce of Asia will flow through our centre. And where has that commerce ever flowed without carrying wealth and dominion with it? . . . In no instance has it failed to carry the nation, or the people which possessed it, to the highest pinnacle of wealth and power, and with it the highest attainments of letters, arts, and sciences.

3. COMMENTARY FROM WILLIAM GILPIN: U.S. DESTINY IN THE PACIFIC

William Gilpin wrote several books, and made uncounted speeches, extolling the virtues of the American destiny in Asia. He was also cited, and quoted at length, in various government publications. (Source: William Gilpin, *Mission of the North American People, Geographical, Social, and Political* [Philadelphia, 1874 (quoting a letter of 1846)], p. 130.)

The *untransacted* destiny of the American people is to subdue the continent—to rush over this vast field to the Pacific Ocean—to animate the many hundred millions of its people, and to cheer them upward—to agitate these herculean masses—to establish a new order in human affairs —to regenerate superannuated nations—to stir up the sleep of a hundred centuries—to teach old nations a new civilization—to confirm the destiny of the human race—to carry the career of mankind to its culminating point—to cause a stagnant people to be reborn—to perfect science—to emblazon history with the conquest of peace—to shed a new and resplendent glory upon mankind—to unite the world in one social family—to dissolve the spell of tyranny and exalt charity—to absolve the curse that weighs down humanity, and to shed blessings round the world.

4. VIETNAMESE ACCOUNT OF FRENCH CONQUEST

This is a radical Vietnamese account of the French conquest of Vietnam. It is important because it reveals the deep national self-consciousness as well as the determination to resist both the Chinese and the French. (Source: Nguyen Khac Vien, *The Long Resistance (1858–1975)* [Hanoi, 1974], pp. 9–18.)

THE CAN VUONG MOVEMENT

On April 15, 1847, French warships sank five armoured junks of the Vietnamese fleet in Da Nang port. On August 31, 1858, a French squadron attacked Da Nang again, thus marking the beginning of a war of colonial conquest by French imperialism, to be waged in many stages from 1858 to 1884, until the total annexation of the country. Facing that aggression, there were, on the Vietnamese side, two parties with opposite views: one standing for compromise, the other for resistance. The king and the high dignitaries of the Court were frightened by the modern weapons used by the French and misjudged the latter's intentions, believing that, coming from so far away, they were less interested in conquering the country than in wresting commercial advantages. Moreover, the Nguyen monarchy, retrograde to the core and constantly busy repressing internal insurrections, was neither able nor willing to mobilize all the energies of the nation to oppose the aggression. All these reasons urged the king and the high dignitaries to practise a policy of peace and negotiation, trying to placate the aggressors with more and more important concessions. On the other hand, a number of mandarins, the great majority of the scholars, and the people as a whole, heirs to a long tradition of struggle for national independence, put up a fierce resistance. While the royal troops offered only weak resistance, that of the popular forces was powerful and protracted, and compelled French imperialism to wage a long and costly war. But the defection of the monarchy, the only force which could then play a guiding role on a national scale, undermined the efforts of the Vietnamese patriots.

The French colonialists used particularly cunning tactics. They began by gaining a foothold on a portion of the territory and having it ceded to them by the Court of Hue through a treaty in due form. The aggressors thus won a springboard to prepare for new annexations, and a respite to annihilate the people's resistance in the occupied zones. They then violated the treaty, and resumed the conquest. New concession by the Court, new treaty. New violation, new conquest. The same scenario recurred again and again until total annexation; from concession to concession the monarchy ended in capitulation and betrayal. The king and the high dignitaries preferred selling out national independence in exchange for a few privileges that the conquerors left them to win them over. Responsible for the safeguarding of national independence and honour, they gradually became agents of the foreigners and put themselves at the latter's service by repressing the people's patriotic movement. The support that the Court of Hue tried to obtain from the Chinese empire—itself on the

13

decline and exposed to Western aggressions—could not deviate the course of events.

LOSS OF SAIGON AND THE THREE EASTERN PROVINCES OF COCHINCHINA

After having occupied Da Nang, the French troops burnt it down, but were not strong enough to threaten the capital city and compel the Court of Hue to make concessions. Bishop Pellerin proposed to the French command to attack the Red River delta where 400,000 Catholics, he said, were ready to rise up in support of the operation. The French command, however, preferred taking its troops to the South, where rice trade was thriving.

Saigon was beleaguered on the morning of February 17, 1859; in the evening the royal troops evacuated it. Meanwhile, reinforcements were pouring in from the neighbouring provinces, among them 5,800 volunteers recruited by local notables. Thus reinforced, the Saigon garrison encircled the French troops who had entered the town, putting them in a difficult position. However, the Court of Hue did not order any counterattack, hoping for a compromise by negotiation. The French took advantage of this indecision to gain time. In 1860, after a new victorious offensive of the Western powers against China, France was able to concentrate the whole of its naval force operating in the Far East to break the siege of Saigon and conquer, in 1861, the three eastern provinces of Cochinchina, which comprised, besides, three western provinces.

The defeat of the royal troops did not put an end to the Vietnamese resistance. Under the direction of patriotic leaders, the population everywhere rose up against the French troops. The French officers who wrote the Military History of Indochina had to recognize that

The defeats of the Annamese army had no effect on the insurrectional state of the occupied territories.

The resistance was general. The French historian Pallu de la Barrière, an eye-witness, wrote:

The fact is that the resistance centre was everywhere, subdivided *ad infinitum,* nearly as many times as there were living Annamese. It would be more exact to consider each peasant who was fastening a sheaf of rice plants as a centre of resistance.

(History of the 1861 Cochinchina Expedition)

The popular character of the resistance was also seen in the change in tactics. Whereas the royal troops operated in close formations and greatly feared French long-range weapons, the popular forces practised guerilla warfare or surprise attacks with close combat. The troops commanded by the patriot Nguyen Trung Truc, attacking at close quarters, succeeded in setting fire to a French warship, *l'Espérance,* and inflicting on the French a bitter defeat at Nhat Tao. The popular forces managed to re-occupy many localities, and the French command had to ask for quick reinforcements.

It was the Court of Hue which got the French troops out of this fix by asking for negotiation. On June 5, 1862, Phan Thanh Gian negotiated with French Admiral Bonard a treaty by which the Court of Hue ceded to France the three eastern provinces of Cochinchina, consented to pay an indemnity of 20 million francs and open three ports of Annam and Tonkin to French trade. The Court immediately ordered the popular forces to withdraw from the aforesaid provinces.

The order was not obeyed. The French historian F. Vial wrote:

> At the very moment the admiral thought he had brought the war to a victorious end, he found that it had become perhaps even more active and redoubtable than a serious war against the King's regular troops.
>
> (The First Years of French Cochinchina)

The insurrection was led by Truong Dinh, who was head of an agricultural settlement when the French attacked Saigon. Together with volunteers he came to the rescue of the town. After its fall he withdrew to Go Cong province where he recruited a 6,000-strong army, and was appointed deputy-commander by the Court. After the signing of the 1862 treaty, the king ordered him to retire to An Giang province and give up the resistance (appointing him commander). Truong Dinh hesitated for a long time. A sincere patriot, he did not want to renounce the struggle, but, brought up as a Confucian, he did not feel he could disobey the king. He was about to obey the latter's order, when delegates of the popular forces and the people flocked to his camp and besought him to remain leader of the movement, dubbing him "Commander-in-Chief, Pacifier of the French." Truong Dinh complied with the people's will and took command of the insurrection.

The patriotic resisters fought heroically.

> The Annamese, armed with weapons ineffective against our carbines, rushed at our men with a blind energy that testified to a rare courage and extraordinary abnegation.
>
> (F. Vial, op. cit.)

Their guerilla tactics put the French troops to a hard test. Pallu de la Barrière wrote:

There is no more painful, dull and tiring sight than that of the French moving over land and water. One of the adversaries is continually in sight, the other never. As the enemy persistently slips away, it seems as though we were hitting only a vacuum.

(op. cit.)

Civil resistance was also organized in all forms. The majority of notables and mandarins refused to collaborate with the enemy. The poet Nguyen Dinh Chieu, though a blind man, left the occupied regions and, together with other scholars, wrote highly patriotic works.

However, the order coming from the Court to stop all resistance sowed confusion in the people's minds. It had sent to France a mission led by Phan Thanh Gian to negotiate the retrocession of the lost provinces. France then, entangled in the Mexican war, gave some promises. On August 20, 1864, Truong Dinh, wounded during an engagement, committed suicide in order not to fall into the enemy's hands. His son Truong Quyen continued the resistance. Meanwhile, in 1863, France had imposed a treaty of protectorate upon the king of Cambodia. Cambodian patriots, led by the bonze Pokumpo, then joined forces with the Vietnamese insurgents against the French.

In 1867, France, having settled the Mexican affair, switched to the offensive in Viet Nam. French troops marched on the three western provinces of Cochinchina. Judging all resistance to be hopeless, Phan Thanh Gian, the governor of these provinces, ceded them to the French, then committed suicide. Popular resistance in the western provinces brought together Vietnamese, Khmers and other nationalities—Cham, Mnong, Stieng—and covered a vast territory extending from the Cambodian Great Lakes to the vicinity of Saigon. From 1866 to 1868, fierce fighting occurred in Tay Ninh province, and Khmer insurgents came very close to Udong, the capital. Unfortunately Pokumpo was killed and the resistance in northwestern Cochinchina and the Cambodian border areas gradually died down. In the west of the Mekong delta two of Phan Thanh Gian's sons took the lead of the popular movement, while the patriot Nguyen Trung Truc, who had set fire to the frigate *l'Espérance* in 1861, conducted the operations. On June 16, 1868, in particular, he seized the Kien Giang post in Rach Gia province. Captured some time later, he refused to submit, and, facing the firing squad, cried out:

"As long as grass grows on our soil, there will be men to resist the invaders."

After the occupation of Cochinchina the French hastened to explore the Mekong river in the hope of draining all the trade of South China towards Saigon. This was soon proved impracticable.

16

THE EMBARRASSING PLIGHT OF THE COURT OF HUE. THE FALL OF HANOI

The loss of Cochinchina caused great concern in Viet Nam. Many patriots sent petitions to King Tu Duc advocating reforms apt to strengthen the defence potential of the country. Nguyen Truong To in particular recommended reforms in all fields: political, administrative, agricultural, commercial, industrial, educational, financial, diplomatic and military. Many urged that the country be opened to international trade, handicrafts renovated, industry and trade developed, the educational system changed, students sent abroad, and the army re-organized along Western lines.

The Court, stuck in its conservatism, refused to take those recommendations into consideration. Ignorant of the international situation, it did not know how to capitalize the difficulties encountered by France and wrest back the initiative of operations. With its policy of "peace and negotiation" it was still hoping to come to terms with the aggressor, and also counted on the support of the Manchu Ching dynasty, then reigning in China.

The deep reason for this conservatism and weakness lay in the fact that the reactionary feudal regime of the Nguyen was facing many popular uprisings. In 1862, near Hanoi, Cai Vang led a movement of protest against waste by the administration; in 1866 the workers and labourers employed in the construction of Tu Duc's tomb revolted. The French missionaries took advantage of this instability to foment unrest within Catholic communities in the Red River delta. This turmoil came to a head with Le Bao Hung's open rebellion.

Another difficulty was the penetration into Viet Nam from China of Taiping bands pursued by Ching troops. Taking refuge in Upper Tonkin, these bands, known as White, Yellow and Black Flags carved out fiefs for themselves. Only the Black Flags led by Luu Vinh Phuc submitted to the authority of the Court of Hue.

Thanks to the Catholic missionaries, the French command was well aware of this situation. The impossibility of reaching southwest China by the Mekong led the French to demand the opening of the Red River and the ports of Tonkin, if need be by force. In 1872, without asking for the permission of the Vietnamese authorities, hundreds of mercenaries headed by the French adventurer Dupuis sailed up the Red River towards Yunnan, carrying weapons for the Chinese general Ma. On his first trip, the mandarins showed conciliation, but on his second passage Dupuis was blocked.

17

The pretext which the French command had been looking for was immediately exploited. Lieutenant-Commander Francis Garnier was at once sent to Hanoi with an armed escort, and soon got in touch with Bishop Puginier, who gathered the routed partisans of the rebel Le Bao Hung. On his own authority, Francis Garnier decreed that henceforth sailing on the Red River was free and customs duties abolished. The Vietnamese authorities refused to comply with this dictate. On November 19, 1873, the French opened fire and seized Hanoi. The old General Nguyen Tri Phuong, defender of Hanoi, wounded and captured, rebuffed all advances by the French, and let himself die of starvation. The French troops rapidly seized Nam Dinh, Hai Duong and other localities in the delta, thanks to the complicity of some Catholic communities. But the Vietnamese forces counter-attacked and encircled Hanoi, and Garnier was killed on December 21, 1873, in an ambush in the vicinity of the town.

Still suffering from the effects of the 1870 French-German war, France stood in dread of committing herself too deeply. King Tu Duc, faithful to his policy of compromise, failed to exploit a favourable military situation; he signed with the French the 1874 treaty, by which France returned the conquered towns but obtained permission to garrison troops in Hanoi and Haiphong, as well as the opening of the Red River for trade.

THE CAPITULATION OF THE MONARCHY AND THE SETTING UP OF THE COLONIAL REGIME

In the last two decades of the 19th century, the Western capitalist economy rapidly developed, the European powers swooped on the other continents, and carried out a partition of the world. France's colonial policy, at times hesitant, began to be conducted in a more energetic and systematic way. The conquest of Burma by Britain speeded up the execution of French plans against Viet Nam.

Violating the 1874 treaty, in 1882 France sent to Tonkin new military units under the command of Henri Rivière. Declaring himself threatened by the "bellicose preparations" of the Vietnamese, he sent an ultimatum to the governor of Hanoi, demanding the destruction of the defence works, and the evacuation of the Vietnamese forces from the town. On April 25, 1882, the French troops attacked and seized Hanoi. Governor Hoang Dieu committed suicide. The mandarins in Tonkin wanted to counter-attack, but King Tu Duc still believed he could recover Hanoi through negotiation. Meanwhile, the French occupied the coal districts of Hon Gai and Cam Pha, then Nam Dinh. Tu Duc, who had little confidence in his own troops, called for help from the Court of Peking. The latter dispatched 10,000 men who came and camped northeast of Hanoi, but did not move any further.

As in 1873, the Vietnamese forces, encircling Hanoi, defeated the French troops in a battle near the town, killing Henri Rivière right at the place where Francis Garnier had died. Paris dispatched 4,000 reinforcement troops, but Tu Duc kept sounding out France for negotiations, and dismissed those mandarins who advocated armed struggle.

In July 1883, Tu Duc died without leaving an heir. In Hue, clans and factions scrambled for power. Within a few months, three kings were successively enthroned, while the high dignitaries were divided over what policy to adopt towards France. Some were partisans of armed resistance, others of negotiation, some openly planned betrayal and collaboration with the aggressors. The Court was not even aware of the military successes recorded in Tonkin by the Vietnamese forces.

Turning to account this confusion, the French command concentrated troops to seize Da Nang and march on Hue. As soon as they heard the boom of French artillery coming from the Thuan An channel which defended the access to the capital city, the mandarins hurriedly accepted all the conditions imposed by the French. Viet Nam, losing her sovereignty, became a French protectorate (August 25, 1883). The mandarins split into two groups. Many disobeyed the Court and resigned their posts so as to continue the resistance, while the remainder, bowing their heads, put themselves at the service of the French.

There remained the Ching troops, sent by the Peking Court which, seriously weakened, did not want a confrontation with France; Paris and Peking signed the Tientsin treaty (May 11, 1884). Regents Ton That Thuyet and Nguyen Van Tuong, hostile to the 1883 accord, had to resign themselves to ratifying the treaty of protectorate in June 1884. However, as the Ching troops withdrew through the Lang Son pass, they clashed at Bac Le with French troops, who were defeated. The French command launched a big attack on China, landed troops on Taiwan (Formosa), and bombarded Foochow port. The Vietnamese forces, co-operating with the Ching, inflicted another defeat on the French at Lang Son in February 1885.

But the Peking Court did not at all want to prolong the hostilities, and signed with France a new treaty (June 9, 1885) by which it renounced all its rights in Viet Nam.

5. THE OPEN DOOR POLICY

These three documents define the Open Door Policy. They are at once simple and majestic. They propose American rules for the imperial competition in Asia and elsewhere. We can be sure that Secretary of State John Hay knew that it would come down to a major war. But one must share with him his pleasure of telling the Germans in the third note that for the moment he had outmaneuvered everyone. (Source: Department of State, *Foreign Relations of the United States, 1899,* pp. 129–30; Ibid., 1900, pp. 299, 344.)

CIRCULAR LETTER OF SEPTEMBER 6, 1899.

. . . Earnestly desirous to remove any cause of irritation and to insure at the same time to the commerce of all nations in China the undoubted benefits which should accrue from a formal recognition by the various powers claiming "spheres of influence" that they shall enjoy perfect equality of treatment for their commerce and navigation within such "spheres," the Government of the United States would be pleased to see His German Majesty's Government give formal assurances and lend its cooperation in securing like assurances from the other interested powers that each within its respective sphere of whatever influence. . . .

First. Will in no way interfere with any treaty port or any vested interest within any so-called "sphere of interest" or leased territory it may have in China.

Second. That the Chinese treaty tariff of the time being shall apply to all merchandise within said "sphere of interest" (unless they be "free ports"), no matter to what nationality it may belong, and that duties so leviable shall be collected by the Chinese Government.

Third. That it will levy no higher harbor dues on vessels of another nationality frequenting any port in such "sphere" than shall be levied on vessels of its own nationality, and no higher railroad charges over lines built, controlled, or operated within its "sphere" on merchandise belonging to citizens or subjects of other nationalities transported through such "sphere" than shall be levied on similar merchandise belonging to its own nationals transported over equal distances. . . .

CIRCULAR LETTER OF JULY 3, 1900.

In this critical posture of affairs in China it is deemed appropriate to define the attitude of the United States as far as present circumstances permit this to be done. We adhere to the policy initiated by us in 1857, of peace with the Chinese nation, of furtherance of lawful commerce, and of protection of lives and property of our citizens by all means guaranteed under extraterritorial treaty rights and by the law of nations. If wrong be done to our citizens we propose to hold the responsible authors to the uttermost accountability. We regard the condition at Pekin as one of virtual anarchy. . . . The purpose of the President is, as it has been heretofore, to act concurrently with the other powers, first, in opening up communication with Pekin and rescuing the American officials, missionaries, and other Americans who are in danger; secondly, in affording all possible protection everywhere in China to American life and property; thirdly, in guarding and protecting all legitimate American interests; and fourthly, in aiding to prevent a spread of the disorders to the other provinces of the Empire and a recurrence of such disasters. It is, of course, too early to forecast the means of attaining this last result; but the policy of the government of the United States is to seek a solution which may bring about permanent safety and peace to China, preserve Chinese territorial and administrative entity, protect all rights guaranteed to friendly powers by treaty and international law, and safeguard for the world the principle of equal and impartial trade with all parts of the Chinese Empire. . . .

HAY TO THE GERMAN AMBASSADOR, OCTOBER 29, 1900.

I have the honor to acknowledge the receipt of your note of the 20th October informing me of the agreement arrived at by the Imperial [German] Ambassador Count von Hatzfeldt and Lord Salisbury [of Great Britain] on the 16th of this month, and inviting the acceptance by the United States of the principles therein laid down. These principles are:

1. It is a matter of joint and permanent international interest that the ports on the rivers and littoral of China should remain free and open to trade and to every other legitimate form of economic activity for the nationals of all countries without distinction, and the two Governments agree on their part to uphold the same for all Chinese territory, so far as they can exercise influence. . . .

The United States have heretofore made known their adoption of . . .

21

these principles. During the last year this Government invited the powers interested in China to join in an expression of views and purposes in the direction of impartial trade with that country and received satisfactory assurances to that effect from all of them. . . .

It is, therefore, with much satisfaction that the President directs me to inform you of the full sympathy of this Government with those of the German Emperor and Her Britannic Majesty in the principles set forth. . . .

6. LUCE'S AMERICAN CENTURY

This is one of the key documents in the history of American foreign relations since the Fall of France. It has echoed down through the rhetoric and policies of every president from Franklin Delano Roosevelt to Ronald Reagan. Written by Henry Luce, the founder and publisher of *Time, Life,* and *Fortune* magazines, it is at once a modern restatement of John Winthrop's sermon about America as the City on a Hill, and a secular call to deploy the power of the United States to realize that vision in China and elsewhere throughout the world.

Luce was not only presenting a powerful sermon that beautifully combined religious and secular themes; he was using the mass communications system that he had created to define the terms of the public and the policy debate. He was the first entrepreneur to manipulate the public consciousness. In this essay he was defining the question that could be asked, and in the process certified the answers that would be allowed into the dialogue. Luce was in that sense a genius. He trapped Americans into his definition of a City on a Hill.

Here are the crucial points of his essay. (Source: Henry R. Luce, *The American Century* [New York, 1941].)

In the field of national policy, the fundamental trouble with America has been, and is, that whereas their nation became in the 20th Century the most powerful and the most vital nation in the world, nevertheless Americans were unable to accommodate themselves spiritually and practically to that fact. Hence they have failed to play their part as a world power—a failure which has had disastrous consequences for themselves and for all mankind. And the cure is this: to accept wholeheartedly our duty and our opportunity as the most powerful and vital nation in the world and in consequence to exert upon the world the full impact of our influence, for such purposes as we see fit and by such means as we see fit.

"For such purposes as we see fit" leaves entirely open the question of what our purposes may be or how we may appropriately achieve them. Emphatically our only alternative to isolationism is not to undertake to police the whole world nor to impose democratic institutions on all mankind including the Dalai Lama and the good shepherds of Tibet.

America cannot be responsible for the good behavior of the entire world. But America is responsible, to herself as well as to history, for the world-environment in which she lives. Nothing can so vitally affect America's environment as America's own influence upon it, and therefore if America's environment is unfavorable to the growth of American life, then America has nobody to blame so deeply as she must blame herself.

In its failure to grasp this relationship between America and America's environment lies the moral and practical bankruptcy of any and all forms of isolationism. It is most unfortunate that this virus of isolationist sterility has so deeply infected an influential section of the Republican Party. For until the Republican Party can develop a vital philosophy and program for America's initiative and activity as a world power, it will continue to cut itself off from any useful participation in this hour of history. And its participation is deeply needed for the shaping of the future of America and of the world.

In 1919 we had a golden opportunity, an opportunity unprecedented in all history, to assume the leadership of the world—a golden opportunity handed to us on the proverbial silver platter. We did not understand that opportunity. Wilson mishandled it. We rejected it. The opportunity persisted. We bungled it in the 1920's and in the confusions of the 1930's we killed it.

To lead the world would never have been an easy task. To revive the hope of that lost opportunity makes the task now infinitely harder than it would have been before. Nevertheless, with the help of all of us, Roosevelt must succeed where Wilson failed.

THE 20TH CENTURY IS THE AMERICAN CENTURY
. . . SOME FACTS ABOUT OUR TIME

Consider the 20th Century. It is ours not only in the sense that we happen to live in it but ours also because it is America's first century as a dominant power in the world. So far, this century of ours has been a profound and tragic disappointment. No other century has been so big

23

with promise for human progress and happiness. And in no one century have so many men and women and children suffered such pain and anguish and bitter death.

It is a baffling and difficult and paradoxical century. No doubt all centuries were paradoxical to those who had to cope with them. But, like everything else, our paradoxes today are bigger and better than ever. Yes, better as well as bigger—inherently better. We have poverty and starvation—but only in the midst of plenty. We have the biggest wars in the midst of the most widespread, the deepest and the most articulate hatred of war in all history. We have tyrannies and dictatorships—but only when democratic idealism, once regarded as the dubious eccentricity of a colonial nation, is the faith of a huge majority of the people of the world.

And ours is also a revolutionary century. The paradoxes make it inevitably revolutionary. Revolutionary, of course, in science and in industry. And also revolutionary, as a corollary in politics and the structure of society. But to say that a revolution is in progress is not to say that the men with either the craziest ideas or the angriest ideas or the most plausible ideas are going to come out on top. The Revolution of 1776 was won and established by men most of whom appear to have been both gentlemen and men of common sense.

Clearly a revolutionary epoch signifies great changes, great adjustments. And this is only one reason why it is really so foolish for people to worry about our "constitutional democracy" without worrying or, better, thinking hard about the world revolution. For only as we go out to meet and solve for our time the problems of the world revolution, can we know how to re-establish our constitutional democracy for another 50 or 100 years.

This 20th Century is baffling, difficult, paradoxical, revolutionary. But by now, at the cost of much pain and many hopes deferred, we know a good deal about it. And we ought to accommodate our outlook to this knowledge so dearly bought. For example, any true conception of our world of the 20th Century must surely include a vivid awareness of at least these four propositions.

First: our world of 2,000,000,000 human beings is for the first time in history one world, fundamentally indivisible. Second: modern man hates war and feels intuitively that, in its present scale and frequency, it may even be fatal to his species. Third: our world, again for the first time in human history, is capable of producing all the material needs of the entire human family. Fourth: the world of the 20th Century, if it is to come to life in any nobility of health and vigor, must be to a significant degree an American Century.

As to the first and second: in postulating the indivisibility of the contemporary world, one does not necessarily imagine that anything like a world state—a parliament of men—must be brought about in this century. Nor need we assume that war can be abolished. All that it is necessary to feel—and to feel deeply—is that terrific forces of magnetic attraction and repulsion will operate as between every large group of human beings on this planet. Large sections of the human family may be effectively organized into opposition to each other. Tyrannies may require a large amount of living space. But Freedom requires and will require far greater living space than Tyranny. Peace cannot endure unless it prevails over a very large part of the world. Justice will come near to losing all meaning in the minds of men unless Justice can have approximately the same fundamental meanings in many lands and among many peoples.

As to the third point—the promise of adequate production for all mankind, the "more abundant life"—be it noted that this is characteristically an American promise. It is a promise easily made, here and elsewhere, by demagogues and proponents of all manner of slick schemes and "planned economies." What we must insist on is that the abundant life is predicated on Freedom—on the Freedom which has created its possibility—on a vision of Freedom under Law. Without Freedom, there will be no abundant life. With Freedom, there can be.

And finally there is the belief—shared let us remember by most men living—that the 20th Century must be to a significant degree an American Century. This knowledge calls us to action now.

No narrow definition can be given to the American internationalism of the 20th Century. It will take shape, as all civilizations take shape, by the living of it, by work and effort, by trial and error, by enterprise and adventure and experience.

And by imagination!

As America enters dynamically upon the world scene, we need most of all to seek and to bring forth a vision of America as a world power which is authentically American and which can inspire us to live and work and fight with vigor and enthusiasm. And as we come now to the great test, it may yet turn out that in all our trials and tribulations of spirit during the first part of this century we as a people have been painfully apprehending the meaning of our time and now in this moment of testing there may come clear at last the vision which will guide us to the authentic creation of the 20th Century—our Century.

Consider four areas of life and thought in which we may seek to realize such a vision:

First, the economic. It is for America and for America alone to determine whether a system of free economic enterprise—an economic order

25

compatible with freedom and progress—shall or shall not prevail in this century. We know perfectly well that there is not the slightest chance of anything faintly resembling a free economic system prevailing in this country if it prevails nowhere else. What then does America have to decide? Some few decisions are quite simple. For example: we have to decide whether or not we shall have for ourselves and our friends freedom of the seas—the right to go with our ships and our ocean-going airplanes where we wish, when we wish and as we wish. The vision of America as the principal guarantor of the freedom of the seas, the vision of America as the dynamic leader of world trade, has within it the possibilities of such enormous human progress as to stagger the imagination. Let us not be staggered by it. Let us rise to its tremendous possibilities. Our thinking of world trade today is on ridiculously small terms. For example, we think of Asia as being worth only a few hundred millions a year to us. Actually, in the decades to come Asia will be worth to us exactly zero—or else it will be worth to us four, five, ten billions of dollars a year. And the latter are the terms we must think in, or else confess a pitiful impotence.

Closely akin to the purely economic area and yet quite different from it, there is the picture of an America which will send out through the world its technical and artistic skills. Engineers, scientists, doctors, movie men, makers of entertainment, developers of airlines, builders of roads, teachers, educators. Throughout the world, these skills, this training, this leadership is needed and will be eagerly welcomed, if only we have the imagination to see it and the sincerity and good will to create the world of the 20th Century.

But now there is a third thing which our vision must immediately be concerned with. We must undertake now to be the Good Samaritan of the entire world. It is the manifest duty of this country to undertake to feed all the people of the world who as a result of this worldwide collapse of civilization are hungry and destitute—all of them, that is, whom we can from time to time reach consistently with a very tough attitude toward all hostile governments. For every dollar we spend on armaments, we should spend at least a dime in a gigantic effort to feed the world—and all the world should know that we have dedicated ourselves to this task. Every farmer in America should be encouraged to produce all the crops he can, and all that we cannot eat—and perhaps some of us could eat less—should forthwith be dispatched to the four quarters of the globe as a free gift, administered by a humanitarian army of Americans, to every man, woman and child on this earth who is really hungry.

But all this is not enough. All this will fail and none of it will happen unless our vision of America as a world power includes a passionate devotion to great American ideals. We have some things in this country which are infinitely precious and especially American—a love of freedom, a feeling for the equality of opportunity, a tradition of self-reliance and independence and also of co-operation. In addition to ideals and notions which are especially American, we are the inheritors of all the great principles of Western civilization—above all Justice, the love of Truth, the ideal of Charity. The other day Herbert Hoover said that America was fast becoming the sanctuary of the ideals of civilization. For the moment it may be enough to be the sanctuary of these ideals. But not for long. It now becomes our time to be the powerhouse from which the ideals spread throughout the world and do their mysterious work of lifting the life of mankind from the level of the beasts to what the Psalmist called a little lower than the angels.

America as the dynamic center of ever-widening spheres of enterprise, America as the training center of the skillful servants of mankind, America as the Good Samaritan, really believing again that it is more blessed to give than to receive, and America as the powerhouse of the ideals of Freedom and Justice—out of these elements surely can be fashioned a vision of the 20th Century to which we can and will devote ourselves in joy and gladness and vigor and enthusiasm.

Other nations can survive simply because they have endured so long—sometimes with more and sometimes with less significance. But this nation, conceived in adventure and dedicated to the progress of man—this nation cannot truly endure unless there courses strongly through its veins from Maine to California the blood of purposes and enterprise and high resolve.

Throughout the 17th Century and the 18th Century and the 19th Century, this continent teemed with manifold projects and magnificent purposes. Above them all and weaving them all together into the most exciting flag of all the world and of all history was the triumphal purpose of freedom.

It is in this spirit that all of us are called, each to his own measure of capacity, and each in the widest horizon of his vision, to create the first great American Century.

7. ROOSEVELT'S INDOCHINA TRUSTEESHIP: DREAM AND REALITY

There are many documents that establish Roosevelt's desire to punish the French and at the same time honor his own concern to establish the United States as a City on a Hill by placing Indochina under a trusteeship that might someday lead to independence. The following items establish those points. (Source: Samuel I. Rosenman, ed., *The Public Papers . . . of Franklin D. Roosevelt, 1941* [New York, 1938–50], pp. 499–502; Ibid., pp. 539–54; Rosenman, ed., *The Public Papers . . . of Franklin D. Roosevelt, 1944–1945*, pp. 556–65.)

PRESS CONFERENCE, NOVEMBER 28, 1941

And as you know, the Secretary of State, with even more patience than I have—which is saying a whole lot—had been holding conversations from, I think it was, April. And in the middle of them came the Japanese expedition to Indo-China, which is very far afield, and caused us very great concern, because it seemed to show a reasonable parallel with the Hitler methods in Europe. As, for example, the infiltration, over a period of several months, of the German armies into Rumania and Hungary, placing themselves in the position where strategically they were all set to attack Yugoslavia and Greece.

And of course the drawing of the parallel made peacefully inclined people over here wonder whether this occupation, with a limited number of troops in Indo-China, was the beginning of a similar action in the Far East, placing obvious American interests in great jeopardy if the drawing of such a parallel was justified. . . .

And we are thinking about what it would mean to this country if that policy were to be used against us in the whole Pacific area. I don't think that anything more can be said at this time. We are waiting. . . .

Q. Mr. President, would this mean that we are working for the status quo?

THE PRESIDENT: Yes. We have been for a long time.

Q. Mr. President—

THE PRESIDENT: *(interposing)* Wait a minute. I wouldn't say working for the status quo, because we—

28

Q. (interposing) Temporary status quo?

THE PRESIDENT: You have got to leave China out of the status quo. We are certainly not working for the status quo in China.

Q. (interjecting) That's right.

THE PRESIDENT: *(continuing)* Or Indo-China, for that matter.

Q. Against further aggression?

THE PRESIDENT: Against further aggression. We are working to remove the present aggression. . . .

Q. That Chinese situation is absolutely solid and set, is it not?

THE PRESIDENT: Absolutely.

Q. No chance of compromise?

THE PRESIDENT: No. . . .

MESSAGE TO CONGRESS, DECEMBER 15, 1941

The American Government, in order to clarify the issues, presented to the Japanese Government, on November 26, a clear-cut plan for a broad but simple settlement.

The outline of the proposed plan for agreement between the United States and Japan was divided into two parts:

In section one there was outlined a mutual declaration of policy containing affirmations that the national policies of the two countries were directed toward peace throughout the Pacific area, that the two countries had no territorial designs or aggressive intentions in that area, and that they would give active support to certain fundamental principles of peace upon which their relations with each other and all other Nations would be based. There was provision for mutual pledges to support and apply in their economic relations with each other and with other Nations and peoples liberal economic principles, which were enumerated, based upon the general principle of equality of commercial opportunity and treatment.

In section two there were outlined proposed steps to be taken by the two Governments. These steps envisaged a situation in which there would be no Japanese or other foreign armed forces in French Indo-China or in China. Mutual commitments were suggested along lines as follows: (a) to endeavor to conclude a multilateral non-aggression pact among the Governments principally concerned in the Pacific area; (b) to endeavor to conclude among the principally interested Governments an agreement to respect the territorial integrity of Indo-China and not to seek or accept preferential economic treatment therein; (c) not to support any Government in China other than the National Government of the Republic of China with capital temporarily at Chungking; (d) to relinquish extraterri-

29

torial and related rights in China and to endeavor to obtain the agreement of other Governments now possessing such rights to give up those rights; (e) to negotiate a trade agreement based upon reciprocal most-favored-Nation treatment; (f) to remove freezing restrictions imposed by each country on the funds of the other; (g) to agree upon a plan for the stabilization of the dollar-yen rate; (h) to agree that no agreement which either had concluded with any third power or powers shall be interpreted by it in a way to conflict with the fundamental purpose of this agreement; and (i) to use their influence to cause other Governments to adhere to the basic political and economic principles provided for in this suggested agreement.

In the midst of these conversations, we learned that new contingents of Japanese armed forces and new masses of equipment were moving into Indo-China. Toward the end of November these movements were intensified. During the first week of December new movements of Japanese forces made it clear that, under cover of the negotiations, attacks on unspecified objectives were being prepared.

I promptly asked the Japanese Government for a frank statement of the reasons for increasing its forces in Indo-China. I was given an evasive and specious reply. Simultaneously, the Japanese operations went forward with increased tempo.

We did not know then, as we know now, that they had ordered and were even then carrying out their plan for a treacherous attack upon us.

MEMO TO HULL, JANUARY 24, 1944

I saw Halifax [Lord Halifax, British Ambassador to the United States] last week and told him quite frankly that it was perfectly true that I had, for over a year, expressed the opinion that Indo-China should not go back to France but that it should be administered by an international trusteeship. France has had the country—thirty million inhabitants for nearly one hundred years, and the people are worse off than they were at the beginning.

As a matter of interest, I am wholeheartedly supported in this view by Generalissimo Chiang Kai-shek and by Marshal Stalin. I see no reason to play in with the British Foreign Office in this matter. The only reason they seem to oppose it is that they fear the effect it would have on their own possessions and those of the Dutch. They have never liked the idea of trusteeship because it is, in some instances, aimed at future independence. This is true in the case of Indo-China.

Each case must, of course, stand on its own feet, but the case of Indo-China is perfectly clear. France has milked it for one hundred years. The people of Indo-China are entitled to something better than that.

PRESS CONFERENCE, FEBRUARY 23, 1945

Q. De Gaulle [Charles de Gaulle, head of the Free French Government] has announced that French Indo-China is to be soon liberated. By whom, Mr. President?

THE PRESIDENT: For two whole years I have been terribly worried about Indo-China. I talked to Chiang Kai-shek in Cairo, Stalin in Teheran. They both agreed with me. The French have been in there some hundred years. The Indo-Chinese are not like the Chinese.

The first thing I asked Chiang was, "Do you want Indo-China?"

He said, "It's no help to us. We don't want it. They are not Chinese. They would not assimilate into the Chinese people."

I said, "What are you going to advocate? It will take a long time to educate them for self-government."

He said they should not go back to the French, that they have been there over a hundred years and have done nothing about educating them, that for every dollar they have put in, they have taken out ten, and that the situation there is a good deal like the Philippines were in 1898.

With the Indo-Chinese, there is a feeling they ought to be independent but are not ready for it. I suggested at the time, to Chiang, that Indo-China be set up under a trusteeship—have a Frenchman, one or two Indo-Chinese, and a Chinese and a Russian because they are on the coast, and maybe a Filipino and an American—to educate them for self-government. It took fifty years for us to do it in the Philippines.

Stalin liked the idea. China liked the idea. The British don't like it. It might bust up their empire, because if the Indo-Chinese were to work together and eventually get their independence, the Burmese might do the same thing to England. The French have talked about how they expect to recapture Indo-China, but they haven't got any shipping to do it with. It would only get the British mad. Chiang would go along. Stalin would go along. As for the British, it would only make the British mad. Better to keep quiet just now.

Q. Is that Churchill's idea on all territory out there, he wants them all back just the way they were?

THE PRESIDENT: Yes, he is mid-Victorian on all things like that.

Q. You would think some of that would be knocked out of him by now.

THE PRESIDENT: I read something Queen Wilhelmina said about the Dutch East Indies. She's got a very interesting point of view. I think it was a public statement concerning the plans about her islands; they differ so from the British plans. The Javanese are not quite ready for self-government, but very nearly. Java, with a little help by other Nations, can probably be ready for independence in a few years. The Javanese are good people—pretty civilized country. The Dutch marry the Javanese, and the Javanese are permitted to join the clubs. The British would not permit the Malayans to join their clubs.

The Queen's idea for some of the Dutch possessions is eventually to give them their independence. When Java is ready for independence, give her help and make her a member of a federation. Sumatra the same.

I asked her, "What about Borneo?"

She said, "We don't talk about that very much. They are still head-hunters. It might be one hundred years before we could educate and civilize the Borneo head-hunter."

I said, "What about New Guinea?"

She threw up both hands and said New Guinea has the lowest form of human life in the world, their skulls have least developed, and they understand civilization probably less than any part of the world. British New Guinea and Papua are probably two hundred years behind the rest of the world.

Q. This idea of Churchill's seems inconsistent with the policy of self-determination?

THE PRESIDENT: Yes, that is true.

Q. He seems to undercut the Atlantic Charter. He made a statement the other day that it was not a rule, just a guide.

THE PRESIDENT: The Atlantic Charter is a beautiful idea. When it was drawn up, the situation was that England was about to lose the war. They needed hope, and it gave it to them. We have improved the military situation since then at every chance, so that really you might say we have a much better chance of winning the war now than ever before.

And when I get back to Washington, I suppose people like Krock [Arthur Krock, New York *Times* correspondent] will write nasty articles about how I always get scooped. That is perfectly true. But I think it is much better to get scooped than to talk all the time. Then there's the time element. The Prime Minister goes before Commons the day he gets home —breaks loads of stuff. People like Krock don't like it.

Q. Do you remember the speech the Prime Minister made about the fact that he was not made the Prime Minister of Great Britain to see the empire fall apart?

THE PRESIDENT: Dear old Winston will never learn on that point. He has made his specialty on that point. This is, of course, off the record.

8. THE VIETNAMESE APPROACH

Once again it is useful to consider how the revolutionary leaders of Vietnam viewed events. This is another selection from *The Long Resistance* by Nguyen Khac Vien. It is all very well to say that it is a biased account; but it nevertheless tells us why Roosevelt's dream of a trusteeship would have failed even if he had managed to control the French determination to reassert their imperial control of Vietnam. (Source: Nguyen Khac Vien, *The Long Resistance (1858–1975)* [Hanoi, 1974], pp. 89, 103.)

THE FRANCO-JAPANESE DOUBLE YOKE

From 1941 to 1945 Viet Nam was subjected to a Franco-Japanese double yoke. The French and the Japanese combined their efforts to exploit the country's resources to the utmost, maintain "law and order," and suppress the revolutionary movement. This collusion, however, did not keep them from pursuing each their own policies to consolidate their respective positions in anticipation of eventual confrontations. Economic exploitation was stepped up to meet both French interests and the requirements of the Japanese war economy. Patriotic movements were repressed with increasing violence while political manoeuvres multiplied in an attempt to hoodwink public opinion and rally reactionary or politically inexperienced Vietnamese elements.

Admiral Decoux, appointed Governor-General of Indochina by the Vichy Government, carried out a double-faced policy of dictatorship and demagogy. At the end of 1940, the few councils which had been set up to give the colonial regime a semblance of democracy were dismissed and all powers fell into the hands of the Governor-General, especially into those of the all-powerful security services. The Decoux administration did its best to launch a cultural movement to promote allegiance to France and reactionary conceptions inspired by Petainism and Confucianism. New schools were opened and enrolment after 1942 increased from 450,000 to 700,000. Money was raised to build the Hanoi Students' Quarters, and Vietnamese mandarins, landowners and bourgeois were encouraged to set up funds to help needy students. The colonial administration strove to seize control of the anti-illiteracy movement until then in the hands of the

33

patriots. It held literary competitions, art exhibitions, gave prizes and sought by all means to enhance French culture.

A particular attempt was made to establish political control over the youth by grouping them into sports associations, para-military and boy-scout organizations. Civil servants were allowed to engage in sports activities on week-ends. A few favours were granted them: increase in salaries and allowances, transfer of certain categories to a metropolitan regime, promotion to higher posts.

The youth and civil servants were even allowed to speak of "patriotism," so long as it was a "local patriotism" within the framework of loyalty to France.

All these measures by no means changed the nature of French policy: complete submission to the Japanese occupier and brutal crack-down on the national movement.

The French had had to agree to the stationing of Japanese troops in Tonkin and to cede 70,000 square kilometers to Thailand, an ally of Japan. The so-called joint defence treaty concluded on December 9, 1941, put the whole of Indochina under Japanese control. Indochina then became a Japanese military base and a supplier of raw materials to the Japanese economy.

First, the French colonial administration supplied Japan with rice: 585,000 tons in 1941, 973,000 tons in 1942, 1,023,000 tons in 1943, 900,000 tons in 1944. At the beginning, Japan paid in gold or industrial goods, but Japanese reserves were quickly exhausted and after December 1942, she paid in "special yen," a sort of worthless military bonds.

In fact, it was the colonial administration that helped cover Japanese war expenditures by putting more and more bank-notes into circulation: 723 million piastres, that is 7 times as much as the 1939 Indochinese budget. In 1944, the total of paper currency in circulation increased to 1,052 million (216 in 1939). As a result, prices spiralled upward.

To meet Japanese needs, the colonial administration stored up a whole range of products: cement, jute, sugar, oil, coal . . . by monopolizing the sale and purchase of a great number of goods. Meanwhile there was a lack of raw materials, equipment and transport to keep the economy going. Only the big colonial firms got huge profits from the new current of exchange with Japan. For them the French surrender to the Japanese was a paying proposition.

The heaviest burden for the people was the compulsory sale of rice to the administration. Even Tonkin, where food was tragically scarce, had to supply 130,205 tons in 1943; 186,130 tons in 1944. Whether the crop was good or bad, each region had to supply a quantity of rice in proportion to the tilled acreage at the derisory price of 19 piastres a quintal. In lean

34

years, the people had to buy rice on the market at 54 piastres a quintal to meet those obligations. To provide gunny bags to the Japanese economy, the peasants were forced to root up rice plants on vast areas and plant jute instead.

In 1944, when the transportation of coal to Saigon was cut off by US bombing, the French and the Japanese used rice and maize as fuel for power stations. They vied with each other in storing up rice. During that time, agriculture was not improved. Dams and dykes were neglected. The slightest natural calamity caused food shortages which developed into horrible famines. Starting in 1943, famine became more and more serious from 1944 onward.

While joining hands with the French administration to exploit to the utmost the resources of the country and harshly repress all revolutionary activity, the Japanese conducted demagogic manoeuvres. They dangled the bait of "national independence" to be won for Viet Nam with Japanese help within the framework of Asian solidarity against the whites and of a co-prosperity zone in Greater Eastern Asia. In particular, they sought to recruit lackeys, either individuals like Tran Trong Kim, Ngo Dinh Diem, Nguyen Van Sam, or tiny groups like the Dai Viet clique in Tonkin. However, until the end of the war, it was more important for Japan to maintain "law and order" with French help than to back any group of puppets. When the French reacted too strongly, the Japanese preferred to send their agents away, to avoid clashes. Even in 1944, after the fall of the Vichy Government in France, they carried on this policy.

THE BIRTH OF VIET MINH

The people were writhing under the Franco-Japanese double yoke. From 1940 to 1944, prices increased by 400%, wages only 20%. In Tonkin and Annam, the peasants starved; in Cochinchina, goods were so scarce: millions of people went about in rags, even clad in leaves. Dissatisfaction mounted among rich peasants and landlords, compelled to sell their products cheap, and among businessmen and industrialists, who lacked raw materials and equipment and were pressed down by Government monopolies. The only ones to profit were the big colonial companies, black-marketeers and professional speculators.

Whereas some patriots at first had harboured illusions about a possible Japanese aid, the Communist Party had the merit of denouncing the Japanese danger and steering the struggle along the right course. In May 1941, Ho Chi Minh convened at Pac Bo (Cao Bang province) the 8th session of the Central Committee which put the Vietnamese revolution unreservedly in the world anti-fascist camp, of which the keystone remained the Soviet Union. The plenum held that Hitlerite fascism would attack the Soviet Union and this would certainly end in its own annihilation. The world war would end with the formation of new socialist countries. It was in this perspective that the strategy of the Vietnamese revolutionary movement was to be defined.

The present essential task was to liberate the country from Franco-Japanese domination, which was bearing hard on the entire people; national liberation must be put above all other things; the interests of all social classes must be subordinated to this primary objective. Broad national union should be achieved against French colonialism and Japanese fascism and a national front be established to rally all social classes and strata, parties, political and religious groups. Lands belonging to the imperialists and traitors should be confiscated and distributed to poor peasants, land rents reduced and communal lands equitably distributed, all these measures to be progressively applied with a view to realizing this slogan: "Land to the tillers." Thus, a national unity could be achieved without the poor peasants' fundamental interests being neglected.

The Central Committee decided to prepare for an armed insurrection and for this purpose to reinforce guerilla and self-defence units and to set up guerilla bases. . . .

The pre-insurrectional mobilization of the masses consisted of three essential aspects:

—Development of guerilla activities in the Highlands and Midlands;
—Capture of rice-stores by the peasants;
—Political agitation in the major towns.

Under the leadership of a National Liberation Committee, liberation committees, the first form of revolutionary power, were set up at different levels: village, district and province. In April, the revolutionary armed force merged into a "Liberation Army" under the command of a Military Committee among whose members were Vo Nguyen Giap, Chu Van Tan, Van Tien Dung. A military school was founded.

After March 9, [1945,] guerilla units overran important posts in Thai Nguyen, Bac Can, Tuyen Quang provinces. In the North, Centre and South, political prisoners who had escaped from prison set about organizing the population in the surrounding areas. Traitors were punished, revolutionary power was established in many localities and regions. By June 1945, most of the six provinces north of the Red River (Lang Son, Cao Bang, Bac Can, Ha Giang, Tuyen Quang, Thai Nguyen) were liberated and served as the main revolutionary bases of the country. The guerilla forces laid ambushes and inflicted serious losses upon the Japanese troops. In Hai Duong and Quang Yen provinces, uprisings took place in some localities and revolutionary power was set up.

In the Centre, an armed insurrection took place in Ba To, Quang Ngai province.

While guerilla warfare was developing, in Tonkin and the northern provinces of Annam, famine took on unprecedentedly tragic proportions: within a few months, two million people died of starvation. Many villages lost half or one-third of their population; in the towns, the streets were littered with dead bodies. The Viet Minh called on the people to count neither on the Japanese nor on the puppet government but on their own efforts, and urged them to capture Japanese rice-stocks and convoys of supplies. This resulted in large-scale mobilization of the people, who grew conscious of their strength. Self-defence units and liberation committees were formed in the course of this struggle. Rice-stocks were seized and distributed to the population, thus lessening the havoc of famine. This was really a pre-revolutionary action.

In the towns—Hanoi, Saigon and Hue in particular—political agitation gained momentum. In Hanoi, though the Town Party Committee was, in the period from 1941 to 1945, five times broken up by the police, each factory, in 1945, had its own workers' organization for national salvation. Self-defence units were formed. Strikes were staged in big factories; meetings, at which orators spoke under armed protection, were held in streets, schools, factories and city-outskirts. Pro-Japanese meetings were turned into ones supporting the revolution. Isolated Japanese soldiers were disarmed and traitors punished in the very heart of the city. Peasants in the neighbourhood of Hanoi, acting in concert with workers, seized rice-stores.

In Saigon, after March 9, the workers' organizations had a membership of 120,000 (3,000 before that date). The Vanguard Youth, led by such well-known intellectuals as Dr. Pham Ngoc Thach and lawyer Thai Van Lung had, in Saigon alone, a membership of 200,000 and of one million all over Cochinchina.

THE AUGUST REVOLUTION

In the summer of 1945, throughout the country, in the North, South and Centre, in the countryside and in the towns, and also among the ethnic minorities of the mountain areas, popular effervescence was at its height and revolutionary activities, both political and military, were on the increase. The decisive factor was that the Viet Minh was leading and co-ordinating all these activities on a nation-wide scale. . . .

The August 1945 Revolution ended 80 years of colonial domination, abolished the monarchy and restored Viet Nam's national independence. A telling blow at the colonial system, it ushered in, together with other movements in the world, a period of break-down of colonial empires. . . .

9. REESTABLISHING THE FRENCH

This policy statement by John Carter Vincent, a top State Department expert on Asia, makes it clear that President Roosevelt had lost his fight to prevent the French from reestablishing their imperial position in Vietnam. The document reveals that liberals were not prepared to support revolutionary change in the East Indies. As Vincent says, "It is our policy to encourage and facilitate the reestablishment of American business in China." (Source: *Department of State Bulletin,* XIII [Oct. 21, 1945], pp. 644–48.)

In southeast Asia a situation has developed to the liking of none of us, least of all to the British, the French, the Dutch, and, I gather, to the Annamese and Indonesians. With regard to the situation in French Indochina, this Government does not question French sovereignty in that area. Our attitude toward the situation in the Dutch East Indies is similar to that in regard to French Indochina. In both these areas, however, we earnestly hope that an early agreement can be reached between representatives of the governments concerned and the Annamese and Indonesians. It is not our intention to assist or participate in forceful measures for the imposition of control by the territorial sovereigns, but we would be prepared to lend our assistance, if requested to do so, in efforts to reach peaceful agreements in these disturbed areas.

In a statement issued by Secretary Hull on March 21, 1944, entitled "Bases of the Foreign Policy of the United States," there occurs the following paragraph in regard to "dependent peoples": "There rests upon the independent nations a responsibility in relation to dependent peoples who aspire to liberty. It should be the duty of nations having political ties with such peoples . . . to help the aspiring peoples to develop materially and educationally, to prepare themselves for the duties and responsibilities of self-government, and to attain liberty." This continues to be American policy. . . .

It is our policy to encourage and facilitate the reestablishment of American business in China. Probably not with all the speed desired, but with all the speed we can generate, we are endeavoring to get businessmen back into China for their sake and for China's sake. We want them back in Shanghai, Hong Kong, Tientsin, and other ports as quickly as possible. We are reopening consulates in these and other cities.

What I have said regarding American businessmen applies with equal force to missionaries and representatives of cultural and philanthropic organizations. We want them back in China as soon as transportation facilities and conditions in China will permit.

10. ROOSEVELT ADMITS DEFEAT

President Roosevelt admits his defeat in these two documents. The President also tells us about the power of the military in the making of American policy. There is a sad note to all of this when Roosevelt asks if the Navy is "trying to grab everything." It does remind one of the Tonkin Gulf Resolution. (Source: Department of State, *Foreign Relations of the United States, 1945,* VI, p. 293.)

MEMORANDUM BY PRESIDENT ROOSEVELT FOR THE SECRETARY OF STATE

WASHINGTON, January 1, 1945.

I still do not want to get mixed up in any Indochina decision. It is a matter for post-war.

By the same token, I do not want to get mixed up in any military effort toward the liberation of Indochina from the Japanese.

You can tell Halifax that I made this very clear to Mr. Churchill. From both the military and civil point of view, action at this time is premature.

F[RANKLIN] D. R[OOSEVELT]

MEMORANDUM OF CONVERSATION, BY THE ADVISER ON CARIBBEAN AFFAIRS (TAUSSIG)

[WASHINGTON,] March 15, 1945.

The President opened the conversation with a reference to the Yalta Conference, saying that he had had a successful time. He then said, apparently referring to our last meeting at luncheon, "I liked Stanley [Oliver Stanley, head of the British Colonial Office]." He thought that Stanley was more liberal on colonial policy than Churchill. He then asked

39

me if Stanley was going to San Francisco. I said I did not know. The President said he hoped he would. I told him that, although Stanley was hard-boiled, I felt there was a genuine streak of liberalism in him, and that under his leadership, the British would make some substantial changes in their whole colonial policy. I told the President of the £120,000,000 appropriation that Parliament had made for Colonial Development over the next ten years, and gave him some little detail of the debate in Parliament (February 7, 1945).

TRUSTEESHIP

I outlined to the President the discussion on the above subject between the General Staffs and the State Department as it had developed in the Committee on Dependent Area Aspects of International Organizations. I outlined the agreement that had been reached on the general category of strategic areas, and told the President that the military had indicated that they would interpret strategic areas as an entire area—for instance, all of the Japanese islands, north of the Equator, that might come under the administration of the United States. I told him that under their interpretation, the entire group of islands irrespective of whether they were fortified or not would be exempt from substantially all of the international agreements pertaining to civilian populations; that the military had been unwilling to agree to divide strategic areas into two categories—closed areas and open areas.

The President said that he would favor these two categories and that the open areas should be subject to international agreements. He said that if the military wanted, at a later date due to change in strategy, to make all or part of the open area a closed area, it should be provided that this could be done with the approval of the Security Council.

The President then asked me, "What is the Navy's attitude in regard to territories? Are they trying to grab everything?" I replied that they did not seem to have much confidence in civilian controls. The President then asked me how I accounted for their attitude.

I said that I thought that the military had no confidence in the proposed United Nations Organization. The President replied that he thought that was so. I told the President of the letter that Admiral Willson showed me addressed to the Secretary of the Navy, referring to the need of sending representatives to San Francisco in order to protect themselves against "the international welfare boys." The President then said that neither the Army nor the Navy had any business administering the civilian government of territories; that they had no competence to do this. . . .

THE PEOPLES OF EAST ASIA

The President said he was concerned about the brown people in the East. He said that there are 1,100,000,000 brown people. In many Eastern countries, they are ruled by a handful of whites and they resent it. Our goal must be to help them achieve independence—1,100,000,000 potential enemies are dangerous. He said he included the 450,000,000 Chinese in that. He then added, Churchill doesn't understand this.

INDO-CHINA AND NEW CALEDONIA

The President said he thought we might have some difficulties with France in the matter of colonies. I said that I thought that was quite probable and it was also probable the British would use France as a "stalking horse."

I asked the President if he had changed his ideas on French Indo-China as he had expressed them to us at the luncheon with Stanley. He said no he had not changed his ideas; that French Indo-China and New Caledonia should be taken from France and put under a trusteeship. The President hesitated a moment and then said—well if we can get the proper pledge from France to assume for herself the obligations of a trustee, then I would agree to France retaining these colonies with the proviso that independence was the ultimate goal. I asked the President if he would settle for self-government. He said no. I asked him if he would settle for dominion status. He said no—it must be independence. He said that is to be the policy and you can quote me in the State Department.

CHARLES TAUSSIG

41

Part II

CRISIS, COMMITMENT, AND COUNTERREVOLUTION

1945–1952

INTRODUCTION
Thomas McCormick

In August 1945, World War II jolted to its heart-stopping, nuclear end in Asia. Vietnam emerged with vivid memories of Japan's subordination and de facto replacement of French authority. The memories produced two lessons: Western colonialism was not omnipotent; and imperialism by any other name was still imperialism—even if Japan preferred to call it an "Asian Co-Prosperity Sphere." Vietnamese nationalism was the beneficiary of both insights, as the movement for an independent, Vietnamese nation topped that society's public agenda. In the movement's vanguard was the Vietminh organization, led by Ho Chi Minh of the Vietnamese Communist Party.

By definition, Vietnam could not act out its historic quest in isolation, for she was a dependent part of a modern world system almost five centuries in the making. At the *core* of that world system—dominating and benefitting—were the powerful, unified, industrial nations of Europe, North America, and Japan: the Trilateral bloc. At the *periphery* of that system—dominated and dependent—were weak, disunified, backward areas like Vietnam itself: the Third World. Marked by a complex, specialized division of international labor, the core-periphery relationships of the system rather resembled a global food chain of nations—each link part of a hierarchical structure among nations of dominance/subordination that tended to reproduce and perpetuate the whole. Vietnam was part of Indochina (along with Laos and Cambodia); Indochina, in turn, was just a portion of the vast Southeast Asia land peninsula (including Thailand, Burma, and Malaya); the peninsula, likewise, was integrally connected to the offshore archipelagoes of Indonesia and the Philippines, and the two together constituted the Southeast Asia region (or SEA as it is noted in American government sources). But even SEA was widely perceived as a functioning part of a larger Asian crescent, anchored by Japan at one end and extending, at the other, as far as India, perhaps as far as Iran and the Persian Gulf. Moreover, prior to World War II, almost all of these peripheral links had been colonial holdings—imperial extensions—of core countries: Britain, France, Holland, Japan, and the United States (the Philippines).

However small and remote, Vietnam was an organic part of this core-periphery structure. Implicitly then, this postwar world order placed certain constraints on the Vietnamese drive for autonomy. On the other hand, the system's capacity to sustain those constraints was seriously called into question by its own self-destructive tendencies. Demoralized by a decade of history's worst economic depression and devastated by six years of one of history's worse wars, the world of 1945 looked like a star on the downhill side of a nova. Therein entered America and its foreign policy—that fixer of universes; the new world once more entering the fray to redress the balance of the old. And that entrance was to set American and Vietnamese societies on a collision course that was to delay Vietnamese independence for three decades and culminate in America's longest and most debated war.

Even before Pearl Harbor and American entrance into World War II, American political and business leaders had largely agreed that two things were necessary to breathe life and energy back into the world system, and that only the United States had the insight and capacity to see them done. First, some political entity had to play the dual role of judge and policeman in the system; to arbitrate differences within the system and to enforce its decisions; to coordinate world affairs in the interests of the whole system, not its specific parts. Since the decline of British hegemony in the late nineteenth century, neither balance-of-power politics nor the League of Nations had successfully done the job. Now, American leaders felt both able and eager to take on the mantle of hegemony themselves, a *Pax Americana* to replace a *Pax Britannia*. Second, the chief task of hegemonic America was to restore economic expansiveness to a system racked and distorted by the Great Depression and ensuing war. A static or contracting economic pie not only threatened world capitalism (and American capitalism) with stagnation, but invited internal strife and aggression to redivide the zero-sum pie by force. Two world wars and three major revolutions made that abundantly clear.

From 1945 to 1949 the core countries of war-devastated Europe and Japan occupied center stage. In an international version of supply-side economics, America's major effort was to restore high levels of productivity—with minimal redundancy and maximum interdependence. The major obstacle was the imbalance within the world system. American capitalism was too strong and that of other core countries too weak—a disequilibrium most acutely demonstrated by the so-called Dollar Gap. Europe and Japan's disastrous balance of payments deficit created such a shortage of dollars that it retarded the level of intra-core trading. Moreover, it tempted them to resort to tariff and convertibility controls that would have retarded it even further. Without a large transfusion of American dollars, the world system seemed more destined to return to the depression of the 1930s than the "normalcy" of the 1920s. The Marshall Plan for Europe and the Special Offshore Procurement Program for Japan were the main American efforts to address this paradox of "progress and poverty."

Southeast Asia was initially of marginal importance to this reconstruction of the industrial core. Indeed, its importance was largely delineated by the impact that the European colonies there seemed to have upon the well-being of their colonizers. In the case of French Indochina, the well-being seemed largely measured in political and psychological terms. French self-esteem apparently required restoration of her overseas empire, and any frustration of that goal might undercut the tenuous stability of French domestic policies to the ultimate benefit of the French Left. (Doc. 1.) Given American concern for France's pivotal role in European recovery, it seemed prudent to set aside America's marginal anticolonialism; refrain from erecting any barriers to French actions in Indochina; and indulge only in occasional sermonettes to the French about giving the "natives" more responsibilities. Indeed, that was the essence of American policy between 1946 and 1949 as France sought to reintegrate Indochina into the French empire in the face of determined opposition from the Vietminh.[1]

The escalation of the French military efforts to reassert colonial control, coupled with the move toward NATO and German rearmament, only reinforced the Eurocentrism of American policy. By 1949 the American ambassador to France believed that continuation of the war was "a severe strain on the French economy and diverted from the defense of Western Europe sizable quantities of French military equipment and personnel."[2] By early 1950 the French diversion of Marshall Plan aid to finance her Vietnam War became such a "great drain" that it "conflicted with her obligations under ECA bilateral [Marshall Plan] and North Atlantic and Brussels Pact [NATO]."[3] Moreover, it impeded French acceptance of German participation in a NATO multilateral army since "a considerable portion of the crack French troops [were] now in Indochina."[4] French leaders encouraged such American perceptions. In thinly veiled diplomatic blackmail, they warned, "Without outside help the future of Indo-China was black."[5] While American counterparts saw through the blackmail, they did accept much of the French analysis. So even before the first formalization of American aid in the spring of 1950, the United States looked the other way while France used surplus American military equipment and Marshall Plan dollars to fight and finance her war. Still, American aid was indirect, its commitment limited and cautious, and its sense of Indochina's importance ephemeral and contingent on France's role in Europe.

The watershed trauma in the last third of 1949 and the first third of 1950 profoundly altered the circumstances of the world system and triggered the curtain's rise on the first act of the long drama of America in Vietnam. What happened between Labor Day 1949 and May Day 1950 was no less than a structural crisis in the world system—a crisis exacerbated by the Cold War and the apparent Russian threat, but not caused by it. George Frost Kennan, chairman of the State Department's Policy Planning Staff (PPS), called attention to that crisis in an August 22 broadcast for CBS radio, which began by defining "the international situation" as in "transition from the immediate posthostilities era, with its short-term problems and demands, to a new stage of affairs which may endure for a long time and many aspects of which we may have to regard as normal." In discussing those new, long-term problems, he put his finger on the central failure of postwar efforts to reconstruct the system: "For it is one thing to produce; it is another thing to sell." The codifier of America's containment policy concluded by alerting his listeners to the "real urgency" of "this problem," and predicted that "coming discussions here in Washington will be devoted to the exploration of possible solutions."[6]

Two key facts produced the beehive of bureaucratic exploration that Kennan anticipated, and ultimately produced commitments at the highest levels by President Truman and Secretary of State Acheson—all with profound relevance for Southeast Asia. One was "the understanding of Congress and the people that the European Recovery Program [Marshall Plan] will be brought to a close in 1952"—and with no prospects for any continuation. The other was the awareness that the structural problem of imbalance in the system—"the problem of the dollar gap"—had not been solved; that "about a third of our exports is being financed by grants. At the end of ERP, European production will have been restored . . . but the problem of payment for American goods and services will remain." Secretary of State Acheson got to the nub of matters in his February 16, 1950, memorandum to the President:

> Put in its simplest terms, the problem is this: as ERP is reduced, and after its termination in 1952, how can Europe and other areas of the world obtain the dollars necessary to pay for a high level of United States exports, which is essential both to their own basic needs and to the well-being of the United States economy? This is the problem of the "dollar gap" in world trade.

The inner working papers of State Department study groups and the Committee of Economic Advisers abound with evidence of the high anxiety that attached to this "problem of crisis magnitude"; "the highest priority"; "the critical and far-reaching decisions of policy arising out of our economic relationships with the rest of the world"; or "the importance to the United States of a successful economic system among the free nations . . . even if it requires adjustments and sacrifices by particular economic groups in the United States in the interest of the nation as a whole."[7] (Doc. 12.)

The structural crisis of 1949–50 produced a tripartite bureaucratic debate, and the ensuing trade-offs were to transform Southeast Asia from an area of marginal, ephemeral concern to one of fundamental, enduring importance. (1) The State Department mainstream, echoing the Council of Economic Advisers, argued that "When all is said and done, it is evident that if exports are to be maintained and there is to be curtailment in extraordinary assistance, the main burden of adjustment in our balance of payments must be accomplished by an increase in our imports of goods and services." (2) The newly emerged "recovery" bureaucracy (like ECA) predictably urged a continuation of their international pump-priming to Europe and expansion to Japan and the Third World via an Asian Marshall Plan and an enlargement of the Point Four program proposed by President Truman. (3) The Pentagon and the MDAP bureaucracy (Mutual Defense Assistance Program) pushed for a militarized version of international Keynesianism: a massive increase in American military spending that could be transferred to Europe either in "direct dollar assistance" or "in kind." Military aid as economic aid to "benefit both military production and the economic situation."[8] The proverbial two birds with one stone. (Doc. 13.)

The militarized option, albeit with modification, largely prevailed. It did so first because it was the only option that was politically viable. Congress showed no willingness to extend or expand foreign economic aid to confront the dollar gap, nor did it respond positively to State Department feelers about liberalizing access to the American market for foreign producers. The legislative branch, in its attitudes and its political constituency, tended to be more nationalistic, and little inclined to jeopardize home-market business and labor in the name of economic internationalism and the world system. But the political side of that congressional nationalism would and did respond positively to initiatives framed in terms of national security. It would vote to prime the military pump. Therein lay common ground. Nationalists and internationalists alike shared fears generated by the Communist triumph in China and, more especially, by the Russian acquisition of the atomic bomb. To be sure, the fears were of a different order. Nationalists focused on the enhanced possibility of direct military aggression by the U.S.S.R. Many internationalists, however, continued to believe that "Soviet history seems to be against military adventures which entail any risk." But they did fear that the Russian atomic bomb would reduce the credibility of the United States to protect and manage the world system, especially in the eyes of Europe and Japan. (Doc. 14.)

This DOD-MDAP bureaucratic triumph found expression in the adoption of NSC 68 in April 1950. (Doc. 15.) But that National Security Council document also was the product of some important trade-offs with the Department of State (DOS) and the "recovery" bureaucracy. First, in proposing "to merge the U.S. organizations and appropriations for military assistance and for economic aid," Army Secretary Tracy Voorhees made clear "that the ECA organizations here and abroad should be the backbone of the combined agency."[9] The "recovery" bureaucracy would not be out of a job. Second, the defense bureaucracy had to address the crucial insight of DOS that "European production has been restored to the point at which the primary problem is now the need for *markets.*" (Emphasis added.)[10] Since domestic politics inhibited access to the major capitalist market (the United States) and since Cold War politics—militarized and heated up—tightly restricted access to socialist markets (Russia and China), where were the markets to be had? Acheson and Kennan were right: that was the structural obstacle to equilibrium in the world system.

The answer, long proposed by area specialists in DOS itself, was the Third World: integrate periphery areas more thoroughly into the market economies of Europe and Japan. But how, when Third World poverty was so high and its productivity so low—"predominantly agricultural and their economies basically self-sufficient or non-complementary at the *present level of their development?*" (Emphasis added.) In stable areas, it was argued that private investment and Point Four technical aid would suffice; the goal, after all, was not industrial development but increasing the productivity of raw materials and foodstuffs to supply core-country needs and purchase core-country manufactured products. But in areas of political instability and civil strife, "the first prerequisite to economic recovery . . . is, not increased production and exports, fiscal reform and economic cooperation as in Europe, but effective solutions for fundamental political and military conflicts which are stifling production and trade. Given these political solutions . . . economic recovery could be attained rapidly, and with relatively little capital expenditure. . . ."[11] The consensus equation was complete: a massive military buildup would not only contain Russia (and/or China), profit America, and provide a short-term solution to the Dollar Gap. It would also create the instrument (the oft-noted "military shield") to pacify and stabilize volatile but important areas of the Third World. And no area was more volatile or more important than Southeast Asia. (Doc. 16.)

Indochina, with its French-Vietminh war, was most in need of pacification. But the rest of Southeast Asia was viewed as so weak and unstable that the National Security Council concluded in February 1950 that the "neighboring countries of Thailand and Burma could be expected to fall under Communist domination if Indochina were controlled by a Communist-dominated government. The balance of Southeast Asia would then be in grave hazard" (i.e., Malaya, the Philippines, and Indonesia).[12] This early version of the famous "falling dominoes" theory posited a regional indivisibility that endowed the Indochina conflict with an importance it otherwise would not have had. Save for its impact on France (and much of that counterproductive), Indochina was of little intrinsic importance or interest. But as perceived linchpin in the crescent that stretched between India and Japan, it was seen as vital. If the region as a whole—this collage of former European, American, and Japanese colonies—was to be reintegrated successfully into the world system, then some military or political solution to the Indochina war was crucial.

The American decision in early 1950 to play a committed and more active role in the Indochina pacification did not flow from direct American interests in the region. Save for the Philippines and, potentially, Indonesia, American economic and military interests were minimal. But power has its price as well as its profit, and American hegemonic leadership in the "free world" did dictate that the United States play surrogate for other core countries—for whom Southeast Asia was of considerable, direct importance. For its Marshall Plan partners in Europe, "Southeast Asia, especially Malaya and Indonesia, is the principal world source of natural rubber and tin . . . Indonesia is a secondary source of petroleum . . . Malaya is the largest net dollar earner for the United Kingdom, and its loss would seriously aggravate the economic problems facing the UK."[13] The last factor was vital. Britain's financial-economic situation was perhaps more complex than any other European power. Her Malayan exports to the dollar bloc constituted her most productive short-term effort to ameliorate her dollar gap; indeed, the American Government helped make it more productive by scaling down its synthetic rubber program and modifying its trade policy on tin imports.[14]

For Japan (and her American occupiers), Southeast Asia commanded even greater present and potential concern. It had "been clear, from the beginning of the occupation, that a revived Japanese foreign trade is an indispensable prerequisite to the reconstruction of a stable economy." The Acting Political Adviser in Japan summed it well in 1947:

Foreign trade historically has been Japan's economic lifeblood. Before the war, Japan ranked fifth among the great nations of the world. With a population of over 70,000,000 living on the small, arable area afforded by the four main islands, and with relatively meager natural resources, Japan maintained herself in large part by importing raw materials, processing them, and exporting the finished products in exchange for food and additional raw materials.[15]

Moreover, "among the major problems facing the healthy development of Japanese commerce is the restriction of economic activities resulting from the unstable political situation in various countries of the Far East [China and SEA] which, rich in natural resources but poor in industry, would naturally be expected to complement Japan's economy by mutually beneficial trade."[16]

By 1947 continuing civil war in China led American leaders to give up on that country as America's postwar "doorman" in Asia, and to turn to Japan as the model of pro-capitalist modernization—Asia's "workshop." The resulting "reverse course" in United States occupation policy strongly supported the revival of heavy industry and its monopoly tendencies. That "workshop" economy approach only intensified the apparent Japanese need for markets and for less distant sources of food and raw materials. Where revolutionary China fit into this need was a matter of debate and concern among American leaders. Occasionally there were suggestions that Sino-Japanese trade might be a good thing—not simply for Japan, but perhaps to wean China herself away from the U.S.S.R. and thus sustain the American dream of an Open Door ("a lever of some utility in our efforts to bring changes within Communist China"). Perhaps reflective of that opinion, COCOM (the Coordinating Committee on Export Control), in 1949–50, exercised restraint in restricting trade with China save in strategic materials that might be transshipped to Russia. Still, the dominant opinion was that Japan ought not be allowed to play her "China card," and if that was to be so, the United States faced the responsibility and necessity of providing Japan an alternative source of markets and primary commodities. Secretary of State Dean Acheson put it crudely in his May 8, 1949, circular telegram to American embassies in ten Far Eastern countries that "Japs will either move toward sound friendly relations with non-Commie countries or into association with Commie system in Asia."[17]

The Acheson position led logically to an American strategy of regionalism—criticized by General MacArthur's occupation headquarters in Japan as "economically similar to those of pre-war Japan in its *Asiatic co-prosperity sphere* plans."[18] On January 10, 1950, the National Security Council (NSC 61) formally subscribed to the principle that "Japan's economic recovery depends upon keeping Communism out of Southeast Asia, promoting economic recovery there and in further developing these countries, together with Indonesia, the Philippines, Southern Korea and India as the *principal trading areas* for Japan." (Doc. 17; emphasis added.) NSC 61, in conjunction with the Special Offshore Procurement Program, constituted a triangular arrangement for the U.S.-Japan-SEA. (1) American economic and military aid programs would be fused into one, directed jointly by DOS-SOS-ECA (the tripartite bureaucracy). (2) Save for some small Point 4 money, American dollar aid would be pumped into Japan rather than Southeast Asia itself. Offshore Procurement would eventually become the main pump-primer by subcontracting the production of military items (jeeps, trucks, uniforms, and the like) to Japanese industry (a key factor in the revival of the Japanese auto industry). (3) The burden of developing the food and raw material productivity of Southeast Asia would fall mainly on Japan—directly through technical aid and war reparations, indirectly through the demand stimulus of Japan's "work-shop" market. The American market, with its demand for rubber, tin, and bauxite (especially in Indonesia and Malaya), would supplement that stimulus. (Doc. 18.) Four months after NSC action, on the eve of President Truman's landmark commitment to the French in Indochina, the Economic and Scientific Staff Section in Tokyo completed a highly detailed projection study entitled "Japan's Export Potential" to South-east Asia, and predicted that "exports to these countries will consider-ably exceed 50% of her total projected export trade" by 1955. Indo-nesia—considered by many Americans as the most important "domino" in the area—was projected as twice as important as any other SEA market. Significantly, French Indochina seemed to possess so little market potential that it ranked last in the country-by-country summary.[19] (Doc. 19.)

This American intent to stabilize Southeast Asia and integrate it more systematically into the world system seemed to run counter to the dominant historical force in the area—that is, nationalism and Pan-Asianism. That movement grew out of and fed off of hostility to three phenomena. The most long-term was European and North American imperialism, which, for more than a half century, had colonized every SEA country save Siam (Thailand). The most recent was Japan's perver-sion of Pan-Asianism (Asia for Asians) into her own blatant imperialism during World War II. The most persistent was economic dependency: that is (in the eyes of a UN economic commission), "the economic insecurity and hazardous exposure of nations whose livelihood was dependent upon the export of raw materials" and, as consequence, the "grossly inferior position compared to predominantly industrialized nations." In short, the subordination to core countries—perceived in political, economic, and racial terms—and the drive to alleviate it and to achieve a real measure of national and regional autonomy. Now, in late 1949 and early 1950, American policy seemed to embrace all three hate symbols of Southeast Asian nationalism: to support residual colonialism of the French in Indochina; to resurrect Japan's co-prosperity sphere but under American aegis; and to perpetuate the region's specialization in primary commodities in a "complementary relationship" with the industrial core.[20] Even as early as 1944, American diplomats in the area had warned the State Department that "there is much bitterness, whether justified or not, among leading and important Asiatics and colonial people toward 'white' imperial or colonial power. Propaganda associating the United States with such powers did not begin with this war and has not always fallen on barren soil."[21] Indeed, by 1950, the soil had produced a bumper crop. As one DOS official put it:

> In this connection, it is a fairly sound if unpleasant generalization to state that the U.S. is feared throughout the whole area, and much of the fear is based upon the notion that our interest in the area originates in large part from conscious programs of economic imperialism. Neither French nor Dutch imperialism is regarded by the sensitive and somewhat xenophobic native nationalism as a serious barrier to their ambitions. We, however, are regarded with considerable apprehension.[22]

American leaders were not insensitive to such apprehension; nor could they be and still succeed in their policy objectives. But the apparent contradictions between those objectives and SEA nationalism created a circle that somehow had to be squared. In a preview of later efforts, "Vietimization" of the Indochina war became the American solution to that problem in political geometry—a sort of pseudo-nationalism to legitimize French efforts. With American encouragement, France created native regimes in Cambodia, Laos, and Vietnam—the latter headed by former Emperor Bao Dai. While these puppet governments were granted nominal autonomy as "free states," the French continued to exercise real authority over them. France's move deceived no one—especially SEA countries like Thailand, who withheld diplomatic recognition of Bao Dai and the other regimes because of "repugnance voluntarily to recognize any regime which in their minds represents perpetuation of colonial rule."[23] (Doc. 20.) In an effort to assuage such views and to facilitate stabilization, the United States did advise France to grant more substantive autonomy, to give some deference to the goal of eventual independence, and to create an indigenous army that would cooperate in the French pacification attempt. But since colonial powers are not known to fight wars with decolonization as their objective, France predictably declined the advice. And since in the American scheme of values, anticolonialism was a minor good alongside the major good of regional stabilization, American leaders perceived but one choice: bed down with France and Bao Dai and do one's best to make the *ménage à trois* look respectable. (Doc. 21.)

One route to relative respectability is to rob one's adversaries of legitimacy. By dismissing European colonialism as dead or dying, and positing that Soviet-directed communism constituted the new imperialism of the postwar era, the United States attempted to define revolutionary communism as the archenemy of Southeast Asian nationalism, and anti-Communist "containment" as its firmest friend. But the empirical question remained: was the Vietminh wholly Communist-dominated, and even if so, was it or would it likely become a lackey for Soviet or Sino-Soviet international policy? Some American area specialists and intelligence people were clearly unsure. (Doc. 22.) Those with greater power were not. As early as May 1949, Secretary of State Acheson dismissed the "question [of] whether Ho [was] as much nationalist as Commie [as] irrelevant. All Stalinists in colonial areas are nationalists."[24] The communist triumph in China only hardened the Secretary's view and led him to predict to the British ambassador in December that "there was likely to be early expansion south and east beyond the borders of China." (Doc. 23.) Chinese and Russian recognition of the Vietminh a month later was all Acheson needed to carry the day over any "doubting Thomases." Plane political geometry gave way to solid: circles squared within circles squared. The choice of stabilization *at the expense* of area nationalism + the rationalization of pseudo-nationalism + the legitimization of anti-communism = the transformation of that choice into a policy *in behalf* of area nationalism.

Many of Southeast Asia's leaders—even staunch non-Communists—did not buy this example of the New Math. Filipino leader Carlos Romulo, presiding head of the UN General Assembly, spoke for many of them in a long, eloquent, and critical letter to Acheson on March 2, 1950. Questioning not only policies but underlying premises, Romulo concluded with the quintessential question. Noting recent Vietminh contact with Yugoslavia, he inquired (Doc. 24):

Suppose now that Vietnamese Communism should assume the shape of Titoism, would the United States still prefer a puppet Bao Dai to a Titoist Ho Chi-minh?

Acheson had, in fact, answered the question nearly a year earlier. While acknowledging a Vietnamese Titoism as a "theoretical possibility," he thought the United States should explore it "only if every other avenue closed."[25] The "puppet Bao Dai" was indeed preferable to a "Titoist Ho Chi-minh," and for the simple reason that pseudo-nationalism was less an obstacle to an Americanized coprosperity sphere than the genuine article. In any case, Acheson declared the issue moot on February 1, 1950, following Russian recognition of the Vietminh regime. Ho, he declared, stood revealed "in his true colors as the mortal enemy of native independence in Indochina."[26]

Acheson's public statement coincided to the day with completion of a DOS "Problem Paper" on "Military Aid for Indochina." In essence, it recommended a dramatic reversal of past American policy (epitomized earlier in PPS 51) that "we are powerless to bring about a constructive solution of the explosive Indochinese situation"; that neither a "French imperialism" nor "militant nationalism" were viable alternatives; and that moral suasion, aimed at reconciling both, was the only available option.[27] (Doc. 25.) A year after that Policy Planning Staff conclusion, the departmental "Working Group" determined that "significant developments" had radically altered the situation, and it made *THE* crucial recommendation (Doc. 26):

The United States should furnish military aid in support of the anti-Communist nationalist governments of Indochina, this aid to be tailored to meet deficiencies toward which the United States can make a unique contribution, *not including United States troops.* [Emphasis added.]

Two weeks later, the French Government formally requested immediate military aid and a commitment of "further military assistances . . . on a very much larger scale and for an *indeterminate period of time.*" (Emphasis added.) On February 27 the National Security Council approved the proposal of military aid in principle and ordered the Joint Chiefs of Staff to "prepare as a matter of priority a program of all practicable measures to protect United States security interests in Indo-china."[28] After six weeks of labor, the JCS report—along with parallel reports from DOS—were submitted to NSC and the President. (Doc. 27.) Finally, on May 1, 1950, President Truman gave new meaning to May Day by announcing the first installment of military and economic aid to bolster the French effort in Indochina.

The final two years of the Truman administration that followed saw that modest seed money of some $15,000,000 transformed into a multibillion-dollar investment that paid about 40 percent of the cost of France's war in Indochina by 1952—and it would continue to expand, not unlike the jungle growth of Vietnam itself. Three related factors prompted that quantum jump: the failure of French suppression in In-dochina, the Korean War, and the continuing problems of the Japanese economy. The French failure is well known. French military fortunes plummeted in 1950, hitting a new low in the Vietminh victory at Cao Bung that cost France some 6,000 troops and a mountain of equip-ment and supplies. French resurgence in the Red River Delta area in early 1951 proved only temporary—prelude to France's worst defeat yet, near Hanoi in late 1951. By 1952, after two years of American military aid, the goal of pacification—as first step to stabilization—was as far away as ever.[29]

In itself, the French failure could as easily have negated the Ameri-can investment as expanded it. Why throw good money after bad—especially when the French effort "will further deplete defenses of Western Europe without—so far as we can tell—solving the Indochina problem"? (Doc. 28.) Or when the long-term consequence might find America "completely committed to direct intervention. These situa-tions, unfortunately, have a way of snowballing"?[30] But the other two factors stimulated the United States to protect its investment rather than liquidate it. The Korean War, for its part, compounded the volatil-ity of Southeast Asia and dictated that only increased commitment had any chance of success. Interpreted as a Soviet venture rather than a civil war, Korea gave credence to the notion of Communist expansion-ism and the possibility that its tactics had moved from Cold War to military aggression. Given Acheson's earlier prediction of Communist expansion south and east from China, it now became increasingly plausible for his subordinates like Dean Rusk—then Assistant Secretary for Far Eastern Affairs—to predict in September 1950 "a probable communist offensive against Indochina in late September or early October . . . carried out by augmented Viet Minh forces" trained and supplied "from Communist China." (Doc. 29.) Chinese entry into the Korea War, arguably done for defensive reasons, nonetheless reinforced a militarized perspective. As early as December 29, 1950, the Central Intelligence Agency made the first of many similar predictions to follow: "Direct intervention by Chinese Communist troops [in Indochina] may occur at any time. It may have already begun." (Doc. 30.) Operating from similar premises, but unwilling and unable to take over the French role directly, the National Security Council (NSC 48/5) could only conclude in May 1951 that the United States should "continue to increase the military effectiveness of French units and the size and equipment of indigenous units," while also encouraging "internal autonomy and progressive social and economic reforms."[31] It was a feeble substitute for earlier PPS advice that France be pressured to promise full independence within a stated two-year period.

If the seeming lesson of Korea was that only enhanced American aid held out any hope for eventual stabilization, then the Japanese situation seemed to teach another one—that the stakes were too high not to make the attempt. General Matthew Ridgway, MacArthur's successor in Korea, summed those stakes up well in recounting a conversation with John Foster Dulles—later Secretary of State in the Eisenhower administration:

Mr. Dulles then stated his view that the two major problems facing the United States in foreign relations were Japan and Germany, of which the former was much more difficult. The problem of weaving Germany into the economic, industrial and security fabric of Western civilization was infinitely easier than that of first bringing Japan into that fabric, and then of keeping her there against the promises of Communism in contiguous Asia.[32]

In the short run, the Korean War eased the problem of Dulles' concern. Enlisting Japanese productivity to meet wartime needs, America's Special Procurement program pumped $860 million (1951) in military purchases into the Japanese economy, and canceled out the $700 million in Japan's dollar deficit resulting from her unfavorable balance of trade with the United States. But in 1952, American anxiety heightened again as its leaders confronted the question of what to do about a "Viable Economy of Japan" once the Korean War ended.[33] What would take the place of American military Keynesianism as a market

59

for Japanese industrial production? The answer was the same as that given Kennan when he first posed the question in late 1949: Southeast Asia. High tariffs inhibited expansion of the American market; declining raw material productivity diminished the sterling bloc market. But "a way to break through is to bestow the purchasing power to Southeast Asian regions."[34]

In a lengthy report on "How to cope with the present dollar deficit of Japan?" the Economic and Scientific Bureau in Tokyo saw economic integration of Japan and SEA as the only viable supplement to a declining procurement operation. Noting that Japan already had a favorable balance of some $100 million with the area, the report argued that Japan could earn dollar exchange by export of its manufactured products to SEA, and reduce its imports of food and raw materials from the United States by substituting those from SEA. None of this could happen, however, unless something was done about political instability and low "purchasing power in these areas." American foreign policy would have to solve the former; "Japan's investment is the only way" to solve the latter.[35] The report's analysis was mirrored in NSC 124/2 (June 1952; Doc. 31):

> In the long run the loss of Southeast Asia, especially Malaya and Indonesia, could result in such economic and political pressures in Japan as to make it extremely difficult to prevent Japan's eventual accommodation to the Soviet Bloc.[36]

The same concern largely motivated American negotiation of the Japanese Peace Treaty formally ending World War II. Designed to integrate Japan politically and to leave open the option of remilitarization, it also sought to facilitate the broadening of Japan's trade relations with her former SEA victims by bestowing upon her the legitimacy of a peace-loving nation. But before Japan—or anyone else—could profitably walk the commercial streets of Southeast Asia, those streets would first have to be made safe. Law and order—pacification and stabilization—was the indispensable prerequisite.

11. DE GAULLE RAISES
THE INDOCHINA ISSUE, 1945

This document is an early illustration of the interrelatedness between affairs in Southeast Asia and in Europe. It is also an early example of French efforts to blackmail the United States into supporting restoration of the French Empire in Indochina. Note that General de Gaulle's manipulation of a shared fear of Soviet communism takes place even as Russia and America allied in the final push to defeat Nazi Germany. (Source: Department of State, *Foreign Relations of the United States, 1945,* VI, p. 300.)

THE AMBASSADOR IN FRANCE (CAFFERY) TO THE SECRETARY OF STATE

PARIS, March 13, 1945—7 p.m.
[Received March 14—1:23 p.m.]

1196. General de Gaulle asked me to come to see him at 6. He spoke in very quiet, affable, friendly fashion, but this is what he said: "We have received word that our troops still fighting in Indochina have appealed for aid to your military authorities in China and the British military authorities in Burma. We have received word that they replied that under instructions no aid could be sent.["] They were given to understand that the British simply followed our lead.

He said also that several expeditionary forces for Indochina had been prepared: Some troops were in North Africa, some in southern France and some in Madagascar, and the British had promised to transport them but at the last minute they were given to understand that owing to American insistence they could not transport them. He observed: "This worries me a great deal for obvious reasons and it comes at a particularly inopportune time. As I told [Harry L. Hopkins, Special Assistant to President Roosevelt] Mr. Hopkins when he was here, we do not understand your policy. What are you driving at? Do you want us to become, for example, one of the federated states under the Russian aegis? The Russians are advancing apace as you well know. When Germany falls they will be upon us. If the public here comes to realize that you are against us in Indochina there will be terrific disappointment and nobody knows to what that will lead. We do not want to become Communist; we do not want to fall into the Russian orbit, but I hope that you do not push us into it."

He then went on to say that difficulties were being created too in regard to the promised armament—difficulties he could not understand unless that were part of our policy too. I told him I had been given to understand that the armament was arriving here as promised.

In any event, I said, I would telegraph at once to Washington all that he had said.

CAFFERY

12. REPORT TO TRUMAN ON THE WORLD ECONOMIC CRISIS, JULY 1950

A member of the Council of Economic Advisers (CEA), Walter Salant was probably more important than any other individual in educating President Truman to the complexities of international economics. In this lengthy and detailed report, excerpted below, Salant elaborated upon the problems and possible solutions only touched upon by Secretary of State Acheson. According to records at the Harry S. Truman Library, the White House received the report on July 12, 1950, just weeks after the outbreak of the Korean War. (Source: Memorandum by Walter Salant entitled "Further Problems for U.S. Foreign Economic Policy," July 10, 1945, Papers of George M. Elsey, Harry S. Truman Library, Independence, Mo.)

THE PROBLEM OF THE U.S. BALANCE OF PAYMENTS

14. In 1949, U.S. government grants and emergency loans financed nearly 40% of our total exports or nearly all of the export surplus of $6 billion. Under present programs, however, in particular the European Recovery Program, the future amount of U.S. economic assistance is scheduled to decline rapidly, and the net addition by this country to the goods and services of other countries will accordingly decrease.

15. *This raises the question whether the amount of dollars, which under present programs is likely to be available to other countries in the*

future, is compatible with the attainment of the economic, political, and security objectives of the U.S. . . .

30. While Western Europe will probably be able to produce a sufficient volume of export goods, *difficulties will be confronted in finding adequate foreign markets, both in the U.S. and in third areas.* The total volume of exports required will be substantially larger than prewar, owing to the loss of Western Europe's income from investment abroad. Available markets are more restricted owing to the sizeable area under Soviet domination. The competitive position of producers in Western Europe is still relatively weak. The prospective difficulties vary greatly among the individual countries, with those facing Western Germany being among the most serious.

31. Even if adequate export markets can be found in third areas, *there is still a question whether sufficient markets can be found in countries which will be able to pay for their additional imports from Europe in dollars (or in currencies convertible into dollars) or in goods which can be substituted for essential goods now paid for in dollars.* Western Europe requires, unavoidably, a "hard core" of dollar imports: goods and services which are essential to its economy and which may not be available in adequate quantities from non-dollar sources within the foreseeable future. For some time these dollar requirements may be substantially greater than the dollars earned by Western Europe.

32. The serious dollar deficit of Western Europe at the present time results from a number of factors: (a) the prewar relationship, whereby Western Europe financed its dollar deficit by dollar earnings in third areas, has not been fully restored . . . ; (b) unrest, lagging recovery, and internal inflation have reduced non-dollar sources of materials which Europe needs, thus forcing reliance on dollar sources where supplies have increased . . . ; (c) Soviet domination of Eastern Europe has drastically curtailed important prewar sources of imports . . . ; and (d) Western European exports to the U.S. are below prewar quantities as well as below prewar proportions of both total Western European exports and total U.S. imports. . . .

35. *The situation of Japan is, in its broad aspects, analogous to that of Western Europe.* It does not appear that *net* aid would be required, if adequate markets could be found for the potential production of exportable goods, and if a sufficient portion of the exports could be paid for in dollars or in goods Japan now obtains from dollar sources.

36. Domestic recovery in Japan has been pronounced (made possible in part by U.S. appropriated aid totalling $1.8 billions through June 1950). Agricultural output now exceeds prewar levels, and the index of industrial activity has currently reached 100 percent of the 1932–1936 base.

Moreover, Japan has manufacturing capacity and a labor force that are not now being utilized fully. It appears that Japan, like Western Europe, could produce goods and services in sufficient volume both to meet domestic requirements and to exchange for the imports it must have from abroad.

37. The actual achievement of a self-supporting status in Japan depends, however, on a combination of circumstances which does not now prevail. To an even greater degree than Western Europe, Japan is dependent upon imported commodities. All its cotton and wool, most of its coking coal and petroleum, and about 20 percent of its basic food requirements must come from abroad. Prewar Japan was able to obtain virtually all of its food imports and a large part of its essential raw material imports from Asiatic sources, within and outside the Japanese Empire. Since the war, many of these sources of imports have dried up almost completely. Korean and Formosan rice exports formerly covered Japan's cereal grain deficit, for example, while Manchuria and China met Japan's needs for coking coal, soybeans, and other commodities. This trade pattern has not been restored and is not likely to be restored in the foreseeable future. . . .

38. The result has been to make Japan heavily dependent upon the U.S. for its indispensable imports. But even before the war, Japan had an import surplus from the U.S. Now that Japan has lost the greatest part of its silk market in the U.S., its dollar earning prospects have deteriorated even further. To achieve self-support Japan must not only seek to expand exports to the U.S., but it must also continue to expand export markets where it can earn dollars or currencies convertible into dollars; and it must also find non-dollar sources from which it can obtain some of its needed imports in exchange for its exports.

39. The U.S. has a profound economic and security interest in achieving a sound solution for these trade problems of the other industrial countries. Failing such a solution, one of two consequences may follow: Either we shall be forced, in order to preserve the progress already achieved, to continue extraordinary dollar aid in substantial amounts; or we are likely to see a deterioration in internal conditions abroad and in international relationships which would be as injurious to us as to the rest of the free world. Consequently, we should be prepared to participate in joint efforts to promote the trade and financial patterns which will use and develop the great productive capacity of Western Europe and Japan. . . .

50. For some countries, such as many of those in Latin America, existing mechanisms may be adequate. For others, new mechanisms and techniques might have to be considered, both to bring about an adequate flow of capital and to have reasonable assurance that such capital is used

effectively for the purpose of economic development. Among the issues involved are the kinds of measures, on the part of both the U.S. and recipient governments, that would tend to accelerate the movement of private capital; the question of the roles to be assigned to various types of foreign assistance; the possibilities of integrating development programs in the underdeveloped areas with U.S. policies toward Western Europe and Japan; and the availability of means for assuring the adoption of appropriate internal policies in underdeveloped countries. Even if effective mechanisms are found, there is a limit to the amounts the underdeveloped countries can absorb efficiently.

51. From the point of view of the defense and security of the free world, Asia differs from underdeveloped areas in Africa and Latin America mainly in that the Communist threat is imminent and may require emergency action. The group of countries principally involved—India, Pakistan, Burma, Ceylon, Malaya, Indonesia, Thailand, Indochina, Formosa, the Philippines, Iran, and Afghanistan—are characterised generally by large populations living at or near the margin of subsistence. This is, of course, not a new condition. What is new is that they have all been affected by postwar political upheavals and by an upsurge of nationalism. Most have achieved political independence since 1945 and their peoples have been led to expect higher levels of material well-being.

52. So far these expectations have largely been disappointed. In many respects, the area as a whole is in a poorer position to meet its people's needs than at any period in modern times. At the same time, Communist military and political aggression, headed by indigenous Communist armed forces and reinforced by the overhanging threat of the new Chinese regime, is a present danger to the stability and independence of some of these countries, and a potential danger to all of them. . . .

54. Critical security situations in underdeveloped areas, such as those of Southeast Asia, and the emergency measures which may be needed to deal with them, should not obscure the nature and importance of the long-range problem. In these countries, as in other underdeveloped countries, self-sustaining economies and democratic societies capable of maintaining their freedom against subversion and aggression can be built in the long run only through internal policies which strengthen their political and social structure, and with the help of the technical skills and capital resources of the industrialized countries of the free world.

13. STATE DEPARTMENT MEMO ON "FAR EASTERN 'MARSHALL PLAN'"

As early as late 1947, there was talk of a "Far Eastern 'Marshall Plan.'" Here, in an internal State Department memorandum, John Allison calls the attention of the Assistant Secretary for Far Eastern Affairs to the advantages of such a regional approach. While focusing on Japanese industrial recovery, an area-wide strategy could appeal to the self-interests of Southeast Asia, while minimizing anti-Japanese sentiments still prevalent in the region. (Source: National Archives, December 17, 1947, 894.50/12-1747.)

CONFIDENTIAL

OFFICE MEMORANDUM   United States Government

TO   : FE—Mr. Butterworth   DATE: December 17, 1947
FROM   : NA—Mr. Allison
SUBJECT: Economic Recovery in Japan (SANACC 381/1 and 381/2)

I believe a strong case can be made for the fact that the economic revival of Japan is dependent upon the economic revival of Asia as a whole and vice-versa. If this is so and if, in fact, Japan is to be the "workshop of Asia" it can only be as a result of a far-reaching, all-embracing program looking toward the restoration not of Japan's economy alone, but of the economy of the whole Far Eastern area. What is needed is, for want of a better term, a Far Eastern "Marshall Plan." It is only by some such imaginative proposal that the United States will be able to obtain the vital whole-hearted cooperation of the other Far Eastern powers in the revival of Japan. I believe under present circumstances it will be useless to go to them with a program which says in effect:

The United States desires to undertake a program to bring about Japanese economic self-support so that American taxpayers will no longer bear the burden of underwriting Japan's economy, that in order to do this we know we must get your cooperation and incidentally your countries will be helped by the revival of Japan.

Rather, it seems to me, it will be necessary to say to the countries of Asia:

We wish to help you people of Asia help yourselves to a better and more abundant standard of living and in order to do this we know it will be necessary along with more direct aid to you to help get Japan back on her feet again economically so that she can buy from you the raw materials and supplies you wish to sell and make available to you the cheap consumers goods and other products which your economy needs.

The above approach is one which can most appropriately be made to China and the countries of south-east Asia. For some time to come it is unlikely that Japan will be able to resume profitable trade relationships with Korea or Manchuria and this makes it most important that every effort be made to enlist the active cooperation of the other Asiatic areas in a program which looks toward making Japan self-supporting. In fact, the cooperation of these south-east Asian areas may become absolutely essential if Japan is to be kept from falling into Soviet arms as a result of offers of economic opportunities in Manchuria, North Korea, Sakhalien and even Siberia.

While it may be argued that any suggestion of a "Marshall Plan" for the Far East is completely impracticable at the present time, I do not think this should prevent the State Department proposing what it believes is right and what it believes is the only program which will, in the long run, be successful. There is considerable Congressional interest in the Far East and the American people have traditionally looked with favor on Far Eastern enterprises. Neither Congress nor the American people, however, will wish to put their money or hopes in a program so narrowly conceived that it is doomed to failure from the beginning. A forthright, positive program which can be shown to make sense economically and which is so designed that it will, of its own nature, attract the cooperation of those nations whose good will and aid is essential, will I believe be possible to "sell" to Congress and the public.

14. STATE DEPARTMENT MEMO ON IMPLICATIONS OF RUSSIAN A-BOMB

The Russian acquisition of the atomic bomb in 1949 unquestionably stimulated the American tendency to define the Cold War and the containment policy in military terms. That tendency, however, grew from fear not that Russia would use the bomb militarily, but that she would use it as a diplomatic tool of intimidation against Western Europe to weaken its solidarity with the United States on policy toward Germany, the Middle East, and the Third World. That whole line of analysis stimulated American thinking that a military shield was necessary to ensure political stability in Europe, necessary in turn to facilitate economic recovery. As we shall see, that same analysis was applied to areas like Southeast Asia that were politically unstable and economically less developed.

The document below represents the internal effort within the State Department to clarify its views on the policy implications of the Russian A-bomb. Parallel efforts were made in the Department of Defense and other groups represented on the National Security Council. (Source: Memorandum by Secretary of State Dean Acheson, December 20, 1949, National Archives, Record Group 59, unnumbered.)

This memorandum was dictated by Secretary Acheson presumably on December 20, 1949. He handed it to Mr. Nitze on the evening of that day. Mr. Nitze made some changes during the evening just before he left for vacation. On the morning of December 21, Mr. Kennan, Mr. Hooker and Mr. Savage made some further changes. The attached memo contains the changes made by the four of us. It was sent to Mr. Acheson on the morning of December 21 and he used it presumably as a basis for the conversation he had during the afternoon with Secretary of Defense Johnson. It is understood that he did not give a copy to Secretary Johnson.

CARLTON SAVAGE

I. It is of immediate importance that the United States Government review and decide its position regarding the essentiality and probable use of weapons of mass destruction—particularly atomic weapons—so far as our security is concerned.

4) It is important to review and decide our position on the use of these weapons because to do so will enable us to identify and possibly decide some major questions affecting foreign policy. Some of these are:

a) Which are the most immediate dangers to our security? Those involved in the cold war or those involved in military aggression?

b) Will military aggression, if it comes, be directed against us or against our allies?

c) If against us, what are the problems involved and how does use or non-use of atomic weapons affect their solution?

d) If against our allies, the same questions.

e) How does the availability of atomic weapons to both sides now affect

68

the possibility of their use? The possibility of precipitating war? The outcome of the cold war? What will be the trend in this respect in the future?

II. Which danger is most imminent and pressing upon us? That which pertains to the cold war, or the danger of military aggression?

1) Soviet theory warns us that their primary attention is directed toward the former.

a) They believe that the capitalist world is doomed by internal decay.

b) They do believe and advocate active and subversive activities within capitalist societies by the communist parties.

c) They do not believe that the overthrow has to come through communist arms in the first instance, but they believe that the capitalist world will not finally surrender power without a resort to arms and that, therefore, at some time they may be attacked.

d) They would prefer a war between capitalist countries in which they intervene at the decisive moment, but in view of the unlikelihood of that coming about might intervene in confused situations created by satellites or subversive groups.

2) Russian history is divided, but Soviet history seems to be against military adventures which entail any risk.

a) The Crimean war, the Russo-Japanese war and World War I show tendencies toward aggressive adventure. So does the Polish affair of 1921 and 1939 and the Finnish war. But these latter may be said to have involved no great risk and to have lessons that risk is hard to estimate. The great care to escape involvement in the "capitalist" war of 1939 supports the thesis that the lesson was learned.

3) A cold appraisal of the world situation would seem to give the Politburo reason to think that their chances in the cold war are not bad, that their dogmas are being proved true, and that military risks to speed the inevitable are not necessary or desirable. They might well conclude that more effort was needed to grease the wheels of economic and social confusion abroad.

4) This would be a sensible conclusion. Our allies are not strong and have a long way to go to get strong. They are divided on some of the essential steps—Germany, colonialism in Asia and Africa, policy in the Middle East. The American people may tire or become confused. Our problems take perseverance of purpose and use of resources. They take a large degree of unity and persistence of purpose. Democracies are not noted for these qualities.

5) This is important. They need and want the people, industry and resources of western Europe. They do not want to destroy them. Success in the cold war achieves these. The hot war may lose all this and more too.

69

6) This is also important. The loss of western Europe or of important parts of Asia or the Middle East would be a transfer of potential from West to East, which, depending on the area, might have the gravest consequences in the long run.

Conclusion on Point II. The weight of the evidence leads to the belief that the Russians will put their chief reliance on the cold war. It is here that we must meet the most pressing dangers and not from military aggression.

Against this is the danger that—

a) They may think they are going to be attacked and foolishly attack first.

b) That failure in the cold war, the growth of Titoism, and the possible instability of the regime may lead to unpredictable action. This seems unlikely but not impossible.

The point made is not to disregard the dangers of military aggression, but to devise policy to give priority to what comes first.

III. In the case of military aggression by the U.S.S.R. is it likely to be directed first against us or against our allies?

The answer would seem to be, either a simultaneous attack against both, or an attack against some other nation or nations. An attack against the U.S. alone seems too difficult, pointless, and hazardous.

The point which the question and answer, if correct, brings out is this: The function of the atomic weapon in regard to the defense of continental United States is to prevent the attack or to stop it by reason of the general punishment inflicted on the enemy—retaliation. It can hardly have, in this field, a more specific military purpose. In the case of a protracted war, other factors would immediately have important bearing.

These other factors would have to do with the course of the war in other areas. Before coming to this, let us appraise the influence of atomic weapons on preventing or stopping the war.

IV. What can be said about the effect of atomic weapons in preventing or stopping the assumed war against the United States?

Without treading on military ground, consider the problem in two parts: (a) a war started against the United States and others simultaneously; and (b) a war started against our allies only.

1) If there were no atomic weapons, it seems unlikely that an attack would be made against the United States. This leaves out of consideration other weapons of mass destruction. If there were none of these, the conclusion that there would be no attack against us seems highly probable, through sheer difficulty.

2) Would the same be true if it were firmly believed on both sides that

such weapons would not be used except in retaliation; but that they would be promptly and vigorously used in retaliation? This involves a calculation as to whether the enemy believed the risks were worth it. In this case it is fair to believe that the risks would not be worth it and there would be no direct attack on the United States, or that the probability of attack would be lessened. This is no inconsiderable consideration to be ignored, if true.

15. NATIONAL SECURITY COUNCIL 68: PIVOTAL REPORT ON THE FUTURE OF THE COLD WAR, APRIL 1950

The following excerpts are from NSC 68, one of the most critical documents in Cold War history. Adopted by the National Security Council in early April 1950 (before the Korean War), it was the fundamental American commitment to the militarization of the Cold War and the most elaborate analysis of the continuous circle of military protection, political stability, and economic growth. Its language, perhaps reflective of Defense Department input, is more strident than that found in State Department study papers (see Doc. 14). Its definition of Soviet-American conflict as global in scope and military in nature had obvious implications for the war in Indochina. (Source: Department of State, *Foreign Relations of the United States, 1950,* I, pp. 234–85.)

A REPORT TO THE NATIONAL SECURITY COUNCIL BY THE EXECUTIVE SECRETARY (LAY)

TOP SECRET   WASHINGTON, April 14, 1950.
NSC 68

NOTE BY THE EXECUTIVE SECRETARY TO THE NATIONAL SECURITY COUNCIL ON UNITED STATES OBJECTIVES AND PROGRAMS FOR NATIONAL SECURITY . . .

[Enclosure 2]

A REPORT TO THE PRESIDENT PURSUANT TO THE PRESIDENT'S DIRECTIVE OF JANUARY 31, 1950

[WASHINGTON,] April 7, 1950.

CONTENTS

TERMS OF REFERENCE

The following report is submitted in response to the President's directive of January 31 which reads:

That the President direct the Secretary of State and the Secretary of Defense to undertake a reexamination of our objectives in peace and war and of the effect of these objectives on our strategic plans, in the light of the probable fission bomb capability and possible thermonuclear bomb capability of the Soviet Union.

The document which recommended that such a directive be issued reads in part:

It must be considered whether a decision to proceed with a program directed toward determining feasibility prejudges the more fundamental decisions *(a)* as to whether, in the event that a test of a thermonuclear weapon proves successful, such weapons should be stockpiled, or *(b)* if stockpiled, the conditions under which they might be used in war. If a test of a thermonuclear weapon proves successful, the pressures to produce and stockpile such weapons to be held for the same purposes for which fission bombs are then being held will be greatly increased. The question of use policy can be adequately assessed only as a part of a general reexamination of this country's strategic plans and its objectives in peace and war. Such reexamination would need to consider national policy not only with respect to possible thermonuclear weapons, but also with respect to fission weapons—viewed in the light of the probable fission bomb capability and the possible thermonuclear bomb capability of the Soviet Union. The moral, psychological, and political questions involved in this problem would need to be taken into account and be given due weight. The outcome of this reexamination would have a crucial bearing on the further question as to whether there should be a revision in the nature of the agreements, including the international control of atomic energy, which we have been seeking to reach with the U.S.S.R.

ANALYSIS

I. BACKGROUND OF THE PRESENT CRISIS

Within the past thirty-five years the world has experienced two global wars of tremendous violence. It has witnessed two revolutions—the Russian and the Chinese—of extreme scope and intensity. It has also seen the collapse of five empires—the Ottoman, the Austro-Hungarian, German, Italian and Japanese—and the drastic decline of two major imperial sys-

73

tems, the British and the French. During the span of one generation, the international distribution of power has been fundamentally altered. For several centuries it had proved impossible for any one nation to gain such preponderant strength that a coalition of other nations could not in time face it with greater strength. The international scene was marked by recurring periods of violence and war, but a system of sovereign and independent states was maintained, over which no state was able to achieve hegemony.

Two complex sets of factors have now basically altered this historical distribution of power. First, the defeat of Germany and Japan and the decline of the British and French Empires have interacted with the development of the United States and the Soviet Union in such a way that power has increasingly gravitated to these two centers. Second, the Soviet Union, unlike previous aspirants to hegemony, is animated by a new fanatic faith, antithetical to our own, and seeks to impose its absolute authority over the rest of the world. Conflict has, therefore, become endemic and is waged, on the part of the Soviet Union, by violent or non-violent methods in accordance with the dictates of expediency. With the development of increasingly terrifying weapons of mass destruction, every individual faces the ever-present possibility of annihilation should the conflict enter the phase of total war.

On the one hand, the people of the world yearn for relief from the anxiety arising from the risk of atomic war. On the other hand, any substantial further extension of the area under the domination of the Kremlin would raise the possibility that no coalition adequate to confront the Kremlin with greater strength could be assembled. It is in this context that this Republic and its citizens in the ascendancy of their strength stand in their deepest peril.

The issues that face us are momentous, involving the fulfillment or destruction not only of this Republic but of civilization itself. They are issues which will not await our deliberations. With conscience and resolution this Government and the people it represents must now take new and fateful decisions. . . .

VII. Present Risks

A. *General*

It is apparent from the preceding sections that the integrity and vitality of our system is in greater jeopardy than ever before in our history. Even if there were no Soviet Union we would face the great problem of the free society, accentuated many fold in this industrial age, of reconciling order, security, the need for participation, with the requirements of freedom. We would face the fact that in a shrinking world the absence of order among nations is becoming less and less tolerable. The Kremlin design seeks to impose order among nations by means which would destroy our free and democratic system. The Kremlin's possession of atomic weapons puts new power behind its design, and increases the jeopardy to our system. It adds new strains to the uneasy equilibrium-without-order which exists in the world and raises new doubts in men's minds whether the world will long tolerate this tension without moving toward some kind of order, on somebody's terms.

The risks we face are of a new order of magnitude, commensurate with the total struggle in which we are engaged. For a free society there is never total victory, since freedom and democracy are never wholly attained, are always in the process of being attained. But defeat at the hands of the totalitarian is total defeat. These risks crowd in on us, in a shrinking world of polarized power, so as to give us no choice, ultimately, between meeting them effectively or being overcome by them.

B. *Specific*

It is quite clear from Soviet theory and practice that the Kremlin seeks to bring the free world under its dominion by the methods of the cold war. The preferred technique is to subvert by infiltration and intimidation. Every institution of our society is an instrument which it is sought to stultify and turn against our purposes. Those that touch most closely our material and moral strength are obviously the prime targets, labor unions, civic enterprises, schools, churches, and all media for influencing opinion. The effort is not so much to make them serve obvious Soviet ends as to prevent them from serving our ends, and thus to make them sources of confusion in our economy, our culture and our body politic. The doubts and diversities that in terms of our values are part of the merit of a free system, the weaknesses and the problems that are peculiar to it, the rights and privileges that free men enjoy, and the disorganization and destruction left in the wake of the last attack on our freedoms, all are but opportunities for the Kremlin to do its evil work. Every advantage is taken of the fact that our means of prevention and retaliation are limited by those principles and scruples which are precisely the ones that give our freedom and democracy its meaning for us. None of our scruples deter those whose only code is, "morality is that which serves the revolution."

Since everything that gives us or others respect for our institutions is a suitable object for attack, it also fits the Kremlin's design that where, with impunity, we can be insulted and made to suffer indignity the opportunity shall not be missed, particularly in any context which can be used to cast dishonor on our country, our system, our motives, or our methods. Thus the means by which we sought to restore our own economic health in the '30's, and now seek to restore that of the free world, come equally under attack. The military aid by which we sought to help the free world was frantically denounced by the Communists in the early days of the last war, and of course our present efforts to develop adequate military strength for ourselves and our allies are equally denounced.

At the same time the Soviet Union is seeking to create overwhelming military force, in order to back up infiltration with intimidation. In the only terms in which it understands strength, it is seeking to demonstrate to the free world that force and the will to use it are on the side of the Kremlin, that those who lack it are decadent and doomed. In local incidents it threatens and encroaches both for the sake of local gains and to increase anxiety and defeatism in all the free world.

The possession of atomic weapons at each of the opposite poles of power, and the inability (for different reasons) of either side to place any trust in the other, puts a premium on a surprise attack against us. It equally puts a premium on a more violent and ruthless prosecution of its design by cold war, especially if the Kremlin is sufficiently objective to realize the improbability of our prosecuting a preventive war. It also puts a premium on piecemeal aggression against others, counting on our unwillingness to engage in atomic war unless we are directly attacked. We run all these risks and the added risk of being confused and immobilized by our inability to weigh and choose, and pursue a firm course based on a rational assessment of each.

The risk that we may thereby be prevented or too long delayed in taking all needful measures to maintain the integrity and vitality of our system is great. The risk that our allies will lose their determination is greater. And the risk that in this manner a descending spiral of too little and too late, of doubt and recrimination, may present us with ever narrower and more desperate alternatives, is the greatest risk of all. For example, it is clear that our present weakness would prevent us from offering effective resistance at any of several vital pressure points. The only deterrent we can present to the Kremlin is the evidence we give that we may make any of the critical points which we cannot hold the occasion for a global war of annihilation.

The risk of having no better choice than to capitulate or precipitate a global war at any of a number of pressure points is bad enough in itself, but it is multiplied by the weakness it imparts to our position in the cold war. Instead of appearing strong and resolute we are continually at the verge of appearing and being alternately irresolute and desperate; yet it is the cold war which we must win, because both the Kremlin design, and our fundamental purpose give it the first priority.

The frustration of the Kremlin design, however, cannot be accomplished by us alone, as will appear from the analysis in Chapter IX, B. Strength at the center, in the United States, is only the first of two essential elements. The second is that our allies and potential allies do not as a result of a sense of frustration or of Soviet intimidation drift into a course of neutrality eventually leading to Soviet domination. If this were to happen in Germany the effect upon Western Europe and eventually upon us might be catastrophic. . . .

POSSIBLE COURSES OF ACTION

D. *The Remaining Course of Action—a Rapid Build-up of Political, Economic, and Military Strength in the Free World.*

A more rapid build-up of political, economic, and military strength and thereby of confidence in the free world than is now contemplated is the only course which is consistent with progress toward achieving our fundamental purpose. The frustration of the Kremlin design requires the free world to develop a successfully functioning political and economic system and a vigorous political offensive against the Soviet Union. These, in turn, require an adequate military shield under which they can develop. It is necessary to have the military power to deter, if possible, Soviet expansion, and to defeat, if necessary, aggressive Soviet or Soviet-directed actions of a limited or total character. The potential strength of the free world is great; its ability to develop these military capabilities and its will to resist Soviet expansion will be determined by the wisdom and will with which it undertakes to meet its political and economic problems.

A program for rapidly building up strength and improving political and economic conditions will place heavy demands on our courage and intelligence; it will be costly; it will be dangerous. But half-measures will be more costly and more dangerous, for they will be inadequate to prevent and may actually invite war. Budgetary considerations will need to be subordinated to the stark fact that our very independence as a nation may be at stake.

A comprehensive and decisive program to win the peace and frustrate the Kremlin design should be so designed that it can be sustained for as long as necessary to achieve our national objectives. It would probably involve:

(1) The development of an adequate political and economic framework for the achievement of our long-range objectives.

(2) A substantial increase in expenditures for military purposes adequate to meet the requirements for the tasks listed in Section D-1.

(3) A substantial increase in military assistance programs, designed to foster cooperative efforts, which will adequately and efficiently meet the requirements of our allies for the tasks referred to in Section D-1-*e.*

77

(4) Some increase in economic assistance programs and recognition of the need to continue these programs until their purposes have been accomplished.

(5) A concerted attack on the problem of the United States balance of payments, along the lines already approved by the President.

(6) Development of programs designed to build and maintain confidence among other peoples in our strength and resolution, and to wage overt psychological warfare calculated to encourage mass defections from Soviet allegiance and to frustrate the Kremlin design in other ways.

(7) Intensification of affirmative and timely measures and operations by covert means in the fields of economic warfare and political and psychological warfare with a view to fomenting and supporting unrest and revolt in selected strategic satellite countries.

(8) Development of internal security and civilian defense programs.

(9) Improvement and intensification of intelligence activities.

(10) Reduction of Federal expenditures for purposes other than defense and foreign assistance, if necessary by the deferment of certain desirable programs.

(11) Increased taxes.

Essential as prerequisites to the success of this program would be *(a)* consultations with Congressional leaders designed to make the program the object of non-partisan legislative support, and *(b)* a presentation to the public of a full explanation of the facts and implications of present international trends.

16. BUTTERWORTH'S ARGUMENT AGAINST A FAR EASTERN MARSHALL PLAN

By late 1948 the Far Eastern desk of the State Department advised Acheson of the importance of Southeast Asia to Japanese recovery and cautioned that political-military solutions had to precede economic development. In this memorandum on "how U.S. aid might contribute effectively to political stability and economic improvement in Asia" Assistant Secretary W. Walton Butterworth develops a fascinating argument against a Far Eastern Marshall Plan—an argument that ultimately prevailed. (Source: National Archives 890.50/10-2748.)

CONFIDENTIAL

OFFICE MEMORANDUM   UNITED STATES GOVERNMENT

TO   : S—The Acting Secretary   DATE: October 27, 1948
THRU   : S/S
FROM   : FE—Mr. Butterworth
SUBJECT: Question of Coordinated U.S. Economic Aid for Asia and
            the Far East

You will recall that I mentioned to you that while in your outer office on Saturday last Mr. William Y. Elliott of the House Foreign Affairs committee indicated preoccupation with the question of coordination of future programs for Korea, China and Japan and, in particular, asked me the direct question as to whether I would favor the giving of ECA a status in Japan similar to that it has in Germany if as seemed likely the ECA legislation would have to be amended to include Korea. I refused to attempt to answer this question indicating it was a highly complicated problem which had to be considered by various offices in the Department.

It seems to me that this suggestion may be considered in the light of broader proposals that are being made rather frequently of late to the effect that the U.S. Government should undertake a coordinated program of aid to Asia and the Far East directed at the economic recovery and development of countries in that area. Such a proposal usually reflects one, or both, of two principal considerations. Secretary Draper's remarks in this connection at a recent meeting of the NSC stemmed from his concern, shared in the Department, that the markets of Asia provide an effective demand for Japanese exports in order that Japan may become self-supporting. The desire of Asiatic countries for industrial growth achieved through U.S. aid comparable to that being extended to western Europe often underlies reports to the effect that a "Marshall Plan" is being formulated for Asia and the Far East. There are indications that Asiatic members of the UN Economic Commission for Asia and the Far East are now actively attempting to work out a coordinated plan of industrial development for the ECAFE area conceived as a necessary prerequisite to the receipt of aid for this purpose.

The question of how U.S. aid might contribute effectively to political stability and economic improvement in Asia has been, and is, of continuing concern in the Department. However, the virtual certainty that the question of coordinated aid to Asia will be introduced at the next session of Congress makes it important that the relevant aspects of the problem be reexamined with a view to formulation of a more definitive policy position.

Without attempting to set forth all of the primary factors bearing on the problem of U.S. economic aid policy towards Asia, I should like to mention certain considerations which occur to me. The most important historical complementary relationship among the economies of Asiatic countries is that between Japanese industry and the raw material producing areas of the Asiatic mainland and the southwest Pacific islands. With the exception of Japan, the countries of Asia are predominantly agricultural and their economies basically self-sufficient or non-complementary at the present level of their development. The first prerequisite to economic recovery in Asia is, not increased production and exports, fiscal reform and economic cooperation as in Europe, but effective solutions for fundamental political and military conflicts which are stifling production and trade. Given these political solutions, and a ready market for Asia's normal exports to the rest of the world, economic recovery could be attained rapidly, and with relatively little capital expenditure, to a large extent through the individual efforts of Asiatic countries themselves.

Thus, the character of Asia's economy indicates that, if political conditions were favorable and demands for its products are maintained at near current levels, economic recovery would not require U.S. economic aid of a magnitude at all comparable to that needed by Europe, nor would such U.S. aid as might be required have to be predicated on the type of joint recovery program developed for the highly industrialized and interdependent economies of western Europe. So long as the present political conflicts exist in China, Indochina, the NEI, Burma, India and Pakistan, the question of U.S. economic aid to those countries presents delicate, if not insuperable, problems which should be considered and dealt with essentially in the light of the unique circumstances existing in each country rather than as components of a common undertaking for Asia as a whole. If large scale U.S. economic aid is extended prior to the achievement of the stability necessary to recovery, such aid should be justified by U.S. political and strategic interests which outweigh the continuing costs to be borne if the political conflicts cannot be solved.

New economic development extending considerably beyond recovery to prewar levels of economic activity is an overriding ambition of the governments of several Asiatic countries. These governments apparently indulge in the hope that the foreign capital required for such development will be made available primarily by western governments. It would seem to me unwise if the U.S. Government, by any gesture which could be interpreted as an Asiatic "Marshall Plan"—even an embryonic one—, were to encourage the idea (1) that present conditions throughout Asia are favorable to the general development of new capital on a significant scale or to the achievement of economic recovery through American aid, (2) that foreign government capital could or should substitute altogether for private foreign capital, or (3) that the progress of new economic development, facilitated by public or private foreign capital, could be expected to overcome severe limitations inherent in the social, political and economic structure of most Asiatic countries. The chronic political instability of many Asiatic countries is, in part, a consequence of the extreme pressure of population on the land. Large scale industrialization offers little prospect for remedying this situation since the amount of domestic capital available for new investment is necessarily small (unless resort were had to extreme exploitation or inflation), and since the growth of population would tend to offset gains in productivity. Obviously, the U.S. Government cannot afford, from the point of view of general policy or economic feasibility, to sponsor in the foreseeable future any aid program, the objective of which is to enable a significant increase in the standard of living of the billion inhabitants of Asia. This is not to say that the gradual development of Asia's resources at a realistic rate (consistent with the availability of capital and of technical and administrative competence) would not contribute to the eventual expansion of world trade. Nor is it to say that some U.S. Government aid for economic development, extended either directly or through the International Bank, should not be considered for those areas of Asia (e.g., the Philippines) in which relatively stable conditions now exist and in which U.S. interests would be supported by such action.

Despite the preceding observations, there may be certain measures which, within the limitations imposed by political circumstances in Asia, could be undertaken to effect some increase of production in Asiatic countries and of the trade of those countries, both among themselves and with other areas of the world. Such measures would be of most immediate and obvious economic advantage, to the U.S. as well as to Asia, if applied to the partial reestablishment of natural economic relations between Japan and the rest of Asia. However, undue emphasis upon reestablishment of trade with Japan would vitiate other important objectives of the U.S. in Asia, and an attempt to promote the economic recovery of Japan through mere provision of dollars to other Asiatic countries with which to purchase Japanese exports would, of course, be tantamount to robbing Peter to pay Paul. Nevertheless, steps to promote the trade of Asiatic countries with Japan, as one aspect of their efforts to increase exports and imports generally, could appropriately be taken, or encouraged, by the U.S. in connection with the unilateral extension of aid to various Asiatic countries.

The formulation and implementation of economic aid measures of this character may require a greater degree of coordination within the U.S. Government than has been effected thus far in our policy toward Asia. However, it should not be necessary to launch a unified program of U.S. aid for all of Asia in order to improve coordination within this Government. Such increased coordination as may be called for should be possible without the creation of elaborate intra- or inter-Departmental machinery.

It is important that the Department have in hand specific proposals regarding such further measures for the rehabilitation of production and trade in Asia as might be undertaken under present conditions. Formulation of such proposals would require careful review and analysis of both particular and general aspects of the Asiatic situation. FE I think can helpfully contribute to this work particularly with respect to the relevant strategic and other policy considerations. I suggest that E be requested to study this problem in collaboration with NEA, U/FAA and FE with a view to arriving at recommendations of the position that the Department should take, and that, if you concur with the general tenor of this memorandum and in this specific recommendation, it be circulated to them for action.

17. STATE AND DEFENSE DEPARTMENT REPORT TO THE NATIONAL SECURITY COUNCIL ON ECONOMIC AID

Entitled "U.S. Economic Aid to Far Eastern Areas," this joint State-Defense Department report to the National Security Council (NSC 61) largely derived from a "Policy Paper on Asia" authored by Tracy Voorhees. Stressing the interdependence between Japanese recovery and Southeast Asian development, Voorhees recommended the same integration of economic and military aid that he also recommended for Europe. Note that NSC 61 predates both NSC 68 and the outbreak of the Korean War. (Source: NSC 61, A Report to the National Security Council by the Departments of State and Defense, January 27, 1950, National Archives, Record Group 59, unnumbered.)

The recommendations in the NSC policy paper on Asia for economic assistance to Southeast Asian areas need to be and can be, I believe, effectively supplemented if they are to result in significant improvement in existing conditions.

This subject is of direct and critical moment to the success of our occupation of Japan. Japan's trade with Russia, Manchuria and Communist China is now exceedingly small. Continuing, or even maintaining, Japan's economic recovery depends upon keeping Communism out of Southeast Asia, promoting economic recovery there and in further developing those countries, together with Indonesia, the Philippines, Southern Korea and India as the principal trading areas for Japan. This is wholly consistent with, and would greatly further the objectives of, the President's "Point Four" policy. It would also be entirely consistent with such countries continuing their existing trade with Europe, as the present proposal would call for increased trade not substitution of sources.

For example, in certain of these areas, such as Siam, it is apparently possible by introducing more irrigated farming to produce two crops of rice per year instead of the prevailing single crop. This additional rice could be bought by Japan with her exports, thereby greatly reducing her dollar deficit, now largely caused by need for dollar purchases of food and cotton from the United States.

The World Bank is now studying possible financing of some such improvements through a mission which just yesterday arrived in Bangkok. I have arranged for a mission including top-level personnel from the Department of Agriculture to survey the food production and trade aspects of the present proposal. This group will reach Bangkok about the middle of January and will correlate its study with that of the World Bank's group. Any detailed formulation of the plan here proposed will, of course, have to await the completion of such studies which should be available in a month to six weeks.

The basic principle should be to merge the present separate requests for appropriated dollars for various projects now operated more or less in separate watertight compartments and, instead to employ the revived Japanese economy to the full.

It is recommended that an immediate study be made as to an economic recovery program for the Southeast Asia area, including Japan and Korea, to be linked with any military assistance programs in that area, upon the basis of unified management of all United States aid, including present GARIOA funds for Japan, ECA funds for Korea, China aid and other incidental United States aid programs for the area covered; that the objectives be (1) to furnish economic assistance required for such backward areas to counter communism without additional dollar cost to the United States through better utilization for these purposes of the Japanese and other economies; (2) to further Japanese economic self-sufficiency; (3) to further the President's "Point Four" policy.

TRACY S. VOORHEES

18. JAPAN'S VIEWS ON SOUTHEAST ASIA

The following document is a fascinating summary of Japanese views about the relationship of Southeast Asia to Japanese well-being. Note the similarity of Japanese and American conceptions of Third World economic development: "better farming is the key." It means more rice ("clearly of vital importance to Japan") and a better "market for Japan's industrial products" ("poor producers make poor customers"). Interesting also is the Japanese willingness to teach "better farming" to Southeast Asia. Japan as the technical aid innovator, the United States as the military shield. (Source: Dispatch, United States Embassy, Tokyo, to the Department of State, "Japan's Participation in the Point IV Program," July 24, 1952, National Archives 834.00-TA/7-2452.)

Mr. Stanley Andrews, Administrator of TCA, spent two days in Tokyo (July 20–22). In the course of his visit he discussed with the Ministry of Agriculture and Forestry (MAF) and the Foreign Office the possibilities of establishing a training center in Japan for agricultural experts of Asian countries receiving technical assistance under the Point IV Program. Both the Foreign Office through Foreign Minister Okazaki, and the MAF through the Minister of Agriculture Hirokawa, assured Mr. Andrews of their readiness to offer all necessary facilities to insure the success of the project. The Japanese Press, too, has displayed the keenest interest in Mr. Andrews' visit. Although the reports lacked some of the more pertinent information regarding the positions taken by Mr. Andrews and the Japanese Government, there is no doubt that the Press as a whole would support any arrangement leading to the active participation of Japan in the Point IV Program.

The MAF presented its views on the subject in a memorandum entitled "Japan's Role in Technical Cooperation for Agricultural Development." The statement, which impressed Mr. Andrews with its thoroughness and concreteness, is summarized as follows.

(1) Japan would benefit from increased agricultural production in Southeast Asia. Japan is the largest importer of rice, and will remain so

with the rise in population. The current short supply of rice with resulting high prices is a heavy financial burden upon the country, and limits its import capacity in other commodities. An increase in the production of rice throughout Asia is clearly of vital importance to Japan.

(2) Higher agricultural productivity in Southeast Asia will augment the market for Japan's industrial products. With the Sino-Japanese trade virtually at a standstill, Japan must rely upon Southeast Asia for the major share of its trade. But since poor producers make poor customers, the market for Japanese goods can be enlarged only through a rising standard of living for the people of that region. The vast majority of the population being agricultural, better farming is the key to increased purchasing power.

(3) Economic and political stability of Asia is essential to Japan's security. Failure to develop Southeast Asian countries affects adversely not only Japan's requirements of rice and trade, but leads to economic and political instability, and, by the same token, to Communist penetration.

(4) Japan is not in a position to give financial assistance, but is capable and eager to extend technical aid to Southeast Asia, which is the very premise upon which Point IV operates. Japanese agricultural specialists believe that it is neither too difficult nor especially time-consuming to apply to agrarian Southeast Asia, with modifications where necessary, their own experience and skill gained from 50 years of scientific farming. They cite the remarkable agricultural developments in Formosa as an example. Apart from assistance along purely technical lines, Japan has much to offer on farm extension, organization of credit cooperatives, and cooperative trading; above all, Japan has acquired intimate knowledge regarding the drafting of land-reform legislation and its implementation. Many Asian countries are in need of land reform and the valuable experience Japan can furnish in this regard. Hence the conclusion: "We firmly believe that the knowledge and experience of Japanese experts and administrators can be utilized to the best advantage of under-developed countries in the field of increasing agricultural output, strengthening or organizing cooperative or extension systems, or in carrying out a sound land reform."

19. JAPAN'S TRADE POTENTIAL

The following is the preamble to a long, detailed report on Japan's trade potential in Southeast Asia. Prepared by the Economic and Scientific Section of the American occupational government in Japan, it was transmitted to both State and Defense in April 1950. (Source: Report from the Tokyo Economic and Commercial Conference, April 1950, National Archives ESS-PTCO-5687.)

JAPAN'S EXPORT POTENTIAL WITH SPECIFIC REFERENCE TO THE ECONOMIC DEVELOPMENT OF THE COUNTRIES OF SOUTH AND SOUTHEAST ASIA

Since the beginning of the Occupation, Japan's export trade with the South and Southeast Asian countries has steadily increased from a postwar low of $24.3 million in 1945–46 to a level of $232.2 million during 1949. During this period the proportion of Japan's total exports flowing to this area increased from 23.5% during 1945–46 to 45.4% in 1949, which shows a pronounced shift of Japan's export markets. Correspondingly, Japan is placing increased emphasis on the procurement from these areas of her food and raw material requirements. . . .

Assuming a fair degree of political and economic stability is achieved in the South and Southeast Asiatic countries over the next few years, it is estimated that Japan's exports to these countries could reach a level of approximately $710 million by 1955. If this potential is realized, exports to these countries will considerably exceed 50% of her total projected export trade. (A detailed analysis of Japan's export potential during the next five years is included in Tab B attached.)

The current and proposed economic programs of the countries of South and Southeast Asia include projects for the greater mechanization of agriculture, the expansion of transportation, communications, and electric power facilities, as well as expanded textile manufacture. With the potential development of industrial resources in view, Japan is looking forward to supplying a major part of the requirements for transportation equipment, including ships and railroad rolling stock, electrical machinery and equipment, agricultural machinery, construction materials and equipment, industrial and textile machinery, thermal and hydro-electric plants, chemicals, etc.

Japan now has the capacity to produce all types of the capital goods and equipment required, and can supply the requirements of these countries without impairment of her domestic economy. Furthermore, in a large measure, payment for such goods can be made through Japan's imports from these countries under existing and proposed trade agreements.

TABLE B
JAPAN'S EXPORT POTENTIAL
FOR SOUTH AND SOUTHEAST ASIAN COUNTRIES
1950–1955

(In U.S. $1,000)

Country	Estimated Exports 1950[1]	1951[1]	Export Potential by 1955[2]
Burma	$ 13,389	$ 27,000	$ 40,000
Ceylon	3,500	3,674	15,000
China	10,000	21,729	100,000
Formosa	21,799	18,155	50,000
Viet Nam including Cambodia	2,000	3,000	10,000
Hong Kong	35,000	40,000	20,000
India	23,962	25,000	50,000
Pakistan	27,691	40,000	70,000
Indonesia	26,000	50,000	100,000
Korea	17,000	59,000	80,000
Malaya including Singapore	13,005	18,000	25,000
Philippine Republic	21,000	35,000	50,000
Thailand	45,000	70,000	100,000
TOTAL	$259,346	$410,558	$710,000

[1] Export estimates for 1950 and 1951 assume unchanged political and economic conditions in South and Southeast Asia.

[2] Export estimates for 1955 represent the potential of Japan's exports which should be attained by that date assuming the achievement of a fair degree of political and economic stability in South and Southeast Asia.

20. THAILAND CRITICIZES BAO DAI GOVERNMENT AS WESTERN PUPPET, FEBRUARY 1950

The following is an intriguing summary of the Thai government's disinclination to recognize the French-created government of Bao Dai. Note that Thailand's Prime Minister and Foreign Minister evidence some concern over communism in the area, but continue to be more anxious about Western colonialism and neocolonialism. (Source: Department of State, *Foreign Relations of the United States, 1950,* VI, pp. 724–25.)

THE AMBASSADOR IN THAILAND (STANTON) TO THE SECRETARY OF STATE

SECRET   BANGKOK, February 8, 1950—8 p.m.

114. Deptel 79, February 4, noon. I have given lengthy exposition to Prime Minister and Foreign Minister of Department's reasons recognition Bao Dai and views concerning IC situation. Following is summary their views:

1. Prime Minister listened most attentively outline situation IC and particularly to my estimate of danger if IC goes completely Communist now that Ho Chi Minh has aligned himself with Moscow and Peiping. Prime Minister stated in reply he fully aware possibility IC going Communist and danger to Thailand from such development, that Thailand Government has definitely taken decision stand with democracy for freedom and independence, and pursuance that policy he and his government would like recognize Bao Dai since his government anti-Communist. He said nevertheless Thai people were Asiatics and in common with other peoples of Asia, they were desirous of seeing those peoples still under colonial domination achieve real freedom and independence. He emphasized the importance of this consideration in thinking of his government, and pointed out that neither the Thai people nor other peoples of this region were convinced that Bao Dai and his government had real freedom and independence, nor a large measure of support from the people. He said in these circumstances seemed in best interests Thailand watch

developments and delay recognition Bao Dai for time being. In reply my query what he thought should be done insure greater popular support Bao Dai, he replied France must grant full independence or at least issue clear-cut statement indicating further and more complete transfer power and authority to Bao Dai in near future. I discussed separately with him question kingdoms Laos and Cambodia. I pointed out no widespread or active opposition to governments these two states seems to exist, and Laos and Cambodia people are supporting existing governments. I stressed recognition by Thailand these two states, immediately adjacent western frontiers this country, would be great encouragement to them. I pointed out if Communism could be kept out Laos and Cambodia these states might, to some extent at least act as buffer Communist expansion into Thailand. Prime Minister displayed considerable interest this idea but seemed feel recognition Cambodia and Laos tied up with recognition Bao Dai. In conclusion Prime Minister said his Cabinet would give whole problem further careful consideration.

2. In long conversation with Foreign Minister he expressed similar views. He spoke very frankly and said thought we and British were making mistake by recognition Bao Dai. He said did not see that our recognition would greatly strengthen Bao Dai unless we and British prepared give military and economic aid sufficient really turn tide inflict crushing defeat on Ho Chi Minh. He reiterated if Bao Dai given full independence and had popular support Thailand would gladly extend recognition as done in case USI.

3. From above evident Thai Government still not prepared extend immediate recognition Bao Dai. Thinking of Thai Government and, I believe, other Asian governments predicated on their strong opposition to colonialism, strong desire to see countries of Asia achieve their independence and their skepticism regarding French intentions. On latter point Thailand particularly skeptical, if not suspicious, in view their past bitter experience with French. I feel we must not forget struggle for independence amongst Asian countries represents strong and deep-seated ideal which has profoundly stirred them for many years. To them recognition Bao Dai seems to mean perpetuation colonialism and they therefore exceedingly reluctant to do so even in face Communist threat which looms. In other words to them colonialism is a foe they understand and have sought to vanquish for many years, whereas Communism is foe whose strength and evil influence not fully known or grasped.

Sent Department 114; repeated Saigon unnumbered, Manila unnumbered, Rangoon unnumbered, New Delhi unnumbered. Department pass Paris.

STANTON

21. TWO STATE DEPARTMENT VIEWS: STICKING WITH BAO DAI OR SWITCHING TO HO CHI MINH, NOVEMBER 1949.

These two memoranda graphically illustrate the polarity of point and counterpoint in American approaches to Indochina. Raymond Fosdick, Consultant to the Department on Far Eastern Affairs, argues that history is on the side of Asian nationalism and against that of Western imperialism, and prefers to take his chances with Ho Chi Minh. Butterworth, Assistant Secretary for Far Eastern Affairs, would rather cast his lot with the French and Bao Dai, however poor the odds. Note their metaphors! Fosdick: "Why, therefore, do we tie ourselves to the tail of [the French] kite?" Butterworth: "Because the odds are heavily against a horse entered in a given race, is no reason to withdraw that horse from the race." Both documents are from NARS. (Sources: Memorandum, Fosdick to Mr. [Philip C.] Jessup, November 4, 1949, National Archives 896.00/11-1849; Memorandum, Butterworth to Fosdick, November 17, 1949, National Archives, Lot Files: PSA, Box 5, Folder: "French-Indochinese relations.")

SECRET

MEMORANDUM FOR: Mr. Jessup

In his memorandum of November 1 on Indochina, Mr. Yost argues that "a further major advance of Communism will be considered as, and will in fact be, a defeat for the United States, whether or not we are directly involved". He therefore recommends, among other steps, support of the Bao Dai government (after the March 8 agreements are ratified) economic assistance to Bao Dai, etc.

It seems to me this point of view fails to take into consideration the possible, and I think the probable, consequences of such a decision. In grasping one horn of the dilemma, it ignores the other. My belief is that the Bao Dai regime is doomed. The compromises which the French are so reluctantly making cannot possibly save it. The Indochinese are pressing toward complete nationalism and nothing is going to stop them. They see all too clearly that France is offering them a kind of semi-colonialism; and to think that they will be content to settle for less than Indonesia has gained from the Dutch or India from the British is to underestimate the power of the forces that are sweeping Asia today.

What kind of independence is France offering the Indochinese today in the March 8th agreements?

(1) The foreign policy of Indochina is to be under the final control of France.

(2) French military bases are to be established and the Indochinese Army in time of war is to be under French direction.

(3) France is to be in charge of the so-called General Services:

    (a) Control of immigration

    (b) Communications

    (c) Industrial development of Indochina

(4) Customs receipts are to be divided between France and Indochina in accordance with a formula to be agreed upon.

(5) Extraterritorial courts for French citizens are to be continued.

This shabby business is a mockery of all the professions we have made in the Indonesian case. It probably represents an improvement over the brutal colonialism of earlier years, but it is now too late in the history of the world to try to settle for the price of this cheap substitute. For the United States to support France in this attempt will cost us our standing and prestige in all of Southeast Asia. A lot of that prestige went down the drain with Chiang Kai-shek; the rest of it will go down with the Bao Dai regime if we support it. Ambassador Stuart calls our relationship to this regime "shameful" and I am inclined to agree with him.

Ev Case argued yesterday that it is too late to do anything else except support Bao Dai. I disagree. It is never too late to change a mistaken policy, particularly when the policy involves the kind of damage that our adherence to the Generalissimo brought us. Why get our fingers burned twice?

Ho Chi Minh as an alternative is decidedly unpleasant, but as was pointed out at our meeting with FE yesterday, there may be unpredictable and unseen factors in this situation which in the end will be more favorable to us than now seems probable. The fundamental antipathy of the Indochinese to China is one of the factors. Faced with a dilemma like this the best possible course is to wait for the breaks. Certainly we should not play our cards in such a way that once again, as in China, we seem to be allied with reaction. Whether the French like it or not, independence is coming to Indochina. Why, therefore, do we tie ourselves to the tail of their battered kite?

RAYMOND B. FOSDICK

91

Mr. Fosdick   November 17, 1949

Mr. Butterworth

Your November 4 Memorandum to Ambassador Jessup Regarding Indochina.

Mr. Jessup has referred to me your memorandum to him of November 4, 1949 regarding Indochina which I have read with much interest.

In general, the considerations which you raise have been very much in the foreground of our thinking. I do not believe, however, that we can necessarily conclude, as you apparently have, that the Bao Dai regime is doomed. There is no doubt in my mind that Bao Dai's chances of establishing a viable non-Communist state are not brilliant, but I feel that under certain circumstances, which admittedly may never arise, he might be successful.

I think I can make our position clear by the following analogy: Because the odds are heavily against a horse entered in a given race, is no reason to withdraw that horse from the race although I agree that there is likewise no reason in these circumstances to back that horse heavily.

I agree that we should not support France in Indochina because such action will damage our standing and prestige in all of Southeast Asia, but I feel that without committing ourselves to another operation similar in some respects to that which took place in China, we must allow Bao Dai his opportunity to succeed and we must do nothing deliberately to eliminate his opportunity.

22. PENTAGON PAPERS ON HO CHI MINH: COULD HE BE AN ASIAN TITO?

Fosdick's willingness to take his chances with Ho Chi Minh was based on the possibility that Ho was as much a nationalist as a communist; someone who would not be subservient to Russia and perhaps even hostile to China. In short, an Asian version of Yugoslavia's Marshall Tito, who had split with Stalin in 1948.

The following selection from the famous *Pentagon Papers* summarizes the official American views of the pros and cons of the "Asian Tito" hypothesis. Pay special attention to the concluding reasoning that led the American government to conclude that it made no real difference whether the hypothesis was true or not. (Source: Department. of Defense, *U.S.-Vietnam Relations (Pentagon Papers),* I, c-1–c-7.)

HO CHI MINH: ASIAN TITO?
SUMMARY

Among the more cogent critiques of U.S. policy toward Vietnam is the contention that the U.S. failed to recognize in Ho Chi Minh a potential Asian "Tito." This view holds that Ho has always been more concerned with Vietnam's independence and sovereign viability than with following the interests and dictates of Moscow and Peking. With U.S. support, the argument runs, Ho would have adopted some form of neutrality in the East-West conflict and maintained the DRV as a natural and durable bulwark against Chinese expansion southward. Thus, were it not for "U.S. communist blinders," Ho would have served the larger purposes of American policy in Asia. Though the focus of inquiry in this study is the period immediately following World War II, when it would have been relatively easy to support an anti-Japanese, anti-colonial Ho, it is often argued that the U.S. neglected another opportunity after the Geneva Conference of 1954—and indeed, that U.S. acceptance of Ho, and a communist dominated Vietnam, may be the only path to peace in Southeast Asia today. The historical (1945–1954) argument has a persuasive ring. In the light of the present costs and repercussions of U.S. involvement in Vietnam, any prior way out can seem attractive. It is possible, however, that a dynamic and unified communist Vietnam under Ho Chi Minh could have been vigorously expansionist, thus causing unanticipated difficult problems in some ways comparable to current ones.

An examination of Ho Chi Minh's political development through 1950 may provide a basis to narrow the range of speculation concerning Ho and U.S. policy. From such a review, it is evident that the man who in 1945 became President of the Democratic Republic of Vietnam was a mature, extraordinarily dedicated revolutionary who had undergone severe hardships serving the cause of Vietnam's freedom from France. Fifty-five years of age in 1945, he had been a communist for twenty-five years—one of the founding members of the French Communist Party—and a Comintern agent in Asia for fifteen years before World War II.

For Ho, now back in Asia, World War II opened new avenues to the attainment of his life-long goals. France discredited itself in Vietnam through Vichy's collaboration with the Japanese, and then in 1945 was toppled from power altogether by Japanese arms. In the meantime, Ho had built the Viet Minh into the only Vietnam-wide political organization capable of effective resistance to either the Japanese or the French. Ho was the only Vietnamese wartime leader with a national following, and he assured himself wider fealty among the Vietnamese people when in August–September, 1945, he overthrew the Japanese, obtained the abdication of Bao Dai, established the DRV, and staged receptions for in-coming allied occupation forces—in which the DRV acted as the incumbent Vietnamese government. For a few weeks in September 1945, Vietnam was—for the first and only time in its modern history—free of foreign domination, and united from north to south under Ho Chi Minh.

Ho, nonetheless, found himself, his movement, and his government under intense pressure. From within the nation, the Chinese-backed Viet parties attacked communist domination of his government. For the sake of national unity, Ho dissolved the Communist Party, avoided communist cant, announced general elections, and assured the contending factions representation in the government well out of proportion to their popular support. External pressures from France and from China proved more difficult. The French capitalized on the relative weakness of the Viet Minh in South Vietnam, and the dissension among the Vietnamese there to overthrow the DRV government in Saigon, and to force the Viet Minh to resort to guerrilla warfare. In famine-wracked North Vietnam, Chinese hordes under booty-minded warlords descended on the DRV, supplanting its local government with committees of their own sponsoring and systematically looting. Ho vainly sought aid abroad; not even the Soviet Union proved helpful. Ho eventually (March, 1946) negotiated with the French, accepting a French military presence in North Vietnam for a period of five years in return for vague French assurances to the DRV as a "Free State within the French Union." When Ho was attacked for this by the pro-Chinese elements within the DRV, he declared:

"You fools! Don't you realize what it means if the Chinese stay? Don't you remember your history? The last time the Chinese came, they stayed one thousand years!

"The French are foreigners. They are weak. Colonialism is dying out. Nothing will be able to withstand world pressure for independence. They may stay for a while, but they will have to go because the white man is finished in Asia. But if the Chinese stay now, they will never leave.

"As for me, I prefer to smell French shit for five years, rather than Chinese shit for the rest of my life."

The unresolved historic problem, of course, is to what extent Ho's nationalist goals over-rode his communist convictions in these maneuvers. Ho seemed to place the former above the latter not solely as a matter of dissemblance, as he might have done in the dissolution of the Party and the simultaneous formation of a "Marxist Association," but possibly as a result of doubts about communism as a political form suitable for Vietnam. Bao Dai is reputed to have said that: "I saw Ho Chi Minh suffer. He was fighting a battle within himself. Ho had his own struggle. He realized communism was not best for his country, but it was too late. Ultimately, he could not overcome his allegiance to communism."

There remains, however, the matter of Ho's direct appeals for U.S. intervention in Vietnam, at which even a Leninist might have scrupled. These occurred (late 1945, early 1946) just after France has reasserted itself militarily in South Vietnam, while Chinese Nationalist warlords were ensconced in Hanoi, and before the 6 March 1946 Accord with France. Desperately, Ho turned to the United States, among other powers, asking for "immediate interference" in Vietnam.

There were, at least, eight communications from Ho to the President of the United States, or to the Secretary of State, from October, 1945, to February, 1946. Ho had conveyed earlier, in August and September, 1945, *via* O.S.S. channels, proposals that Vietnam be accorded "the same status as the Philippines," for an undetermined period of tutelage preliminary to independence. With the outbreak of hostilities in South Vietnam, September–October 1945, he added formal requests for U.S. and U.N. intervention against French aggression, citing the Atlantic Charter, the U.N. Charter, and a foreign policy address of President Truman in October, 1945, endorsing national self-determination. Ho's last direct communication with the U.S. was in September, 1946, when he visited the U.S. Ambassador in Paris to ask vaguely for U.S. assistance in obtaining independence for Vietnam within the French Union.

There is no record of U.S. reply to any of Ho's appeals for aid. Extant instructions to a U.S. diplomat in contact with Ho in December, 1946, reveal U.S. preoccupation with his known communist background, and apprehension that he might establish a "communist-dominated, Moscow-oriented state." Two months later, when the Franco-Viet Minh war in North Vietnam was underway, Secretary of State Marshall emphasized that "we do not lose sight [of the] fact that Ho Chi Minh has direct Communist connections and it should be obvious that we are not interested in seeing colonial empire administrations supplanted by philosophy and political organizations emanating from and controlled by the Kremlin." In May, 1949, Secretary of State Acheson admitted that as a "theoretical possibility" the establishment of a "National Communist state on pattern Yugoslavia in any area beyond reach [of the] Soviet Army," but pointed out that:

"Question whether Ho as much nationalist as Commie is irrelevant. All Stalinists in colonial areas are nationalists. With achievement national aims (i.e., independence) their objective necessarily becomes subordination state to Commie purposes and ruthless extermination not only opposition groups but all elements suspected even slightest deviation. . . ."

When, in early, 1950, Ho's DRV lay within reach of Mao's Chinese Army, and Ho had openly embraced communism, Secretary Acheson declared that bloc recognition of the DRV "should remove any illusion as to the nationalist character of Ho Chi Minh's aims and reveals Ho in his true colors as the mortal enemy of native independence in Vietnam."

The simple truth seems to be that the U.S. knew little of what was transpiring inside Vietnam, and certainly cared less about Vietnam than about France. Knowing little and caring less meant that real problems and variety of choices were perceived but dimly. For example, the U.S. could have asked itself—"Did we really have to support France in Southeast Asia in order to support a non-communist France internally and in Europe?" Another question we could have asked ourselves was—"If the U.S. choice in Vietnam really came down to either French colonialism or Ho Chi Minh, should Ho automatically be excluded?" Again, "If the U.S. choice was to be France, did France have any real chance of succeeding, and if so, at what cost?"

French representations to the contrary notwithstanding, Ho Chi Minh possessed real political strength among the people of Vietnam. While calling Ho another George Washington may be stretching the point, there is no doubt about his being the only popularly-recognized wartime leader of the Vietnamese resistance, and the head of the strongest and only Vietnam-wide political movement. There can be no doubt either that in a test by ballot only Ho's Viet Minh could have delivered votes at the hamlet level. Washington and Paris, however, did not focus on the fact of Ho's strength, only on the consequences of his rule. Paris viewed Ho as a threat to its regaining French economic, cultural and political prerogatives in Indochina. The U.S., wary of Ho's known communist background, was apprehensive that Ho would lead Vietnam into the Soviet, and later Chinese, orbit. President Eisenhower's later remark about Ho's winning a free election in Vietnam with an 80% vote shone through the darkness of our vision about Vietnam; but U.S. policy remained unillumined.

In the last speculation, U.S. support for Ho Chi Minh would have involved perspicacity and risk. As clear as national or independent or neutral communism may seem today, it was a blurred vision in 1945–1948. Even with the benefit of seeing Tito successfully assert his independence, it would have been hard for Washington to make the leap from there to an analogy in Asia. Recourse to "national communism" in Vietnam as an eventual bulwark against China, indeed, would have called for a perspicacity unique in U.S. history. The risk was there, too. The reality of Ho's strength in Vietnam could have worked seriously against U.S. interests as well as against Chinese Communist interests. Ho's well-known leadership and drive, the iron discipline and effectiveness of the Viet Minh, the demonstrated fighting capability of his armies, a dynamic Vietnamese people under Ho's control, could have produced a dangerous period of Vietnamese expansionism. Laos and Cambodia would have been easy pickings for such a Vietnam. Ho, in fact, always considered his leadership to extend to Indochina as a whole, and his party was originally called the Indochinese Communist Party. Thailand, Malaya, Singapore, and even Indonesia, could have been next. It could have been the "domino theory" with Ho instead of Mao. And, it could have been the dominoes with Mao. This may seem implausible, but it is only slightly less of a bad dream than what has happened to Vietnam since. The path of prudence rather than the path of risk seemed the wiser choice.

23. ACHESON ON ASIA: AN AMAZING DINNER CONVERSATION WITH THE SECRETARY OF STATE

This telegram is stunning both in its content and in its timing. It recounts a lengthy and private dinner conversation with Secretary of State Acheson on December 17, 1949. Six months before the start of the Korean War, Acheson previews the primacy of Asia in the world affairs of 1950. A month before Chinese recognition of Ho Chi Minh, he has already set forth his hard-line views of Chinese expansionism in Southeast Asia. And five months before President Truman's commitment to aid France in Indochina, the Secretary argues for American responsibility to "look after" not only Indochina but Indonesia and the Philippines, with Britain responsible for Burma and Malaya, and both responsible for Thailand (Siam). (Source: Telegram, Sir Oliver Franks, British Ambassador in Washington, to Foreign Office, No. 5855, December 17, 1949, British Public Records Office, FO371, F18982/10345/61. We wish to thank Professor Andrew Rotter for sharing this document with us.)

IMMEDIATE
SECRET

For Secretary of State from Oliver Franks.

At dinner with Hume Wrong and myself Acheson made several remarks about the Far East and the Indian Ocean. He was talking at large so that to my mind importance attaches to the drift of his thoughts rather than their detailed expression.

2. He started off by saying that he thought the world across the Pacific Ocean would be the principal preoccupation of the State Department in 1950. He and his advisers had changed their views on what were likely to be the immediate consequences of the successful conquest and occupation of China by the Communists. They now thought there was likely to be early expansion south and east beyond the borders of China. This expansion would be especially dangerous, if it took place, where there were considerable Chinese settlements.

3. He had been scratching together what dollars he could and believed he could lay hands on about 75 millions. He expected to use this in Indonesia and Indo-China with possibly a little bit of help to spare for Siam. With the aid these dollars represented, quite a job could be done in building up the régimes in these countries. At this point Acheson interpolated a paean of praise about French achievements in Indo-China. They had done far more than they had ever let on. Bao Dai had a good chance and the thing to do was to press early recognition on the French. The American Government in distinction from its earlier views would be ready to recognise and help Indo-China as soon as the French had acted.

4. He then said that all this made the Colombo Conference a most important event. His mind was moving in terms of some rough geographical division of responsibilities. The Americans would look after Indonesia, Philippines, Indo-China with a little to spare for Siam. The Commonwealth would see to the help of the countries in the Indian Ocean. He had in mind especially Burma: then there was our own position in Malaya and our interest overlapping theirs in Siam. Acheson clearly was hoping that in some way India and the United Kingdom would be able to tidy up the mess in Burma so as to prevent the Chinese appearing over the hump.

5. He said that he would like to talk with Mike Pearson about these ideas before the Colombo Conference and this was tentatively arranged with Hume Wrong.

6. I did not take very much part in this expression of views. I did ask what evidence there was to account for the American change of view about the behaviour of the Chinese. The only reply I got was that the Communists would, by aggrandisement in the south, direct the gaze of

the Chinese people from Manchuria. I also said that I personally had doubts about spheres of influence rather than joint policies and operations. To start with Hong Kong did not fit in and I did not want Acheson to feel that now the Americans have at last got interested in South East Asia they need not think at all about the Indian Ocean. We may want them to think a good deal about some of the countries round that Ocean, for example in connexion with the tripartite talks. I therefore discouraged any sharp divisions of interest or function.

24. AN ASIAN STATESMAN QUESTIONS AMERICAN SUPPORT FOR FRENCH COLONIALISM, MARCH 1950

This "private and confidential" letter to Secretary Acheson came from the hand of Carlos Romulo, President of the UN General Assembly, Filipino political leader, and an Asian nationalist with strong anti-Communist sentiments. This lengthy, impassioned, and sometimes eloquent letter questions the whole direction of America's policy in Southeast Asia and concludes that "in all friendship I think that America's problem at the moment is how to clear herself of the suspicion of pro-imperialism rather than how to keep faith with Bao Dai." It bears closer reading now than Acheson gave it at the time. (Source: Carlos Romulo to Dean Acheson, March 2, 1950, Papers of Dean Acheson, Harry S. Truman Library, Independence, Mo.)

My dear Secretary Acheson:

I am taking this liberty of writing you as a private person, involving neither my Government, whose policy on the question I do not yet know, nor the United Nations over whose General Assembly I have had the honor of presiding during its fourth regular session. At the same time, I trust you will understand that I am a friend—your friend whose admiration for you has been enhanced by your integrity of character as evidenced by your fidelity under all circumstances, and a friend of this great Republic under whose flag I served, with faith and loyalty, in one of the darkest hours of its history. You will recall that we were to have gotten together in Washington sometime last January but owing to my illness we were obliged to postpone our meeting for another day. I have since felt therefore that I must communicate my thoughts to you somehow and I need not say how this feeling has increased under the impact of events which cannot but involve my country.

The franker I am in my views the better, I trust, you will appreciate what I have to say; but if I should overstate some of my points, as likely I will, you as an understanding man will know how to charge it against my desire alone to see your Government stronger, and more deserving of the faith of the peoples of the world in this most critical of all times. You will forgive me if I claim to know Oriental psychology as well as the complex realities of Oriental politics. I had the distinct advantage to have felt the pulse of Asia's peoples and to have known the convictions of their leaders, during a survey I made of their countries before the war, and my series of articles based on that survey have been borne out by subsequent events. While I may not therefore be necessarily right in my conclusions, I feel that I can speak with some authority on a situation the historical circumstances of which I have known from first hand sources. I am also emboldened to address you this letter because when the Indonesian crisis was coming to a head General Marshall and I had conferred lengthily on the problem in the American embassy in Paris, and I had occasion then to volunteer to give him what I thought was the proper Oriental slant on the subject and which he so graciously accepted.

I have particularly in mind your Government's recognition of Bao Dai in Indo-China and the situation that has resulted because of it. To be frank, may I suggest that the attitudes of the neighboring countries might have been different if the political implications of the act had been more cautiously weighed. Perhaps, if the act did not appear as having been timed in retaliation for Moscow's recognition of Ho Chi-minh's regime and in deliberate contrast with American non-recognition of Communist China, it would not now look to the rest of Asia that the United States, in fighting Communism, may have unwittingly espoused even the demonstrated iniquity of colonial imperialism.

It would be difficult to prove that Bao Dai is even pseudo-independent when the whole world knows that he is helpless without the French. His neighbors are well aware of what you and I very well know: that his government is good only in the limited areas occupied by French troops, that outside those areas he has no leg to stand on. If it should be the aim of his sponsors to extend his dominion beyond his present foothold, then that has to be with an exertion of military effort far I am afraid beyond the present fire and armor of the French occupation army. In such an event would the United States be willing to commit itself to extending the armed assistance which the French would require to achieve victory against the stubborn guerrilla resistance which they have failed in the last five years to overcome?

In the eyes of the great mass of the people of Indo-China and of Asia, the French army, particularly its ex-Nazi units, is a hostile army, an enemy of Viet Nam independence. This is the explanation for its eminent failure to subdue the Vietnamese. And supposing now that this army should receive the aircraft and field weapons needed for effective action, does it not follow that it will devastate larger areas and kill more people than it has done heretofore? Is it not logical then to assume that as the French achieve their military goals, the greater the resentment will be against them?

It is extremely to be doubted that a feat so gigantic as a reconquest of the country—and this is nothing short of what it would amount to—can be accomplished by the French without breaking their backs. On the other hand, Communist China could reasonably be expected to rush to the aid of the Vietnamese. Also, it would be well to bear in mind that whatever Vietnamese forces Bao Dai might be able to muster under his dubious banner are as likely as not to be extremely unreliable.

As I see it, everything seems to militate against the French in Indo-China and as the days pass the weakness of the Bao Dai set-up becomes more evident. One could cite the renewed turbulence of the last few days in the state of Thailand to be impressed by the fact that the proximate cause of it all is the recognition of Bao Dai, and it might be well also to remember the swift manner in which Siamese politics have tended to move around crucial issues such as the current one which has forced the Foreign Minister to resign.

If I may venture to state the position of the countries surrounding Indo-China, they have plainly enough gone hard against the line pursued by the United States with regard to Bao Dai. India, Burma, Pakistan, and Indonesia, which are definitely not for aligning themselves against Peiping, could hardly be expected to climb Bao Dai's band-wagon. And for that matter, I have a feeling that the Philippine Government—and again I assure you I am not officially informed—much as it would like to do so, would most probably be forced by pressure of public opinion to think twice before acting favorably on the question. If I interpret the sentiment of my people right, they will not rally to the Tricolor and chant the Marseillaise in an eminently colonial setting as Bao Dai's empire. Regardless of who is on the other side, this is the hard political fact which must be given its proper weight in evaluating the different factors affecting this question.

The Communist threat is fully appreciated in my country. Probably no other people stand to lose as much as mine under a police state. The

101

Filipino way of life, with the Christian family as its cornerstone, can expect but crucifixion under the communist Lucifer. This is the compelling reason why the Filipinos will always be against Communism, and it is in obedience to this sentiment that I have painstakingly sought a common ground with the country that has inspired me most for its high-minded aims, a common ground at least of political consistency in the defense of the democratic way of life in the Asian world.

That common ground unfortunately is not to be found in the American policy in Indo-China. However convinced the State Department may be that Bao Dai is an "independent nationalist," the facts as they appear to Asian eyes do not bear out that conviction. What is plain enough is a case of combined operations with the French army. To the countries of Asia remote or recent history offers nothing to support the notion that this army is in Indo-China to free the people. On the other hand, the Communists have been given the enormous advantage of plausible and logical insistence on anti-Communism being pro-imperialism, and on the Communists, and the Communists alone, being anti-imperialist.

The unfortunate result is the virtual isolation of American policy from the sentiment of Asian countries. Politically, the United States has suffered a signal reverse which has made Bao Dai's position more untenable in the eyes of his neighbors. Undoubtedly, the peoples of Asia would want to have a common ground with the United States, undoubtedly they all want to resist the Communists in close friendship with the United States; but if the price is association with the French army in Indo-China, that price would be hard to pay.

The sending of American economic missions to Southeast Asia which I proposed unofficially a year ago will not, I think, help extricate America from the accomplished fact of alliance with a surviving remnant of colonial imperialism in our part of the world. Asian leaders will no doubt welcome American aid, but they will certainly do nothing in the way of political commitments sure to damage their position, not only vis-a-vis the Communist opposition, but in the eyes of sincere nationalists as well. Ambassador Jessup has seen this very point when he declared at Karachi (A.P., Feb. 28, 1950) that "full independence of Viet Nam will not be assured until French troops are withdrawn."

And I come now to what possibly is the only way out of the difficulty of the American position: the United States Government should ask the French Government for a clean-cut declaration of good faith toward the people of Indo-China. In this declaration independence should be promised and a date set for its proclamation. It should also state that Bao Dai is the true commander-in-chief of all troops in Indo-China taking orders from no one but himself. Nothing in this suggestion is inconsistent with the glorious tradition in American history as exemplified by America's record in the Philippines.

As you already know, I have for nearly a year now, under the inspiration of President Quirino, been trying to establish the basis for some effective union of Southeast Asian countries along non-Communist lines. Although in the beginning the Quirino proposal did not sweep your Department's policy-makers off their feet, perhaps because it was accidentally linked with Chiang Kai-shek and Sygman [Syngman] Rhee, it has since been clear that the Philippine initiative had your support and that of your staff. In this connection, I must say that I have lived up to all commitments I had made to Messrs. Jessup and Butterworth sometime before I left for Manila last year and that those commitments are faithfully reflected in President Quirino's instructions to me. After a series of conferences with them, Messrs. Fosdick and Case, like Jessup and Butterworth, have assured me of the State Department's support and you yourself have expressed your approbation. Now, however, I must admit that your move in Indo-China has made my task very difficult and I regret very much that it had not been possible for me to square my plans with your subsequent decisions. A great deal of complication would have been avoided and the Southeast Asia Union project should now be sailing smoothly.

In view of what must be admitted is the unenviable position of the United States, I am wondering whether it is not the better part of wisdom to hold any military assistance to Bao Dai in abeyance pending a more thorough exploration of the situation. Ho Chi-minh's political initiative in Belgrade is a new complication. Not only does it appear to be in complete harmony with America's own policy toward Tito but, more important, it proves that Ho Chi-minh, whom I met personally during my Asian survey and who impressed me as a man who could make all sorts of trouble for Stalin, may not allow himself to be a tool of the Kremlin. Suppose now that Vietnamese Communism should assume the shape of Titoism, would the United States still prefer a puppet Bao Dai to a Titoist Ho Chi-minh?

If I may suggest, Mr. Secretary, the present situation with regard to Southeast Asia calls for urgent discussion, for in all friendship I think that America's problem at the moment is how to clear herself of the suspicion of pro-imperialism rather than how to keep faith with Bao Dai. I personally am convinced that this suspicion is unjustified, but how could it be otherwise in the untutored minds of Asia's discontented masses? A great deal is to be gained from getting a better appraisal of Ho Chi-minh's political plans and from consulting the views of the various friendly Governments in Southeast Asia before policy decisions are finally made.

Just in case you have not yet read the enclosed article of mine in the

103

New York Times Magazine, I am sending it to you in the hope that it will serve as background material in your study of the Asian situation.

I have written at length, Mr. Secretary, and I am most grateful to you for your kind attention. May I add that I deeply appreciate the cooperation of your staff since I last discussed the Southeast Asia Union project with Ambassador Jessup during the last session of the General Assembly. Needless to say, I am always at your disposal and would be pleased to meet you any time at your convenience on Monday, March 6, in Washington, where your secretary may reach me at my home. My telephone number is Ordway 0215.

With the best of wishes, I am

Sincerely yours,

Carlos P. Romulo

Enclosure:
    as stated

The Honorable Dean C. Acheson
Secretary of State
Department of State
Washington, D.C.

25. STATE DEPARTMENT'S INITIAL POSITION ON SOUTHEAST ASIA, MARCH 1949

For almost a year, the State Department's "Paper on United States Policy Toward Southeast Asia" (PPS 51) provided the general framework and assumptions for U.S. policy. Read this March 29, 1949, document carefully, then compare it with Doc. 26 of ten months later. (Source: Department of State, *Foreign Relations of the United States, 1949,* VII, pp. 1128–33.)

POLICY PLANNING STAFF PAPER ON UNITED STATES POLICY TOWARD SOUTHEAST ASIA

SECRET   [WASHINGTON,] March 29, 1949.
PPS 51

THE PROBLEM

1. To define U.S. policy toward Southeast Asia, including Indonesia, Indochina, Burma, Malaya, Siam and the Philippines. . . .

76. We should accept the fact that the crucial immediate issue in Southeast Asia—that of militant nationalism in Indonesia and Indochina—cannot be resolved by any of the following policies on our part:

(1) full support of Dutch and French imperialism,

(2) unlimited support of militant nationalism, or

(3) evasion of the problem.

Because the key to the solution of this issue lies primarily with the Netherlands and France, we should as a matter of urgent importance endeavor to induce the Dutch and the French to adapt their policies to the realities of the current situation in Southeast Asia, as set forth in this paper. Our first step should be, in conjunction with the British, to set forth to the Dutch and French in candor, detail, and with great gravity our interpretation of the situation in and intentions with regard to SEA. We should make a major effort to persuade them to join us and the states mentioned in the following paragraph in a constructive overall approach to the region as a whole.

77. Having done this, we should promptly discuss with the British, Indians, Pakistanis, Filipinos and Australians a cooperative approach based on the principles laid down in paragraph 75. We should be prepared subsequently to work with a wider group, always recognizing that while the area concerned is primarily Asian it is in our interest to leaven the oriental nature of the collaboration with sympathetic western influence. We should at the same time attempt to discourage the extension of this cooperative effort to include Middle and Near Eastern countries on the grounds that they constitute a separate natural regional group.

78. We should avoid at the outset urging an area organization. Rather, our effort should initially be directed toward collaboration on joint or parallel action and then, only as a pragmatic and desirable basis for more intimate association appears, should we encourage the area to move step by step toward formal organization. If Asian leaders prematurely precipitate an area organization, we should not give the impression of attempt-

105

ing to thwart such a move but should go along with them while exerting a cautiously moderating influence.

79. We should, of course, seek to cast the multilateral approach recommended in the preceding four paragraphs within the framework of the U.N. insofar as our Charter obligations require it and, where there is no requirement, insofar as we consider it appropriate. We should, however, be willing to act cooperatively outside of that framework when that would be consistent with our Charter obligations and when to proceed through U.N. mechanisms would constitute a serious impediment to the achievement of our objectives.

80. In order to minimize suggestions of American imperialist intervention, we should encourage the Indians, Filipinos and other Asian states to take the public lead in political matters. Our role should be the offering of discreet support and guidance. Politically, Japan should be kept in the background.

81. We should seek vigorously to develop the economic interdependence between SEA, as a supplier of raw materials, and Japan, western Europe and India, as suppliers of finished goods, with due recognition, however, of the legitimate aspirations of SEA countries for some diversification of their economies. To achieve these ends we should emphasize primarily the fourth point of the President's inaugural address. Every effort should be made to initiate and expand programs of technical assistance both through bilateral arrangements and through international agencies. The propaganda value of the President's fourth point should be fully exploited.

To achieve our objectives, efforts should also be made to supplement conservatively private investment, with Governmental assistance.

82. We should greatly expand our cultural and informational program. It should be directed at developing an appreciation and respect for the humanistic values of western civilization and an understanding of international political and economic realities. . . .

INDOCHINA

84. Because we are powerless to bring about a constructive solution of the explosive Indochinese situation through unilateral action, the determination of our future policy toward Indochina should await the outcome of the *démarche* recommended in paragraph 76 and the earliest feasible consultation with India and the Philippines.

26. STATE DEPARTMENT "PROBLEM PAPER" OF 1950

This State Department "Problem Paper" of February 1, 1950, set in motion the formal decision-making process that ultimately produced President Truman's basic decision to underwrite the French military pacification in Indochina. Again, compare its assumptions, assessments, and recommendations with those of PPS-51. (Source: Department of State, *Foreign Relations of the United States, 1950,* VI, pp. 711–15.)

PROBLEM PAPER PREPARED BY A WORKING GROUP IN THE DEPARTMENT OF STATE

SECRET   [WASHINGTON,] February 1, 1950

MILITARY AID FOR INDOCHINA
I. THE PROBLEM

Should the United States provide military aid in Indochina and, if so, how much and in what way.

II. ASSUMPTION

A. There will not be an effective split between the USSR and Communist China within the next three years.

B. The USSR will not declare war on any Southeast Asian country within the next three years.

C. Communist China will not declare war on any Southeast Asian country within the next three years.

D. The USSR will endeavor to bring about the fall of Southeast Asian governments which are opposed to Communism by using all devices short of war, making use of Communist China and indigenous communists in this endeavor.

III. FACTS BEARING ON THE PROBLEM

1. When the Mutual Defense Assistance Act of 1949 was being written, the question of providing military aid to Southeast Asia was examined and

107

it was decided not to include specific countries in that area, other than the Republic of the Philippines.

2. The attitude of the Congress toward the provision of military and economic aid to foreign countries recently has stiffened due to both economy and to policy considerations.

3. At the same time, the Congress has shown considerable dissatisfaction with policies which are alleged to have contributed to the Communist success in China and which are involved in the current United States' approach toward the question of Formosa.

4. Section 303 of the Mutual Defense Assistance Act of 1949 makes available to the President the sum of $75 million for use, at the President's discretion, in the general area of China to advance the purposes and policies of the United Nations.

5. Section 303 funds are unrestricted in their use.

6. The British Commonwealth Conference recently held at Colombo recognized that no SEA regional military pact now exists due to divergent interest and that such an arrangement was now unlikely.

7. Communism has made important advances in the Far East during the past year.

8. Opposition to Communism in Indochina is actively being carried on by the three legally-constituted governments of Vietnam, Cambodia and Laos.

9. Communist-oriented forces in Indochina are being aided by Red China and the USSR.

IV. Discussion

1. Indochina has common border with China and Burma, thus making it subject to invasion by Red China.

2. Its population is some 27 million concentrated in the delta regions of the Mekong and Red Rivers. Of the total population, Chinese account for between 600,000 and a million, concentrated largely in the cities.

3. Indochina has an agricultural economy based principally on rice of which it is an exporter. World War II and its aftermath seriously disrupted the national economy. The country presently has an annual trade deficit of about $85 million.

4. There are three subdivisions of Indochina: Vietnam, Laos, and Cambodia. An agreement was signed March 8, 1949, between France and Vietnam which provides for the latter to become an Associated State within the French Union. Ratification of the Agreement, followed by the recognition of Vietnam by the West, is expected in the near future. French policy aims at making Laos and Cambodia Associated States within the French Union at the same time.

5. Governmental stability is poor in Indochina. In Vietnam, less than one-third of the country is controlled by the legal government with the French in control of the major cities; in Cambodia and Laos, the French maintain order but unrest is endemic. Before World War II Indochina was made up of four French Protectorates (Tonkin, Annam, Laos and Cambodia) and the colony of Cochinchina. It was occupied after the war by Chinese troops in the north (Tonkin) and by British and later French in the south. In 1946 a (nationalist coalition) government headed by the Moscow-trained Communist agent Ho Chi Minh consented to the return to the north (Tonkin) of the French upon promises of independence within the French Union. French negotiations with Ho were broken off following the massacre of many foreigners in Tonkin and Cochinchina in December 1946 by Ho's forces. Hostilities have continued to date.

6. The French are irrevocably committed in Indochina and have sponsored Bao Dai as a move aimed at achieving non-Communist political stability. It was a case of backing Bao Dai or accepting the Communist government of Ho Chi Minh. This latter alternative was impossible not only because it would obviously make their position in Indochina untenable but would also open the door to complete Communist domination of Southeast Asia. Such a communist advance would have severe repercussions in the non-communist world.

7. Military operations in Indochina represented a franc drain on the French Treasury of the equivalent of approximately $475 million in 1949. This constitutes nearly half of the current French Military Budget.

8. Ho Chi Minh, a Moscow-trained Communist, controls the Viet Minh movement which is in conflict with the government of Bao Dai for control of Vietnam. Ho actually exercises control of varying degree over more than two-thirds of Vietnam territory and his "government" maintains agents in Thailand, Burma and India. This communist "government" has been recognized by Communist China and the USSR.

9. Most Indochinese, both the supporters of Bao Dai and those of Ho Chi Minh, regard independence from the French as their primary objective. Protection from Chinese Communist imperialism has been considered, up to now, a secondary issue.

10. Unavoidably, the United States is, together with France, committed in Indochina. That is, failure of the French Bao Dai "experiment" would mean the communization of Indochina. It is Bao Dai (or a similar anti-communist successor) or Ho Chi Minh (or a similar communist successor); there is no other alternative. The choice confronting the United States is to support the French in Indochina or face the extension of Communism over the remainder of the continental area of Southeast Asia and, possibly, farther westward. We then would be obliged to make stag-

gering investments in those areas and in that part of Southeast Asia remaining outside Communist domination or withdraw to a much-contracted Pacific line. It would seem a case of "Penny wise, Pound foolish" to deny support to the French in Indochina.

11. The US plans on extending recognition to the newly-created states of Vietnam, Laos and Cambodia, following French legislative action which is expected in early February 1950.

12. Another approach to the problem is to apply the practical test of probability of success. In the present case we know from the complex circumstances involved that the French are going to make literally every possible effort to prevent the victory of Communism in Indochina. Briefly, then, we would be backing a determined protagonist in this venture. Added to this is the fact that French military leaders such as General Cherrière are soberly confident that, in the absence of an invasion in mass from Red China, they (the French) can be successful in their support of the anti-Communist governments in Indochina.

13. Still another approach to the problem is to recall that the United States has undertaken to provide substantial aid to France in Europe. Failure to support French policy in Indochina would have the effect of contributing toward the defeat of our aims in Europe.

V. Conclusions

A. Significant developments have taken place in Indochina since the Mutual Defense Assistance Act of 1949 was drawn up, these changes warranting a reexamination of the question of military aid.

B. The whole of Southeast Asia is in danger of falling under Communist domination.

C. The countries and areas of Southeast Asia are not at present in a position to form a regional organization for self-defense nor are they capable of defending themselves against militarily aggressive Communism, without the aid of the great powers. Despite their lack of military strength, however, there is a will on the part of the legal governments of Indochina toward nationalism and a will to resist whatever aims at destroying that nationalism.

D. The French native and colonial troops presently in Indochina are engaged in military operations aimed at denying the expansion southward of Communism from Red China and of destroying its power in Indochina.

E. In the critical areas of Indochina France needs aid in its support of the legally-constituted anti-Communist states.

VI. RECOMMENDATIONS

1. The United States should furnish military aid in support of the anti-Communist nationalist governments of Indochina, this aid to be tailored to meet deficiencies toward which the United States can make a unique contribution, not including United States troops.

2. This aid should be financed out of funds made available by Section 303 of the Mutual Defense Assistance Act of 1949.

27. THE JOINT CHIEFS OF STAFF ARTICULATE AMERICAN INTERESTS IN SOUTHEAST ASIA, APRIL 1950

This April 14, 1950, letter from the Secretary of Defense to the Secretary of State chiefly summarizes the recommendations of the Joint Chiefs of Staff called for by NSC 64. Almost more interesting than the Joint Chiefs' military recommendations is their analysis of American national interests in Southeast Asia. Section 2 (a–g) may well constitute the best, single, short answer to the basic question of this book: Why were we in Vietnam? What was the root, the underlying basis of the American commitment? (Source: Department of State, *Foreign Relations of the United States, 1950,* VI, pp. 780–85.)

THE SECRETARY OF DEFENSE (JOHNSON) TO THE SECRETARY OF STATE

TOP SECRET   WASHINGTON, 14 April 1950.

My Dear Mr. Secretary:

1. In the light of U.S. strategic concepts, the integrity of the offshore island chain from Japan to Indonesia is of critical strategic importance to the United States.

2. The mainland states of Southeast Asia also are at present of critical strategic importance to the United States because:

a. They are the major sources of certain strategic materials required for the completion of United States stock pile projects;

b. The area is a crossroad of communications;

111

c. Southeast Asia is a vital segment in the line of containment of communism stretching from Japan southward and around to the Indian Peninsula. The Security of the three major non-Communist base areas in this quarter of the world—Japan, India, and Australia—depends in a large measure on the denial of Southeast Asia to the Communists. If Southeast Asia is lost, these three base areas will tend to be isolated from one another;

d. The fall of Indochina would undoubtedly lead to the fall of the other mainland states of Southeast Asia. Their fall would:

(1) Require changing the Philippines and Indonesia from supporting positions in the Asian offshore island chain to front-line bases for the defense of the Western Hemisphere. It would also call for a review of the strategic deployment of United States forces in the Far East; and

(2) Bring about almost immediately a dangerous condition with respect to the internal security of the Philippines, Malaya, and Indonesia, and would contribute to their probable eventual fall to the Communists.

e. The fall of Southeast Asia would result in the virtually complete denial to the United States of the Pacific littoral of Asia. Southeast Asian mainland areas are important in the conduct of operations to contain Communist expansion;

f. Communist control of this area would alleviate considerably the food problem of China and would make available to the USSR important strategic materials. In this connection, Soviet control of all the major components of Asia's war potential might become a decisive factor affecting the balance of power between the United States and the USSR. "A Soviet position of dominance over Asia, Western Europe, or both, would constitute a major threat to United States security"; and

g. A Soviet position of dominance over the Far East would also threaten the United States position in Japan since that country could thereby be denied its Asian markets, sources of food and other raw materials. The feasibility of retention by the United States of its Asian offshore island bases could thus be jeopardized.

3. In the light of the foregoing strategic considerations pertaining to the area of Southeast Asia, the Joint Chiefs of Staff, from the military point of view, concur in the conclusions in NSC 64. . . .

5. It appears obvious from intelligence estimates that the situation in Southeast Asia has deteriorated and, without United States assistance, this deterioration will be accelerated. In general, the basic conditions of political and economic stability in this area, as well as the military and internal security conditions, are unsatisfactory. These factors are closely interrelated and it is probable that, from the long-term point of view, political and economic stability is the controlling factor. On the other hand, the

military situation in some areas, particularly Indochina, is of pressing urgency. . . .

15. In view of the considerations set forth in paragraph 14 above, the Joint Chiefs of Staff recommend the immediate establishment of a small United States military aid group in Indochina, to operate in conformity with the requirements in paragraph 9 above. The Joint Chiefs of Staff would expect the senior member of this group to sit in consultation with military representatives of France and Vietnam and possibly of Laos and Cambodia. In addition to screening requests for matériel, he would be expected to insure full coordination of military plans and efforts between the French and Vietnamese forces and to supervise the allocation of matériel. The Joint Chiefs of Staff believe in the possibility of success of a prompt coordinated United States program of military, political, and economic aid to Southeast Asia and feel that such a success might well lead to the gaining of the initiative in the struggle in that general area. . . .

17. The Joint Chiefs of Staff suggest the following measures with military implications:

a. An increased number of courtesy or "show the flag" visits to Southeast Asian states;

b. Recognition of the "port closure" of Communist China seaports by the Nationalists as a *de facto* blockade so long as it is effective. Such action should remove some of the pressure, direct and indirect, upon Southeast Asia; should be of assistance to the anti-Communist forces engaged in interference with the lines of communication to China; and should aggravate the economic problems and general unrest in Communist China;

c. A program of special covert operations designed to interfere with Communist activities in Southeast Asia; and

d. Long-term measures to provide for Japan and the other offshore islands a secure source of food and other strategic materials from non-Communist held areas in the Far East.

28. THE STATE DEPARTMENT REASSESSES THE INDOCHINA SITUATION, AUGUST 1950

Failures in the field periodically produced reexamination of American policy in Indochina. The following memorandum, authored by the State Department's Policy Planning Staff, is almost more similar to PPS 51 (March 1949) than NSC 64 (February 1950) in its concern for impact on European affairs, its awareness of Asian nationalism, and its willingness to countenance the possibility of French failure in Indochina. (Source: Department of State, *Foreign Relations of the United States, 1950,* VI, pp. 857–58.)

MEMORANDUM PREPARED IN THE POLICY PLANNING STAFF

TOP SECRET   [WASHINGTON,] August 16, 1950.

UNITED STATES POLICY TOWARD INDOCHINA IN THE LIGHT OF RECENT DEVELOPMENTS

The receipt of Paris's telegram no. 783 of August 12, on top of reports received from General Erskine and Melby, together with telegrams from our representatives stationed in Indochina, suggests that the situation in Indochina is more serious than we have reckoned. The question then arises—is our present policy toward Indochina realistic?

The French are seeking a solution of the Indochina problem on a military plane. Coping only with indigenous Viet Minh resistance, which has thus far not been supported by significant Chinese aid, the French have enjoyed notable success through resort to arms. But now it has been revealed that the French have no confidence in their ability to maintain a position should the Chinese Communists seriously go to the aid of the Viet Minh, either directly or indirectly. The reports which we have been receiving from our own representatives, including the MDAP Mission, give us no reason to believe that the French are unduly alarmist in this appraisal. If the French send reinforcements to Indochina, as they are reportedly planning to do, they will further deplete defenses of Western Europe without—so far as we can tell—solving the Indochina problem.

If what Bruce was told and what Erskine and Melby have reported is true, it is questionable whether such air and naval support as we could muster would, in the light of our Korean experience, balance the scales in favor of France and its associated states. The question inevitably arises: "Can we then supply supplementary ground forces"? The answer, subject to check with the Defense Department, would seem to be in the negative.

All of this being the case, the French position in Indochina is indeed imperiled. We would be deceiving the French Government were we to offer encouragement of decisive military support. Furthermore, we would be undertaking a responsibility for the course of military events in Indochina which could be flung back in our face with recriminations should the military effort fail. The conclusion, therefore, is that if the

French—and we—are to be spared a humiliating debacle in Indochina, some means other than reliance on military force must be found.

What political moves can be made?

The French Government's inclination to appease Peiping is not only futile but a disturbing commentary on the general state of mind in Paris. Obviously, we should give the French no encouragement along such lines.

A dispassionate examination of the Indochina problem leads one to the familiar conclusion that the only hope for a solution lies in the adoption of certain drastic political measures by the French themselves. We recognize that those measures would be extremely distasteful to the French. But the only foreseeable alternative would seem to be even more disagreeable and embarrassing. This is a matter for voluntary decision by the French Government. The American Government should not take the responsibility for pressing Paris to any decision on this score. To do so would only lead to misunderstandings and mutual reproaches between allies.

We would, however, be less than frank with the French if we did not expose to them our views regarding a possible new approach to the problem of Indochina. Such an approach might be along the following general lines: It would seem that the March 8 agreements are an inadequate basis for attacking the Indochina problem on a political plane. It appears that genuine nationalism in Indochina would not, in view of the embittered atmosphere, be satisfied with anything less than independence by a definite date—perhaps two years hence, at a maximum. If the French make such a commitment, we can visualize the removal of much of the suspicion among the Indochinese and other Asians, leading to a greater degree of spontaneous cooperation, both within Indochina and from South Asians, with the current French military efforts. Subsequent to such a declaration, were Paris to pass a large measure of responsibility for the Indochinese problem to the United Nations, it might well enlist an even wider support from free Asian countries and inhibit somewhat Chinese Communist support to Ho. Such developments would make our own military and economic aid role in Indochina more popular in this country.

An approach along the foregoing lines would in our estimation tend to (1) reduce the political appeal of Ho, (2) increase the support throughout Indochina of the Viet Nam regime, (3) raise the morale of the Viet Nam forces to a level approaching that of the ROK army, (4) provide for international surveillance of the border, (5) bring the Western powers and the new national states of Asia into closer alignment, (6) reduce our commitments in what is for us at best a tertiary theater, and (7) provide the French the least humiliating means for their inevitable retirement from the Indochina scene.

115

If Paris does not feel that it can adopt a bolder political approach with respect to Indochina, we must recognize that the French and we may well be heading into a debacle which neither of us can afford. For our part, it will become necessary promptly to reexamine our policy toward Indochina.

29. THE FAR EASTERN DESK REAFFIRMS THE AMERICAN COMMITMENT, SEPTEMBER 1950

Each reexamination in turn produced a reaffirmation of policy direction. The following internal memorandum to Secretary Acheson is revealing not only in content but in its authorship. It was penned by the Assistant Secretary of State for Far Eastern Affairs, Dean Rusk. Rusk, of course, was to become Secretary of State for Presidents Kennedy and Johnson during the American military escalation of the 1960s. (Source: Department of State, *Foreign Relations of the United States, 1950,* VI, pp. 878–79.)

MEMORANDUM BY THE ASSISTANT SECRETARY OF STATE FOR FAR EASTERN AFFAIRS (RUSK) TO THE SECRETARY OF STATE

SECRET   [WASHINGTON,] September 11, 1950.
Subject: Possible Invasion of Indochina.

The following brief staff study is intended to sum-up the current situation in Indochina for your information:

1. *Military*

All indications point to a probable communist offensive against Indochina in late September or early October. While there is a possibility that this offensive would be directed by the Chinese Communists, who maintain approximately 100,000 troops on or near the border, we believe it more likely that the attack will be carried out by augmented Viet Minh forces under Ho Chi Minh, supplemented by material and possibly technical assistance from Communist China.

While the Viet Minh's capability has been increased during the past four months by the cooperation of Communist China, where an estimated 30,000 Viet Minh troops are now in training, there has not been a comparable increase in the ability of the anti-communist forces in Indochina to withstand a possible attack.

In the event of an attack by the Viet Minh, augmented by Chinese Communist assistance, we believe that the northern border area of Indochina could be overrun within a short time. In the event of a mass attack by Chinese Communist forces, augmented by the Viet Minh, we believe that by sheer numbers such a force could occupy perhaps the northern half of Indochina within a matter of weeks. In both cases, communist forces would then be in position along the Burma–Laos border; in the latter case, along the Burma–Laos and Thai–Laos borders, both relatively undefended by Burma and Thailand.

American military assistance consisting of equipment for twelve infantry battalions (less small arms) for the State forces, as well as aircraft and naval equipment for the French Union forces will be in Indochina by the end of October. It is expected that further equipment will be in the pipe line as soon as more funds are available.

The impact of the arrival of this equipment will be partially political since the build-up of the States forces by American assistance will have a salutary effect upon the morale of the three State Governments, with a concurrent increase in their abilities to withstand aggression from either internal or external sources. This effect, however, cannot be apparent by October, 1950, since a period of months will be required to train and equip the State forces. The air and naval equipment for the French Union forces, however, will be almost immediately effective since it will be used by trained personnel.

Although M. Pleven has informally suggested that the United States assume the financial burden of raising and maintaining larger State forces which would permit the withdrawal of French troops to Europe, and at the same time satisfy the new States' appetite for evidence of sovereignty represented by large national forces, such a program, even if adopted immediately, could not have an effect by October, 1950.

2. *Political*

The anticipated timing of the communist attack would take advantage of a partial political vacuum resulting from the transfer of powers from the French to the new State Governments. The new States have thus far failed to develop a solid anti-communist front. Their efforts and fears remain largely anti-colonial, a form of government which they know and dislike, rather than anti-communist, which is to them still a relatively unknown and unrecognized threat. They have devoted most of the nine months since their formation to gradually and haltingly assuming the powers granted to them. It seems doubtful that by the time of the possible offensive they will be sufficiently strong, or public opinion sufficiently concerned with the threat of communism to become effectively organized against it.

Although the non-communist nationalist leaders and "fence sitters" have continually pressed the French Government for further extension of sovereignty, such as a "timetable" statement promising complete autonomy at a future date, the French have informed us that they are opposed to any further extension of the March 8 Accords at this time. It is doubtful whether France, which is spending $500,000,000 a year in Indochina and has suffered approximately 50,000 military casualties since 1945, would be in a political mood to continue such an effort if a definite withdrawal date of French authority were announced. This view, however, cannot reduce the continuing French responsibility for the defense of the area against communist aggression. It would not seem reasonable or desirable for this Government to ask for the withdrawal of French support and troop strength from Indochina in view of the communist threat to that area outlined above. The presence of French and French controlled native troops in the area represents the only effective bulwark against communist encroachment.

3. *Conclusion*

The dilemma which has always faced American policy in Indochina is considerably heightened by the development set forth above. If the area of Southeast Asia is to be preserved from communist domination, it appears necessary for continued American assistance to be extended to the forces now opposing that aggression. At the same time the extension of American support to the Governments of the three States, which were established under French patronage, will continue to give rise to charges of imperialism, not only from the Kremlin and its satellites, but by other Asian countries in whose minds the threat of colonialism is still more vivid than that of communism.

By continuing our present policy of assisting the forces in Indochina which are opposed to communist aggression, we will assist in the preservation of the area from communist domination. We note, however, that American assistance alone cannot ensure the area against communist aggression if the desires and capabilities of the peoples and governments do not provide the main effort against it. So far and for the predictable future, French forces appear to be the sole effective guarantee that communist forces will be resisted.

30. CIA MEMO ANALYZING CHINESE INTENTIONS

The following CIA memorandum (NIE–5) was written shortly after Chinese entry into the Korean War. It is not only of passing interest as an assessment of the Indochina situation in late 1950, but of more enduring importance as a quintessential statement of American fears about Chinese intentions in Southeast Asia and a restatement and elaboration of the "falling dominoes" theory. (Source: Department of State, *Foreign Relations of the United States, 1950*, VI, pp. 958–63.)

MEMORANDUM BY THE CENTRAL INTELLIGENCE AGENCY

SECRET   [WASHINGTON,] 29 December 1950.
NIE–5

NATIONAL INTELLIGENCE ESTIMATE
INDOCHINA: CURRENT SITUATION AND PROBABLE DEVELOPMENTS

CONCLUSIONS

1. The French position in Indochina is critically endangered by the Viet Minh, a Communist movement that has exploited native nationalism. The Chinese Communist regime is already furnishing the Viet Minh matériel, training and technical assistance. Official French sources report that Chinese Communist troops are already present in Tonkin in some strength. If this aid continues and French strength and military resources are not substantially increased above those presently programmed, the Viet Minh probably can drive the French out of North Viet Nam (Tonkin) within six to nine months. French loss of Tonkin, even assuming the evacuation of French forces in substantial numbers, would jeopardize the French position in the remainder of Viet Nam, Laos, and Cambodia.

2. Under these circumstances there is only a slight chance that the French can maintain their military position long enough to build up an independent Vietnamese government and an effective national army which might win the support of non-Communist nationalists, and, in

conjunction with French forces, contain the Viet Minh. For these and other reasons there are grounds for questioning the French will to remain in Indochina.

3. The intervention of Chinese Communist troops in force in support of the Viet Minh would render the military position of the French untenable. At present there are about 185,000 Chinese Communist troops in the Tonkin border area, and approximately half of these could be committed to operations in Indochina. Even a relatively small number of Chinese Communist troops (25,000–50,000) would enable the Communist forces to drive the French out of Tonkin in a relatively short time.

4. Direct intervention by Chinese Communist troops may occur at any time. It may have already begun (see para. 1). It is almost certain to occur in strength whenever there is danger either that the Viet Minh will fail to attain its military objective of driving the French out of Indochina, or that the Bao Dai government is succeeding in undermining the support of the Viet Minh. The scale of Chinese Communist intervention, however, would be limited mainly by anti-Communist activities in China and by Chinese military commitments elsewhere.

5. The expulsion of the French by the Viet Minh, with or without Chinese Communist intervention, would almost certainly lead to the transformation of Indochina into a Communist satellite.

6. We believe that control of Indochina by the Viet Minh would eventually entail Communist control of all mainland Southeast Asia in the absence of effective Western assistance to other countries of the area. . . .

9. There is little doubt that a Viet Minh victory would lead to the transformation of Indochina into a Communist satellite. Ho Chi Minh is a Moscow-trained professional revolutionary and there have always been Communists in his government. At the present time, the Viet Minh regime is openly Communist in ideology and pro-Soviet in statements on foreign affairs. The recognition of the Ho regime by various international Communist groups as a full-fledged "people's democracy," formal recognition of the regime by Communist China and the Soviet bloc, and the failure of the Viet Minh to acknowledge the recognition tendered by Yugoslavia, all offer reasonably clear indications of the alignment of the Viet Minh leadership with the USSR, with Communist China, and the international Communist movement.

10. The strong probability is that the loss of Indochina to Communist control would mean the eventual loss of all mainland Southeast Asia, in the absence of Western assistance to the other countries of the area. Without such assistance, the proximity of well-trained Viet Minh forces would place nearly irresistible pressure upon Thailand, increasing the proclivity of Thai officialdom to accommodate itself to the winning side. If

Thailand were under Communist control, the Communist rebels in Malaya could be furnished military assistance that would be very likely to cause the British to lose control of the area. The Burmese government, already plagued by internal Communist problems, would find it difficult to resist diplomatic pressures backed up by both Chinese and Indochinese Communist forces on the borders of Burma. In addition, in Indonesia and the Philippines, the principal effect of Communist control of Indochina would be to strengthen indigenous Communist movements. Moreover, there might be a trend in Indonesia toward accommodation with the Communist bloc in Asia. As each successive country came under Communist influence, the non-Communist resistance in the remaining countries would be weakened.

31. THE STATE DEPARTMENT UPDATES AND CLARIFIES AMERICAN POLICY, MARCH 1952

This State Department memorandum was later incorporated as the basis for NSC 124/2 (June 1952)—the first major, overall restatement of American approaches to Southeast Asia since NSC 64 (February 1950). It is significant for its reaffirmation of increased aid to France, for its continued unwillingness to employ U.S. troops directly (out of fear of Chinese intervention), and for its refinement of the "falling dominoes" theory. It makes clear that the loss of Indochina would be serious but tolerable; but the loss of Malaya and Indonesia (the most important dominoes) was not acceptable. ("The West would suffer economic losses of major importance, and the Western orientation of Japan would be seriously jeopardized.") (Source: Department of State, *Foreign Relations of the United States, 1952–1954*, XIII, pp. 82–89.)

PAPER PREPARED IN THE DEPARTMENT OF STATE

TOP SECRET   [WASHINGTON, March 27, 1952.]

DRAFT—INDOCHINA SECTION OF NSC PAPER

Problem: To determine the policy of the United States toward the countries of Southeast Asia, and in particular, the courses of action which may be taken by the United States to strengthen and coordinate resistance to communism on the part of the governments and peoples of the area.

Assumption: That identifiable Chinese Communist aggression against Southeast Asia does not take place.

Analysis:

IMPORTANCE OF INDOCHINA

The strategic importance of Indochina derives from its geographical position as a key to the defense of mainland Southeast Asia; its economic value as a potential large scale exporter of rice; and its political importance as an example of Western resistance to Communist expansion.

a. It is generally accepted that should Indochina fall to Communist control, Thailand and Burma could be expected soon to make their own accommodations with the Communist bloc. . . .

If, however, the loss of Indochina were accompanied by the loss of Malaya and Indonesia as well, the West would suffer economic losses of major importance, and the Western orientation of Japan would be seriously jeopardized. Malaya and Indonesia are major sources of tin and rubber. Malaya is an important source of dollar earnings for the UK. Indonesia is an important secondary source of oil for the West. Communist control of all of Southeast Asia would remove the chief potential area for Japanese commercial development, and would so add to the already powerful mainland pulls upon Japan as to make it dubious that Japan could refrain from reaching an accommodation with the Communist bloc.

c. Communist successes in Indochina would, in any event, have major political and psychological consequences for the West. Southeast Asia and South Asia certainly, and possibly important areas of the Middle East would be influenced toward alignment with the Communist bloc. Japan, economic pressures aside, would be more disposed to accommodate itself to the Communist bloc by reason of its altered evaluation of the relative balance of power. Western European confidence in the strength and future of the West would be further undermined.

PRESENT SITUATION IN INDOCHINA

5. In the long run, the security of Indochina against communism will depend upon the development of native governments able to command the support of the masses of the people and national armed forces capable of relieving the French of the major burden of maintaining internal security. The Vietnamese Government has been slow to assume its responsibilities and has continued to suffer from a lack of strong leadership. It has had to contend with: *(a)* lingering Vietnamese suspicion of any French-

supported regime, combined with the apathetic and "fence-sitting" attitude of the bulk of the people; *(b)* the difficulty, common to all new and inexperienced governments, of training the necessary personnel and building an efficient administration; *(c)* the failure of factional and sectional groups to unite in a concerted national effort; and *(d)* the relatively ineffective character of Bao Dai's administration.

The French Government is increasingly concerned over France's ability to maintain its position in Indochina. There is a growing official feeling in France that it cannot simultaneously support presently projected military efforts in both Europe and Asia without greater U.S. aid. If the French were unable, by remaining in Indochina, to secure financial assistance for both their European and Indochinese operations, and were forced to choose between the two, they would probably view their Indochinese commitment as of lesser importance. Moreover, there has been a growing popular feeling that the distant and costly Indochinese war offers few rewards even if won. This feeling is increasing political pressure for some alleviation of the French burden in Indochina.

Strong factors, however, still hold the French to their present commitments. These include: *(a)* the intangible but powerful factor of prestige; *(b)* the knowledge that withdrawal from Indochina would have repercussions elsewhere in the French Union; *(c)* the concern over the fate of French nationals and investments in Indochina; *(d)* the official feeling that no settlement with the VietMinh or with Communist China could be achieved that would reserve any French interests in Indochina; and *(e)* the physical and technical difficulties of a withdrawal operation.

On balance it appears probable that the French will continue the effort to maintain their position in Indochina, but will attempt to alleviate their burden by insisting that the U.S. undertake an increased share of financial responsibility for the defense of the area. The French may, in due course, also press for U.S. armed assistance, either directly, or through the UN, and may also press for U.S. or international support. The French will probably attempt to convince the U.S. that the alternatives to U.S. assumption of an important share of at least financial support for the Indochina operation will be either French withdrawal, or a negotiated settlement with the VietMinh which would be tantamount to acceptance of a Communist Indochina. It is, however, quite possible that if the French are unsuccessful in securing greater U.S. financial assistance they will in fact seriously consider withdrawal from Indochina, or, as a more likely alternative, will explore the possibilities of extricating themselves as gracefully as possible from their Indochina entanglement through a negotiated settlement with the Communists, following an achievement of a truce similar to that now being sought in Korea.

123

CONSIDERATIONS AFFECTING U.S. ASSUMPTION OF INCREASED RESPONSIBILITY FOR INDOCHINA

Important as the maintenance and development of an anti-communist position in Indochina is to the interests of the U.S., a U.S. decision to undertake greater responsibility in Indochina should be made only in the light of *(a)* the possibility that any U.S. course of action, short of actual employment of U.S. armed forces, may in the long run prove inefficacious; *(b)* the possibility that a marked improvement in the anti-communist position in Indochina which threatened to eliminate the VietMinh might occasion Chinese Communist intervention; *(c)* the possibility that U.S. assumption of responsibility in Indochina might occasion a rapid and extensive loss of interest in the situation on the part of the French; and *(d)* U.S. ability to assume increased burdens in Indochina in view of its present world-wide commitments.

U.S. OBJECTIVES

In the light of the considerations described above, U.S. courses of action with regard to Indochina should be designed to:

(a) Enable the French to continue to fulfill French responsibilities for Indochina without sacrificing development of French strength under NATO;

(b) Supplement rather than supplant French efforts in Indochina, and minimize any increase of U.S. responsibility for the area;

(c) Assist in development of the fullest degree of political and military independence of the Associated States which may be consistent with continuation of French efforts in the area, and assist in the development of stable and competent indigenous governments, strong national armies, and sound economies.

(d) Minimize possibilities of Chinese Communist intervention.

POSSIBLE U.S. COURSES OF ACTION

The courses of action which the U.S. might consider following to maintain the Franco-Vietnamese position in Indochina and to prevent deterioration of that position include: *(a)* increase of present types of U.S. assistance; *(b)* assumption of a portion of the French burden by financial assistance to metropolitan France, or by financial assistance to the national armies of Indochina; *(c)* exertion of U.S. influence for a broadening of the base of the governments of Indochina; *(d)* employment of U.S. forces in Indochina; and *(e)* stabilization of the present situation through the achievement of a truce which, *inter alia*, would secure anti-communist Indochinese control of territories now administered by them. . . .

b. The current cost to France of the Indochina military operation is approximately U.S. $1,200,000,000 a year. U.S. assumption of a major portion of these costs might be undertaken either by provision of budgetary assistance to metropolitan France, or by U.S. underwriting of all or part of the costs of the development of the Indochinese national armies, which currently account for some $400,000,000 of French costs in Indochina. If it were estimated to be in U.S. interest to undertake responsibility for a portion of the French costs in Indochina, either of these methods could be used to good effect. Direct budgetary assistance to France would have the advantage of limiting direct U.S. responsibility for the Indochina situation and thus might be better calculated to preserve French will for continuing French efforts in Indochina. Assumption of part or all of the costs of the national Indochinese armies would increase U.S. involvement in Indochina, and would undoubtedly to some degree increase U.S. responsibility for the area. This course of action might, however, be more attractive to the U.S. domestically and thus make U.S. appropriations more feasible. It would give the U.S. a greater voice in a particularly useful sector of Indochinese political and military development, and might be so carried out as to minimize the danger of reducing French interest in Indochina.

c. French political concessions to Indochinese nationalism have been considerable and as of now the Associated States probably have more privileges than they can effectively exercise. The French have not offered the Associated States freedom of choice as to whether they wish to be in or out of the French Union. Such an offer might have some utility as a gesture to Indochinese nationalism but the desirability of such a French move, from the point of view of the U.S., depends almost completely on whether or not it would result in a slackening of French will to carry on the defense of Indochina. At present it appears inadvisable for the U.S. to exert its influence to secure such an offer from the French.

The U.S., however, might usefully exert its influence to induce the French and the new States to move towards a broadening of the present overly narrow base of the new governments. In the key area of Vietnam the present government represents primarily the members of a small, relatively pro-French, faction. Important political groups such as the Dai Viets, and Cao Daists, are not adequately represented in the cabinet or government. Without U.S. assumption of major responsibility for Indochina it must be estimated that U.S. influence in the political developments of the area will necessarily remain to some degree limited, but the considerable political influence that the U.S. does possess might well be directed toward the development of governments in Indochina which adequately represent all non-Communist groups.

d. The Chinese Communists have demonstrated in Korea their sensitivity to the presence of U.S. forces near their borders and their willingness to accept major risks and casualties to prevent the approach of U.S. forces to the Manchurian frontier. It must be estimated that the Chinese Communists have the same sensitivity about their southern border as they have demonstrated in the case of Manchuria and it is probable therefore that the intervention of U.S. armed forces in Indochina would occasion a full scale Chinese Communist military intervention. The employment of U.S. armed forces in Indochina, without a prior Chinese Communist intervention, would also have the disadvantage of tending to relieve the French of their basic military responsibility for Indochina and thus of providing the French with a possible means of exit from Indochina which might not too greatly involve French prestige. Aside from the dislocation which use of U.S. forces in Indochina would impose upon U.S. military dispositions elsewhere in the world, therefore, there is good reason to consider it inadvisable for the U.S. to employ its own armed forces in Indochina on the assumption, to which this paper is addressed, that Chinese Communist identifiable aggression does not take place.

e. If it is assumed that a truce in Indochina is *ipso facto* desirable it must also be recognized that none of the political prerequisites of a satisfactory truce are present in the situation. Unlike the situation in Korea, the opposing forces do not face each other across a line of battle; to the contrary large territories are only sporadically subjected to the administrative control of either force. As a practical matter it would be virtually impossible to secure agreement on a "cease fire line" and upon the territories which the opposing forces should control and regard as their own. Correlatively, in the circumstances it would be virtually impossible to set up safeguards for any truce, since observation commissions, neutral or otherwise, would have no "front" to patrol. A situation not unlike but even more unsatisfactory than that which obtained in Indonesia from 1947 to 1949 would doubtless develop. Finally, the concession on the part of Franco-Vietnamese forces of any important territory to the Communists would unquestionably be regarded by the Indochinese people as a confession of great weakness and would have a deleterious effect on the political climate of Indochina.

Recommendations

The U.S. should:

1. Continue and increase its military and economic assistance programs for Indochina;

2. Continue to provide substantial financial assistance for the French effort in Indochina either through direct budgetary assistance to France

or through assumption of financial responsibility for the Indochinese national armies, or a combination of both.

3. Continue to exert its influence to promote constructive political developments in Indochina, and in particular to promote a broadening of the base of the governments of the Associated States.

4. Continue to stress French responsibility for Indochina and oppose any decrease of French efforts in Indochina.

5. The U.S. should not employ U.S. armed forces in Indochina.

6. The U.S. should not exert its influence for the achievement of a truce in Indochina.

Part III

DOMINOES, DIEM, AND DEATH

1952–1963

INTRODUCTION
Lloyd Gardner

No foreign policy issue is ever considered in isolation, of course, but the all-absorbing concern of the 1960s and 1970s—not to be the President who lost Indochina—has somewhat obscured a clear understanding of the origins of the Vietnam War and its development from a broad spectrum of concerns: military, political, economic, and psychological. Indochina was always part of a Cold War whole. Thus the struggle of the French in Southeast Asia to retain their colonial position posed a number of questions and difficulties for the new Eisenhower administration.

First was Korea. In December 1952 the President-elect had fulfilled a Republican campaign pledge to go to Korea to see for himself what could be done to end the fighting. After visiting the front lines and hearing the pleas of South Korean President Syngman Rhee for an all-out attack on the North, Eisenhower then rendezvoused with his key military and political advisers on the cruiser *Helena* off Wake Island. For several days Eisenhower conducted a seminar. "There was general agreement with my conclusion that we could not tolerate the indefinite continuance of the Korean conflict," he would write of these conversations; "the United States would have to prepare to break the stalemate."[1]

In that case, what about Indochina? To the extent that any settlement short of victory encouraged the "other side" to shift to another "front," the possibilities of a safe exit from Korea diminished rapidly.[2] "We discussed gravely the problem of Indochina," Secretary of State John Foster Dulles would recall nearly two years later in the midst of the Geneva Conference. The Soviet "program," he had warned his colleagues on board the *Helena,* aimed at exhausting American resources and patience by "mounting a series of local actions around the world at times and places of their choosing." Korea and Indochina, as

131

well as the vulnerable points in decolonizing Africa, were all included in the Soviet master plan. "They [Soviet strategists] *expect* the Republican Administration to be tougher. If it is not tougher, they will enlarge their estimate of what they can get away with. Our future plight will be worse than our past."[3]

The Dulles "world view," so well stated in the above quotation, did not presume that American ability to influence events was without limit, however much the Secretary of State sometimes seemed to suggest so in his public rhetoric. (Doc. 42.) If American leaders feared that the Soviet Union would seize upon a Korean cease-fire to step up pressures on the West elsewhere, they also suffered from chilling premonitions of an extended land war in Southeast Asia. "No more Koreas" was a watchword of both military and political spokesmen in the 1950s. That persistent concern led, at times, to an almost desperate groping for some alternative to sending foot soldiers into the forbidding mists and elephant grasses of the Vietnamese hinterland. Atomic bombs were considered, with the Air Force Chief of Staff, General Nathan Twining, arguing that a "clean" nuclear weapon dropped outside the besieged Dienbienphu fortress in 1954 could save the situation. Eisenhower rejected the idea.[4]

Contradictory assumptions about the nature of the war also exerted a limiting influence upon American involvement. (Doc. 32.) Vietminh leader Ho Chi Minh had favorably impressed American OSS officers near the end of World War II, and even his supposed subservience to the Russians had not completely replaced the concern in policy-makers' minds that they were fighting a genuinely "nationalist" leader at the head of a powerful anticolonial movement with worldwide implications. Americans despaired, moreover, of French willingness (or even ability) to abandon their "imperial" pretensions. "I have never talked or corresponded with a person knowledgeable in Indochinese affairs," was Eisenhower's frequently quoted judgment, "who did not agree that had elections been held as of the time of the fighting, possibly 80 per cent of the population would have voted for the Communist Ho Chi Minh as their leader rather than Chief of State Bao Dai."[5]

But because Vietnam *was* part of a larger reality, in the perceptions of American policy-makers, the gamble to resolve these fears and contradictions was deemed an essential risk. Eisenhower and Dulles both believed, for example, that Communist China, acting with Moscow's approval, had embarked upon a *jihad* to drive the white man from

Asia. (Doc. 33.) Marxist-inspired, the Chinese drive was thought to have pre–Cold War roots in an entirely separate ideological conflict. "The Japanese war lords adopted a similar slogan when they sought to subject Asia to their despotic rule," Dulles liked to say.[6] "Asia for the Asians" appealed, he thought, to peoples under colonial domination regardless of who was championing the cause, reactionaries or revolutionaries. One very powerful motive for the construction of an Asian security pact, therefore, was to foil the purposes of those who said that the West would cooperate only on terms of degradation for Asian peoples. (Doc. 45.)

When Dulles suggested to President Eisenhower on March 24, 1953, that Indochina "had probably the top priority in foreign policy, being in some ways more important than Korea because the consequences of loss there could not be localized, but would spread throughout Asia, and Europe," he had all these things in mind—and more.[7] Americans had long worried about French morale, and the debilitating nature of the Indochina struggle: how it weakened the French commitment to NATO. Even more serious, perhaps, was the concern felt about Japan's fate in an Asia dominated by Peking. (Doc. 36.)

Indeed, Secretary Dulles had first encountered this latter problem at the time he undertook to draft the peace treaty with Japan. Economic recovery in the former "workshop of Asia" was a high priority in Washington by 1950. Without the China market to stimulate Japanese enterprise, and lacking the ability to guarantee that Japan could enter into American and European markets, American diplomats felt that their former enemy needed all the help it could get. "We believe that there is a big market for Japanese industrial output in Southeast Asia," the Secretary wrote in October 1950. Two years later, moreover, he would recall that it had fallen "to my lot" to invite the three Associated States of Indochina, Vietnam, Laos, and Cambodia, to sign the treaty as "independent sovereign states."[8]

They were not, of course, and that was the problem. The effort to boost the status of the Associated States had a dual purpose: to encourage the French to move faster in granting independence, and thus remove the stigma of a "colonial" war from the Western effort in Indochina, and to establish a "connection" between Japan and Southeast Asia. The Japanese "connection" was to prove an enduring concern, and was incorporated most famously by Eisenhower in his "domino theory" of April 7, 1954. (Doc. 36). The Japanese connection also linked Indochina to the American effort to put the dynamic forces of the modern world on the same side in the Cold War. In the Truman years the Cold War in Europe had occupied center stage, but the Chinese Revolution changed all that. Efforts to portray the Chinese followers of Mao-Tse-tung as Moscow's puppets had not made policy-makers oblivious to the obvious reality about them. The center of the ideological conflict was now in what was becoming known as the Third World.

Japan's industrial capacity would have to be used to the fullest if the economic problems encountered in those areas were to be overcome by non-Communist methods. (Doc. 48.) "I have become personally convinced that it is going to be very difficult to stop Communism in much of the world," the Secretary wrote the Eisenhower administration's specialist in psychological warfare, C. D. Jackson,

> if we cannot in some way duplicate the intensive Communist effort to raise productive standards. They themselves are increasing their own productivity at the rate of about 6% per annum, which is about twice our rate. In many areas of the world such as Southeast Asia, India, Pakistan and South America, there is little, if any, increase. That is one reason why Communism has such great appeal in areas where the slogans of "liberty," "freedom" and "personal dignity" have little appeal.[9]

Although estimates of Soviet successes in raising living standards at home proved to be overdrawn, the concern about "Peaceful Co-Existence" as a new method for fighting the Cold War persisted. (Doc. 50.) The static colonial powers, Britain and France, with their traditional narrow concerns, stood in the way of so many things: Japanese integration in the free world economy, independence for colonial areas, and, as a result, the development of a sound international economy.

At least, so it seemed in 1953 when the Eisenhower administration took over stewardship of American foreign policy. "Ike" had called upon the Soviet Union to make a new beginning, to demonstrate an interest in ending the Cold War by not taking advantage of a Korean armistice. "Any armistice in Korea that merely released aggressive armies to attack elsewhere would be a fraud."[10] None of his advisers imagined for a minute, however, that if the Soviets withdrew their aid, or the Chinese Communists decided to withhold support, the war could be won by current French methods. These were, Washington believed, too defensive and controlled by strategies designed to keep the Associated States dependent upon Paris. The stalemate in Indochina—if not outright military defeat—could only be corrected in Paris.

On July 3, 1953, after lengthy consultations with French political and military leaders, the United States participants in the discussions signaled their willingness to aid the so-called Navarre Plan. It might have a chance to succeed, they reported, if it was faithfully carried out. Named for General Henri Navarre, it involved creating a "nationalist" Vietnamese army of at least 200,000 men, a project Paris had previously resisted, and a promise to renegotiate 1949 accords with the Associated States with a view "to perfecting their independence and sovereignty." Admiral Arthur W. Radford was satisfied especially because he sensed a turning point. All he wanted to know was if the Administration had the money. "A change of concept on the part of the French could do a lot," said the chairman of the Joint Chiefs of Staff. "I think if we can send [Lieutenant General John W.] O'Daniel out to ride herd on them, he might be able to talk Navarre into really pushing forward."[11]

In all, the Administration committed nearly $1.4 billion to aid the Indochina effort in fiscal year 1954, an increase of $1.1 billion over the average for the previous three years. By the end of 1953, moreover, the United States was paying approximately 80 percent of the cost of the war. Military supplies sent to Vietnam from the end of World War II through 1954 included 554 aircraft, 347 naval vessels, 182 tanks, 1,498 combat vehicles, 20,593 trucks, 280,349 small arms and machine guns, 4,753 artillery pieces, 442,360,000 rounds of small-arms machine-gun ammunition, and 8,212,000 rounds of artillery ammunition.[12]

The Navarre Plan became famous, however, not for its training of a Vietnamese army or its "forward" strategy, but for what happened at an isolated outpost in northwest Vietnam near the Laotian border. In early 1954 General Navarre placed a garrison of nearly 12,000 men in a fortress at Dienbienphu. Never fully explained to the end of the Vietnam War in 1975, the battle of Dienbienphu that resulted from this decision has been called a decisive turning point in world history. Navarre gambled. And so did the Vietminh, explains historian Bernard Fall. If they chose not to attack, the new American aid "would make

135

itself felt in Indochina and would permit the French vastly to expand the native Indochinese armies.''[13]

Whatever degree of desperation led the Vietminh to risk so much on this throw of the dice, the situation in Paris was worse. The war had lasted nearly eight years. No amount of American aid could make up for the dreary reality of a war that was costing more in human and psychological terms every day, almost every hour. Over strenuous American objections, French delegates to the Berlin Foreign Ministers' Conference in January 1954 sought to have Indochina put on the agenda of a Five Power Conference to be held in Geneva.

American policy-makers assumed, perhaps correctly, that the Russians were eager to use this lever to persuade the French to renounce the latest plan for rearming West Germany, the proposed European Defense Community (EDC). Russian behavior is explainable on those terms. But it is also true that both Moscow and Peking had been sending out signals since the summer of 1953 that they would welcome an Indochinese settlement.[14] Ironically, moreover, the greater the American support, the harder the war was to sell at home. The French left was critical of American "neocolonialism," while the right saw little reason to continue a struggle simply for the "honor" of making Indochina independent. Only a few years later, General Charles de Gaulle would find a way to remold French politics around a concept of European integrity and its special mission to the world. In 1954 the task for French statesmen was less well defined and concerned almost entirely with limiting damage caused by the war.

As the crisis at Dienbienphu worsened, President Eisenhower was repeatedly asked to state how far the United States would go to save the situation. On February 10, 1954, he appeared to rule out any active participation. "No one could be more bitterly opposed to ever getting the United States involved in a hot war in that region than I am; consequently, every move that I authorize is calculated, as far as humans can do it, to make certain that that does not happen."[15] Little room there, it would seem, for additional questions about Ike's intentions; but they kept coming all the same, and, in fact, a debate within the Administration was just getting going, triggered by a visit from a new French military commander, General Paul Ely.

Ely's discussions with Admiral Radford and Secretary Dulles made it clear that without a dramatic change, not only would Dienbienphu fall to the Vietminh, but the psychological consequences would make defeat a certainty. Radford was responsive to suggestions of direct American engagement, beginning with air strikes to relieve the garrison at Dienbienphu. The Secretary of State did not rule out such a course, but felt it "appropriate to remind our French friends" that if the American flag was to be engaged, it must be in a successful effort. And that meant "a greater degree of partnership than had prevailed up to the present time, notably in relation to independence for the Associated States and the training of indigenous forces."[16]

Instead of clarifying the situation, therefore, the Ely mission produced confusion in both Paris and Washington. Complaints of bad faith and unfulfilled promises were heard in each capital as time for the opening of the Geneva Conference neared. While Radford continued discussing air strikes, now given the name Operation Vulture, and leaving the impression with Ely that Eisenhower would back him up, Secretary Dulles was in New York adding another condition to the list of requirements for American intervention. The threatened imposition of the Communist "political system . . . by whatever means," Dulles said, "would be a grave threat to the whole free community." It should not be passively accepted, "but should be met by united action."[17]

On April 3, 1954, Dulles and Radford met with congressional leaders. The Chairman of the Joint Chiefs went into considerable detail in regard to Dienbienphu, while Dulles drew out the ominous consequences of what would happen if Indochina fell "and nothing was done about it." Dulles later complained that Radford's purpose was to secure approval for a specific set of actions, while his own was aimed at building support for "united action." However that may be, the feeling was unanimous that "we want no more Koreas with the United States furnishing 90% of the manpower."[18] (Doc. 34.)

The conference with congressional leaders reaffirmed Eisenhower's belief that he could get no mandate from the legislators unless the nation's allies agreed to participate fully in any military intervention. At first Dulles was perfectly happy with that caveat. He had already briefed allied ambassadors on his "united action" speech, and its implications, and was hard at work lining up the support of Asian nations thought to be friendly to the idea as well as from Asian members of the British Commonwealth. Upon his departure for London on a hurried mission to secure British and French participation in this collective security organization, as yet unnamed, Dulles told reporters, "Our purpose is not to prevent a peaceful settlement at the forthcoming Geneva Conference, but to create the unity of free wills needed to assure a peaceful settlement which will in fact preserve the vital interests of us all."[19] (Doc. 37.)

Dulles' statement was a masterful piece of *double entendre*. In between the lines, argue French observers, what he wanted "was to establish a political and strategic framework where, as in NATO, France and England would no longer be able to take any diplomatic initiatives (such as negotiating peace in Indochina) without Washington's formal agreement. The 'solidarity of the free world' would transcend all national interests."[20] Hence the necessity of obtaining commitments before the Geneva Conference met, or, perhaps more urgently, before the fall of Dienbienphu. But there was another reason for Dulles' actions: the creation of a Southeast Asia collective security organization would, once and for all, remove the Indochina war from the category of "colonialism." (Doc. 38.)

Echoes from another era reverberated in Dulles' mind during these troubled moments. Flying over the Atlantic, he may have recalled what he said at the most recent National Security Council meeting:

> The situation was not unlike that which existed in 1932 when Stimson tried so desperately with Sir John Simon to get the United Kingdom to join with the United States in trying to slow down the Japanese. The British, of course, had refused to follow Stimson's course. Secretary Dulles said he believed, however, that if we put our case to them strongly they may come along this time.[21]

Preliminary soundings in the British capital brought forth a commitment to consider a collective security organization—but not until diplomacy had been given its chance. The Secretary did not help his case at a Paris NATO meeting several days later, when, during the course of a discussion on hydrogen weapons, he suggested that they must now be treated as having become "conventional." An effort to contain the Soviet threat around a 20,000-mile perimeter, he said, "would impose critical strains upon the economic, social and fiscal orders of many of the free nations and expose them to serious instability and unrest within their own borders." The United States would make every effort to consult, but, "under certain contingencies, time would not permit consultation without itself endangering the very security we seek to protect."[22]

When coupled with recent American statements about Chinese "aggression," and rumors of Franco-American military decisions, Dulles' thoughts on hydrogen weapons were not a little disquieting. Indeed, the Secretary would himself report to President Eisenhower that a main obstacle to British acquiescence was precisely the fear that intervention would trigger a nuclear countdown in Asia.[23] Nothing Dulles or Eisenhower could say—the President tried a personal letter to Prime Minister Winston Churchill—could budge the British from their original position. (Doc. 35.) The essential condition having gone unsatisfied, Eisenhower spoke the final words on the pre-Geneva effort to stave off defeat by "collective" security. The United States could not police the world, he told the National Security Council on April 29, 1954. Without Allied support such an attempt would cost "all our significant support in the free world. . . . Without allies and associates the leader is just an adventurer like Genghis Khan."[24]

Dulles, meanwhile, had gone to Geneva. He would stay only a week, "and while there conducted himself with the pinched distaste of a puritan in a house of ill repute," refusing to shake hands with Chou En-lai, the Chinese Foreign Minister, and ordering the American delegation to ignore the presence of the Chinese delegation.[25] The incident made for good news copy, but Dulles remained a firm believer in the value of ignoring such "old world" conventions. America, he was trying to say, was different.

The Secretary escaped the depressing environment he found at Geneva before the fall of Dienbienphu on May 7, 1954. The impact was instantaneous. French Foreign Secretary Georges Bidault began to speak to the conference about the heroism of its defenders, but when he looked up all he saw around him was the downcast eyes of fellow Western diplomats and an unblinking stare from the Communist delegates. "He was the very picture of France's loneliness in her defeat," remarked one observer. Buried in the last part of his text was a short paragraph proposing a "general cessation of hostilities." France had sued for peace on the ninth anniversary of V-E Day.[26]

Pressed by their Russian and Chinese "seconds," the Vietminh representatives at Geneva accepted the temporary partition of Vietnam at the 17th Parallel—surrendering almost a third of the territory they held. The West had not hoped to attain so much, nor to find the Russians willing to allow Laos and Cambodia to seek outside military assistance as part of a formal agreement. Nevertheless, the term "Geneva Agreement of 1954" is something of a misnomer. All that was signed was a series of armistices, and particularly not the so-called Final Declaration of July 21, 1954.[27] (Docs. 43, 44.)

The terms of the Vietnamese armistice—controversial from the beginning—provided for a temporary partition of the country at the 17th Parallel, evacuation of French forces from the North, a ban on increasing any military matériel in either part of the country, the creation of an international control commission, and the organization of elections to reunify the country before the deadline of July 20, 1956. The American delegate, Under Secretary of State Walter Bedell Smith, issued a statement on the final day pledging on behalf of the United States not to interfere with the operation of these terms. (Doc. 44.)

No sooner had the diplomats closed their briefcases in Switzerland, however, than Dulles led a parade of Western statesmen into the Philippines, there to meet with certain Asian counterparts to sign the articles of the Southeast Asia Treaty Organization.[28] (Doc. 45.) If SEATO came too late to save Dienbienphu, or to keep Chinese Foreign Minister Chou En-lai out of Geneva "society," American policy-makers now had something they valued highly: a clean slate. The principle behind SEATO was set forth in the document as collective security. South Vietnam, Laos, and Cambodia were barred from becoming members under the terms of the Geneva armistice agreements, yet Secretary Dulles explained that a protocol to the SEATO pact extended an "umbrella" to those three "nations." (Doc. 46.)

Almost immediately, therefore, Washington had made known to the world an intention of disregarding the "election" clause of the Vietnam armistice terms and Final Declaration. Perhaps all-Vietnamese elections would be held one day—just as all-German elections might be held, or all-Korean elections. Anything was possible, but it was safest not to bet.[29] (Doc. 40.) The American "candidate" to lead the new "nation" of South Vietnam was Ngo Dinh Diem, an exile whose "nationalist" credentials had impressed a remarkably diverse number of Americans, including later critics of the American buildup such as Senator Mike Mansfield of Montana. Diem had even been offered a position in Ho Chi Minh's government at one time before he became an exile in America. Installed as head of the South Vietnamese Government on June 17, 1954, Premier Diem made no effort to send any functionaries north of the 17th Parallel to negotiate with Ho Chi Minh's about the elections—or anything else.[30] And with the aid of two American "pro-consuls," Generals Edward Geary Lansdale and J. Lawton Collins, Premier Diem went about the task of "nation-building." Lansdale, an expert on counterinsurgency, arrived in Saigon on June 1, 1954, with little more than a battered typewriter. He quickly made himself known to Diem by means of a memorandum he had drafted on statesmanship and how-to recommendations on winning the hearts and minds of the people. "We saw each other more and more frequently in the weeks and months that followed until we fell into the habit of meeting nearly every day. Our association gradually developed into a friendship of considerable depth, trust, and candor."[31]

Collins had a more strictly military mission. At the end of six months he had achieved his primary objective: an agreement with the French that the training of the Vietnamese army would pass into American hands. Collins had doubts about Diem originally, but he soon came to like the "George Washington" of this new country. "It was . . . apparent that he was not only strongly anti-Communist but quite strongly anti-French."[32] (Docs. 47, 50.) In less than two years, the South Vietnamese military, including irregular forces, totaled 280,000. American military aid rose steadily between 1956 and 1962 in order to sustain this force, and in 1961 came to $300 million. By 1960 the American military mission had swollen from the handful of men under Collins' command to more than 4,000.[33]

Diem's survival, once rated by Dulles as a one-in-ten chance, seemed assured. Indeed, Americans talked about South Vietnam as a "showcase" example of nation-building. Among those least happy about the course of events in Vietnam were the French, who resented what they said was displacement, and who made no effort to conceal for the sake of SEATO unity their belief that President Diem was an American puppet. Of course Dulles denied the charges. Washington did not control the Diem government, the Secretary told a background press conference on May 12, 1955. If it were the kind of government that could be controlled, it would not succeed. "The only government that can succeed there is a government which is independent of foreign controls and which is really operating on a national basis."[34]

Eerily prophetic, the Secretary's words would come back to haunt his successors. But in 1956, Diem's final refusal to consider all-Vietnamese elections was supported and seconded by a steady stream of American visitors to Saigon. "The militant march of communism has been halted," Vice-President Richard M. Nixon congratulated the South Vietnamese Constituent Assembly. Before he left, Nixon invited Diem to visit Washington, where he was welcomed by a bipartisan crowd of celebrants, all of whom were eager to lavish praise upon the man whose inspired leadership put him in the front ranks of defenders of the "cause of the free world."[35]

The White House communiqué issued at the end of his visit in May 1957 hinted, however, that certain difficulties had yet to be overcome. Foremost among these was the "continued military buildup of the Chinese Communists," which was cited as the main justification for continuing American military aid. The only references to the growing insurgency Diem faced in the countryside was the communiqué's oblique warning about "continuing Communist subversive capabilities" and that "aggression or subversion" against "the Republic of Viet Nam would be considered as endangering peace and stability."[36]

The combination of forces building up against Diem was indeed formidable, though it did not include any direct threat from China. Desertions from his army, peasant resistance to Saigon, growing evidence of corruption in the American aid program, offered a fertile ground for the new insurgency led by the Vietcong. Exactly when the North Vietnamese joined in the fight against Diem remains a matter of dispute. Some observers claim that the origins of the insurgency can be traced to Northerners who stayed behind in 1954 for the specific purpose of engineering a "revolution." Others insist that the documents reveal that as late as 1959 (and later) the North placed first priority on a political struggle and that armed force was to be used only for "self-defense."[37] (Doc. 51.) In any case, by mid-1959 Ho was sending arms and advisers into the South in significant numbers.

Whatever the level of assistance from the North, Diem had compiled an abysmal record in agriculture and production in the South. The bulwarks of a sound economy were simply never constructed. Despite an American aid program that was larger than any other save for that granted Korea, the Vietnamese economy not only did not progress, it went backward. In 1958 South Vietnam imported $232 million in American, French, and Japanese goods, but sold only $57 million abroad. The deficit had to be made up by funds from the U.S. Treasury. Congressional investigators learned all of this from reliable witnesses, but so strong was Diem's American reputation, now boosted again as winner of the Valley Forge Freedom Foundation's award for "effective resistance to communism," that it was considered almost disloyal even to whisper that Diem's government was less than perfect.[38]

Indeed, the more perilous his predicament, the firmer the words used in Washington promising support. Eisenhower, for example, now told a Gettysburg College audience on April 4, 1959, that it had become a question of South Vietnam's survival, and promised that America stood ready to provide "the military strength necessary to its continued existence in freedom."[39] (Doc. 51.)

In these "transition" years, 1959–61, Vietnam was perceived as a primary "target area" for Russian-sponsored "wars of national liberation." Thus Democratic candidate John F. Kennedy made the 1960 race a contest with Nikita Khrushchev, insofar as he could, with the "world" as the prize to the winner. Little or nothing was said about Vietnam specifically, because there was hardly time to talk about anything else besides Cuba. But Kennedy's new look in foreign policy envisioned an America ready to take on the Russians anywhere, at any level from counterinsurgency to nuclear counterforce. (Docs. 52, 53.)

A parallel "national security" effort was to be mounted in the political area: Third World nations lacking an adequate "infrastructure" were to be redesigned from bottom to top according to blueprints provided by a new breed of "action intellectuals" who flocked to Washington to answer Kennedy's summons. "It was the golden age for development theorists," recalled a skeptical observer inside the new administration. "Some university faculties were almost denuded as professors left their tranquil campuses to instruct the natives in the dank far reaches of the world."[40]

Instructed by the "experts," Third World leaders would modernize their countries, economically and politically, and, "with American hardware and technical help, acquire an appropriate military capability."[41] "Vietnamization," associated with Richard M. Nixon, was really an invention of these years that went haywire. Kennedy sensed the trap. Commenting on Diem's appeal for American ground forces, he told an aide about his doubts. "The troops will march in; the bands will play; the crowds will cheer; and in four days everyone will have forgotten. Then we will be told we have to send in more troops. It's like taking a drink. The effect wears off, and you have to take another."[42]

Prompted by the advisers he had appointed standing at his elbow, Kennedy took the first drink. How could he do otherwise? he half-

143

complained, half-asked once. "I can't take a 1954 defeat today." Eisenhower could blame the French, he said to Walt W. Rostow, and take shelter behind America's disinclination to support colonialism. Besides, Ike was a military hero, and Kennedy possessed no such reputation to still critics.[43] There was something else: to lose in Vietnam would put the stigma of "colonialism" back on American policy in the Third World, because it was axiomatic to that policy that the French had lost because they fought such a war, and where did that leave the Americans if they also lost? (Docs. 54, 55.)

By the end of 1963 the number of U.S. military personnel had grown to more than 16,000. Air Force sorties had increased from 2,334 in 1962 to 6,929 in 1963. Economic assistance in the Kennedy years rose only slightly from $145 million annually in 1961 to $186 million in 1963; but military aid climbed from $65 million to $185 million in the same period.[44]

Looking at these figures, one does not sense that a great effort was being made to redesign Vietnam's "infrastructure" in the thousand days of the New Frontier. Nevertheless, after the war, complaints were heard that a fatal mistake had been made early on when the "development theorists" had too much say. Put crudely, Vietnam was fought from the beginning as a "liberals' war." Their critics charged that nation-building hampered, then undid, the good work of the military mission. Kennedy's favorite general, Maxwell D. Taylor, later expressed himself in a fashion that could be taken in such a way: "We should have learned from our frontier forebears that there is little use planting corn outside the stockade if there are still Indians around in the woods outside."[45] But the brunt of these post facto judgments really bear upon the events leading to the November 1963 coup d'etat and the assassination of President Diem.

Discontent with Diem had been growing in Washington for some time. It came to a head between May 8 and August 21, 1963, when the South Vietnamese Government moved against Buddhist protesters. (Doc. 56.) On the latter date, forces loyal to Diem's brother, Ngo Dinh Nhu, raided Buddhist pagodas throughout the country, triggering a series of self-immolations by Buddhist priests that were televised into American homes. On August 23, General Tran Van Don, Chief of Staff of South Vietnam's Joint General Staff, contacted a CIA officer to inquire if the United States would support the ARVN (South Vietnamese Army) if it acted against Nhu and Diem.[46] (Doc. 57.)

The ensuing debate in Washington centered on whether the war could be won with Diem or not. Even those who wanted to stand by the flawed "Washington" of Southeast Asia (or "Winston Churchill," as Vice-President Lyndon Johnson once called Diem), now had to consider that the generals might rebel on their own—and then what?

These were tricky questions. They led through fog-laden areas, along "certain half-deserted streets" imagined by T. S. Eliot, and back again to "a tedious argument of insidious intent." Postponed several times by the generals, who feared on their side that Washington might not support them, the coup was staged on November 1, 1963. Diem's and Nhu's deaths followed. American responsibility remains a moot proposition. The South Vietnamese generals had been given to understand that U.S. aid—absolutely necessary to military success—was now conditional upon reforms Diem had so far refused or evaded. Such a signal might not be a shining green light, but the generals would have been dullards indeed (especially since they were being coached by CIA contacts), not to perceive the dangers involved in a protracted contest of wills between the American Embassy and the presidential palace. Sooner or later it must come to a point of decision. And in the meantime opportunities in the field would slip away, morale would decline disastrously, and, perhaps, the battle for American public support would be lost. (Docs. 55, 56, 57.)

General Taylor's observation, offered as one of several lessons from the Vietnam War, illustrates how the 1963 coup deepened American involvement even more than the troops Kennedy had sent up to that point: "In the post-Diem period when the political turbulence in South Vietnam offered the United States an excuse to withdraw from its involvement, the realization of our role in creating the Vietnamese predicament was a strong deterrent to anyone inclined to make such a proposal."[47]

Three weeks after Diem's overthrow, President Kennedy was shot to death in Dallas, Texas. The next day, his first as President, Lyndon B. Johnson was given a gloomy assessment of the situation in Saigon Thus far, at least, the coup had changed nothing, and there was a "neutralist" trend growing in South Vietnam. Difficult decisions had to be made right away, ended Ambassador Henry Cabot Lodge, and "you will have to make them." LBJ hesitated not a second. "I am not going to lose Vietnam," he said. "I am not going to be the President who saw Southeast Asia go the way China went."[48]

145

32. WHAT KIND OF WAR?

In his first briefing of the Senate Foreign Relations Committee on April 29, 1953, Dulles was asked several probing questions about Indochina and, in secret executive session, gave some very frank answers. (Source: United States Senate, Committee on Foreign Relations, *Executive Sessions of the Senate Foreign Relations Committee, 1953* [Historical Series], V, 1953 [Washington, 1977], pp. 385–88.)

SENATOR GILLETTE. . . . What do you conceive to be the Indo-China affair? A civil war, an attempt to secure liberty from the imperialism, or a Communist invasion that the United Nations should take cognizance of?

What do you consider the excuse for our participation in the Indo-China affair?

SECRETARY DULLES. Well, the excuse for our participation in the Indo-China affair is that if Indo-China is lost to communism and the non-Communist government is driven out, and a totally Communist government is installed, it is almost certain that the next operation will be in Siam, which is already weak; the next operation may be in Northern Malaya or Burma, or both; and the next operation will be Indonesia, and by that time all of Southeast Asia will be lost.

That will then put Japan in an extremely serious situation, both from the standpoint of morale and the standpoint of economics, because the only area of the world which it hopes to develop trade with to advantage is Southeast Asia. It has been denied trade with Manchuria and Communist Red China.

If that goes, Japan will be in a very precarious situation, and to sustain Japan will require very long operations by sea largely from the United States, to supply food and raw materials which, to some extent, at least, they are now getting from Southeast Asia. Food, rice they get from Siam, iron ore from Malaya, tin and so forth from Indonesia, which they use to fabricate goods which, in turn, are sold back into that area.

So if they lose that Southeast Asia, as a source of food and a source of raw materials, on top of the loss of Manchuria and China, then we face a very costly operation to try and hold Japan.

It will be even more costly so that in terms of money you asked for our excuse for doing it, I am talking now just in terms of the direct self-interest of the United States. If our influence can develop a strategy or tactics and

146

their implementation in Indo-China with which to hold that situation, with the French still carrying the bulk of the burden, I believe that the interests of the United States would be much better served than if we pulled out and let go without supporting them.

SENATOR FERGUSON. Mr. Secretary, why did not the United Nations take a step when Laos was taken over by the Communists? That was an invasion of an independent nation.

SECRETARY DULLES. That is being very actively considered. I impressed on the French, when I was in Paris—we met with the French at the Quai d'Orsay Sunday afternoon for a couple of hours. I got Mr. [René] Meyer, the French Premier, to come back from Africa, and spent an hour with him before I took my plane Saturday night.

SENATOR FERGUSON. Didn't they know it was going to happen?

SECRETARY DULLES. Yes, and I had a long talk again yesterday with the French Ambassador.

SENATOR FERGUSON. Are they against the United Nations?

SECRETARY DULLES. What they are afraid of is, if they take the United Nations, that many, many people will raise the point which Senator Gillette suggests, and say that this really isn't an international affair at all, just a revolution against colonialism and then they will develop an attack on French colonialism.

On the other hand, if the French say, "If that's the way the world looks at it, we will just get out, and let the world see that we are not colonialists," there is quite a movement in favor of quitting there, in France, and it is precipitated both from the left and the extreme right.

SENATOR HICKENLOOPER. They might answer that criticism by making a clear declaration of their intention, and the ways and means by which they have given complete freedom or would give complete freedom to the country, once the revolution has been put down. It seems to me that will answer the colonialism charges.

SECRETARY DULLES. Yes. They have gone quite a ways in that direction, and I think that it would practically be quite a long time before it would be safe actually for the French to pull out of there, because those people of Laos and Viet Nam are a long way removed, really, from having a capacity of establishing a type of government that will be strong, up against the constant pressure and infiltrations that will occur from Communist China.

SENATOR GILLETTE. Mr. Secretary, may I just pursue that a bit further, on the question I raised.

In discussions with people of this periphery to which you refer, there is a strong feeling that the United States in several instances is coming in to bolster up decadent imperialism.

147

THE CHAIRMAN. To what?

SENATOR GILLETTE. Decadent imperialism, bolster it up, and coming to their support.

That is why I asked the question, with such a situation as has developed in Indo-China and Laos, and why it is justified for us to initiate an incursion into that area, as the United States, instead of a member of the United Nations taking cognizance of a threat to world peace.

SECRETARY DULLES. Let me make it clear, Senator Gillette, I am not talking about any form of U.S. direct military intervention in that war.

SENATOR GILLETTE. There would be no troops.

SECRETARY DULLES. No sending of troops or anything of that sort there. We are supplying the French, and to some extent the local people, the Vietnamese, with certain end items, in the way of equipment, machine guns, and things of that sort; and we are encouraging the French to put up a resistance there.

Now, the problem you raise is, of course, a very real one and a very difficult one. I would say that in a relatively peaceful world, where we did not face the threat of Soviet Communism, we could do very much more in the way of promoting the reforms and advancing self-government than we can do under present conditions. I think we have to take a realistic view of the situation and recognize that at this time, to support a somewhat backward situation, it is the lesser of two evils, because the possibility of a peaceful change is very much diminished by the fact that you have constantly with you, for instance, the tactics of the Soviet Communist forces which take advantage of every opportunity to capture and lead the so-called reform and revolutionary movement. They are extremely adroit at that.

Now, in this area of the world I speak about, I recognize full well that there are plenty of social problems and unrest which would exist if there were no such thing as Soviet Communism in the world, but what makes it a very dangerous problem for us is the fact that wherever those things exist, whether it is in Indo-China or Siam or Morocco or Egypt or Arabia or Iran, for that matter, even in South America, the forces of unrest are captured by the Soviet Communists because they are smart at that, just as in this country, for a long while they captured the labor unions. When there was a strong labor situation which led to unrest, you would find immediately the Communists had moved in and gotten control, and that makes it very difficult to concentrate on reforms.

It is the same problem you faced when you were faced with the question of—are you going to support Syngman Rhee, Chiang Kai-Shek, and so forth. They are not the people, under normal circumstances, that we would want to support. We would be trying to get somebody else, but in times like these, in the unrest of the world today, and the divided spirit, we know that we cannot make a transition without losing control of the whole situation.

Now, that is my philosophy.

SENATOR GREEN. May I ask a question?

THE CHAIRMAN. Senator Green.

SENATOR GREEN. Mr. Secretary, have your negotiations with the French given any indication that they are willing to go any farther toward home rule toward Indo-China than the concessions they have already made?

SECRETARY DULLES. Further toward independence?

SENATOR GREEN. Yes.

SECRETARY DULLES. No, they have not; but our analysis of the situation, Senator Green, is that the moves taken, from the standpoint of the juridical, constitutional position go really very far. I don't think—our advisers from out there do not think there would be any great gain in going much further in that direction.

THE PROBLEM IS LOCAL AND PRACTICAL

Where the trouble comes is not in the constitutional changes which give it a very large degree of self-government, at least as a juridical matter, to the peoples of the three states. Their tie with France is a very loose one indeed. If this were carried out, it would be, but the trouble comes when you come practically to translating that change of attitude into the life of the community.

What you have got there is a bunch of people who have been colonialists all their lives, and it is in the actual working relations, who has what house, do you bring them into your clubs, and do you allow them to be trained in units larger than a battalion, and what is the officer relationship, or social relationship—all of those matters are what really make the difference, and they all tell me, from the standpoint of getting the loyalty and support of the native people, what is needed are changes in that respect, and that merely writing a new decree in Paris is not appreciably going to change the situation.

Now, I talked very frankly, more frankly than would be done usually to a Minister from the Associated States, and I told him the same thing I am saying to you here today. I don't think he liked it very well, but I think it is time for frank speaking, because it is too critical for less, and I hope things can be changed some, in some way; but we all know how difficult it is to change social relations which have grown up over a long period of years, which reflect the white man's sense of superiority, the ruler's sense of superiority over the natives, and that is a situation which, as I say, cannot be effectively changed merely by writing a new decree.

Decrees are pretty good as far as they go. It is a question in terms of living relationships with the people, giving them, in a sense, more that they are in their own home and fighting for their own homes. That requires a change in the personal attitudes of thousands of people. That cannot be brought about overnight.

33. A WARNING TO CHINA

On September 2, 1953, after clearing the wording with President Eisenhower, Secretary Dulles delivered this warning to China. He had always questioned the terms for settling the Korean War, largely because they left the United States at a psychological as well as a military "disadvantage." Although Dulles was really not an advocate of preventive war against China, these words and other declarations would hinder his pre-Geneva efforts to secure Allied agreement to an Asian Collective Security Pact. (Source: Department of State, *American Foreign Policy, 1950–1955,* 2 vols. [Washington, 1957], II, pp. 2370–71.)

We do not make the mistake of treating Korea as an isolated affair. The Korean war forms one part of the worldwide effort of communism to conquer freedom. More immediately it is part of that effort in Asia.

A single Chinese-Communist aggressive front extends from Korea on the north to Indochina in the south. The armistice in Korea, even if it leads to a political settlement in Korea, does not end United States concern in the western Pacific area. As President Eisenhower said in his April 16 speech, a Korean armistice would be a fraud if it merely released Communist forces for attack elsewhere.

In Indochina a desperate struggle is in its eighth year. The outcome affects our own vital interests in the western Pacific, and we are already contributing largely in material and money to the combined efforts of the French and of Viet-Nam, Laos, and Cambodia.

We Americans have too little appreciated the magnitude of the effort and sacrifices which France has made in defense of an area which is no longer a French colony but where complete independence is now in the making. This independence program is along lines which the United

States has encouraged and justifies increased United States aid, provided that will assure an effort there that is vigorous and decisive.

Communist China has been and now is training, equipping, and supplying the Communist forces in Indochina. There is the risk that, as in Korea, Red China might send its own army into Indochina. The Chinese Communist regime should realize that such a second aggression could not occur without grave consequences which might not be confined to Indochina. I say this soberly in the interest of peace and in the hope of preventing another aggressor miscalculation.

We want peace in Indochina, as well as in Korea. The political conference about to be held relates in the first instance to Korea. But growing out of that conference could come, if Red China wants it, an end of aggression and restoration of peace in Indochina. The United States would welcome such a development.

34. CONGRESSIONAL RESTRAINTS

On April 3, 1954, Dulles and Admiral Arthur W. Radford, Chairman of the Joint Chiefs, met with congressional leaders. In preparation for this conference, the Secretary had drafted a proposed resolution granting the President power "to employ the Naval and Air Forces of the United States to assist the forces which are resisting aggression in Southeast Asia. . . ." Among those in attendance was Senator Lyndon B. Johnson, who would seek exactly such a grant of authority ten years later. On this occasion, however, the legislative leaders made it plain that a precondition of any such resolution must be commitments from America's closest Allies. (Source: Department of State, *Foreign Relations of the United States, 1952–1954,* XIII, *Indochina,* 2 parts, Part 2, pp. 1224–25.)

MEMORANDUM FOR THE SECRETARY'S FILE

SUBJECT: Conference with Congressional Leaders concerning the crisis in Southeast Asia, Saturday, April 3, 1954.

Those in attendance were:

Senators Knowland, Millikin, Johnson of Texas, Russell, Clements, Speaker Martin, Congressmen McCormack, Priest

From the Department of Defense: Admiral Radford, Kyes, Anderson;

From the Department of State: The Secretary, the Under Secretary (part of the time), and Thruston B. Morton.

Admiral Radford gave a very comprehensive briefing of the military situation in Indochina. He went into particular detail in connection with the battle now raging at Dien Bien Phu.

The Secretary explained the significance of Indochina, pointing out that it was the key to Southeast Asia, that if the Communists gained Indochina and nothing was done about it, it was only a question of time until all of Southeast Asia falls along with Indonesia, thus imperiling our western island of defense.

The Secretary then said that he felt that the President should have Congressional backing so that he could use air and seapower in the area if he felt it necessary in the interest of national security. Senator Knowland expressed concurrence but further discussion developed a unanimous reaction of the Members of Congress that there should be no Congressional action until the Secretary had obtained commitments of a political and material nature from our allies. The feeling was unanimous that "we want no more Koreas with the United States furnishing 90% of the manpower."

Both the Secretary and Admiral Radford pointed out that the Administration did not now contemplate the commitment of land forces. The Congressmen replied that once the flag was committed the use of land forces would inevitably follow.

The Secretary said that he had already initiated talks to secure unity of action. He had spoken with the British Ambassador yesterday and was meeting with Bonnet in a few minutes. He had talked with Romulo but he could not go further without knowing that he could expect U.S. action if the others responded.

Admiral Radford was asked if airpower could save Dien Bien Phu today. He replied that it was too late but that if we had committed airpower three weeks ago, he felt reasonably certain that the Red forces would have been defeated. It was apparent that the Congressional group, especially Senator Russell, had very little confidence in the French. There was less criticism of the British, but it was nevertheless substantial. Senator Russell said that if the U.K. flinched in this matter, it would be necessary to reconsider our whole system of collective security from the standpoint of dependability. Admiral Radford pointed out the extensive British military deployment in Malaya and elsewhere throughout that area.

It was decided that the Secretary would attempt to get definite commitments from the English and other free nations. If satisfactory commitments could be obtained, the consensus was that a Congressional resolution could be passed, giving the President power to commit armed forces in the area.

35. EISENHOWER'S APPEAL TO A WAR COMRADE

The campaign to win British support began with this letter to Prime Minister Churchill, hurriedly drafted twenty-four hours after the meeting with congressional leaders. The final paragraph, which Eisenhower did not reproduce in his memoirs, *Mandate for Change,* indicates the growing feeling that France's role had declined in American calculations and in world power. (Source: Department of State, *Foreign Relations of the United States, 1952–1954,* XIII, *Indochina,* 2 parts, Part 2, pp. 1239–41.)

Dear Winston: Washington, April 4, 1954

I am sure that like me you are following with the deepest interest and anxiety the daily reports of the gallant fight being put up by the French at Dien Bien Phu. Today, the situation there does not seem hopeless.

But regardless of the outcome of this particular battle, I fear that the French cannot alone see the thing through, this despite the very substantial assistance in money and matériel that we are giving them. It is no solution simply to urge the French to intensify their efforts, and if they do not see it through, and Indochina passes into the hands of the Communists, the ultimate effect on our and your global strategic position with the consequent shift in the power ratio throughout Asia and the Pacific could be disastrous and, I know, unacceptable to you and me. It is difficult to see how Thailand, Burma and Indonesia could be kept out of Communist hands. This we cannot afford. The threat to Malaya, Australia and New Zealand would be direct. The offshore island chain would be broken. The economic pressures on Japan which would be deprived of non-Communist markets and sources of food and raw materials would be such, over a period of time, that it is difficult to see how Japan could be prevented from reaching an accommodation with the Communist world which would combine the manpower and natural resources of Asia with the industrial potential of Japan. This has led us to the hard conclusion that the situation

153

in Southeast Asia requires us urgently to take serious and far-reaching decisions.

Geneva is less than four weeks away. There the possibility of the Communists driving a wedge between us will, given the state of mind in France, be infinitely greater than at Berlin. I can understand the very natural desire of the French to seek an end to this war which has been bleeding them for eight years. But our painstaking search for a way out of the impasse has reluctantly forced us to the conclusion that there is no negotiated solution of the Indochina problem which in its essence would not be either a face-saving device to cover a French surrender or a face-saving device to cover a Communist retirement. The first alternative is too serious in its broad strategic implications for us and for you to be acceptable. Apart from its effects in Southeast Asia itself, where you and the Commonwealth have direct and vital interests, it would have the most serious repercussions in North Africa, in Europe and elsewhere. Here at home it would cause a widespread loss of confidence in the cooperative system. I think it is not too much to say that the future of France as a great power would be fatally affected. Perhaps France will never again be the great power it was, but a sudden vacuum wherever French power is, would be difficult for us to cope with.

Somehow we must contrive to bring about the second alternative. The preliminary lines of our thinking were sketched out by Foster in his speech last Monday night when he said that under the conditions of today the imposition on Southeast Asia of the political system of Communist Russia and its Chinese Communist ally, by whatever means, would be a grave threat to the whole free community, and that in our view this possibility should now be met by united action and not passively accepted. He has also talked intimately with Roger Makins.

I believe that the best way to put teeth in this concept and to bring greater moral and material resources to the support of the French effort is through the establishment of a new, *ad hoc* grouping or coalition composed of nations which have a vital concern in the checking of Communist expansion in the area. I have in mind in addition to our two countries, France, the Associated States, Australia, New Zealand, Thailand and the Philippines. The United States Government would expect to play its full part in such a coalition. The coalition we have in mind would not be directed against Communist China. But if, contrary to our belief, our efforts to save Indochina and the British Commonwealth position to the south should in any way increase the jeopardy to Hong Kong, we would expect to be with you there. I suppose that the United Nations should somewhere be recognized, but I am not confident that, given the Soviet veto, it could act with needed speed and vigor.

I would contemplate no role for Formosa or the Republic of Korea in the political construction of this coalition.

The important thing is that the coalition must be strong and it must be willing to join the fight if necessary. I do not envisage the need of any appreciable ground forces on your or our part. If the members of the alliance are sufficiently resolute it should be able to make clear to the Chinese Communists that the continuation of their material support to the Viet Minh will inevitably lead to the growing power of the forces arrayed against them.

My colleagues and I are deeply aware of the risks which this proposal may involve but in the situation which confronts us there is no course of action or inaction devoid of dangers and I know no man who has firmly grasped more nettles than you. If we grasp this one together I believe that we will enormously increase our chances of bringing the Chinese to believe that their interests lie in the direction of a discreet disengagement. In such a contingency we could approach the Geneva conference with the position of the free world not only unimpaired but strengthened.

Today we face the hard situation of contemplating a disaster brought on by French weakness and the necessity of dealing with it before it develops. This means frank talk with the French. In many ways the situation corresponds to that which you describe so brilliantly in the second chapter of "Their Finest Hour", when history made clear that the French strategy and dispositions before the 1940 breakthrough should have been challenged before the blow fell.

I regret adding to your problems. But in fact it is not I, but our enemies who add to them. I have faith that by another act of fellowship in the face of peril we shall find a spiritual vigor which will prevent our slipping into the quagmire of distrust.

If I may refer again to history, we failed to halt Hirohito, Mussolini and Hitler by not acting in unity and in time. That marked the beginning of many years of stark tragedy and desperate peril. May it not be that our nations have learned something from that lesson?

So profoundly do I believe that the effectiveness of the coalition principle is at stake that I am prepared to send Foster or Bedell to visit you this week, at the earliest date convenient to you.* Whoever comes would spend a day in Paris to avoid French pique, the cover would be preparation for Geneva.

* Walter Bedell Smith, Under Secretary of State.

36. COUNTING THE DOMINOES

In this famous press conference, Eisenhower introduced the domino thesis. On other occasions he used the phrase "the cork in the bottle" to describe the situation and its dangerous implications. Eisenhower returned here, as he often did, to the Japanese connection. The date was April 7, 1954. (Source: United States Government, *Public Papers of the Presidents of the United States: Dwight D. Eisenhower, 1954* [Washington, 1958], pp. 381–90.)

Q. ROBERT RICHARDS, COPLEY PRESS: Mr. President, would you mind commenting on the strategic importance of Indochina to the free world? I think there has been, across the country, some lack of understanding on just what it means to us.

THE PRESIDENT: You have, of course, both the specific and the general when you talk about such things.

First of all, you have the specific value of a locality in its production of materials that the world needs.

Then you have the possibility that many human beings pass under a dictatorship that is inimical to the free world.

Finally, you have broader considerations that might follow what you would call the "falling domino" principle. You have a row of dominoes set up, you knock over the first one, and what will happen to the last one is the certainty that it will go over very quickly. So you could have a beginning of a disintegration that would have the most profound influences.

Now, with respect to the first one, two of the items from this particular area that the world uses are tin and tungsten. They are very important. There are others, of course, the rubber plantations and so on.

Then with respect to more people passing under this domination, Asia, after all, has already lost some 450 million of its peoples to the Communist dictatorship, and we simply can't afford greater losses.

But when we come to the possible sequence of events, the loss of Indochina, of Burma, of Thailand, of the Peninsula, and Indonesia following, now you begin to talk about areas that not only multiply the disadvantages that you would suffer through loss of materials, sources of materials, but now you are talking really about millions and millions and millions of people.

Finally, the geographical position achieved thereby does many things.

It turns the so-called island defensive chain of Japan, Formosa, of the Philippines and to the southward; it moves in to threaten Australia and New Zealand.

It takes away, in its economic aspects, that region that Japan must have as a trading area or Japan, in turn, will have only one place in the world to go—that is, toward the Communist areas in order to live.

So, the possible consequences of the loss are just incalculable to the free world.

37. SEEKING COMMITMENTS

Dulles thought he had pinned down the British to an immediate commitment when he talked with reporters at a background press conference on April 13, 1954. His comments at these sessions were always directed toward building support for a specific policy. If necessary, he could disavow the stories that resulted. (Source: *Dulles MSS.*)

Q: When you speak of collective defense within the framework of the United Nations, obviously that means military defense if necessary. Are we to take it, then, that you do not exclude the possibility of American participation in such an armed defense—that is, American soldiers actually fighting there, ground forces—either on an ad hoc or any other arrangement?

A: Well, obviously, if you create a defense association, if there is occasion for it to act, you have to act through military strength. Whether that would involve American ground forces in Asia or not is, I think, quite problematic. I have never been a believer myself in having United States forces fighting on the Asian mainland.

Q: Do you consider that this communique amounts to an agreement in principle for the British Government to associate itself with the security backing in Southeast Asia?

A: I should think so, very clearly.

Q: How many countries do you envisage as participating in this?

A: There has been talk of ten. I have never used that figure, but if France and the three Associated States come along, that makes four; Thailand and The Philippines both indicated their disposition to come along, that makes six; the UK with its interest in Malaya has indicated its desire to come along—seven; Australia and New Zealand would make nine; and the United States would make ten.

157

Q: What about Japan? Would they be eligible?

A: I do not think that this arrangement in its initial phase would be extended as far north as Japan.

Q: Could you foresee any circumstances in which the defense of Southeast Asia may require an extension of Anzus in Britain and France?

A: As I indicated, it is possible that if the arrangement which is referred to here—this collective defense—if it took the form of permanent treaty arrangement, it might be an extension, you might say, of Anzus or a merger of Anzus into this new arrangement. The same would apply to the Philippine treaty.

Q: With regard to a conceivably successful outcome at the Geneva conference, could you indicate what you would regard as a reasonably satisfactory settlement of the Indochina situation?

A: The removal by the Chinese communists of their apparent desire to extend the political system of communism to Southeast Asia.

Q: That means a complete withdrawal of the Communists from Indochina?

A: That is what I would regard as a satisfactory solution.

Q: Is there any other compromise that might be offered if that is not entirely satisfactory to the communists?

A: I had not thought of any.

Q: Does this communique commit us to try to achieve victory over the communists in Indochina itself or leave it open to establish a line of defense somewhere else in Southeast Asia?

A: It talks about establishing the collective defense to assure the peace, security and freedom of Southeast Asia and the Western Pacific. It is clear from what goes before that Indochina is regarded as part of Southeast Asia . . . if that answers your question.

Q: Could you define the area a little further? What is Southeast Asia as comprised within the understanding of this comment?

A: At the moment, it does not lend itself to a precise definition. I have indicated already the area that I would think should certainly be included. I indicated France and the three Associate States, Thailand (or Siam as it is generally called here, Malaya, Australia, New Zealand, Philippines.

Q: What about the Republic of China on Formosa?

A: I would doubt whether you would include that in there, the same as Japan—I doubt that they include it in there.

Q: What about going in the other direction—India, Indonesia, Burma?

A: Indonesia would certainly be eligible. Burma would also. When you start these things you never know when they end. NATO was set up and Turkey is quite a long way off from the North Atlantic.

Q: Has Indonesia been approached?
A: I had a talk with the Indonesian Ambassador.
Q: What system would activate this defense arrangement, Chinese intervention in Indochina?
A: The present situation activates it. I think this is the beginning of a plan which ought to proceed.
Q: Is it true that the Chinese have very substantially increased in the last two or three months supplies to the Viet Minh?
A: Yes.
Q: I understand they built two major roads also. Is that true?
A: I think it is.

38. DISAPPOINTMENT AT GENEVA

After two weeks of futile effort trying to get the Southeast Asia Collective Security Pact "on track" before the French made any irreversible commitment at Geneva, Dulles had a heated conversation with British Foreign Secretary Anthony Eden. The conversation took place in the wake of Prime Minister Churchill's statement to the Commons that the United Kingdom was not prepared "to give any undertakings about United Kingdom military action in Indochina in advance of the results of Geneva." The statements about American discomfort in backing European colonialism emphasize another key theme of the era. This conversation occurred in Geneva on April 30, 1954. (Source: Department of State, *Foreign Relations of the United States, 1952–1954,* XVI, *The Geneva Conference,* pp. 622–25.)

MEMORANDUM OF CONVERSATION WITH MR. EDEN

I said to Mr. Eden that I was greatly disturbed over the present position and its bearing upon the cooperation of our two countries. We had, I thought, agreed to sit down with other directly interested countries to try to work out a common defense for the southeast Asia area, but now the British were unwilling to go ahead with the agreement which Mr. Eden and I had reached at London. On top of that was the fact that in the face of the vicious attacks by Molotov, Chou En-lai and Nam Il on the United States for what it had done in Korea, there was not a single Western European power which was prepared to get up and say a word in defence

159

of the UN or United States position. The only speakers on the non-Communist side had been South Korea, Colombia, the United States and Australia, and no one else was inscribed to speak.

I said it was particularly galling to the United States to have to accept this attack on it as being an "imperialist" power. I said that the United States was eager to beat the Communists at their own game and to sponsor nationalism in the independent colonial areas, which was in accordance with our historic tradition, but that we were restrained from doing so by a desire to cooperate with Britain and France in Asia, in North Africa and in the Near and Middle East. This, however, did not seem to be paying any dividends because when the chips were down there was no cohesion between us. Here at Geneva we were presenting a pathetic spectacle of drifting without any agreed policy or purpose. The United States had presented a program which, after it had been apparently accepted, had been repudiated and there was no alternative offered.

I said as far as the Korean problem was concerned, we were being forced by our western allies to abandon our original position of backing the UN resolutions so that western leaders could show how generous they were at south Korea's expense. I thought, however, that it was rather pathetic that we had to make our concessions to our allies before even starting to negotiate with the Communists, where the concessions might have some negotiating value. If the effort to develop a united position with reference to southeast Asia collapsed, we would be faced by the problem of going it alone. This would probably mean increasing the close relations with Syngman Rhee and Chiang Kai-shek, who, whatever their defects, were at least willing to stand strong against the Communists. I mentioned that there was considerable pressure for the United States to complete a mutual security treaty covering Formosa. This had been deferred and I felt that its negotiation at the time of the Geneva conference and after my proposal for a united defense of southeast Asia might be embarrassing. However, if there was to be no united defense for southeast Asia and no agreed program for Geneva, then we would have to consider who there was upon whom we could depend.

I emphasized that despite what I gathered the British might have inferred from Radford's talks, the United States was not seeking either war with China or a large scale intervention in Indo-China. In fact these were the two things we were seeking to avoid and thought could be avoided if we had a show of common strength.

I greatly feared that if I return to Washington under present conditions and had to meet with the Congressional Committees and give explanations as to what had happened, the consequences would be disastrous for the close UK-US relations which we wanted to maintain. . . .

39. A GLOOMY REPORT

As he had told Eden, Dulles went home from Geneva to report to congressional leaders. In a White House session on May 5, 1954, the Secretary tried to outline the next steps after the expected loss of Vietnam. It emerged in the question period that he thought the best thing would be to wipe the slate clean, concede an election victory as well as a military triumph to the Vietminh, and prepare the next line of defense. (Source: *Dulles MSS.*)

The Secretary said he would like to finish his discussion by explaining certain conclusions he had reached from the events of the past few weeks. In the first place we should not intervene in Indochina unless the preconditions he had enumerated earlier had been fulfilled. The French have not even made a firm or formal request for United States intervention or the internationalization of the war. In fact there was much opposition in France to do such action because it would mean the loss of French influence in Asia, the Colonial issue would be again raised as it was on North Africa if the action should take the form of UN intervention, and some Frenchmen felt that internationalization was merely a scheme to keep France in the war. [Prime Minister Joseph] Laniel had almost apologized yesterday before the French Assembly for his earlier request for US intervention. In the Secretary's view the French have not yet fulfilled the prerequisites we need from them. Further, if we do intervene, conditions must exist for a successful conclusion of the war. The French might be able to work out the preconditions of independence for the associated states, effective training of the native troops and a sensible and offensive military plan; but we should not intervene until they do.

We also have a hostile or disinterested attitude on the part of other nations regarding participation, particularly on the part of the UK and Australia. After the Australian elections the Australians will quite probably come along with us and will pressure the British to the extent that they also may have to join in. However this aspect of intervention is largely academic until the other preconditions are met. The Secretary said that this in essence was the Administration's position on intervention.

The second conclusion which the Secretary had reached was that we should proceed as fast as we can to build up a Southeast Asian community, which would probably not include Vietnam, although we would hope to include Laos and Cambodia. Parenthetically, the Secretary remarked that the most hopeful formula for peace in Vietnam was for an agreement with the Vietminh on the withdrawal of all foreign troops, the establishment of a coalition government, and the holding of elections in six months, all of which would probably result in the loss of Vietnam to the Communists. Partition was not a likely solution because either side agreeing to partition of the country would lose the support of the people of the area.

The Secretary said that we may get the help of the British and other governments to strengthen the defense of Southeast Asia. The British may want to bring in Burma, to which the US agrees if it is possible to do so, and also India. The Secretary felt that this plan for a Southeast Asian Community might offer a fair chance to insulate the rest of Southeast Asia against the possible loss of Vietnam.

The Secretary's third conclusion was that in spite of the weakness of the British and French, we should not write them off. Although they were weak in Asia, they, and the UK in particular, had the possibility for strength in Europe. The Secretary said we have had to take a licking at Geneva because of British and French press briefings there which resulted in false and harmful interpretations of our position. In spite of our disappointment, however, he would agree with the President's remark to him this morning that you would never win a battle if you got rid of all those who are timid, because 90 per cent of all troops were afraid under fire. . . .

Senator [Leverett] *Saltonstall* asked whether we should not soon stop our aid to Vietnam since we apparently believed that it would be soon lost to the Communists. *The Secretary* said he would agree with this viewpoint in general. *Senator* [William] *Knowland* asked what steps we could take to recover the arms we have given the Vietnamese to prevent the Communists from capturing them and using them against Thailand, et cetera. *The Secretary* said this was one of the things he had taken up with Secretary Wilson this morning and that he was having lunch with Admiral Radford and Secretary Wilson tomorrow to discuss the problem. He personally saw no reason why we could not simply remove our arms from Vietnam if a peace settlement were agreed to.

Representative [John] *Vorys* asked whether it was likely that the Vietnamese people might throw over Bao Dai, form a new government and ask for US assistance without the French. *The Secretary* said that the problem was that there was little effective leadership in Vietnam and although he would agree that Bao Dai was not an impressive leader there was no one else whom the French had developed who could take over.

Representative [Walter F.] *Judd* asked whether there was any chance the French might pull out of Indochina and whether this would be good or bad for us. He said he did not think the military situation was too bleak because the rains would save us by stopping the fighting. *The Secretary* stated he was not so sure that the rains would stop the fighting. . . .

40. THE ELECTION ISSUE

In the wake of the fall of Dienbienphu, Dulles reconsidered his position on Vietnamese elections. He had told congressional leaders on May 5, 1954, that partition would be the worst alternative. Now he was reconsidering that, too, although at his press conference on May 11, 1954, he was also trying to prepare the public for the "loss" of all Indochina. (Source: Verbatim transcript in *Dulles MSS.*)

Q. Mr. Secretary, if I can return for a moment to my previous question, if I understood you correctly, you believed that Southeast Asia could if necessary be held without Indochina. Does that represent a modification of what has been variously called the domino or cork-in-the-bottle theory?

A. The situation in that area, as we found it was that it was subject to the so-called "domino theory." That means that if one went, another would go. We are trying to change it so that that would not be the case. That is the whole theory of collective security. That is the theory of the North Atlantic Treaty. As nations come together, then the "domino theory," so-called, ceases to apply. What we are trying to do is create a situation in Southeast Asia where the domino situation will not apply. And while I see it might be said that I felt that Southeast Asia could be secured even without perhaps Vietnam, Laos, and Cambodia, I do not want for a minute to underestimate the importance of these countries. Neither do I want for a minute to give the impression that we believe that they are going to be lost or that we have given up trying to prevent their being lost. On the contrary, we recognize that they are extremely important and that the problem of saving Southeast Asia is far more difficult if they are lost. But I do not want to give the impression either that if events that we could not control, and which we do not anticipate, should lead to their being lost that we would consider the whole situation hopeless and we would give up in despair. We do not give up in despair. Also, we do not give up Vietnam, Laos or Cambodia.

Q. Mr. Secretary, would you favor genuinely free elections in Indochina?

A. I would favor genuinely free elections under conditions where there would be an opportunity for the electorate to be adequately informed as to what the issues are. At the present time in a country which is politically immature, which has been the scene of civil war and disruption, we would doubt whether the immediate conditions would be conducive to a result which would really reflect the will of the people.

Q. You said the other day, Mr. Secretary, that it was the Government's policy to oppose a communist advance in Indochina by whatever means. What would be your attitude toward a victory of Ho Chi-Minh or a coalition in a free election in Indochina? Would you recognize that or would you consider that to also be barred by your formula?

A. I said that I thought that the United States should not stand passively by and see the extension of communism by any means into Southeast Asia. We are not standing passively by.

Q. I asked you what would be your attitude toward a victory of Ho Chi-Minh or a coalition in a genuinely free election in Indochina. Would you be prepared to recognize such a government?

A. I have just said that I don't think the present conditions are conducive to a free election there and I don't care now to answer the hypothetical situation of what might result if they did have elections. . . .

Q. Mr. Secretary, if you regard the Indochinese people as too immature politically for free elections, do you regard them as politically mature enough for independence at this point?

A. I did not say that the people were too immature for free elections; I said that conditions were not conducive to it. When we had the discussion of the possibility of having elections in the eastern part of Germany, it was the plan—the so-called Eden Plan—that the elections should not take place until there had been a preparatory period, because it was felt that the people were so terrorized, so misinformed, that quick elections held there under existing conditions could not be expected accurately to reflect the real views of the people and their intelligent judgment. If we felt that as regards eastern Germany, certainly we are entitled to feel the same as regards Indochina.

Q. Then do you favor independence for Indochina at this time? For Cambodia, Laos, and Vietnam?

A. I believe that their complete independence should be absolutely assured. Now the question as to the exercise of complete independence under present conditions is another matter. I have spoken to their representatives. I had a long talk with Bao Dai. They don't, any of them, feel at the moment they would want the French to withdraw or want to sever their relations with the French Union because they know that there would have to be a transitory period during which they can build up the strength necessary to exercise independence. Today, if they attempted to be wholly independent and if the French were withdrawn, which is the Vietminh proposal, their independence would not last probably for more than a few days. Just as the United States would not have granted independence to the Philippines in the middle of the Second World War, it would be foolish to expect, and, in fact, the governments of those countries do not expect, that they can instantly exercise full independence. But there should not be any doubt whatever but what their independence is assured under times and conditions so that they will actually be able to exercise it and enjoy it.

41. WALKING SOFTLY

Dulles was concerned that certain statements (including some of his own) would scare off Allies from making a commitment to SEATO. This conversation with the President also suggests that the collective security organization was intended primarily as a way for the United States to "re-do" the colonial empires along liberal lines, and not to prepare a war against China. (Source: *Dulles MSS.)*

MEMORANDUM OF CONVERSATION WITH THE PRESIDENT

Deputy Secretary Anderson and I discussed with the President the prospective five-power military talks. I said that I was concerned lest the JCS viewpoint should be presented in a way which would have undesirable political repercussions. Their judgment had been that there was little use discussing any "defense" of the Southeast Asia area or any substantial committal of U.S. force to this area; that United States power should be directed against the source of the peril which was, at least in the first instance, China, and that in this connection atomic weapons should be used.

The British at least wanted to discuss the establishment of a defensive line, assuming the loss of all or part of Indochina.

I said that while I did not question Admiral Radford's military judgment, I did not believe that it was serving our political objectives to present it at this time; that it would lead to U.S. isolation, and indeed it had already done so to some extent in connection with Admiral Radford's last trip to Paris and London.

If there was U.S. intervention as part of a coalition, no one could, of course, tell what the consequences might be or whether the initial theater would be enlarged. However, it was not politically good judgment to take it for granted that any defensive coalition would be bound to become involved in a general war with China, and perhaps with Russia, and that this would be an atomic war.

The President said he wholly agreed with me and that he was strongly opposed to any assumption that it was necessary to have a war with China. He said that the JCS should not act in any way which would interfere with the political purposes of the Government, and that he would try to find an occasion to make this clear. He also said that he might plan himself to talk with the military representatives of the other four nations so that they would get directly from him the political position of the United States.

42. ANSWERING CRITICS

The Eisenhower administration faced a "two-front" assault on its inability to change the outcome of the Geneva Conference. Conservative Republicans were joined by others, including Senator Mike Mansfield, a Democratic "spokesman" on the Far East. Dulles' proposed answer to Mansfield, never used, offers a good insight into his thinking, and also reveals that his public "briefs" sometimes concealed a recognition on the limits of power. The date of the draft is July 9, 1954. (Source: *Dulles MSS.*)

American diplomacy is, of course, a potent force. But it is not sufficiently potent to overcome the consequences of growing French weakness and the fact that as a result of two world wars France has been weakened to a point where its overall commitments in the world are beyond its capability. The United States could, of course, push in to fill the vacuum created by the decline of French power. This would, however, have involved us in the case of Indochina of fighting the French for the privilege of getting in to fight the Vietminh. I do not understand that Senator Mansfield advocates this course. This Administration was alert to try to fill the vacuum to the maximum extent possible. We agreed in substance to pay the entire cost of the war. We agreed to supply the French and the Vietnam forces with military equipment and we agreed that we would share in an "internationalizing" of the war if the French were willing to put it on an international basis with the backing of the United Nations and with conditions for the independence of the Associated States which would make it sure that it was not a colonial power. In these respects we went to the limit. If this was not enough, and it was not enough, the reason was not that the United States could properly have done more but that the French weakness was too great to be bolstered even by the maximum potential of American diplomacy.

The fundamental blunder with respect to Indochina was made after 1945 when the French as the colonial power in Indochina had been ousted by the Japanese. The question then was whether or not the United States as a victor over Japan would use its power to put the French back into Indochina. Originally, President Roosevelt was against this on the ground that France did not have a good record as a colonial power and its return would not be accepted by the people. Nevertheless, our Government allowed itself to be persuaded in this matter by the French and the British and we acted to restore France's colonial position in Indochina. The French only maintained their position by bloody massacres which started the colonial war, which the Communists subsequently took control of, and the result has been a bleeding of France and the giving to the Communists of a popular issue against which the French were unable to prevail.

Senator Mansfield says "Geneva was a mistake; and the result was a failure of American policy. It is a profoundly humiliating result." Geneva may have been a mistake but if so it was not a United States mistake. The United States has not the power and if it had could not wisely exercise the power to force France to go on fighting after its will and power to fight had gone. We might ourselves have stepped in and taken over the fighting but that apparently is not what Senator Mansfield wanted us to do. Certainly it is not what the American people wanted us to do. There is not the slightest reason why the United States should feel "humiliated" as a result of what is happening at Geneva. It has taken throughout a clear, strong and honorable position. If our position, for understandable reasons, is not shared by others, that may be a reflection upon them but surely it is not a reflection upon the United States.

The Secretary of State, speaking at Seattle on June 10, 1954, pointed out that while the United States does have a large measure of responsibility in the world "that is far short of saying that the United States has responsibility for all that takes place throughout the world. We do not accept the view that whenever there is trouble anywhere that is the fault of the United States and we must quickly fix it. The United States does not believe that it can alone solve problems elsewhere. The possibilities of

167

solution lie primarily with the peoples directly concerned." It is a grave disservice to the United States to assume the contrary view and that it is a "failure" of the United States if anywhere in the world others fail. The United States is not throughout the world "Mr. Fixit."

43. GENEVA DECLARATIONS

The final declarations of the Geneva Conference attempted to spell out on July 21, 1954, a program for converting the armistice in Indochina into a lasting peace. (Source: Democratic Republic of Viet-nam, Ministry of Foreign Affairs, Press and Information Department, *Documents Related to the Implementation of the Geneva Agreements Concerning Viet-nam* [Hanoi, 1956], pp. 181–83.)

1. The Conference takes note of the Agreements ending hostilities in Cambodia, Laos, and Viet-nam and organizing international control and the supervision of the execution of the provisions of these agreements.

2. The Conference expresses satisfaction at the ending of hostilities in Cambodia, Laos and Viet-nam; the Conference expresses its conviction that the execution of the provisions set out in the present Declaration and in the Agreements on the cessation of hostilities will permit Cambodia, Laos and Viet-nam henceforth to play their part, in full independence and sovereignty, in the peaceful community of nations.

3. The Conference takes note of the declarations made by the Governments of Cambodia and of Laos of their intention to adopt measures permitting all citizens to take their place in the national community, in particular by participating in the next general elections, which, in conformity with the constitution of each of these countries, shall take place in the course of the year 1955, by secret ballot and in conditions of respect for fundamental freedoms.

4. The Conference takes note of the clauses in the Agreement on the cessation of hostilities in Viet-nam prohibiting the introduction into Viet-nam of foreign troops and military personnel as well as all kinds of arms and munitions. The Conference also takes note of the declarations made by the Governments of Cambodia and Laos of their resolution not to request foreign aid, whether in war material, in personnel or in instructors except for the purpose of the effective defence of their territory and, in the case of Laos, to the extent defined by the Agreements on the cessation of hostilities in Laos.

5. The Conference takes note of the clauses in the Agreement on the cessation of hostilities in Viet-nam to the effect that no military base under the control of a foreign State may be established in the regrouping zones of the two parties, the latter having the obligation to see that the zones allotted to them shall not constitute part of any military alliance and shall not be utilized for the resumption of hostilities or in the service of an aggressive policy. The Conference also takes note of the declarations of the Governments of Cambodia and Laos to the effect that they will not join in any agreement with other States if this agreement includes the obligation to participate in a military alliance not in conformity with the principles of the Charter of the United Nations or, in the case of Laos, with the principles of the Agreement on the cessation of hostilities in Laos or, so long as their security is not threatened, the obligation to establish bases on Cambodian or Laotian territory for the military forces of foreign powers.

6. The Conference recognizes that the essential purpose of the Agreement relating to Viet-nam is to settle military questions with a view to ending hostilities and that the military demarcation line is provisional and should not in any way be interpreted as constituting a political or territorial boundary. The Conference expresses its conviction that the execution of the provisions set out in the present Declaration and in the Agreement on the cessation of hostilities creates the necessary basis for the achievement in the near future of a political settlement in Viet-nam.

7. The Conference declares that, so far as Viet-nam is concerned, the settlement of political problems, effected on the basis of respect for principles of independence, unity and territorial integrity, shall permit the Vietnamese people to enjoy the fundamental freedoms, guaranteed by democratic institutions established as a result of free general elections by secret ballot. In order to ensure that sufficient progress in the restoration of peace has been made and that all the necessary conditions obtain for free expression of the national will, general elections shall be held in July 1956, under the supervision of an international commission composed of representatives of the Member States of the International Supervisory Commission, referred to in the Agreement on the cessation of hostilities. Consultations will be held on this subject between the competent representative authorities of the two zones from 20 July, 1955 onwards.

8. The provisions of the Agreements on the cessation of hostilities intended to ensure the protection of individuals and of property must be most strictly applied and must, in particular, allow everyone in Viet-nam to decide freely in which zone he wishes to live.

9. The competent representative authorities of the Northern and Southern zones of Viet-nam, as well as the authorities of Laos and Cambo-

dia, must not permit any individual or collective reprisals against persons who have collaborated in any way with one of the parties during the war, or against members of such persons' families.

10. The Conference takes note of the declaration of the Government of the French Republic to the effect that it is ready to withdraw its troops from the territory of Cambodia, Laos and Viet-nam, at the request of the governments concerned and within periods which shall be fixed by agreement between the parties except in the cases where, by agreement between the two parties, a certain number of French troops shall remain at specified points and for a specified time.

11. The Conference takes note of the declaration of the French Government to the effect that for the settlement of all the problems connected with the re-establishment and consolidation of peace in Cambodia, Laos and Viet-nam, the French Government will proceed from the principle of respect for the independence and sovereignty, unity and territorial integrity of Cambodia, Laos and Viet-nam.

12. In their relations with Cambodia, Laos and Viet-nam, each member of the Geneva Conference undertakes to respect the sovereignty, the independence, the unity and the territorial integrity of the above-mentioned States, and to refrain from any interference in their internal affairs.

13. The members of the Conference agree to consult one another on any question which may be referred to them by the International Supervisory Commission, in order to study such measures as may prove necessary to ensure that the Agreements on the cessation of hostilities in Cambodia, Laos and Viet-nam are respected.

44. THE AMERICAN CAVEAT

Under Secretary of State Walter Bedell Smith delivered the American response to the Geneva Declaration. Perhaps the most significant part of the statement was not the final pledge that the United States would do nothing to "disturb" the agreements, but the caveat about elections. (Source: United States Senate, Committee on Foreign Relations, *Background Information Relating to Southeast Asia and Vietnam,* 90th Cong., 1st Sess. [Washington, 1967], p. 83.)

As I stated on July 18, my Government is not prepared to join in a declaration by the Conference such as is submitted. However, the United States makes this unilateral declaration of its position in these matters:

Declaration

The Government of the United States being resolved to devote its efforts to the strengthening of peace in accordance with the principles and purposes of the United Nations takes note of the agreements concluded at Geneva on July 20 and 21, 1954 between (a) the Franco-Laotian Command and the Command of the Peoples Army of Viet-Nam; (b) the Royal Khmer Army Command and the Command of the Peoples Army of Viet-Nam; (c) Franco-Vietnamese Command and the Command of the Peoples Army of Viet-Nam and of paragraphs 1 to 12 inclusive of the declaration presented to the Geneva Conference on July 21, 1954 declares with regard to the aforesaid agreements and paragraphs that (i) it will refrain from the threat or the use of force to disturb them, in accordance with Article 2 (4) of the Charter of the United Nations dealing with the obligation of members to refrain in their international relations from the threat or use of force; and (ii) it would view any renewal of the aggression in violation of the aforesaid agreements with grave concern and as seriously threatening international peace and security.

In connection with the statement in the declaration concerning free elections in Viet-Nam my Government wishes to make clear its position which it has expressed in a declaration made in Washington on June 29, 1954, as follows:

In the case of nations now divided against their will, we shall continue to seek to achieve unity through free elections supervised by the United Nations to insure that they are conducted fairly.

With respect to the statement made by the representative of the State of Viet-Nam, the United States reiterates its traditional position that peoples are entitled to determine their own future and that it will not join in an arrangement which would hinder this. Nothing in its declaration just made is intended to or does indicate any departure from this traditional position.

We share the hope that the agreements will permit Cambodia, Laos and Viet-Nam to play their part, in full independence and sovereignty, in the peaceful community of nations, and will enable the peoples of that area to determine their own future.

45. SEATO: DULLES EXPLAINS THE PURPOSES

No secret document says anything more about the SEATO organizing conference than this press statement Dulles gave out on his arrival in Manila on September 6, 1954. Each theme in American policy is spelled out: "mobile striking power," regional economic planning, nationalism, and the effort to blunt any talk about all-Vietnamese elections by constant references to other divided Cold War states. (Source: Department of State, Press Release 492, September 6, 1954.)

We have come here to establish a collective security arrangement for Southeast Asia. In so doing we are acting under the authority, and in accordance with the principles, of the United Nations Charter. What we do is directed against no nation and no peoples. We exercise what the Charter refers to as the inherent right of collective self-defense.

The United States has itself no direct territorial interests in Southeast Asia. Nevertheless, we feel a sense of common destiny with those who have in this area their life and being.

We are united by a common danger, the danger that stems from international communism and its insatiable ambition. We know that wherever it makes gains, as in Indochina, these gains are looked on, not as final solutions, but as bridgeheads for future gains. It is that fact which requires each of us to be concerned with what goes on elsewhere.

The danger manifests itself in many forms. One form is that of open armed aggression.

We can greatly diminish that risk by making clear that an attack upon the treaty area would occasion a reaction so united, so strong and so well-placed that the aggressor would lose more than it could hope to gain.

So our association should bind the members to develop both individual and collective capacity to resist armed attack. The United States is itself seeking to do that and we note with satisfaction the efforts which are being made in this direction in other countries here, such as the Philippines, Thailand and Pakistan. We welcome the historic declaration by the Prime Minister of Australia that Australia was prepared to accept, even in time of peace, overseas military commitments.

It will be necessary to assure that the individual efforts of the various parties to the treaty are used to the best common advantage. Those nations which are represented here cannot match the vast land armies, of which international communism disposes in Asia. For the free nations to attempt to maintain or support formidable land-based forces at every danger point throughout the world would be self-destructive.

Insofar as the United States is concerned, its responsibilities are so vast and so far flung that we believe we serve best by developing the deterrent of mobile striking power, plus strategically placed reserves.

I am confident that through prospective treaty members, by adequate and well-coordinated efforts which are within our capacity, we can establish a power that protects us all.

In addition to the danger of open armed attack there is the danger from subversion and indirect aggression. There is no simple or single formula to cover such risks. To meet them requires dedication, fortitude and resourcefulness, such as was shown here by President Magsaysay.

The opportunities of communism will diminish if trade relationships help the free nations to strengthen their economies. This will require the participation of countries additional to those which are particularly concerned with the security of Southeast Asia. Economic planning, to be adequate, must stimulate trade not only within the Southeast Asia area, but also between that area and South Asia and the West Pacific. Such planning is obviously beyond the scope of this conference. But this conference would not do its duty toward the many who place hope in us if we did not leave here with a well-conceived resolve to unite our efforts with those of others to make the free countries of this area stronger and more vigorous, not only militarily, but also socially and economically.

Some countries, which have a close relationship to the prospective treaty area, are not here. Among these are Cambodia, Laos and Vietnam. Their governments and people can know that we shall have them much in mind, and I hope we shall be able to throw over them some mantle of protection. There are other countries which may subsequently desire to join our defensive grouping. To that end our treaty will, I hope, make provision for the adherence of new members.

There is one aspect of our problem which should always be remembered. That is the yearning of the Asian peoples to be free of "colonialism."

International Communism uses "nationalism" as a slogan for gaining control, and then imposes its own brutal form of imperialism, which is the negation of nationalism.

We are rightly zealous against that Communist threat. But we should be careful lest that zeal lead us inadvertently to offend those who still associate colonialism with the Western powers.

It must be made abundantly clear that we each and all intend to invigorate the independence of the new nations and to promote the processes whereby others become capable of winning and sustaining the independence they desire. Only then can the West and the East work together in true fellowship.

We gather here with some differences to be resolved. That is nothing frightening. Differences are inherent in a society of freedom.

I do not doubt that out of our initial differences we shall develop an area of significant agreement. That is our high duty, both to ourselves and others.

We see that duty dramatically defined as in Northern Vietnam hundreds of thousands are today abandoning their ancient homes to start life anew where they believe they will be free. We are seeing another exodus, such as took millions out of Communist East Germany and millions out of Communist North Korea.

Those of us who are free and strong and not yet instantly imperiled are bound in honor to prove that freedom can protect those who, at immense sacrifice, are faithful to freedom.

Let that be the dedication of our conference.

46. THE SEATO TREATY

Signed on September 8, 1954, this treaty became the "legal" basis for American involvement in Vietnam. (Source: Department of State, *American Foreign Policy, 1950–1955,* 2 vols. [Washington, 1950], I, pp. 912–16.)

The Parties to this Treaty,

Recognizing the sovereign equality of all the Parties,

Reiterating their faith in the purposes and principles set forth in the Charter of the United Nations and their desire to live in peace with all peoples and all governments,

Reaffirming that, in accordance with the Charter of the United Nations, they uphold the principle of equal rights and self-determination of peoples, and declaring that they will earnestly strive by every peaceful means to promote self-government and to secure the independence of all countries whose peoples desire it and are able to undertake its responsibilities,

Desiring to strengthen the fabric of peace and freedom and to uphold the principles of democracy, individual liberty and the rule of law, and to promote the economic well-being and development of all peoples in the treaty area,

Intending to declare publicly and formally their sense of unity, so that any potential aggressor will appreciate that the Parties stand together in the area, and

Desiring further to coordinate their efforts for collective defense for the preservation of peace and security,

Therefore agree as follows:

ARTICLE I

The Parties undertake, as set forth in the Charter of the United Nations, to settle any international disputes in which they may be involved by peaceful means in such a manner that international peace and security and justice are not endangered, and to refrain in their international relations from the threat or use of force in any manner inconsistent with the purposes of the United Nations.

ARTICLE II

In order more effectively to achieve the objectives of this Treaty, the Parties, separately and jointly, by means of continuous and effective self-help and mutual aid will maintain and develop their individual and collective capacity to resist armed attack and to prevent and counter subversive activities directed from without against their territorial integrity and political stability.

ARTICLE III

The Parties undertake to strengthen their free institutions and to cooperate with one another in the further development of economic measures, including technical assistance, designed both to promote economic progress and social well-being and to further the individual and collective efforts of governments toward these ends.

ARTICLE IV

1. Each Party recognizes that aggression by means of armed attack in the treaty area against any of the Parties or against any State or territory which the Parties by unanimous agreement may hereafter designate, would endanger its own peace and safety, and agrees that it will in that event act to meet the common danger in accordance with its constitutional processes. Measures taken under this paragraph shall be immediately reported to the Security Council of the United Nations.

2. If, in the opinion of any of the Parties, the inviolability or the integrity of the territory or the sovereignty or political independence of any

Party in the treaty area or of any other State or territory to which the provisions of paragraph 1 of this Article from time to time apply is threatened in any way other than by armed attack or is affected or threatened by any fact or situation which might endanger the peace of the area, the Parties shall consult immediately in order to agree on the measures which should be taken for the common defense.

3. It is understood that no action on the territory of any State designated by unanimous agreement under paragraph 1 of this Article or on any territory so designated shall be taken except at the invitation or with the consent of the government concerned.

ARTICLE V

The Parties hereby establish a Council, on which each of them shall be represented, to consider matters concerning the implementation of this Treaty. The Council shall provide for consultation with regard to military and any other planning as the situation obtaining in the treaty area may from time to time require. The Council shall be so organized as to be able to meet at any time.

ARTICLE VI

This Treaty does not affect and shall not be interpreted as affecting in any way the rights and obligations of any of the Parties under the Charter of the United Nations or the responsibility of the United Nations for the maintenance of international peace and security. Each Party declares that none of the international engagements now in force between it and any other of the Parties or any third party is in conflict with the provisions of this Treaty, and undertakes not to enter into any international engagement in conflict with this Treaty.

ARTICLE VII

Any other State in a position to further the objectives of this Treaty and to contribute to the security of the area may, by unanimous agreement of the Parties, be invited to accede to this Treaty. . . .

ARTICLE VIII

As used in this Treaty, the "treaty area" is the general area of Southeast Asia, including also the entire territories of the Asian Parties, and the general area of the Southwest Pacific not including the Pacific area north of 21 degrees 30 minutes north latitude. The Parties may, by unanimous agreement, amend this Article to include within the treaty area the territory of any State acceding to this Treaty in accordance with Article VII or otherwise to change the treaty area.

ARTICLE IX

1. This Treaty shall be deposited in the archives of the Government of the Republic of the Philippines. . . .

2. The Treaty shall be ratified and its provisions carried out by the Parties in accordance with their respective constitutional processes. . . .*

ARTICLE X

This Treaty shall remain in force indefinitely, but any Party may cease to be a Party one year after its notice of denunciation has been given to the Government of the Republic of the Philippines, which shall inform the Governments of the other Parties of the deposit of each notice of denunciation. . . .

UNDERSTANDING OF THE UNITED STATES OF AMERICA

The United States of America in executing the present Treaty does so with the understanding that its recognition of the effect of aggression and armed attack and its agreement with reference thereto in Article IV, paragraph 1, apply only to communist aggression but affirms that in the event of other aggression or armed attack it will consult under the provisions of Article IV, paragraph 2.

In witness whereof, the undersigned Plenipotentiaries have signed this Treaty.

Done at Manila, this eighth day of September, 1954.

PROTOCOL TO THE TREATY, SEPTEMBER 8, 1954

DESIGNATION OF STATES AND TERRITORY AS TO WHICH PROVISIONS OF ARTICLE IV AND ARTICLE III ARE TO BE APPLICABLE.

The Parties to the Southeast Asia Collective Defense Treaty unanimously designate for the purposes of Article IV of the Treaty the States of Cambodia and Laos and the free territory under the jurisdiction of the State of Vietnam.

The Parties further agree that the above mentioned states and territory

* Thailand deposited its instrument of ratification Dec. 2, 1954; the remaining signatories (the United States, Australia, France, New Zealand, Pakistan, the Philippines, and the United Kingdom) deposited their instruments Feb. 19, 1955.

shall be eligible in respect of the economic measures contemplated by Article III.

This Protocol shall enter into force simultaneously with the coming into force of the Treaty.

IN WITNESS WHEREOF, the undersigned Plenipotentiaries have signed this Protocol to the Southeast Asia Collective Defense Treaty.

Done at Manila, this eighth day of September, 1954.

47. A SLIGHT UPGRADE

Appearing in executive session before the Senate Foreign Relations Committee on January 13, 1955, Secretary Dulles gave a cautiously optimistic report on Vietnam, and confirmed that the military burden had, indeed, fallen to Washington. Military cooperation in SEATO, he now also argued, would help to create a good impression throughout the Third World. (Source: United States Senate, Committee on Foreign Relations, *Executive Sessions of the Senate Foreign Relations Committee* [Historical Series], VII, 1955 [Washington, 1978], pp. 7–15.)

I would only say at this point that the trend in that area is, I think, slightly more favorable than has been the case. At the beginning we were on a sharp downgrade. We have just been flattened out, and we are on a slight upgrade at the present time.

I would not want to express complete confidence in the outcome by any means, but I believe it is one of the situations where I think we should probably continue to give our support, recognizing as I think we must that there are a number of situations in the world where I think you should put up a good stout effort, even though it is by no means certain that we will succeed.

I do not think we should only exert ourselves where there is only a 100-percent chance of success, because if we do that we will miss a good many opportunities where in fact we can get a success out of apparent defeat.

There were moments both in Iran and Guatemala when many people thought the situation was hopeless, but we kept a stout heart, kept our courage up, and then all of a sudden things began to go better, and that is a possibility in Vietnam. . . .

It is not, of course, certain yet that that conference will be held, but it is at least a likely possibility, and I believe that to have had preceding that conference, which is limited to the nonwhite, non-Western countries, a conference at which a certain number of Western powers and a certain number of Asian powers met together and showed they could work together in common interest, that will be a very useful antidote to the Afro-Asian conference that was held, where there may be a tendency, certainly will be on the part of the Communist participants in that conference, to persuade the Afro-Asian peoples that they can get along better without any association at all with the Western white powers.

I think we have got to show that the Western powers and the Asian powers can work together usefully, and I believe that to hold that conference at Bangkok, as is planned the latter part of February, will be an extremely important demonstration which will have a big psychological value throughout Asia, and to a lesser extent in Africa itself. . . .

There has been no decision reached as to the extent to which we would try to build up forces in Vietnam. That is one of the matters being discussed between General Collins and General Ely.

However, I can say there that generally it is the feeling that we should reduce in numbers but improve in quality the present strength in Vietnam.

There is at the present time, on paper at least, an army of approximately 175,000. The present plan being discussed is to bring that down to approximately in the neighborhood of 100,000, with the belief that a better training and better arming of that lesser number will be better than the larger number in its present state, and because of the fact that the estimates of cost of this thing are very considerable.

To put an army as big as 175,000 into good fighting condition in a country like southern Vietnam would entail not only a very considerable direct military expenditure but, above all, a very large defense support item, because the economy of the country cannot stand the subtraction of that number of people from productive uses and a rough estimate, as I recall it, is it would cost approximately $1 billion a year to carry as large a force as approximately 200,000 for that area.

So the plan is being considered to cut that number down.

We believe that a well-trained and equipped force of approximately half that size, which can be created at less than half the cost of the larger figure, is probably a more prudent use of our money.

48. SEATO IN OPERATION

Following the formal signing of the SEATO alliance, Dulles reported on a meeting he had had with American Chiefs of Mission in Asia at yet another background press conference. His statement speaks for itself, as do his answers to questions. The date is March 2, 1955; the place is Manila. (Source: *Dulles MSS.)*

I gave a two-hour presentation this morning at which I tried to make clear to our people from these different posts the broad outlines of our policy for this area and to make clear the connection of what we do in one country with the interests of another. This is an extremely difficult thing to get across through the normal exchange of diplomatic cables and instructions. We fall into the habit of dealing with each Chief of Mission in relation to the problems of his country, and we don't often adequately, I am afraid, explain, for instance, to our Ambassador to Australia the meaning to Australia of what we may be doing in Korea or Japan. This gave me an opportunity to outline our basic philosophy and to point out that in this part of the world, at least, the United States does occupy a position of central power and influence and that we have an overall strategy which [takes into account] each of these countries, but does not, necessarily, try to solve the problems in terms of that country alone. I pointed out the broad strategy which underlies our desire to maintain at least a potential of three fronts against the Chinese Communists if they should commit open aggression—the one in Korea, the one in Formosa, and the one in Indochina—and the fact that we have those three fronts is far more protective of everybody than if, for example, we concentrated on an effort on any one of those three fronts. I outlined the military strategy which dictates a mobility of power rather than a segregation of power by dividing it up between different areas. There is a capacity to move rapidly into whatever area we chose as circumstances indicate desirable, and that it is much better to have all our power available for that purpose than to have it split up into fractions no one of which might be adequate to do the job. I reviewed the economic policies which lead us to try to develop the economic health of the area as a whole and not just concentrate on one country or even a group of countries represented at the Manila Pact; and particularly I emphasized the economic problem with Japan. That, incidentally, is the problem certain aspects of which meet us right away in

Indochina, as was, I guess, remarked at the time we had our Saigon meeting. As Indochina becomes independent and has dollars directly available to it, there exists a competitive situation and there is a good chance of Japanese textile goods, for instance, moving into Indochina. The French are somewhat concerned about that, and I don't blame the French for being concerned about it but I don't think you can go on indefinitely having a protected preferential market for the French if Indochina . . . , particularly Vietnam, is to be an independent country and have its own sources of dollars. You see, in the past we have given the dollars to the French and the French have in turn given French francs to Vietnam so that the purchases of Vietnam almost had to be made in the franc area. Now with us giving the dollars direct they will have the currency which is good for use anywhere and the situation becomes competitive. . . .

I also spoke about one thing that had impressed me very greatly when I was at Saigon, and that was of reports I had heard about this Brotherhood Movement which is backed here, I think, largely by the Philippine Junior Chamber of Commerce. They are sending people largely in the medical field—doctors and nurses—to Saigon and they are working with the refugees that come in there from the north and are doing, according to all the information I get, a very amazing job. They are on the job day and night. They've got little signs saying, "We are open 24 hours a day." People are standing in line to get the advice and counsel of these doctors and nurses, and it is a very fine demonstration not only of humanitarianism but also it is interesting to me as indicating to me how one thing leads to another. We granted independence to the Philippines and now after they get their independence they in turn are helping another country, Vietnam, to become independent. There is a certain drama about it which appeals to me, at least, and it is having an excellent effect in Vietnam. President Diem spoke to me about it there when we had lunch together in Saigon. Then, later, this afternoon, the Ambassador was kind enough to give a reception for the personalities of the American Colony and leading figures of the Republic of the Philippines, Senators and Representatives. I guess that's a pretty substantial account of the day. . . .

Q: Do you anticipate, Mr. Secretary, that in addition to Japanese textiles other goods will likely be bought in increasing numbers from Japan by the Vietnamese once their dollars become available?

A: We have always felt that a major market for Japanese goods would be and, in fact, should be the Southeast Asia area, including not only Indochina but Indonesia, Thailand, Burma, and also perhaps South Asia, India and Pakistan. The Japanese make a type of goods which find a ready market. It's a cheaper type of goods than is desired really in our own markets and is within the capacity of people to buy. Also, they should be able to contribute some heavy industry goods in the way of machinery and things of that sort, so that we have always looked forward to a development of the Japanese market in that area and I think what is taking place there is a logical and almost inevitable development. And if you take the French situation—if you take the overall picture—I don't have the figures in mind, but by and large the French trade that may be dislocated will not seriously affect the French economy. The French economy is getting along very well despite political crises and governmental crises their economy moves along in a pretty satisfactory way, so that France does not face any serious economic crisis and I do not think the increasing independence, both political and economic, of Indochina will have any serious effect on the French economy as a whole. It may not be pleasant for some individual concerns in France, but by and large the impact on French economy will not be serious. As I said to you in Saigon, there is no desire on the part of the United States to try to displace French influence in that area. A certain displacement is, I think, inevitable.

Q: You mentioned the French fears of this thing. Have you run into any indication of similar apprehension on the part of the British?

A: No. I discussed this somewhat with Eden when we were there and I think that he recognized that the British interests had to be prepared to accept a certain competition of Japanese goods in that area and that it would probably be better to meet the competition there than to try to meet it by having Japanese goods going directly into the United Kingdom.

If the reciprocal trade agreements act is extended, and I hope it will be, and when we carry through our negotiations under that act, and when we have got operating our more complete economic program, for Southeast Asia and South Asia, which will be geared to promoting trade with Japan to that area, I think the combination of those things will really pretty well take care of the Japanese economic problem. That, of course, assumes that the Southeast Asia and South Asia area does not go Communist.

49. SHOWDOWN IN PARIS

The encouragement that the United States gave Diem not to go ahead with preparations for all-Vietnamese elections in the absence of "safeguards" the North Vietnamese were likely to reject, and indeed the support Washington showed for Diem in general, led to a Franco-American argument, the main points of which were summarized by

Dulles at the beginning of this response he drafted for a Foreign Ministers Conference held in Paris in May 1955. (Source: *Dulles MSS.)*

The French Memorandum suggests that the French Government can accept the formula proposed by Secretary Dulles on certain conditions. These conditions are:

1. An enlargement of the Diem Government and acceleration of an electoral process.
2. Peaceful solution of the problem of the sects.
3. Cessation of anti-French propaganda.
4. Continuance of the present role of Bao Dai.
5. Reciprocal removal from Vietnam of French and US functionaries who are deemed disturbing to Franco-US harmony.
6. US assurance that French economic, cultural and financial relations in Vietnam will be nurtured.

The foregoing conditions seem to the US to involve a basically different judgment of the situation from that which is entertained by the US.

There exists in Vietnam a revolutionary spirit. That spirit can perhaps be guided and moderated, but it cannot be put down. We believe that Diem represents the best hope of a moderate, tolerable and anti-Communist evolution; but that, if an attempt is made to remove him by joint or separate pressure from the US or France, the result may well be that he will be used by, and ultimately replaced by, a violently revolutionary movement under the control of the Communists.

The US believes that Diem can perhaps succeed precisely because he has a large measure of independence, coupled with moral conviction. During recent days he has exerted his influence in favor of the more moderate of the revolutionary gatherings, and has not given his support to those who would have instantly deposed Bao Dai.

We believe that the best and perhaps only chance is to back Diem *unconditionally* on the gamble that he can succeed, and that if he does succeed, there will be an anti-Communist government in Vietnam which will treat tolerably the French and other foreign interests which are there.

Admittedly, this is a gamble, but it is in our judgment far less of a gamble than to attempt to turn Diem into a puppet taking orders and direction from outside the country, whether it be from Bao Dai, France or the US.

The US cannot undertake to give any assurances to the French that Diem will do the things enumerated above. We do not have that power over Diem, and if Diem subjected himself to that power, he would not in our opinion have the qualities needed for survival.

The US in the common interest would of course give advice provided advice were sought and acceptable in the sense of many of the French proposals.

We would like to see the Government of Diem strengthened, and we believe that the Cabinet additions announced on May 10 do strengthen its capacity to govern: We are not confident that the Government is necessarily strengthened by enlarging it in the sense of bringing in political opponents on the theory that a coalition government can function.

We believe that the problem of the sects should be worked out peacefully so long as they do not forcibly challenge the Government. We do not, however, consider that the Binh Xuyen is a sect, and we believe that it should be outlawed and that it is necessary that the Diem Government should have full support in taking over control of the National Police.

Next, we hope that the Diem Government will moderate its anti-French propaganda just as we hope the French will moderate the anti-Diem and often anti-American propaganda which is carried on by various French agencies in Saigon.

We believe that the relationship of Bao Dai [the head of state installed by the French at the end of World War II] to Vietnam must be worked out by the Vietnamese themselves. While we would prefer to see the thread of legitimacy preserved, we believe that that preservation depends primarily upon the avoidance by Bao Dai of such activities as those he has engaged in in recent weeks, which have greatly aroused public sentiment against him and which have exposed the feebleness of his power. The US, itself a revolutionary government, could not be expected to commit itself never to recognize or deal with a Government of Vietnam which established itself independently of Bao Dai.

If there are American officials in Vietnam whose presence is deemed by the French to be injurious to our common cause, we would be glad to be so informed, and we would be glad to reciprocate; but we believe that neither government could give any undertaking to put the disposal of its personnel under the direction of another government.

We do not believe that there is any possibility of guaranteeing good relations between the Vietnamese and French commercial, cultural and financial institutions in Vietnam. We believe that there must inevitably be a period when these relations become less advantageous than was the case when Vietnam was a French colony. On the other hand, as the experience of the US with the Philippines and of the UK with its former colonies has shown, recognition of real independence and support of a national government can lead to even better commercial, cultural and financial relations than before. We believe that this natural process, rather than any artificial means, must be the principal French reliance.

The US is glad to note that the French Government does not now contemplate an abrupt withdrawal of its forces, but merely contemplates some continuing reduction in their numbers and their redeployment so that they will not be conspicuous in political centers.

In conclusion, we again emphasize that the salvation of Vietnam depends upon the presence there of a government which cannot be controlled by extraneous forces, but which is demonstrably nationalistic. Such a government cannot be coerced. It can perhaps be influenced by those whom it trusts as being genuinely dedicated to its vigorous survival. It is the belief of the US that if France and the US qualify in that respect, then there is a good chance, though by no means a certainty, that the other results which we want will in fact be obtainable, though that result cannot be stipulated or assured in advance.

May 11, 1955

50. VIETNAM'S EXAMPLE

The "gamble" paid off early. At least that was the American consensus at the time Dulles testified before a Senate committee in executive session in 1956. The elections had been held—but only in South Vietnam. (Source: United States Senate, Committee on Foreign Relations, *Executive Sessions of the Senate Foreign Relations Committee* [Historical Series], VIII, 1956 [Washington, 1978], pp. 159–61.)

Diem has done a wonderful job, of course with our help, in cleaning up his sect armies. There were three independent groups: the Binh Xuyen, who had charge of the police in Saigon, and who dispensed the prostitution and the gambling privileges; and then there were the Hoa/Hao and the Cao Dai.

All of them now have been liquidated, at least as far as their independent army or police was concerned, and there are small mopping-up operations still to be done. But the back of the problem has been broken, and Diem's authority throughout the area is now generally accepted.

That, as I say, has been done with the great help from the United States in training and equipping his national forces. They have performed loyally and efficiently, and have brought central authority into the country to a degree which is really quite amazing.

I don't want to suggest that their problems are over, or that there is ground for complacency. . . .

They have had there the general elections, and the day I left, they were holding their first constituent assembly convention meeting, and the foundation has just been laid for a representative form of government.

Bao Dai has been eliminated, and there is a chance for really building a strong and effective anti-Communist regime in an area where for a time it looked as though it would be swept away as a result of the French defeat in the Hanoi area, notably, at Dienbienphu, and by the unfavorable armistice terms.

51. IKE CHANGES HIS WILL

On January 19, 1961, Eisenhower entertained President-elect Kennedy and his advisers for some last-minute words of advice. And what words they were! In the wake of an attempted coup by American-supported rightist Kong Le in Laos, it looked as if Communist insurgents would succeed instead in replacing the "neutralist" government of Souvanna Phouma. Eisenhower thus bequeathed a new legacy to JFK, one that provided the incoming occupant of the White House with many difficulties. (Source: Clark Clifford Memorandum of September 29, 1967, reprinted in The Senator Gravel Edition, *The Pentagon Papers,* 4 vols. [Boston, 1971], II, pp. 635–37.)

President Eisenhower opened the discussion on Laos by stating that the United States was determined to preserve the independence of Laos. It was his opinion that if Laos should fall to the Communists, then it would be just a question of time until South Vietnam, Cambodia, Thailand and Burma would collapse. He felt that the Communists had designs on all of Southeast Asia, and that it would be a tragedy to permit Laos to fall.

President Eisenhower gave a brief review of the various moves and coups that had taken place in Laos involving the Pathet Lao, Souvanna Phouma, Boun Oum, and Kong Le. He said that the evidence was clear that Communist China and North Vietnam were determined to destroy the independence of Laos. He also added that the Russians were sending in substantial supplies in support of the Pathet Lao in an effort to overturn the government.

President Eisenhower said it would be fatal for us to permit Communists to insert themselves in the Laotian government. He recalled that our experience had clearly demonstrated that under such circumstances the Communists always ended up in control. He cited China as an illustration.

At this point, Secretary of State Herter intervened to state that if the present government of Laos were to apply to SEATO for aid under the Pact, Herter was of the positive opinion that the signatories to the SEATO Pact were bound. President Eisenhower agreed with this and in his statement gave the impression that the request for aid had already come from the government of Laos. He corroborated the binding nature of the obligation of the United States under the SEATO Pact.

President Eisenhower stated that the British and the French did not want SEATO to intervene in Laos, and he indicated that they would probably continue to maintain that attitude. President Eisenhower said that if it were not appropriate for SEATO to intervene in Laos, that his next preference would be the International Control Commission. He was sure, however, that the Soviet Union did not want the ICC to go into Laos. President Eisenhower stated that if this country had a choice as to whether the task should be assumed by SEATO or the ICC, that he personally would prefer SEATO.

Secretary Herter stated that we possibly could work out some agreement with the British, if they could be persuaded to recognize the present government in Laos. The chances of accomplishing this, however, appeared to be remote.

Secretary Herter stated, with President Eisenhower's approval, that we should continue every effort to make a political settlement in Laos. He added, however, that if such efforts were fruitless, then the United States must intervene in concert with our allies. If we were unable to persuade our allies, then we must go it alone.

At this point, President Eisenhower said with considerable emotion that Laos was the key to the entire area of Southeast Asia. He said that if we permitted Laos to fall, then we would have to write off all the area. He stated that we must not permit a Communist take-over. He reiterated that we should make every effort to persuade member nations of SEATO or the ICC to accept the burden with us to defend the freedom of Laos.

As he concluded these remarks, President Eisenhower stated it was imperative that Laos be defended. He said that the United States should accept this task with our allies, if we could persuade them, and alone if we could not. He added that "our unilateral intervention would be our last desperate hope" in the event we were unable to prevail upon the other signatories to join us. . . .

Commenting upon President Eisenhower's statement that we would have to go to the support of Laos alone if we could not persuade others to proceed with us, President-elect Kennedy asked the question as to how long it would take to put an American division into Laos. Secretary Gates replied that it would take from twelve to seventeen days but that some of that time could be saved if American forces, then in the Pacific, could be utilized. Secretary Gates added that the American forces were in excellent shape and that modernization of the Army was making good progress.

President-elect Kennedy commented upon the seriousness of the situation in Laos and in Southeast Asia and asked if the situation seemed to be approaching a climax. General Eisenhower stated that the entire proceeding was extremely confused but that it was clear that this country was obligated to support the existing government in Laos.

The discussion of Laos led to some concluding general statements regarding Southeast Asia. It was agreed that Thailand was a valuable ally of the United States, and that one of the dangers of a Communist take-over in Laos would be to expose Thailand's borders. In this regard, it was suggested that the military training under French supervision in Thailand was very poor and that it would be a good idea to get American military instructors there as soon as possible so the level of military capability could be raised.

President Eisenhower said there was some indication that Russia was concerned over Communist pressures in Laos and in Southeast Asia emanating from China and North Vietnam. It was felt that this attitude could possibly lead to some difficulty between Russia and China.

This phase of the discussion was concluded by President Eisenhower in commenting philosophically upon the fact that the morale existing in the democratic forces in Laos appeared to be disappointing. He wondered aloud why, in interventions of this kind, we always seem to find that the morale of the Communist forces was better than that of the democratic forces. His explanation was that the Communist philosophy appeared to produce a sense of dedication on the part of its adherents, while there was not the same sense of dedication on the part of those supporting the free forces. He stated that the entire problem of morale was a serious one and would have to be taken into consideration as we became more deeply involved.

52. CUBA AND VIETNAM

Immediately after the fiasco at the Bay of Pigs in April 1961, Kennedy added yet another reason for American involvement in South Vietnam, the "message of Cuba." The missions he sent to investigate conditions in Southeast Asia all had in mind this speech to the American Society of Newspaper Editors on April 20, 1961. (Source: United States Government, *Public Papers of the Presidents of the United States: John F. Kennedy, 1961* [Washington, 1962], pp. 305–6.)

". . . [T]here are from this sobering episode useful lessons for us all to learn. Some may be still obscure, and await further information. Some are clear today.

First, it is clear that the forces of communism are not to be underestimated, in Cuba or anywhere else in the world. The advantages of a police state—its use of mass terror and arrests to prevent the spread of free dissent—cannot be overlooked by those who expect the fall of every fanatic tyrant. If the self-discipline of the free cannot match the iron discipline of the mailed fist—in economic, political, scientific and all the other kinds of struggles as well as the military—then the peril to freedom will continue to rise.

Secondly, it is clear that this Nation, in concert with all the free nations of this hemisphere, must take an ever closer and more realistic look at the menace of external Communist intervention and domination in Cuba. The American people are not complacent about Iron Curtain tanks and planes less than 90 miles from their shore. But a nation of Cuba's size is less a threat to our survival than it is a base for subverting the survival of other free nations throughout the hemisphere. It is not primarily our interest or our security but theirs which is now, today, in the greater peril. It is for their sake as well as our own that we must show our will.

The evidence is clear—and the hour is late. We and our Latin friends will have to face the fact that we cannot postpone any longer the real issue of survival of freedom in this hemisphere itself. On that issue, unlike perhaps some others, there can be no middle ground. Together we must build a hemisphere where freedom can flourish; and where any free nation under outside attack of any kind can be assured that all of our resources stand ready to respond to any request for assistance.

Third, and finally, it is clearer than ever that we face a relentless strug-

189

gle in every corner of the globe that goes far beyond the clash of armies or even nuclear armaments. The armies are there, and in large number. The nuclear armaments are there. But they serve primarily as the shield behind which subversion, infiltration, and a host of other tactics steadily advance, picking off vulnerable areas one by one in situations which do not permit our own armed intervention.

Power is the hallmark of this offensive—power and discipline and deceit. The legitimate discontent of yearning people is exploited. The legitimate trappings of self-determination are employed. But once in power, all talk of discontent is repressed, all self-determination disappears, and the promise of a revolution of hope is betrayed, as in Cuba, into a reign of terror. Those who on instruction staged automatic "riots" in the streets of free nations over the efforts of a small group of young Cubans to regain their freedom should recall the long roll call of refugees who cannot now go back—to Hungary, to North Korea, to North Viet-Nam, to East Germany, or to Poland, or to any of the other lands from which a steady stream of refugees pours forth, in eloquent testimony to the cruel oppression now holding sway in their homeland.

We dare not fail to see the insidious nature of this new and deeper struggle. We dare not fail to grasp the new concepts, the new tools, the new sense of urgency we will need to combat it—whether in Cuba or South Viet-Nam. And we dare not fail to realize that this struggle is taking place every day, without fanfare, in thousands of villages and markets—day and night—and in classrooms all over the globe.

The message of Cuba, of Laos, of the rising din of Communist voices in Asia and Latin America—these messages are all the same. The complacent, the self-indulgent, the soft societies are about to be swept away with the debris of history. Only the strong, only the industrious, only the determined, only the courageous, only the visionary who determine the real nature of our struggle can possibly survive.

No greater task faces this country or this administration. No other challenge is more deserving of our every effort and energy. Too long we have fixed our eyes on traditional military needs, on armies prepared to cross borders, on missiles poised for flight. Now it should be clear that this is no longer enough—that our security may be lost piece by piece, country by country, without the firing of a single missile or the crossing of a single border.

We intend to profit from this lesson. We intend to reexamine and reorient our forces of all kinds—our tactics and our institutions here in this community. We intend to intensify our efforts for a struggle in many ways more difficult than war, where disappointment will often accompany us.

For I am convinced that we in this country and in the free world possess the necessary resource, and the skill, and the added strength that comes from a belief in the freedom of man. And I am equally convinced that history will record the fact that this bitter struggle reached its climax in the late 1950's and the early 1960's. Let me then make clear as the President of the United States that I am determined upon our system's survival and success, regardless of the cost and regardless of the peril!

53. LYNDON JOHNSON'S REPORT

Not long after his speech on the Bay of Pigs failure, when he had warned that "regardless of the peril" the American "system" must survive, JFK sent his Vice-President on a fact-finding mission to Asia. The Vice-President was not at all optimistic about the way the system was faring out there. (Source: Department of Defense, *United States–Vietnam Relations, 1945–1967* [Washington, 1971], Book 2, part B, pp. 53–57.)

Beyond question, your judgment about the timing of our mission was correct. Each leader—except Nehru—publicly congratulated you on the "timing" of this mission. Chiang [Kai-shek, President of the Republic of China on Taiwan] said—and all the others privately concurred—that the mission had the effect of "stabilizing" the situation in the Southeast Asian nations. . . .

Our mission arrested the decline of confidence in the United States. It did not—in my judgment—restore any confidence already lost. The leaders were as explicit, as courteous and courtly as men could be in making it clear that deeds must follow words—soon.

We didn't buy time—we were given it.

If these men I saw at your request were bankers, I would know—without bothering to ask—that there would be no further extensions on my note. . . .

I took to Southeast Asia some basic convictions about the problems faced there. I have come away from the mission there—and to India and Pakistan—with many of those convictions sharpened and deepened by what I saw and learned. I have also reached certain other conclusions which I believe may be of value as guidance for those responsible in formulating policies.

These conclusions are as follows:

1. The battle against Communism must be joined in Southeast Asia

with strength and determination to achieve success there—or the United States, inevitably, must surrender the Pacific and take up our defenses on our own shores. Asian Communism is compromised and contained by the maintenance of free nations on the subcontinent. Without this inhibitory influence, the island outposts—Philippines, Japan, Taiwan—have no security and the vast Pacific becomes a Red Sea.

2. The struggle is far from lost in Southeast Asia and it is by no means inevitable that it must be lost. In each country it is possible to build a sound structure capable of withstanding and turning the Communist surge. The will to resist—while now the target of subversive attack—is there. The key to what is done by Asians in defense of Southeast Asia freedom is confidence in the United States.

3. There is no alternative to United States leadership in Southeast Asia. Leadership in individual countries—or the regional leadership and cooperation so appealing to Asians—rests on the knowledge and faith in United States power, will and understanding.

4. SEATO is not now and probably never will be the answer because of British and French unwillingness to support decisive action. Asian distrust of the British and French is outspoken. Success at Geneva would prolong SEATO's role. Failure at Geneva would terminate SEATO's meaningfulness. In the latter event, we must be ready with a new approach to collective security in the area.

We should consider an alliance of all the free nations of the Pacific and Asia who are willing to join forces in defense of their freedom. Such an organization should:

a) have a clear-cut command authority

b) also devote attention to measures and programs of social justice, housing, land reform, etc.

5. Asian leaders—at this time—do not want American troops involved in Southeast Asia other than on training missions. American combat troop involvement is not only not required, it is not desirable. Possibly Americans fail to appreciate fully the subtlety that recently-colonial peoples would not look with favor upon governments which invited or accepted the return this soon of Western troops. To the extent that fear of ground troop involvement dominates our political responses to Asia in Congress or elsewhere, it seems most desirable to me to allay those paralyzing fears in confidence, on the strength of the individual statements made by leaders consulted on this trip. This does not minimize or disregard the probability that open attack would bring calls for U.S. combat troops. But the present probability of open attack seems scant, and we might gain much needed flexibility in our policies if the spectre of combat troop commitment could be lessened domestically.

192

6. Any help—economic as well as military—we give less developed nations to secure and maintain their freedom must be a part of a mutual effort. These nations cannot be saved by United States help alone. To the extent the Southeast Asian nations are prepared to take the necessary measures to make our aid effective, we can be—and must be—unstinting in our assistance. It would be useful to enunciate more clearly than we have—for the guidance of these young and unsophisticated nations— what we expect or require of them.

7. In large measure, the greatest danger Southeast Asia offers to nations like the United States is not the momentary threat of Communism itself, rather that danger stems from hunger, ignorance, poverty and disease. We must—whatever strategies we evolve—keep these enemies the point of our attack, and make imaginative use of our scientific and technological capability in such enterprises.

8. Vietnam and Thailand are the immediate—and most important— trouble spots, critical to the U.S. These areas require the attention of our very best talents—under the very closest Washington direction—on matters economic, military and political.

The basic decision in Southeast Asia is here. We must decide whether to help these countries to the best of our ability or throw in the towel in the area and pull back our defenses to San Francisco and a "Fortress America" concept. More important, we would say to the world in this case that we don't live up to treaties and don't stand by our friends. This is not my concept. I recommend that we move forward promptly with a major effort to help these countries defend themselves. I consider the key here is to get our best MAAG people to control, plan, direct and exact results from our military aid program. In Vietnam and Thailand, we must move forward together.

a. In Vietnam, Diem is a complex figure beset by many problems. He has admirable qualities, but he is remote from the people, is surrounded by persons less admirable and capable than he. The country can be saved —if we move quickly and wisely. We must decide whether to support Diem—or let Vietnam fall. We must have coordination of purpose in our country team, diplomatic and military. The Saigon Embassy, USIS, MAAG and related operations leave much to be desired. They should be brought up to maximum efficiency. The most important thing is imaginative, creative, American management of our military aid program. The Vietnamese and our MAAG estimate that $50 million of U.S. military and economic assistance will be needed if we decide to support Vietnam. This is the best information available to us at the present time and if it is confirmed by the best Washington military judgment it should be supported. Since you proposed and Diem agreed to a joint economic mission, it should be appointed and proceed forthwith.

b. In Thailand, the Thais and our own MAAG estimate probably as much is needed as in Vietnam—about $50 million of military and economic assistance. Again, should our best military judgment concur, I believe we should support such a program. Sarit is more strongly and staunchly pro-Western than many of his people. He is and must be deeply concerned at the consequence to his country of a communist-controlled Laos. If Sarit is to stand firm against neutralism, he must have—soon—concrete evidence to show his people of United States military and economic support. He believes that his armed forces should be increased to 150,000. His Defense Minister is coming to Washington to discuss aid matters.

The fundamental decision required of the United States—and time is of the greatest importance—is whether we are to attempt to meet the challenge of Communist expansion now in Southeast Asia by a major effort in support of the forces of freedom in the area or throw in the towel. This decision must be made in a full realization of the very heavy and continuing costs involved in terms of money, of effort and of United States prestige. It must be made with the knowledge that at some point we may be faced with the further decision of whether we commit major United States forces to the area or cut our losses and withdraw should our other efforts fail. We must remain master in this decision. What we do in Southeast Asia should be part of a rational program to meet the threat we face in the region as a whole. It should include a clear-cut pattern of specific contributions to be expected by each partner according to his ability and resources. I recommend we proceed with a clear-cut and strong program of action.

I believe that the mission—as you conceived it—was a success. I am grateful to the many who labored to make it so.

54. THE EDGE OF COMMITMENT

Throughout the summer and fall of 1961, President Kennedy received the recommendations of various investigators and advisers. They all pointed in the same direction: the need to commit American ground forces. Kennedy held back from a final "yes" to a massive increase in force levels, but requested Secretary of State Dean Rusk and Secretary of Defense Robert McNamara to prepare an alternative plan. Their memorandum of November 11, 1961, scaled down earlier recommendations from Defense and stressed the dangers of overinvolvement. Kennedy approved this version, but warned President Diem that Washington would henceforth "expect to share in the decision-making process in the political, economic and military fields as they affect the security situation." (Source: Department of Defense, *United States–Vietnam Relations, 1945–1967* [Washington, 1971], Book 2, part B, pp. 125–33.)

1. United States National Interests in South Viet-Nam.

The deteriorating situation in South Viet-Nam requires attention to the nature and scope of United States national interests in that country. The loss of South Viet-Nam to Communism would involve the transfer of a nation of 20 million people from the free world to the Communist bloc. The loss of South Viet-Nam would make pointless any further discussion about the importance of Southeast Asia to the free world; we would have to face the near certainty that the remainder of Southeast Asia and Indonesia would move to a complete accommodation with Communism, if not formal incorporation with the Communist bloc. The United States, as a member of SEATO, has commitments with respect to South Viet-Nam under the Protocol to the SEATO Treaty. Additionally, in a formal statement at the conclusion session of the 1954 Geneva Conference, the United States representative stated that the United States "would view any renewal of the aggression . . . with grave concern and seriously threatening international peace and security."

The loss of South Viet-Nam to Communism would not only destroy SEATO but would undermine the credibility of American commitments elsewhere. Further, loss of South Viet-Nam would stimulate bitter domestic controversies in the United States and would be seized upon by extreme elements to divide the country and harass the Administration. . . .

3. The United States' Objective in South Viet-Nam.

The United States should commit itself to the clear objective of preventing the fall of South Viet-Nam to Communist [sic]. The basic means for accomplishing this objective must be to put the Government of South Viet-Nam into a position to win its own war against the Guerillas. We must insist that that Government itself take the measures necessary for that purpose in exchange for large-scale United States assistance in the military, economic and political fields. At the same time we must recognize that it will probably not be possible for the GVN to win this war as long as the flow of men and supplies from North Viet-Nam continues unchecked and the guerillas enjoy a safe sanctuary in neighboring territory.

We should be prepared to introduce United States combat forces if that should become necessary for success. Dependent upon the circumstances, it may also be necessary for United States forces to strike at the source of the aggression in North Viet-Nam.

4. The Use of United States Forces in South Viet-Nam.

The commitment of United States forces to South Viet-Nam involves two different categories: (A) Units of modest size required for the direct support of South Viet-Namese military effort, such as communications, helicopter and other forms of airlift, reconnaissance aircraft, naval patrols, intelligence units, etc., and (B) larger organized units with actual or potential direct military mission. *Category (A) should be introduced as speedily as possible.* Category (B) units pose a more serious problem in that they are much more significant from the point of view of domestic and international political factors and greatly increase the probabilities of Communist bloc escalation. Further, the employment of United States combat forces (in the absence of Communist bloc escalation) involves a certain dilemma: if there is a strong South-Vietnamese effort, they may not be needed; if there is not such an effort, United States forces could not accomplish their mission in the midst of an apathetic or hostile population. Under present circumstances, therefore, the question of injecting United States and SEATO combat forces should in large part be considered as a contribution to the morale of the South Vietnamese in their own effort to do the principal job themselves.

5. Probable Extent of the Commitment of United States Forces.

If we commit Category (B) forces to South Viet-Nam, the ultimate possible extent of our military commitment in Southeast Asia must be faced. The struggle may be prolonged, and Hanoi and Peiping may overtly intervene. It is the view of the Secretary of Defense and the Joint Chiefs of Staff that, in the light of the logistic difficulties faced by the other side, we can assume that the maximum United States forces required on the ground in Southeast Asia would not exceed six divisions, or about 205,000 men. . . . This would be in addition to local forces and such SEATO forces as may be engaged. It is also the view of the Secretary of Defense and the Joint Chiefs of Staff that our military posture is, or, with the addition of more National Guard or regular Army divisions, can be made, adequate to furnish these forces and support them in action without serious interference with our present Berlin plans. . . .

In the light of the foregoing, the Secretary of State and the Secretary of Defense recommend that:

1. We now take the decision to commit ourselves to the objective of preventing the fall of South Viet-Nam to Communism and that, in doing so, we recognize that the introduction of United States and other SEATO

forces may be necessary to achieve this objective. (However, if it is necessary to commit outside forces to achieve the foregoing objective our decision to introduce United States forces should not be contingent upon unanimous SEATO agreement thereto.)

2. The Department of Defense be prepared with plans for the use of United States forces in South Viet-Nam under one or more of the following purposes:

(a) Use of a significant number of United States forces to signify United States determination to defend Viet-Nam and to boost South Viet-Nam morale.

(b) Use of substantial United States forces to assist in suppressing Viet Cong insurgency short of engaging in detailed counter-guerrilla operations but including relevant operations in North Viet-Nam.

(c) Use of United States forces to deal with the situation if there is organized Communist military intervention.

3. We immediately undertake the following actions in support of the GVN:

. . . (c) Provide the GVN with small craft, including such United States uniformed advisers and operating personnel as may be necessary for quick and effective operations in effecting surveillance and control over coastal waters and inland waterways. . . .

(e) Provide such personnel and equipment as may be necessary to improve the military-political intelligence system beginning at the provincial level and extending upward through the Government and the armed forces to the Central Intelligence Organization.

(f) Provide such new terms of reference, reorganization and additional personnel for United States military forces as are required for increased United States participation in the direction and control of GVN military operations and to carry out the other increased responsibilities which accrue to MAAG under these recommendations. . . .

(i) Provide individual administrators and advisers for insertion into the Governmental machinery of South Viet-Nam in types and numbers to be agreed upon by the two Governments. . . .

5. Very shortly before the arrival in South Viet-Nam of the first increments of United States military personnel and equipment proposed under 3., above, that would exceed the Geneva Accord ceilings, publish the "Jorden report" as a United States "white paper," transmitting it as simultaneously as possible to the Governments of all countries with which we have diplomatic relations, including the Communist states.

6. Simultaneous with the publication of the "Jorden report," release an exchange of letters between Diem and the President.

(a) Diem's letter would include: reference to the DRV violations of

Geneva Accords as set forth in the October 24 GVN letter to the ICC and other documents; pertinent references to GVN statements with respect to its intent to observe the Geneva Accords; reference to its need for flood relief and rehabilitation; reference to previous United States aid and the compliance hitherto by both countries with the Geneva Accords; reference to the USG statement at the time the Geneva Accords were signed; the necessity of now exceeding some provisions of the Accords in view of the DRV violations thereof; the lack of aggressive intent with respect to the DRV; GVN intent to return to strict compliance with the Geneva Accords as soon as the DRV violations ceased; and request for additional United States assistance in framework foregoing policy. The letter should also set forth in appropriate general terms steps Diem has taken and is taking to reform Governmental structure.

(b) The President's reply would be responsive to Diem's request for additional assistance and acknowledge and agree to Diem's statements on the intent promptly to return to strict compliance with the Geneva Accords as soon as DRV violations have ceased. . . .

55. TWO INTERVIEWS

Kennedy's Vietnam difficulties began to take their toll. In television interviews a week apart, the President first said that the situation was one that would be determined by the Vietnamese themselves, and then warned against impatience, promising that the United States would not withdraw. (Source: United States Senate, Committee on Foreign Relations, *Background Information Relating to Southeast Asia and Vietnam,* 90th Cong., 1st. Sess. [Washington, 1967], pp. 112–14.)

PRESIDENT KENNEDY'S TV INTERVIEWS, SEPTEMBER 2 AND 9, 1963 (EXCERPTS)

(A) CBS INTERVIEW, SEPTEMBER 2

MR. CRONKITE. Mr. President, the only hot war we've got running at the moment is of course the one in Viet-Nam, and we have our difficulties here, quite obviously.

PRESIDENT KENNEDY. I don't think that unless a greater effort is made by the Government to win popular support that the war can be won out there. In the final analysis, it is their war. They are the ones who have to win it or lose it. We can help them, we can give them equipment, we can send our men out there as advisers, but they have to win it—the people of Viet-Nam—against the Communists. We are prepared to continue to assist them, but I don't think that the war can be won unless the people support the effort, and, in my opinion, in the last 2 months the Government has gotten out of touch with the people.

The repressions against the Buddhists, we felt, were very unwise. Now all we can do is to make it very clear that we don't think this is the way to win. It is my hope that this will become increasingly obvious to the Government, that they will take steps to try to bring back popular support for this very essential struggle.

MR. CRONKITE. Do you think this Government has time to regain the support of the people?

PRESIDENT KENNEDY. I do. With changes in policy and perhaps with personnel, I think it can. If it doesn't make those changes, I would think that the chances of winning it would not be very good.

MR. CRONKITE. Hasn't every indication from Saigon been that President Diem has no intention of changing his pattern?

PRESIDENT KENNEDY. If he does not change it, of course, that is his decision. He has been there 10 years, and, as I say, he has carried this burden when he has been counted out on a number of occasions.

Our best judgment is that he can't be successful on this basis. We hope that he comes to see that; but in the final analysis it is the people and the Government itself who have to win or lose this struggle. All we can do is help, and we are making it very clear. But I don't agree with those who say we should withdraw. That would be a great mistake. That would be a great mistake. I know people don't like Americans to be engaged in this kind of an effort. Forty-seven Americans have been killed in combat with the enemy, but this is a very important struggle even though it is far away.

We took all this—made this effort to defend Europe. Now Europe is quite secure. We also have to participate—we may not like it—in the defense of Asia.

(B) NBC INTERVIEW, SEPTEMBER 9

MR. HUNTLEY. Mr. President, in respect to our difficulties in South Viet-Nam, could it be that our Government tends occasionally to get locked into a policy or an attitude and then finds it difficult to alter or shift that policy?

THE PRESIDENT. Yes, that is true. I think in the case of South Viet-Nam we have been dealing with a Government which is in control, has been in control for 10 years. In addition, we have felt for the last 2 years that the struggle against the Communists was going better. Since June, however—

the difficulties with the Buddhists—we have been concerned about a deterioration, particularly in the Saigon area, which hasn't been felt greatly in the outlying areas but may spread. So we are faced with the problem of wanting to protect the area against the Communists. On the other hand, we have to deal with the Government there. That produces a kind of ambivalence in our efforts which exposes us to some criticism. We are using our influence to persuade the Government there to take those steps which will win back support. That takes some time, and we must be patient, we must persist.

MR. HUNTLEY. Are we likely to reduce our aid to South Viet-Nam now?

THE PRESIDENT. I don't think we think that would be helpful at this time. If you reduce your aid, it is possible you could have some effect upon the government structure there. On the other hand, you might have a situation which could bring about a collapse. Strongly in our mind is what happened in the case of China at the end of World War II, where China was lost—a weak government became increasingly unable to control events. We don't want that.

MR. BRINKLEY. Mr. President, have you had any reason to doubt this so-called "domino theory," that if South Viet-Nam falls, the rest of Southeast Asia will go behind it?

THE PRESIDENT. No, I believe it. I believe it. I think that the struggle is close enough. China is so large, looms so high just beyond the frontiers, that if South Viet-Nam went, it would not only give them an improved geographic position for a guerrilla assault on Malaya but would also give the impression that the wave of the future in Southeast Asia was China and the Communists. So I believe it.

MR. BRINKLEY. In the last 48 hours there have been a great many conflicting reports from there about what the CIA [Central Intelligence Agency] was up to. Can you give us any enlightenment on it?

THE PRESIDENT. No.

MR. HUNTLEY. Does the CIA tend to make its own policy? That seems to be the debate here.

THE PRESIDENT. No, that is the frequent charge, but that isn't so. Mr. [John A.] McCone, head of the CIA, sits in the National Security Council. We have had a number of meetings in the past few days about events in South Viet-Nam. Mr. McCone participated in every one, and the CIA coordinates its efforts with the State Department and the Defense Department.

MR. BRINKLEY. With so much of our prestige, money, so on, committed in South Viet-Nam, why can't we exercise a little more influence there, Mr. President?

THE PRESIDENT. We have some influence. We have some influence and we are attempting to carry it out. I think we don't—we can't expect these countries to do everything the way we want to do them. They have their own interest, their own personalities, their own tradition. We can't make everyone in our image, and there are a good many people who don't want to go in our image. In addition, we have ancient struggles between countries. In the case of India and Pakistan, we would like to have them settle Kashmir. That is our view of the best way to defend the subcontinent against communism. But that struggle between India and Pakistan is more important to a good many people in that area than the struggle against the Communists. We would like to have Cambodia, Thailand, and South Viet-Nam all in harmony, but there are ancient differences there. We can't make the world over, but we can influence the world. The fact of the matter is that with the assistance of the United States and SEATO [Southeast Asia Treaty Organization], Southeast Asia and indeed all of Asia has been maintained independent against a powerful force, the Chinese Communists. What I am concerned about is that Americans will get impatient and say, because they don't like events in Southeast Asia or they don't like the Government in Saigon, that we should withdraw. That only makes it easy for the Communists. I think we should stay. We should use our influence in as effective a way as we can, but we should not withdraw.

56. FIRST YES, THEN NO—THEN MAYBE

Although President Kennedy told TV interviewers that the United States had made it clear that repressing the Buddhists was not the way to win the war, the Administration was actively considering a much more forceful step. Advised by South Vietnamese generals that a coup was being planned, Washington gave its approval to the idea, then had second thoughts. This discussion on August 31, 1963, which is concluded by Lyndon Johnson's statement that it was time to stop playing cops and robbers, illustrates the dilemma. (Source: The Senator Gravel Edition, *The Pentagon Papers,* 4 vols. [Boston, 1971], II, pp. 741–43.)

AUGUST 31, 1963.

MEMORANDUM FOR THE RECORD

Subject: Meeting at the State Department, 1100, 31 August 1963; Subject; Vietnam.

Present: The Vice President, Secretary Rusk, Secretary McNamara, Mr.
   Gilpatric, Mr. Bundy, General Taylor, Mr. Murrow, General Carter,
   Mr. Helms, Mr. Colby, Ambassador Nolting, Mr. Hilsman, Mr. Kat-
   tenburg, General Krulak.

1. Secretary Rusk stated that, in his judgment, we were back to where
we were about Wednesday of last week, and this causes him to go back to
the original problem and ask what in the situation led us to think well of a
coup. Ruling out hatred of the Nhus, he said, there would appear to be
three things:

a. The things that the Nhus had done or supported, which tended to
upset the GVN internally.

b. The things that they had done which had an adverse external effect.

c. The great pressures of U.S. public opinion.

2. Mr. Rusk then asked if we should not pick up Ambassador Lodge's
suggestion in his message of today (Saigon 391) and determine what steps
are required to re-gird solidarity in South Vietnam—such as improvement in conditions concerning students and Buddhists and the possible
departure of Madame Nhu. He said that we should determine what additional measures are needed to improve the international situation—such
as problems affecting Cambodia—and to *improve the Vietnamese position
wherein U.S. public opinion is concerned.* He then said that he is reluctant
to start off by saying now that Nhu has to go; that it is unrealistic.

3. Mr. McNamara stated that he favored the above proposals of the
Secretary of State, with one additional step—that is to establish quickly
and firmly our line of communication between Lodge, Harkins and the
GVN. He pointed out that at the moment our channels of communication
are essentially broken and that they should be reinstituted at all costs.

4. Mr. Rusk added that we must do our best not to permit Diem to
decapitate his military command in light of its obviously adverse effect on
the prosecution of the war. At this point he asked if anyone present had
any doubt in his mind but that the coup was off.

5. Mr. Kattenburg said that he had some remaining doubt; that we
have not yet sent the generals a strong enough message. . . .

6. Mr. Hilsman commented that, in his view, the generals are not now
going to move unless they are pressed by a revolt from below. In this
connection Ambassador Nolting warned that in the uncoordinated Vietnamese structure anything can happen, and that while an organized
successful coup is out, there might be small flurries by irresponsible dissi-
dents at any time.

7. Mr. Hilsman undertook to present four basic factors which bear
directly on the problem confronting the U.S. now. They are, in his view:

a. The mood of the people, particularly the middle level officers, non-commissioned officers and middle level bureaucrats, who are most restive. Mr. McNamara interrupted to state that he had seen no evidence of this and General Taylor commented that he had seen none either, but would like to see such evidence as Hilsman could produce. Mr. Kattenburg commented that the middle level officers and bureaucrats are uniformly critical of the government, to which Mr. McNamara commented that if this is indeed the fact we should know about it.

b. The second basic factor, as outlined by Hilsman, was what effect will be felt on our programs elsewhere in Asia if we acquiesce to a strong Nhu-dominated government. In this connection, he reported that there is a Korean study now underway on just how much repression the United States will tolerate before pulling out her aid. Mr. McNamara stated that he had not seen this study and would be anxious to have it.

c. The third basic factor is Mr. Nhu, his personality and his policy. Hilsman recalled that Nhu has once already launched an effort aimed at withdrawal of our province advisors and stated that he is sure he is in conversation with the French. He gave, as supporting evidence, the content of an intercepted message, which Mr. Bundy asked to see. Ambassador Nolting expressed the opinion that Nhu will not make a deal with Ho Chi Minh on Ho's terms.

d. The fourth point is the matter of U.S. and world opinion, Hilsman stated that this problem was moving to a political and diplomatic plane. Part of the problem, he said, is the press, which concludes incorrectly that we have the ability to change the things in Vietnam of which they are critical. To this Mr. Murrow added that this problem of press condemnation is now worldwide.

8. Mr. Kattenburg stated that as recently as last Thursday it was the belief of Ambassador Lodge that, if we undertake to live with this repressive regime, with its bayonets at every street corner and its transparent negotiations with puppet bonzes, we are going to be thrown out of the country in six months. He stated that at this juncture it would be better for us to make the decision to get out honorably. He went on to say that, having been acquainted with Diem for ten years, he was deeply disappointed in him, saying that he will not separate from his brother. It was Kattenburg's view that Diem will get very little support from the military and, as time goes on, he will get less and less support and the country will go steadily down hill.

9. General Taylor asked what Kattenburg meant when he said that we would be forced out of Vietnam within six months. Kattenburg replied that in from six months to a year, as the people see we are losing the war, they will gradually go to the other side and we will be obliged to leave.

Ambassador Nolting expressed general disagreement with Mr. Kattenburg. He said that the unfavorable activity which motivated Kattenburg's remarks was confined to the city and, while city support of Diem is doubtless less now, it is not greatly so. He said that it is improper to overlook the fact that we have done a tremendous job toward winning the Vietnam war, working with this same imperfect, annoying government.

10. Mr. Kattenburg added that there is one new factor—the population, which was in high hopes of expelling the Nhus after the VOA announcement regarding cessation of aid; now, under the heel of Nhu's military repression, they would quickly lose heart.

11. Secretary Rusk commented that Kattenburg's recital was largely speculative; that it would be far better for us to start on the firm basis of two things—that we will not pull out of Vietnam until the war is won, and that we will not run a coup. Mr. McNamara expressed agreement with this view.

12. Mr. Rusk then said that we should present questions to Lodge which fall within these parameters. He added that he believes we have good proof that we have been winning the war, particularly the contrast between the first six months of 1962 and the first six months of 1963. He then asked the Vice President if he had any contribution to make.

13. The Vice President stated that he agreed with Secretary Rusk's conclusions completely; that he had great reservations himself with respect to a coup, particularly so because he had never really seen a genuine alternative to Diem. He stated that from both a practical and a political viewpoint, it would be a disaster to pull out; that we should stop playing cops and robbers and get back to talking straight to the GVN, and that we should once again go about winning the war. He stated that after our communications with them are genuinely reestablished, it may be necessary for someone to talk rough to them—perhaps General Taylor. He said further that he had been greatly impressed with Ambassador Nolting's views and agreed with Mr. McNamara's conclusions.

14. General Taylor raised the question of whether we should change the disposition of the forces which had been set in motion as a result of the crisis. It was agreed that there should be no change in the existing disposition for the time being.

57. DIEM'S ELIMINATION

Two days before the coup, on October 30, 1963, Washington informed Ambassador Henry Cabot Lodge of its continuing doubts about the plan of the South Vietnamese generals. Yet Washington's previous signals, the cutting off of aid, and the constant pressure on Diem to reform his government forced the issue to a head. (Source: The Senator Gravel Edition, *The Pentagon Papers,* 4 vols. [Boston, 1971], II, pp. 782–83.)

30 Oct 1963

FROM: MCGEORGE BUNDY

TO: LODGE

CAS 79109

1. Your 2023, 2040, 2041 and 2043 examined with care at highest levels here. You should promptly discuss this reply and associated messages with Harkins whose responsibilities toward any coup are very heavy especially after you leave (see para. 7 below). They give much clearer picture group's alleged plans and also indicate chances of action with or without our approval now so significant that we should urgently consider our attitude and contingency plans. We note particularly Don's curiosity your departure and his insistence Conein be available from Wednesday night on, which suggests date might be as early as Thursday.

2. Believe our attitude to coup group can still have decisive effect on its decisions. We believe that what we say to coup group can produce delay of coup and that betrayal of coup plans to Diem is not repeat not our only way of stopping coup. We therefore need urgently your combined assessment with Harkins and CAS (including their separate comments if they desire). We concerned that our line-up of forces in Saigon (being cabled in next message) indicates approximately equal balance of forces, with substantial possibility serious and prolonged fighting or even defeat. Either of these could be serious or even disastrous for U.S. interests, so that we must have assurance balance of forces clearly favorable.

3. With your assessment in hand, we might feel that we should convey message to Don, whether or not he gives 4 or 48 hours notice that would

(A) continue explicit hands-off policy, (B) positively encourage coup, or (C) discourage.

4. In any case, believe Conein should find earliest opportunity express to Don that we do not find presently revealed plans give clear prospect of quick results. This conversation should call attention important Saigon units still apparently loyal to Diem and raise serious issue as to what means coup group has to deal with them.

5. From operational standpoint, we also deeply concerned Don only spokesman for group and possibility cannot be discounted he may not be in good faith. We badly need some corroborative evidence whether Minh and others directly and completely involved. In view Don's claim he doesn't handle "military planning" could not Conein tell Don that we need better military picture and that Big Minh could communicate this most naturally and easily to Stillwell? We recognize desirability involving MACV to minimum, but believe Stillwell far more desirable this purpose than using Conein both ways.

6. Complexity above actions raises question whether you should adhere to present Thursday schedule. Concur you and other U.S. elements should take no action that could indicate U.S. awareness coup possibility. However, DOD [Department of Defense] is sending berth-equipped military aircraft that will arrive Saigon Thursday and could take you out thereafter as late as Saturday afternoon in time to meet your presently proposed arrival Washington Sunday. You could explain this being done as convenience and that your Washington arrival is same. A further advantage such aircraft is that it would permit your prompt return from any point en route if necessary. To reduce time in transit, you should use this plane, but we recognize delaying your departure may involve greater risk that you personally would appear involved if any action took place. However, advantages your having extra two days in Saigon may outweigh this and we leave timing of flight to your judgment.

7. Whether you leave Thursday or later, believe it essential that prior your departure there be fullest consultation Harkins and CAS and that there be clear arrangements for handling (A) normal activity, (B) continued coup contacts, (C) action in event a coup starts. We assume you will wish Truehart as charge to be head of country team in normal situation, but highest authority desires it clearly understood that after your departure Harkins should participate in supervision of all coup contacts and that in event a coup begins, he become head of country team and direct representative of President, with Truehart in effect acting as POLAD. On coup contacts we will maintain continuous guidance and will expect equally continuous reporting with prompt account of any important divergencies in assessments of Harkins and Smith.

8. If coup should start, question of protecting U.S. nationals at once arises. We can move Marine Battalion into Saigon by air from Okinawa within 24 hours—if available. We are sending instructions to CINCPAC [Commander in Chief, Pacific] to arrange orderly movement of seaborne Marine Battalion to waters adjacent to South Vietnam in position to close Saigon within approximately 24 hours.

9. We are now examining post-coup contingencies here and request your immediate recommendations on position to be adopted after coup begins, especially with respect to requests for assistance of different sorts from one side or the other also request you forward contingency recommendations for action if coup (A) succeeds, (B) fails, (C) is indecisive.

10. We reiterate burden of proof must be on coup group to show a substantial possibility of quick success; otherwise, we should discourage them from proceeding since a miscalculation could result in jeopardizing U.S. position in Southeast Asia.

58. CODA

As the coup began, Ambassador Lodge reported on a telephone conversation with Diem. The exchange took place at 4:30 P.M. Saigon time. As Lodge indicates, furthermore, these are not the words that would sound an American withdrawal—but the beginning of a new commitment more profound than SEATO. (Source: The New York *Times* Edition, Neil Sheehan, et al., eds., *The Pentagon Papers* [New York, 1971], p. 232.)

DIEM: Some units have made a rebellion and I want to know what is the attitude of the U.S.?

LODGE: I do not feel well enough informed to be able to tell you. I have heard the shooting, but am not acquainted with all the facts. Also it is 4:30 a.m. in Washington and the U.S. Government cannot possibly have a view.

DIEM: But you must have some general ideas. After all, I am a Chief of State. I have tried to do my duty. I want to do now what duty and good sense require. I believe in duty above all.

LODGE: You have certainly done your duty. As I told you only this morning, I admire your courage and your great contributions to your country. No one can take away from you the credit for all you have done. Now I am worried about your physical safety. I have a report that those in charge of the current activity offer you and your brother safe conduct out of the country if you resign. Had you heard this?

DIEM: No. (And then after a pause) You have my telephone number.

LODGE: Yes. If I can do anything for your physical safety, please call me.

DIEM: I am trying to re-establish order.

59. THE "OTHER" SIDE

The argument over whether North Vietnam "invaded" the South will always be difficult to resolve. These excerpts from an article in an internal Lao Dong (Vietminh) Party journal dated February 1960 indicate how the struggle looked from the other side. (Source: Gareth Porter, ed., *Vietnam: A History in Documents* [New York, 1981], pp. 197–99.)

HOW MUST WE CONCEIVE THE PATH OF GENERAL UPRISING TO SEIZE POLITICAL POWER?

The path of general uprising to seize political power is the path of long-term political struggle combined with armed struggle. Because purely political struggle or purely armed struggle are equally incapable of achieving the objective and line of general uprising to seize political power. Therefore political struggle must be combined with armed struggle. Political struggle and armed struggle must advance side by side. But political struggle must still be fundamental and primary. Armed struggle is aimed at serving the political struggle, at guiding the political struggle movement of the masses forward, helping the struggle movement of the workers and the poor strata in the cities, and the struggle movement of the peasants and other strata and classes. At the same time, it aims chiefly at building the political forces of the working class peasants and poor urban strata to become political forces making the enemy weaken every day and making him suffer defeats and becoming decisive political forces during the general uprising to seize political power.

During the process of preparing to advance according to the objective and line of general uprising to seize political power, what possibilities could develop which we must see in order to know how to use them and to guard against them?

The process of advancing to achieve the objective and line of general uprising to seize political power is a process taking political struggle as primary, and is a process of political, economic, and cultural struggle combined with armed struggle. So the political forces and power of the Party and the masses will rise and the power of the enemy will diminish with each day. In that process, the situation becomes complex, and two possibilities may develop as follows:

First: a peaceful possibility could develop. Although this possibility is small, our party does not reject it but must know how to use it. The strength of the struggle of the people could force U.S.-Diem into circumstances in which they are forced to carry out a number of conditions in our government's diplomatic note, acquiescing in economic, cultural, and postal exchanges and travel, etc. We must know how to use that possibility, and must not cause the masses to stray from the objective and line of the general uprising to seize political power.

Second: the possibility of long-term armed struggle could also develop if our leadership and guidance leans in the direction of arms and defending a base area but not stretching out, not paying attention to helping the political struggle movement in the cities and the countryside rise and not building the political forces of the workers, poor urban strata, peasants and other classes. In those circumstances, we cannot have a strong political force in order to make the enemy weak and make him suffer defeats and cannot be determined to seize political power when there is an opportune moment for the general uprising.

But on the other hand, the possibility of long-term armed struggle could develop due to the bellicose, insane nature of American imperialism. If it were to jump in and intervene directly with military force, the situation would finally become a long-term struggle between our people and imperialism. But the final victory would be ours. However, we must also assess correctly the possibility of intervention by the U.S. imperialists, which is very limited at present.

We must see all the above mentioned possibilities, in order to conduct the revolutionary struggle correctly toward the objective and line we have fixed, in order to use to the correct degree the possibility of peace and also in order to vigilantly prepare to take the initiative and deal with the enemy.

The situation in the world and in the country changes daily to the advantage of the revolution and unfavorably for the enemy. There are many opportunities, as well as many difficulties. But under the leadership of the party, we must be more determined, overcome difficulties, correct weaknesses and mistakes and develop strong points to make every effort to correctly execute the direction, line and policy of the party. In this way we will definitely change the situation for the better, obstruct and push the enemy's schemes back step by step, and advance to overturning the entire U.S.-Diem scheme and structure in order to complete the revolutionary task before us.

HOW MUST WE CONCEIVE OF THE ARMED STRUGGLE?

The concept of armed struggle at present is in accordance with the line of general uprising to seize political power and not armed struggle as during the period of resistance war in which we took the countryside to surround the cities and finally liberated cities. Armed struggle at the present time is not guerrilla war, nor is it protracted interzonal warfare, fighting for a liberated area and to establish a government as during the resistance period.

Armed struggle at the present time means the whole people armed for self-defense and propaganda. If we wish to achieve the objective of the whole people armed and propagandizing, we must rely on the political forces of the masses, rely on the organized masses and on that basis arm the masses, with the main factor being arms for the people. The people must get their own arms, in order to defend themselves, oppose and annihilate puppet personnel, militia, security agents, spies, and cruel and stubborn landlords in order to protect their rights and their homes, preserve the country and keep their own land. They must not passively sit and wait but must stand up and liberate themselves. But on the other hand, the people must also have armed self-defense units in order to join with the people and help them destroy the stubborn and cruel group within the government and army of U.S.-Diem and, with the forces of the entire people, make the U.S.-Diem army disintegrate in terms of morale and organization.

The task and requirement of armed self-defense activity is to serve the interests of the political struggle. But on the other hand, the political struggle also has the significance and objective of guarding and pushing forward the armed struggle. But the main task and requirement of the armed struggle is to serve the political struggle, to build, assemble, organize and develop the political forces of workers, peasants, and other classes. On the other hand, the armed struggle must also aim at destroying security agents, spies, militia, puppet officials, cruel and stubborn landlords, reducing the influence of the enemy, causing the enemy to shrink, clearing out and destroying concentration centers of the enemy, raising high the political influence of the Party and masses, and maintaining the long-term legal position of the masses.

To a certain degree and in a certain number of localities, our armed forces must also oppose the mop-up and terror operations of the enemy and when necessary thrust deep to fight battles and carry out armed propaganda to affect the morale of the enemy in order to advance the political struggle of the masses in the rural area and the cities, creating favorable conditions to promote more strongly the building, assembling and organizing of the political forces of the masses.

The line of operation of the armed forces is that they must assemble and disperse quickly, be lively, secret, quick, hide and not show off, not make the enemy vigilant, take precautions against commandoes, avoid attrition, know how to consolidate and develop the armed forces in accordance with the possibilities of each locality, and avoid negligence.

Speaking generally, only when we have built the political forces and led the political struggle movement of the working class and urban poor and the political struggle movement of the peasants in the rural area with the vast majority of the population can we protect, strengthen, and develop the armed forces and push the armed struggle movement forward. On the contrary, only by pushing armed force and coordinating it correctly can we conduct the political struggle movement forward.

Part IV

THE RISE AND FALL OF AMERICAN POWER

1963–1975

INTRODUCTION
Walter LaFeber

Within hours after taking control of the earth's greatest military and economic power, President Lyndon Johnson uttered his first words on the war: "I am not going to lose Vietnam. I am not going to be the President who saw Southeast Asia go the way China went."[1] With that historical memory (that is, that the United States truly has a manifest destiny in Asia), and political lesson (Americans do not reelect those who lose territory to Communists), Johnson set out with incredible military might and the overwhelming support of Congress and the American people to climax 130 years of U.S. involvement in the distant Pacific region.

He seemed the perfect leader to cap the era. Few could match his ability to sway audiences, especially with off-the-cuff, colorful remarks. In nearly two centuries of American history, none surpassed his ability to lead Congress. As Senate Majority Leader in the 1950s, Johnson had mastered governmental processes and exerted a personal force that was "elemental," in the word of his shrewd, long-time associate George Reedy. "He may have been a son-of-a-bitch but he was a colossal son-of-a-bitch," Reedy recalled.[2] Johnson's "elemental" force controlled another kind of force: a nuclear superiority so great that the Soviets had first tried to blunt and then bowed to it in the 1962 Cuban Missile Crisis, and a powerful conventional force so mobile that by merely picking up the phone, Johnson could station 100,000 of those troops in South Vietnam in a matter of weeks.

This enormous power worked, as always, at the pleasure of history —or, more accurately, the history as understood by Americans and their President. In this sense, Johnson believed he had inherited from Presidents Eisenhower and Kennedy (indeed, from McKinley and Truman), a commitment to prevent Southeast Asia from being closed off. From Truman, whom Johnson idolized, he also inherited the doctrine of Containment. In this case, Chinese communism and its supposed surrogates in North Vietnam had to be contained. Otherwise China would rule supreme in Southeast Asia and U.S. credibility would be ruined worldwide. Few Americans questioned this view of Containment in 1965 or later.[3] If Chinese power was not contained, the theory continued, non-Communist areas would fall like dominoes. The domino theory made little distinction between Asian nations, their histories, or their nationalisms. In the words of one U.S. official of the mid-1960s, this theory perhaps "resulted from a subconscious sense that, since 'all Asians look alike,' all Asian nations will act alike."[4] The domino theory rested on a view of history that was totally ahistorical, but Lyndon Johnson never questioned it.

He did not do so because to him history was to be manipulated, not studied. As Reedy observed, "His whole life was lived in the present and he was tenacious in his conviction that history always conformed to current necessities." Johnson's political needs dictated his view of historical reality.[5] He interpreted Vietnam within two historical contexts. The first was the 1930s, the years when as a young congressman he used the New Deal to help the poor of Texas, but also watched European powers "appease" Hitler's territorial demands at the 1938 Munich conference. Johnson believed ever after that the New Deal could work anywhere, but only if appeasement was tolerated nowhere.

His determination to stop disorder also arose out of a second, more general, historical framework: his view of the American frontier and himself as an actor in that ongoing drama. Asia, he declared in 1967, was "the outer frontier of disorder." It had to be civilized as the pioneers had civilized his home region of Texas: with "a rifle in one hand and an axe in the other." One of his close friends, Congressman Wright Patman of Texas, called Johnson "the last Frontiersman." Acting the cowboy in the late twentieth century could create problems. Ronnie Dugger, a distinguished Texas journalist who knew Johnson, observed that "the one great trouble with a foreign policy for pioneers is that you need savages for it. For Communists the savages may be capitalists; for Americans, Communists."[6] There was also another problem with Johnson's approach. He attempted to bring order to Vietnam not with sailing ships and Gatling guns, but with B-52 bombers that carpet-bombed miles of territory in an instant, defoliants that destroyed jungles and humans alike, and ground firepower unequaled

216

in the history of warfare. In 1907 the great historian Henry Adams watched another "cowboy in the White House," Theodore Roosevelt, and quietly warned that it is a dangerous thing to put unlimited power in the hands of limited minds.[7] Vietnam became a test of Adams's insight.

Johnson focused this unparalleled power on a situation that, as his Secretary of Defense Robert McNamara told him in early 1964, was disintegrating rapidly in the wake of Diem's assassination. (Doc. 60.) By late summer both civilian and military advisers believed that only a full-scale conventional bombing campaign could save a South Vietnamese government that displayed little effectiveness and less stability. Few questioned whether such a bombing attack could work in a bitter civil war that had lasted for decades. When one lower-level official suggested to his superior that "in some ways, of course, it *is* a civil war," an Assistant Secretary of State angrily retorted, "Don't play word games with me!"[8] It was more Johnson's consuming desire to win a landslide victory in the 1964 election than a realistic view of Vietnam's history that prevented him from triggering a major escalation during midyear.

He was opposed in the race by the Republican senator from Arizona, Barry Goldwater. The Republican nominee so vigorously demanded applying military force (he even mentioned how satisfying it would be to lob a nuclear-tipped missile "down into the gent's room in the Kremlin,"[9]) that Americans turned away from him in droves. Johnson gathered up these voters by keeping his voice low: "Sometimes our folks get a little impatient. Sometimes they rattle their rockets some. . . . But we are not about to send American boys nine or ten thousand miles away from home to do what Asian boys ought to be doing for themselves."[10] The President, however, had it both ways. Promising no U.S. troop involvement, he seized upon two incidents— North Vietnamese torpedo boats supposedly attacking U.S. warships in the Gulf of Tonkin—that allowed him to obtain congressional approval for escalating the war. (Doc. 61.) Later investigations revealed that the alleged second attack that led Johnson to submit his Tonkin Gulf Resolution to Congress probably never occurred. It also turned out, contrary to his assertions that the attacks were "unprovoked," that U.S. warships were actually monitoring Communist positions while South Vietnam commandos carried out raids in North Vietnam.[11] The revelations appeared several years later, too late to save either Goldwater (who went down to a landslide defeat), Congress's reputation as an easy mark for Presidents who justified any foreign policy with "anticommunism," or, finally, Lyndon Johnson himself.

By the autumn of 1964 the President actively considered escalating the U.S. involvement. Not any limit of American power but the weakness of the South Vietnam Government and the fear of possible Chinese intervention prevented escalation at that time. (Doc. 62.) In February 1965, however, Johnson believed he had no alternative. He launched Operation Rolling Thunder, a massive bombing of North Vietnam. The President's motives were complex. He had concluded that only a greater application of U.S. power could save the shattered South Vietnam regime. But at home he wanted to be the President who, through his so-called Great Society programs, fulfilled the New Deal's promises to the minorities, poor, elderly, and ill in America. Johnson believed his programs stood little chance of passing Congress and taking effect if he lost South Vietnam to Communists. The Goldwater right wing would destroy his administration, he feared, as the right wing had destroyed Truman after China fell to communism and the Korean War stalemated. Johnson's Vietnam and Great Society plans became linked, first for mutual protection, then—by 1967—as a sharklike struggle in which each tried to survive by killing the other.

In early 1965 another danger also appeared. A year earlier the United States had helped install General Nguyen Khanh in power. But Khanh had proved ineffective militarily and politically in the eyes of Washington officials, and they now moved to oust him. Khanh struck back by obtaining support from powerful Buddhist leaders and then making contact with the National Liberation Front (the South Vietnamese Communists) for the purpose of finding a neutral solution. That solution would have required a U.S. withdrawal from Vietnam. Johnson countered Khanh's plans by launching the bombing raids, then claiming they were in retaliation for Communist attacks on U.S. quarters at Pleiku that had killed 7 and wounded 109 Americans. But as Johnson's National Security Adviser, McGeorge Bundy, observed, "Pleikus are like streetcars—such an opportunity for retaliation arose regularly."[12] The President seized this "streetcar" in the hope the bombing would strengthen the Saigon regime's will to continue fighting, stop South Vietnamese neutralization initiatives, and demonstrate his determination to doubters in Congress.

Shortly before the bombing raids began, Khanh's regime fell to a

U.S.-supported coup led by right-wing army officers. Many of those officers were Roman Catholic, a religion that represented only about 10 percent of the population. Most important to the White House, the new government willingly went along with Johnson's plans.[13] Not surprisingly, within two months the situation worsened. The President ordered U.S. Marines to protect the air bases and, when the bombing failed to be effective, gave the troops an actual combat role. By April 1965 he had ordered U.S. forces into battle, but did so secretly so the American people would not think it was a desperate throw of the dice.

Johnson did not believe these momentous steps would win the war, but only prevent him and his South Vietnamese allies from losing it. His advisers assumed, wrongly, that bombing would severely reduce Communist supplies moving into the South and improve Saigon's morale, thus making possible a negotiated settlement on Washington's terms.[14] Johnson thus announced his commitment to "unconditional discussions" in a major speech at Johns Hopkins University in April 1965. (Doc. 63.) The address was largely for American public opinion. U.S. officials privately believed that no discussions (the term "negotiate" was carefully not used) were possible at the time because the Saigon regime was too weak to make deals.[15] The Communists then issued their own program. (Doc. 64.) It little resembled Johnson's.

U.S. officials began to understand they were locked in a battle that, as Secretary of Defense Robert McNamara privately remarked, might require the use of nuclear weapons to prevent a "Red Asia." (Doc. 65.) Faced with that terrible alternative, Johnson followed the logic of the policy he had accepted in late 1963: he began a massive buildup of U.S. ground forces. This decision in July 1965 occurred only after intense discussion. (Doc. 66.) Johnson understood, as he put it, he was jumping "off the diving board." He could believe, however, that he was aiming for the middle of the pool—neither "turning tail and running," nor fighting a fully declared, perhaps nuclear, war that would bring China and maybe even the Soviet Union into the conflict. The Great Society could also be shielded from political attack. The United States, Johnson assumed in the language of the day, was so rich that it could produce "both guns and butter."[16]

The President, indeed most Americans, also assumed U.S. power to be so great that North Vietnam had to reach an early breaking point and settle on Johnson's terms. At a Washington dinner party a guest suggested to an administration official that it might take as long to rid

Vietnam of Communists as the decade it took the British to banish them in Malaya. The official arched an eyebrow and retorted, "We are *not* the British."[17] He meant that Americans did not bear the horrible onus of being colonialists in Asia, and their military power was infinitely greater than the British. The colonial issue, however, blurred as the number of U.S. troops reached the 200,000 level and Americans virtually took over the responsibility for running South Vietnam. This policy now less resembled the traditional U.S. open-door approach (see Part I) than British rule in India. Unlike the British in the nineteenth century, however, the United States was immersed in a mass, anti-foreign revolution. No matter how large the scale of the U.S. buildup, it could not solve the complex political deterioration in the South. Indeed, the buildup actually worsened the deterioration, for it gave nationalists in North and South Vietnam a handy foreign target. It weakened the power of South Vietnamese officials and, in the eyes of many nationalists, smeared them for working with the foreigners. In a classic form of political jujitsu, the Communists could use the buildup of U.S. strength to defeat the American effort.

The Communists also matched Johnson's buildup on the ground. U.S. ground forces grew from 14,000 in 1963 to 267,000 in 1966. Regular Vietcong (often referred to as the National Liberation Front) strength grew during those years from 25,000 to 101,000, with another 170,000 irregulars in reserve by 1966. North Vietnam regular army units grew in the South from zero in 1963 to 30,000 by 1966. The U.S. bombing had only accelerated the infiltration of Communist troops.

Politically and militarily Johnson could not solve the revolution. In December 1965 he announced with fanfare that he was dispatching diplomats to world capitals in a search for peace. This "flying circus," as it was soon labeled, meant little. The two opponents disagreed too fundamentally and the U.S. negotiating position was too weak to allow meaningful talks.[18] As American resources disappeared into an apparently bottomless pit, debate sharpened in the United States. Senator J. William Fulbright (Dem.-Ark.), a longtime advocate of a strong presidency, turned against his former close friend in the White House. Fulbright concluded that Johnson had deliberately misled Congress on several foreign policy issues, especially Vietnam. In early 1966 the senator summoned Secretary of State Dean Rusk before the Foreign Relations Committee. Americans now heard a full debate by Washington officials. (Doc. 67.) It occurred as South Vietnamese troops deserted in greater numbers.[19]

America's European allies also quietly withdrew, especially as Johnson's fixation on China tightened. Quoting Theodore Roosevelt that this was to be the "Pacific era," the President warned that a "hostile China must be discouraged from aggression."[20] That remark made at least three questionable assumptions: that China, whom the North Vietnamese had fought and feared for a thousand years, controlled the Vietnamese Communists; that China, not mass revolution, was thwarting U.S. efforts; and that China, bitterly divided internally by its own problems, wanted to fight the United States. The Peking government did provide large supplies of war matériel to North Vietnam. But the Chinese carefully explained in 1967 that they would intervene in Vietnam with combat troops only if Americans invaded North Vietnam and approached "our borders," or if there was a highly unlikely "sellout" peace by Ho Chi Minh.[21] A great irony appeared: Johnson focused on the Chinese threat, but in 1967 also moved toward lessening tensions with the Soviet Union. It was the Russians, however, who supplied increasingly larger amounts of war matériel to North Vietnam than did the Chinese.[22]

The battle at home went no better and had as much irony. As war costs spiraled upward, Johnson frantically pushed for completion of his Great Society programs. "This may be the last chance we have to get some of these things done," he prophetically told an aide in 1966.[23] At the same time, he had to admit publicly, "Because of Vietnam we cannot do all that we should, or all that we would like to do." As battle costs soared, he cut nearly every budget item but defense.[24] Having gone into Vietnam partly to save the Great Society program, Johnson now sacrificed the program to Vietnam. But the irony did not stop there. Key sections of the program that were passed to help blacks and other minorities in 1965–66 failed to prevent riots that killed thirty-four blacks in Watts (a suburb of Los Angeles) and spread to other ghettos. By 1967 antiwar protests that disrupted college campuses were accompanied by race riots in Tampa, Cincinnati, Atlanta, and then in Detroit, where forty-three people died and parts of the city were destroyed. Devastation in American urban areas mirrored on a much smaller scale the destruction of Vietnamese towns. Johnson wanted to end "that bitch of a war" so he could court "the woman I really loved"—the Great Society.[25] In the end, he lost both.

Meanwhile the world's greatest economy stumbled. It was being victimized by war costs that produced a startling inflation rate of nearly 5 percent and large budget deficits. The value of the dollar, the currency that had long undergirded world trade, began to crumble under the burden of war. In 1966 the New York Stock Exchange panicked when it appeared that an economy increasingly dependent on military contracts might be damaged by possible peace in Vietnam.[26] The peace scare soon passed, however. As an exchange between Johnson and Ho Chi Minh indicated in early 1967, an end to the war was not in sight. (Doc. 68.)

A lack of U.S. power did not cause these dilemmas. Johnson increased his own authority until top aides could taunt Congress with the "imperial presidency." (Doc. 69.) The President could also call upon an ever-larger storehouse of military might. But such power was not ending the conflict on Johnson's terms. As an increasingly discouraged McNamara secretly told a Senate committee, "We could take out all their power systems, all of their oil, all of their harbors, destroy their dams," and the North Vietnamese could still send in "men and equipment necessary to support some level of operations in the South."[27] By late 1967, however, Johnson believed the right moment might have arrived to make a deal. The U.S. presidential campaign of 1968 appeared on the horizon. The massive U.S. effort had come closer to stabilizing the military situation than during the previous two years. Something had to be done, moreover, to stop what some were calling the "Vietnamization" of American cities and campuses.

In September 1967 Johnson proposed in San Antonio, Texas, that he would halt the bombing if Ho Chi Minh would negotiate and not attempt to build up militarily in South Vietnam during the halt. The speech was also notable for the absence of references to China. (Doc. 70.) The Administration was finally glimpsing Asian realities: the growing hatred between China and Russia, growing mistrust between China and North Vietnam, and growing Vietnamese dependence on Russia as U.S. military efforts escalated. These realities were unfortunately glimpsed at least several years too late. The great difference—whether South Vietnam was to be in the U.S. camp or part of a unified, Communist Vietnam—continued to divide Johnson and Ho. But U.S. military policies were reported (erroneously as it turned out) to be more successful, and a happy Administration passed all the good news on to the American people.

In this context occurred the turning point of the United States involvement. On January 31, 1968, the Communists launched an offensive during the Tet (New Year's) holiday. For a remarkable moment, Ho's forces actually controlled parts of Saigon. They captured provincial capitals as well as the ancient capital of Hue. Only intense U.S. bombing of those cities and bloody battles waged by South Vietnamese and American troops finally repulsed the Communists. (It was during these terrible days that U.S. officials offered a famous explanation of how they were having to fight the war: "We had to destroy the village to save it.") Ho's forces lost 30,000 to 40,000 men. Many Communist cadres were wiped out. The South Vietnamese, moreover, had refused to join in an uprising against the Saigon Government.

General William Westmoreland, commander of U.S. forces in Vietnam, declared a triumph, but then secretly asked Johnson for 206,000 more troops to win a final victory. The President was stunned. Publicly he said the Tet offensive had been "anticipated . . . and met," but privately he and his advisers were shocked. They had believed Westmoreland's upbeat speeches of late 1967 and discounted McNamara's warning that, despite U.S. efforts, Ho's ability to fight on had not been weakened. Johnson's top advisers now wondered whether accomplishing their goals required 500,000 to one million additional Americans in Vietnam. McNamara agreed that such numbers at least focused on the price that might have to be paid. He had little use for Westmoreland's recommendation, for 206,000 men "is neither enough to do the job, nor an indication that our role must change." Johnson's former NSC adviser, McGeorge Bundy, agreed: "We must also prepare for the worst. [South Vietnam] is very weak."[28]

Many Americans shared the shock felt in Washington. The general feeling was well expressed by Benjamin Read, a top aide to Rusk. "The fact that screamed at you . . ." Read later observed, "was [the Communists'] ability to just romp at will over that much of the landscape of that miserable country." In such a context, Westmoreland's request for 206,000 more Americans made Vietnam look "like an endless engagement and an endless rathole."[29]

In the years since the Tet disaster, U.S. officials and many of their supporters have blamed the American media, especially television, for misrepresenting the results of the offensive and thus undermining Johnson's effort in Vietnam.[30] As the McNamara, Bundy, and Read quotes indicate, however, the media did not shape the pessimism of Johnson's top aides. Blaming television neglects more fundamental realities both in Washington and Vietnam. American public opinion appears to have had little if any effect on Johnson's decision to change course sharply after the Tet offensive. That decision was shaped by other forces.[31] His own top military officers warned him that Tet had been "a very near thing," and that the war could become much more costly than it had been before Tet. (Doc. 71.) The South Vietnamese people doubted now that Americans could protect them, while their government remained unsteady and sharply divided between the factions of President Nguyen Van Thieu and Vice-President Nguyen Cao Ky.

Johnson heard some of the most surprising news from the home front. McNamara, about to leave the Defense Department, warned the President that U.S. forces had to be kept at home "to meet the possibility of widespread civil disorder in the United States in the months ahead."[32] Inflation, race riots, antiwar protests threatened to rip apart the society. McNamara's successor, Clark Clifford (an influential Washington lawyer whose deep involvement in White House politics went back to the 1940s), then discovered that for all their outward optimism, the military chiefs had no plan to win the war in Vietnam. The chiefs complained bitterly about civilian restraints not allowing them to fight the war as they wished, but Clifford learned that—restraints or no restraints—the Pentagon had no tenable ideas about gaining victory, at least short of destroying most of the country that Johnson had promised to save.[33] Clifford also knew firsthand that the war was devastating the American economy and business community,[34] as well as the crucial alliance system with Western Europe and Japan. His view was shared by a group of so-called Wisemen whom Johnson had begun to consult in 1967. Powerful members of the corporate community, former top government officials, and men who had been instrumental in waging the Cold War since the 1940s, they had wanted no retreat from Vietnam just six months earlier. In March 1968, however, they warned Johnson that an independent South Vietnam could not be built, at least not without unacceptable costs. (Doc. 72.)

On March 31, 1968, the President told a nationwide television audience that he was stopping the bombing of North Vietnam in the hope that this gesture would lead Ho to begin negotiations. To show his earnestness, Johnson dramatically announced he would not run for a second term so that he could instead concentrate on bringing peace to Southeast Asia. (Doc. 73.) Preliminary talks did begin, but ground fighting continued. Johnson even secretly raised the level of U.S. troops from 486,000 to 535,000 during the summer. North Vietnam matched the buildup until by early 1969, one year after their terrible losses of Tet, the Communists had their party structure and/or important influence in 80 percent of South Vietnam's hamlets, and among 65 percent of the total population.[35] Neither side had given up hope of winning South Vietnam.

Negotiations quickly deadlocked on three key issues that killed hopes for peace during the next four years: the U.S. insistence that Ho withdraw all his troops from South Vietnam; Ho's insistence that U.S. forces fully withdraw before he would agree to a cease-fire; and the Thieu-Ky regime's insistence that it not have to enter into any governing coalition with the more powerful Communists. The peace talks appeared as fruitless as the battlefield action. The military draft of young Americans continued. Then in late spring 1968 Martin Luther King and Robert Kennedy were murdered—King as he led blacks and whites alike toward change through nonviolence, Kennedy as he seemed about to win the Democratic presidential nomination on an antiwar platform. Riots erupted throughout the nation. Among the worse were those in Chicago during the Democrats' presidential nominating convention. (Doc. 74.)

In November, Republican nominee Richard Nixon barely defeated Vice-President Hubert Humphrey by 0.7 percent of the popular vote. Stressing law and order in American streets, Nixon refused to discuss Vietnam. He would only say he had a "plan" for handling the war. Nixon privately admitted, however, "I've come to the conclusion that there's no way to win the war. But we can't say that, of course."[36] The pessimism of the new President and his National Security Adviser, Henry Kissinger, deepened when they surveyed the facts and possible policy alternatives in early 1969. One survey revealed that knowledgeable State Department officials estimated it could take thirteen more years to control the Communists in South Vietnam. The war was costing Americans $30 billion a year and two hundred dead each week by this time.[37]

Given such a sad assessment, Nixon could have begun rapid withdrawal of those forces. He instead decided on a two-prong policy that aimed at concluding the war on his terms. First, the President tried to work through Russia and China in the hope that the two Communist giants, who now hated and feared each other, could somehow force

North Vietnam to make peace. This policy assumed, wrongly as it turned out, that Moscow and Peking could pressure Hanoi to follow their wishes. Second, Nixon attempted to salvage South Vietnam and —of much greater importance to him and Kissinger—what they believed to be the credibility of U.S. global commitments, by slowly withdrawing Americans while beefing up South Vietnam's army to do the fighting. In addition, Nixon decided to rely on massive air strikes, the kind that in three years would give him the name of "the mad bomber." (Nixon actually did not mind the label because he believed the Communists would be more careful if they thought he was indeed slightly unbalanced.) The President's overall policy became known as "Vietnamization."[38]

Vietnamization required more time. As it turned out, the policy required four years and 26,000 more American lives, as well as hundreds of thousands of Vietnamese casualties, before the last U.S. combat troops left in 1973. Nixon believed he could buy time. Despite massive antiwar protests, polls showed that nationwide some 58 percent of those surveyed approved his policies. Public opinion was not forcing the President's hand.[39] His appeal to the "great silent majority of Americans" won him time, even as he laid out a Nixon Doctrine that explained how the United States would remain deeply involved in Asian affairs. (Doc. 75.) This new version of Vietnamization, however, seemed to resemble the old one of 1949–50 when it had been intended only to legitimize foreign power in the region. (See Part II.)

The President withdrew the first contingent of U.S. troops during 1969. He thus set in motion an irreversible policy. South Vietnamese forces could now be protected only by their own efforts or U.S. bombing. During that year Nixon followed this logic by ordering repeated bombing raids on Cambodia, which Communist troops used for supplies and passage into South Vietnam. The President wanted the raids to be kept secret (he was, after all, devastating parts of a neutral country friendly to the United States). The Pentagon even kept two sets of records so that if the press or Congress became too curious, they could be satisfied with lies supported by hollow figures. When news of the raids did leak in May 1969, Nixon created a "plumbers' unit" to fix the leaks and spy on the Administration's supposed enemies. His decision led directly to the break-in of Democrat Party headquarters in 1972 at the Watergate Hotel in Washington, and, when Nixon tried to cover up that crime, his resignation in 1974. Vietnamization, much like Dr.

Frankenstein's monster, turned on its creator. Nixon could not keep the effects of the war limited to Southeast Asia.[40]

That lesson appeared tragically in April–May 1970. Claiming that North Vietnamese and Vietcong bases in Cambodia could be destroyed, the President launched a major assault into South Vietnam's neighbor. His reasoning came under immediate fire from U.S. experts on Southeast Asia who used history as a weapon to attack the President's entire Southeast Asian policy. (Doc. 76.) The operation failed either to capture the Communists' headquarters or to stop their use of Cambodian bases. But the effects rippled to American campuses. Four students were killed by Ohio National Guardsmen during antiwar protests at Kent State University. In a special report to Nixon, two distinguished educators emphasized that the disturbances signaled a deep national, not merely college, crisis. (Doc. 77.) A new protest group, Vietnam veterans, began to attack U.S. policy at home as well as in Asia, and did so with a passion and insight unsurpassed by other antiwar voices. (Doc. 78.) These veterans illustrated how the costs of the war went far beyond casualty figures. Some of the costs even escaped accurate calculation. (Doc. 79.) Nixon himself nearly lost control during one night of the Cambodian–Kent State crisis. He made forty-nine phone calls after 10:30 P.M., then, in early morning light, drove to the Lincoln Memorial to talk with protesting students. Kissinger feared the President was "on the edge of a nervous breakdown."[41]

The full impact of the war, however, was only beginning to be felt. For the first time Congress passed laws tying the President's hands in Asia. He could not again send troops into Cambodia. In 1971 Nixon nevertheless tried to save his Vietnamization policy by attacking Communist bases and trails in neighboring Laos with South Vietnamese troops backed by U.S. artillery and air power. The assault again failed to destroy the camps. The South's troops performed so poorly that Vietnamization appeared doomed. Nixon had brought nearly 300,000 U.S. men home and, by 1971, silenced part of the antiwar movement by halting the draft. But he left behind a crippled ally whose prices skyrocketed because of uncontrollable inflation, whose population suffered spreading hunger, whose economy crumbled under deficits and corruption.[42] All that remained for Nixon to do was to bomb massively, as he had hoped to do in 1969.

First, however, he and Kissinger tried to protect Vietnamization by making deals with the North's two giant allies. The President extended better relations and valued U.S. goods to the Soviets, while offering a reversal of twenty-two years of enmity and a new relationship to China if the two nations would help, as Kissinger phrased it, "in settling the war."[43] A strange reversal had taken place: Eisenhower, Kennedy, and Johnson had argued that the defeat of North Vietnam was necessary to contain China and Russia. Now Nixon and Kissinger argued that the friendship of China and Russia was necessary to contain North Vietnam. The second approach, however, worked no better than the first. Neither Peking nor Moscow could force Hanoi to bend to U.S. wishes, even if the two giants wished to do so. Kissinger discovered North Vietnamese stubbornness firsthand when he conducted a series of secret talks with Hanoi's diplomats in 1970–71 and made little progress.

The logjam broke in 1972. In the spring the Communists launched a full-scale conventional assault complete with 120,000 men and Soviet-made tanks. The South Vietnamese and U.S. forces drove back the invasion, inflicting casualties that may have run as high as 100,000. Nixon proceeded to put his 1969 plan into effect. He launched large-scale B-52 attacks on civilian as well as military areas in the North, and even mined Haiphong harbor, despite Russian and other foreign shipping unloading at the docks. He did all this without massive protests in the United States. The Communists had suffered a major military and political defeat. Such a setback again misled, however: the war was one of revolution, not conventional battle (as in Korea or World War II), and in this struggle the Communists continued to display amazing strength. (Doc. 80.)

U.S. leverage was, meanwhile, hardly growing. The presidential election loomed and Nixon needed to show that his Vietnamization plans had produced peace, not merely military stalemate. Kissinger and the North Vietnamese negotiated feverishly during 1972 and finally struck a deal that required a cease-fire, final withdrawal of U.S. troops, the return of all American prisoners of war, and elections administered by a group made up of Communists, the South Vietnam Government, and neutralists.

Kissinger obtained the deal just days before Nixon faced the Democratic (and antiwar) nominee for President, Senator George McGovern of South Dakota. The agreement helped undercut McGovern's campaign. But in late October, Nixon suddenly decided he wanted no agreement. Public opinion polls showed that nearly half those surveyed opposed any U.S. recognition of Communist political power in

South Vietnam, but to obtain his agreement Kissinger had recognized the North Vietnamese Communists' right to stay in the area. The President wanted to appear tough. He was also becoming jealous of Kissinger's growing fame. Nixon passed the word to his negotiator that "it will hurt—not help us—to get the settlement before the election." He also used General Alexander Haig, Kissinger's top aide in the talks, as an agent to undercut Kissinger's attempt to make peace.[44] The critical blow was finally struck by President Thieu of South Vietnam. He flatly refused to accept any deal that left the North's troops in his country. Kissinger was furious with Thieu: "We'll kill the son-of-a-bitch if we have to," he supposedly told his aides late one night.[45] Nixon, however, now had it both ways: a peace to demonstrate the success of his Vietnamization policies, and an ongoing war to show his toughness. McGovern went down to one of the greatest defeats in U.S. political history.

Nixon proceeded to launch another massive bombing attack. His purpose was twofold: to soften up the Communists for new talks, and —perhaps more important—to show Thieu that South Vietnam could accept peace in full confidence that in a crisis the Americans would be fully willing to act, in Nixon's words, like a "mad man." American military officers became deeply concerned at the number of bombers lost during the raids. Some U.S. airmen rebelled against flying the missions. "My conscience told me not to," was the way one pilot explained it. Court-martials were secretly ordered and at least one officer found guilty.[46] Against this background, Kissinger and the North Vietnamese hammered out a final accord in Paris during January 1973.

The agreement included: (1) a cease-fire; (2) U.S. recognition of the "unity" of all Vietnam; (3) withdrawal of U.S. forces and the dismantling of American bases in Indochina; (4) the return of U.S. prisoners and the intention of working out an agreement between the Vietnamese parties to exchange political prisoners; (5) South Vietnam's right to self-determination; (6) Thieu's remaining in power in Saigon until an election could be held by a "National Council" that included representatives of his government, the Communists, and neutralists; (7) a demilitarized zone between North and South that would act as a provisional military demarcation line; and (8) allowing North Vietnamese troops to remain in the South. Thieu now accepted the deal. He had to accept it: Nixon was prepared to desert his regime if he did not. But the American President also offered a carrot. In a secret agreement, he assured

Thieu that "we will respond with full force should the settlement be violated by North Vietnam." (Doc. 81.) He also offered a carrot to the Communists: billions of dollars for economic reconstruction if they followed through on the settlement.

The deal reflected the military and political realities in South Vietnam. The Communists were an accepted force in the country, and they built their strength by moving heavy reinforcements down the Ho Chi Minh Trail into South Vietnam. Nixon could do little in response. In July and August 1973 the U.S. Congress prohibited the use of funds to "support directly or indirectly combat activities in or over Cambodia, Laos, North Vietnam, and South Vietnam." In Kissinger's words, "any American military action anywhere in or around Indochina became illegal."[47] Nor was the President in any position to ignore Congress and carry through his secret deal with Thieu. Investigations of the break-in at the Watergate Hotel complex revealed that Nixon and some of his top aides had tried to cover up the crime. In August 1974 he became the first U.S. President to resign from office.

By that time the South Vietnamese were on their own. To drive home that point, the U.S. Congress, besieged by other crises and a faltering domestic economy, cut back assistance to Thieu's government. (Doc. 82.) The fighting meanwhile escalated. Thieu's forces, fearful of competing politically with the Communists, tried to salvage their position by ignoring the cease-fire and attacking the Communists in order to expand their territorial control. In late 1973 the Communists began retaliating. The 160,000 Communist troops of early 1973 became a 220,000-man force by January 1975 when it launched an offensive that aimed to conquer all of South Vietnam in two years.[48] After initial resistance, Thieu's forces began to disintegrate. Kissinger, now Secretary of State for President Gerald Ford, asked Congress for more aid. Everyone understood this was only a gesture, but it gave Kissinger and Congress an opportunity to reflect on how the United States had ended up in such a dead end. (Doc. 83.) The Communists needed only four months, not two years, before they marched into Saigon. By May 1975, Vietnam was united and Communist. So was Laos. Cambodia fell under the control of the Khmer Rouge, a brutal Communist group that hated the Vietnamese and within three years were driven out of power by an invading Vietnamese force.

So ended the quarter-century-long U.S. war in Southeast Asia. It was the longest war in U.S. history. The conflict cost over 57,000 American men and women, but the price also included beliefs—the very beliefs that Americans had long accepted without question as they grew into the world's leading power. Because of those lives lost, that power wasted, and those beliefs threatened, the debate over the U.S. role in Vietnam will long continue. That debate will revolve around the beliefs—the views of U.S. history and values—that carried Americans into the struggle.

One belief dated to the 1950s and before: only U.S. power could keep Southeast Asia open, free from Chinese control, and safe for allied (especially Japanese) investments and markets. By the 1980s, however, Vietnam itself excluded Chinese power from the area, while the Japanese—who had criticized U.S. policy during the post-1961 years—profited more handsomely from Southeast Asia after the United States departed than while the war went on. A second belief assumed that if Vietnam fell to communism, all of Southeast Asia, and perhaps even Japan, would follow in what Eisenhower had called a "domino" effect. Laos and Cambodia did become Communist, but the United States as well as South Vietnam had made those two small nations part of the war in the post-1961 years. The dominoes could fall in a certain direction, journalist Richard Rovere warned in 1967, *"because we set them up that way."*[49] Other nations that refused to become dominoes (Thailand, Malaysia, and Singapore, not to mention Japan), never wobbled. The domino theory was (and remains) one of the most dangerous of ideas that attract Americans. As experts on Asia tried to tell Johnson in 1965, "A first reality to bear in mind: Despite elements of similarity, no Southeast Asian nation is a replica of any other."[50]

American supporters of the effort in Vietnam also held to a third idea: that if the United States did not respond to the situation, American "credibility" would disappear. Allies would stop trusting U.S. commitments. The Soviets and Chinese would then take advantage of this U.S. loss of will (or what Nixon called the "pitiful, helpless giant") and expand their power indefinitely. A variation of this view was that the Chinese (or Soviets, or North Vietnamese) resembled Hitler's Germany. If the aggressor was "appeased" as Hitler had been in the 1930s, he would only move on insatiably to new conquests.[51] In the Vietnam War, however, U.S. allies questioned Washington's credibility for quite different reasons. As Professor Lawrence Kaplan has phrased it, "The apparent American obsession with the defense of South Viet-

231

nam raised doubts [among allies] about the wisdom of American leadership in any part of the world."[52] Henry Kissinger recognized this truth by 1972: "We have fought for four years, have mortgaged our whole foreign policy to the defense of one country."[53]

A fourth idea is especially important because it has become increasingly popular years after the war: the United States lost because it did not use enough power. A variation of this view is that civilian officials never allowed the U.S. military to win the war. Another variation is that the antiwar, pro-peace movement of the 1960s undermined the military effort and prevented a U.S. victory.[54]

It should be pointed out, however, that the United States dropped three times the amount of bombs on these small Southeast Asian countries than it dropped on both Europe and Asia during all of World War II. Two million Vietnamese, Cambodians, and Laotians died in the post-1946 era, and twice that number were wounded. The United States, according to recently released documents, did not escalate rapidly in 1964-65 because Johnson feared the weak South Vietnamese Government would collapse and China might retaliate. The supposed limits of U.S. military power and the actions of antiwar protesters did not restrain him. By 1968-69 the United States had committed over a half-million men who controlled the most advanced technology for killing in a conventional war that science had ever devised. As journalist Michael Herr observed, "There was such a dense concentration of American energy there, American and essentially adolescent, if that energy could have channeled into anything more than noise, waste and pain, it would have lighted up Indochina for a thousand years."[55]

Those who believe that greater force should have been applied might recognize that such an application would have required either invading North Vietnam (thus running the risk of Chinese response) or —more likely—that the United States would have had to send in a million or more men, employ nuclear weapons, and remove all bombing restrictions. McNamara saw those possibilities as early as 1965. The United States would have literally had to destroy Vietnam to save it. Fortunately no U.S. policy-maker in the 1960s and 1970s was that irrational. Officials instead hoped to raise force levels until they found a point at which the North Vietnamese would "break" and agree to negotiate on U.S. terms. That point could never be found. The Vietnamese were willing to take one of the highest casualty rates in proportion to population in history—indeed, at twice the rate of the supposedly suicidal Japanese forces of World War II. By 1971, Dean Rusk admitted he had "underestimated the resistance and determination of the North Vietnamese." They had taken the killing of "almost the equivalent of—what? Ten million Americans? And they continue to come."[56]

The United States never lost a major battle against North Vietnamese troops, but it lost the war because the struggle was a revolution, not just a war. It involved political ideals for which Vietnamese Communists were willing to die in large numbers: the ideals of national unity and independence from foreign domination. The Communists constructed a totalitarian regime that efficiently used those ideals as the dynamic to drive out the French, then the Americans. The United States had no comparable ideals to appeal to the mass of Vietnamese. The more U.S. officials tried to impose their values, the more they Americanized the war, thus giving the Communists "foreign devils" to target. As early as 1966, Senator Fulbright worried over the U.S. ability "to go into a small, alien, undeveloped Asian nation and create stability where there is chaos, the will to fight where there is defeatism, democracy where there is no tradition of it, and honest government where corruption is almost a way of life."[57]

The United States tried to impose its values on Vietnam in such a way that it succeeded only in corrupting those values at home. The Nixon years, the "imperial presidency," the Watergate scandal that shocked the political and economic system, were all products of Vietnam. So was the inflation that tore apart the U.S. economy, destroyed much of the dollar's value by 1971, and helped bring on the quadrupling of gasoline prices in 1973–74 as oil producers tried to maintain the dollar value of their mineral. Some 200,000 Americans became draft evaders rather than go to Vietnam. The duty of dying in the war, moreover, fell disproportionately on blacks and poor whites.

The U.S. failure in Vietnam had little to do with the use or the lack of American military power. It had much to do with Americans' failure to understand their own history, their own two-century-old revolution, and their own long relationship with Asia. (Doc. 84.)

60. JOHNSON'S DILEMMA IN EARLY 1964

President Lyndon Johnson inherited a bleak situation in Vietnam. Secretary of Defense Robert McNamara described the problems and offered suggestions for solutions in March 1964, including the possibility of striking North Vietnam. The report arrived on Johnson's desk as the 1964 presidential campaign heated up in the United States. (Source: Memorandum entitled "South Vietnam," from McNamara to Johnson, March 16, 1964, reprinted in the New York *Times* Edition, Neil Sheehan, et al., eds., *The Pentagon Papers* [New York, 1971], pp. 277–80.)

I. U.S. OBJECTIVES IN SOUTH VIETNAM

We seek an independent non-Communist South Vietnam. We do not require that it serve as a Western base or as a member of a Western Alliance. Vietnam must be free, however, to accept outside assistance as required to maintain its security. This assistance should be able to take the form not only of economic and social pressures but also police and military help to root out and control insurgent elements.

Unless we can achieve this objective in South Vietnam, almost all of Southeast Asia will probably fall under Communist dominance (all of Vietnam, Laos, and Cambodia), accommodate to Communism so as to remove effective U.S. and anti-Communist influence (Burma), or fall under the domination of forces not now explicitly Communist but likely then to become so (Indonesia taking over Malaysia). Thailand might hold for a period with our help, but would be under grave pressure. Even the Philippines would become shaky, and the threat to India to the west, Australia and New Zealand to the south, and Taiwan, Korea, and Japan to the north and east would be greatly increased.

All these consequences would probably have been true even if the U.S. had not since 1954, and especially since 1961, become so heavily engaged in South Vietnam. However, that fact accentuates the impact of a Communist South Vietnam not only in Asia, but in the rest of the world, where the South Vietnam conflict is regarded as a test case of U.S. capacity to help a nation meet a Communist "war of liberation."

Thus, purely in terms of foreign policy, the stakes are high. They are increased by domestic factors.

II. PRESENT U.S. POLICY IN SOUTH VIETNAM

We are now trying to help South Vietnam defeat the Viet Cong, supported from the North, by means short of the unqualified use of U.S. combat forces. We are not acting against North Vietnam except by a very modest "covert" program operated by South Vietnamese (and a few Chinese Nationalists)—a program so limited that it is unlikely to have any significant effect. In Laos, we are still working largely within the framework of the 1962 Geneva Accords. In Cambodia we are still seeking to keep Sihanouk from abandoning whatever neutrality he may still have and fulfilling his threat of reaching an accommodation with Hanoi and Peking. As a consequence of these policies, we and the GVN have had to condone the extensive use of Cambodian and Laotian territory by the Viet Cong, both as a sanctuary and as infiltration routes.

III. THE PRESENT SITUATION IN SOUTH VIETNAM

The key elements in the present situation are as follows:

A. The military tools and concepts of the GVN-US efforts are generally sound and adequate. Substantially more can be done in the effective employment of military forces and in the economic and civic action areas. These improvements may require some selective increases in the U.S. presence, but it does not appear likely that major equipment replacement and additions in U.S. personnel are indicated under current policy.

B. The U.S. policy of reducing existing personnel where South Vietnamese are in a position to assume the functions is still sound. Its application will not lead to any major reductions in the near future, but adherence to this policy as such has a sound effect in portraying to the U.S. and the world that we continue to regard the war as a conflict the South Vietnamese must win and take ultimate responsibility for. Substantial reductions in the numbers of U.S. military training personnel should be possible before the end of 1965. However, the U.S. should continue to reiterate that it will provide all the assistance and advice required to do the job regardless of how long it takes.

C. The situation has unquestionably been growing worse, at least since September:

1. In terms of government control of the countryside, about 40% of the territory is under Viet Cong control or predominant influence. . . .

2. Large groups of the population are now showing signs of apathy and

235

indifference, and there are some signs of frustration within the U.S. contingent. . . .

a. The ARVN and paramilitary desertion rates, and particularly the latter, are high and increasing.

b. Draft-dodging is high while the Viet Cong are recruiting energetically and effectively.

c. The morale of the hamlet militia and of the Self Defense Corps, on which the security of the hamlets depends, is poor and failing.

3. In the last 90 days the weakening of the government's position has been particularly noticeable. . . .

4. The political control structure extending from Saigon down into the hamlets disappeared following the November coup. . . .

5. North Vietnamese support, always significant, has been increasing. . . .

D. The greatest weakness in the present situation is the uncertain viability of the Khanh government. . . .

61. THE TONKIN GULF DEBATE AND RESOLUTION

During the first four days of August 1964, the Johnson administration claimed that U.S. warships were twice attacked by North Vietnamese torpedo boats in international waters (the Gulf of Tonkin, off North Vietnam). Johnson ordered immediate retaliatory air raids on North Vietnam, then asked the U.S. Congress for the powers embodied in the following resolution. Congress overwhelmingly passed the resolution. Senator J. William Fulbright (Dem.-Ark.), later a leading antiwar voice, helped his close friend, the President, pass the resolution over a few scattered, but ominous, questions. Evidence later revealed that the Administration had not told the full truth about the attacks, but Johnson nevertheless received a virtual blank check in waging the war. (Source, *Congressional Record,* August 5–7, 1964, pp. 18132–33, 18406–7, 18458–59, 18470–71.)

THE RESOLUTION: Whereas naval units of the Communist regime in Vietnam, in violation of the principles of the Charter of the United Nations and of international law, have deliberately and repeatedly attacked

United States naval vessels lawfully present in international waters, and have thereby created a serious threat to international peace;

Whereas these attacks are part of a deliberate and systematic campaign of aggression that the Communist regime in North Vietnam has been waging against its neighbors and the nations joined with them in the collective defense of their freedom;

Whereas the United States is assisting the peoples of southeast Asia to protect their freedom and has no territorial, military or political ambitions in that area, but desires only that these peoples should be left in peace to work out their own destinies in their own way: now, therefore, be it

Resolved by the Senate and House of Representatives of the United States of America in Congress assembled, That the Congress approves and supports the determination of the President, as Commander in Chief, to take all necessary measures to repel any armed attack against the forces of the United States and to prevent further aggression.

Sec. 2. The United States regards as vital to its national interest and to world peace the maintenance of international peace and security in southeast Asia. Consonant with the Constitution and the Charter of the United Nations and in accordance with its obligations under the Southeast Asia Collective Defense Treaty, the United States is, therefore, prepared, as the President determines, to take all necessary steps, including the use of armed force, to assist any member or protocol state of the Southeast Asia Collective Defense Treaty requesting assistance in defense of its freedom.

Sec. 3. This resolution shall expire when the President shall determine that the peace and security of the area is reasonably assured by international conditions created by action of the United Nations or otherwise, except that it may be terminated earlier by concurrent resolution of the Congress.

— — — — — — — — — — — — — — — — —

AUG. 6, 1964. [Debate in the U.S. Senate]

MR. NELSON [Gaylord Nelson, Dem.-Wisc.] . . . Am I to understand that it is the sense of Congress that we are saying to the executive branch: "If it becomes necessary to prevent further aggression, we agree now, in advance, that you may land as many divisions as deemed necessary, and engage in a direct military assault on North Vietnam if it becomes the judgment of the Executive, the Commander in Chief, that this is the only way to prevent further aggression"?

MR. FULBRIGHT [J. William Fulbright, Dem.-Ark.]. As I stated, section 1 is intended to deal primarily with aggression against our forces. . . . I

237

believe section 2 deals with the SEATO area, which we are committed to protect under our treaties, particularly when they ask for our assistance. . . .

I do not know what the limits are. I do not think this resolution can be determinative of that fact. I think it would indicate that he [the President] would take reasonable means first to prevent any further aggression, or repel further aggression against our own forces, and that he will live up to our obligations under the SEATO treaty and with regard to the protocol states. I do not know how to answer the Senator's question and give him an absolute assurance that large numbers of troops would not be put ashore. I would deplore it. And I hope the conditions do not justify it now. . . .

AUG. 7, 1964

MR. NELSON. In view of the differing interpretations which have been put upon the joint resolution with respect to what the sense of Congress is, I should like to have this point clarified. I have great confidence in the President. However, my concern is that we in Congress could give the impression to the public that we are prepared at this time to change our mission and substantially expand our commitment. If that is what the sense of Congress is, I am opposed to the resolution. I therefore ask the distinguished Senator from Arkansas if he would consent to accept an amendment [that explicitly says Congress wants no extension of the present military conflict and no U.S. direct military involvement].

MR. FULBRIGHT . . . The Senator has put into his amendment a statement of policy that is unobjectionable. However, I cannot accept the amendment under the circumstances. I do not believe it is contrary to the joint resolution, but it is an enlargement. I am informed that the House is now voting on this resolution. The House joint resolution is about to be presented to us. I cannot accept the amendment and go to conference with it, and thus take responsibility for delaying matters. . . .

MR. GRUENING [Ernest Gruening, Dem.-Alaska] . . . Regrettably, I find myself in disagreement with his [the President's] southeast Asian policy. . . . The serious events of the past few days, the attack by North Vietnamese vessels on American warships and our reprisal, strikes me as the inevitable and foreseeable concomitant and consequence of U.S. unilateral military aggressive policy in southeast Asia. . . .

We now are about to authorize the President if he sees fit to move our Armed Forces . . . not only into South Vietnam, but also into North Vietnam, Laos, Cambodia, Thailand, and of course the authorization includes all the rest of the SEATO nations. That means sending our American boys into combat in a war in which we have no business, which is not our war, into which we have been misguidedly drawn, which is steadily being escalated. This resolution is a further authorization for escalation unlimited. I am opposed to sacrificing a single American boy in this venture. We have lost far too many already. . . .

MR. MORSE [Wayne Morse, Dem.-Ore.] . . . I believe that history will record that we have made a great mistake in subverting and circumventing the Constitution of the United States, article I, section 8 [which gives Congress the power to declare war] thereof by means of this resolution . . . I believe [this resolution] to be a historic mistake. I believe that within the next century, future generations will look with dismay and great disappointment upon a Congress which is now about to make such a historic mistake. Our constitutional rights are no better than the preservation of our procedural guarantees under the Constitution. . . . [The Resolution passed 88–2, Gruening and Morse voting against.]

62. THE FATAL CONTRADICTIONS OF U.S. POLICY

During the 1964 presidential campaign, President Johnson denied that he intended to escalate the war. The following discussion, however, indicates that escalation was under active consideration. This discussion of September 14, 1964, raises serious doubts about the claims of later critics, such as Ronald Reagan, that U.S. officials should have struck major blows in 1964–66 and gotten the war over with, but did not because of domestic opposition in the United States. The participants include Robert McNamara, Secretary of Defense; John McCone, Director of the Central Intelligence Agency; General Earle Wheeler, Chairman of the Joint Chiefs of Staff; General Maxwell Taylor, Ambassador to South Vietnam, and President Johnson. "General Khanh" is the head of the South Vietnam Government at the time. (Source: "Memorandum for the Record," September 14, 1964, Meeting Notes File, Box 1, Lyndon B. Johnson Library, Austin, Texas.)

The meeting began with the President's review of a memorandum, "Courses of Action for South Vietnam," dated September 8, 1964. Initial attention was concentrated on the four specific recommendations in this paper. The Secretary of Defense reported that these recommendations, with minor adjustments, had the approval of the Joint Chiefs, but he reported also that there was an important division among the Chiefs, in that the Chief of Staff of the Air Force and the Commandant of the Marine Corps believed that it was now necessary in addition to execute extensive U.S. air strikes against North Vietnam. General Wheeler explained that these two officers now felt that the situation would continue to deteriorate unless such drastic action was taken now. He said that he and the other two colleagues were persuaded by the argument of Ambassador Taylor— the man on the spot—that it was important not to overstrain the currently weakened GVN by drastic action in the immediate future. General Taylor repeated that this was indeed his view, but he emphasized that he also believed that in the long run the current in-country program would not be sufficient. He had held this view for many months, but it had been reinforced by recent events in the field. . . .

The President asked Director McCone for his opinion and the Director replied that in the judgment of his Agency the four recommended actions were appropriate, and that a sustained air attack at present would be dangerous because of the weakness of the GVN. Such an attack might also trigger major increases in Chinese Communist participation. The Agency remained very gravely concerned by the internal situation in South Vietnam, which the Director estimated a shade more pessimistically than Ambassador Taylor.

The President asked the Ambassador whether we could stop internal feuding. The Ambassador replied that it was very difficult with a group of men who turned off their hearing aids in the face of appeals to the public weal. These people simply did not have the sense of responsibility for the public interest to which we were accustomed, and regularly estimated matters in terms of their own personal gains and losses. The President then asked the Secretary of State for his judgment. Mr. Rusk said that a major decision to go North could be taken at any time—"at 5-minutes' notice." He did not recommend such decision now. He thought we should take the four recommended actions and play for the breaks. The split in the Communist bloc was deepening and would probably be sharpened by the forthcoming December meeting. As that split grew more severe, there might be real inhibitions upon adventures by Peking and Hanoi in Southeast Asia. . . .

The President said that in his judgment the proper answer to those advocating immediate and extensive action against the North was that we should not do this until our side could defend itself in the streets of Saigon. We obviously wanted to strengthen the GVN. We believed it could be strengthened. But what specifically were we going to do in this direction?

Ambassador Taylor replied that we needed to move on in meshing our team with the GVN. This had been well started before the unrest of August. The problem was not in planning but in execution, and in the quality of the individuals in the GVN. Nevertheless we should continue to seek better individuals and continue to strengthen our cooperative effort with them.

The President accepted this as a first purpose and then asked whether we needed additional equipment as well. Ambassador Taylor said that while the additional U.S. advisers would be helpful, there was currently no equipment need beyond that which was being supplied.

Secretary McNamara emphasized the importance of politico-economic action in the urban areas . . . to lower the level of student and Buddhist pressure and increase the political base of support for the GVN. Mr. McCone endorsed this judgment. He further expressed his opinion that Hanoi and Peking now believed that they were doing very well and that they were not having second thoughts about their basic policy (an implied disagreement with the Secretary of State). The Agency was also disturbed by the prospect that internal movement toward negotiations might be increasing, and that there was some sign also of anti-American feeling in South Vietnam. It could happen that the President would find that the purposes originally set forth in Eisenhower's 1954 letter were no longer supported by the people of Vietnam themselves. . . .

The President asked whether the situation was better or worse than when Ambassador Taylor went out. Ambassador Taylor said he thought it was somewhat worse, but made it clear in response to a further question that this weakening was political, not military. Ambassador Taylor also emphasized his belief that sooner or later we would indeed have to act more forcefully against the North. He simply did not think now was the best time.

The President asked if anyone doubted whether it was worth all this effort. Ambassador Taylor replied that we could not afford to let Hanoi win, in terms of our overall position in the area and in the world. General Wheeler supported him most forcefully, reporting the unanimous view of the Joint Chiefs that if we should lose in South Vietnam, we would lose Southeast Asia. Country after country on the periphery would give way and look toward Communist China as the rising power of the area. Mr. McCone expressed his concurrence and so did the Secretary of State, with considerable force.

The President indicated that the reason for waiting, then, must be simply that with a weak and wobbly situation it would be unwise to attack until we could stabilize our base. Secretary McNamara added that the price of waiting was low, and the promise of gain substantial. . . .

The President asked Ambassador Taylor to compare Khanh and Diem in the people's affections. The Ambassador replied the people did not care for either one.

63. LBJ EXPLAINS HIS DECISION:
THE JOHNS HOPKINS UNIVERSITY SPEECH
APRIL 7, 1965

Debate had already erupted in the United States over the President's escalation of the war as he explained the situation and his policies in a public speech on April 7. Especially notable was a long last section on developing Vietnam. Johnson had admired Franklin D. Roosevelt and the New Deal for developing large parts of the South and Southwest in the United States, and LBJ now urged that the New Deal be carried to Asia. (Source: United States Government, *Public Papers of the Presidents of the United States: Lyndon B. Johnson, 1965* [Washington, 1967], pp. 394–99.)

Viet-Nam is far away from this quiet campus. We have no territory there, nor do we seek any. The war is dirty and brutal and difficult. And some 400 young men, born into an America that is bursting with opportunity and promise, have ended their lives on Viet-Nam's steaming soil.

Why must we take this painful road?

Why must this Nation hazard its ease, and its interest, and its power for the sake of a people so far away?

We fight because we must fight if we are to live in a world where every country can shape its own destiny. And only in such a world will our own freedom be finally secure. . . .

The first reality is that North Viet-Nam has attacked the independent nation of South Viet-Nam. Its object is total conquest.

Of course, some of the people of South Viet-Nam are participating in attack on their own government. But trained men and supplies, orders and arms, flow in a constant stream from north to south.

This support is the heartbeat of the war.

And it is a war of unparalleled brutality. Simple farmers are the targets of assassination and kidnapping. Women and children are strangled in the night because their men are loyal to their government. . . .

Over this war—and all Asia—is another reality: the deepening shadow of Communist China. The rulers in Hanoi are urged on by Peking. This is a regime which has destroyed freedom in Tibet, which has attacked India, and has been condemned by the United Nations for aggression in Korea.

It is a nation which is helping the forces of violence in almost every continent. The contest in Viet-Nam is part of a wider pattern of aggressive purposes.

Why are these realities our concern? Why are we in South Viet-Nam?

We are there because we have a promise to keep. Since 1954 every American President has offered support to the people of South Viet-Nam. We have helped to build, and we have helped to defend. Thus, over many years, we have made a national pledge to help South Viet-Nam defend its independence.

And I intend to keep that promise. . . .

We are also there to strengthen world order. Around the globe, from Berlin to Thailand, are people whose well-being rests, in part, on the belief that they can count on us if they are attacked. To leave Viet-Nam to its fate would shake the confidence of all these people in the value of an American commitment and in the value of America's word. The result would be increased unrest and instability, and even wider war.

We are also there because there are great stakes in the balance. Let no one think for a moment that retreat from Viet-Nam would bring an end to conflict. The battle would be renewed in one country and then another. The central lesson of our time is that the appetite of aggression is never satisfied. To withdraw from one battlefield means only to prepare for the next. We must say in southeast Asia—as we did in Europe—in the words of the Bible: "Hitherto shalt thou come, but no further." . . .

Our objective is the independence of South Viet-Nam, and its freedom from attack. We want nothing for ourselves—only that the people of South Viet-Nam be allowed to guide their own country in their own way.

We will do everything necessary to reach that objective. And we will do only what is absolutely necessary.

In recent months attacks on South Viet-Nam were stepped up. Thus, it became necessary for us to increase our response and to make attacks by air. This is not a change of purpose. It is a change in what we believe that purpose requires. . . .

A COOPERATIVE EFFORT FOR DEVELOPMENT

These countries of southeast Asia are homes for millions of impoverished people. Each day these people rise at dawn and struggle through until the night to wrestle existence from the soil. They are often wracked by disease, plagued by hunger, and death comes at the early age of 40. . . .

For our part I will ask the Congress to join in a billion dollar American investment in this effort as soon as it is underway.

And I would hope that all other industrialized countries, including the

Soviet Union, will join in this effort to replace despair with hope, and terror with progress.

The task is nothing less than to enrich the hopes and the existence of more than a hundred million people. And there is much to be done.

The vast Mekong River can provide food and water and power on a scale to dwarf even our own TVA. . . .

CONCLUSION

We often say how impressive power is. But I do not find it impressive at all. The guns and the bombs, the rockets and the warships, are all symbols of human failure. They are necessary symbols. They protect what we cherish. But they are witness to human folly. . . .

Every night before I turn out the lights to sleep I ask myself this question: Have I done everything that I can do to unite this country? Have I done everything I can to help unite the world, to try to bring peace and hope to all the peoples of the world? Have I done enough?

Ask yourselves that question in your homes—and in this hall tonight. Have we, each of us, all done all we could? Have we done enough? . . .

This generation of the world must choose: destroy or build, kill or aid, hate or understand.

We can do all these things on a scale never dreamed of before.

Well, we will choose life. In so doing we will prevail over the enemies within man, and over the natural enemies of all mankind.

64. THE NORTH VIETNAMESE POSITION APRIL 1965

As President Johnson committed U.S. combat troops in large numbers, the North Vietnam Communist Government issued its position on the conflict. That government's reading of the 1954 Geneva Agreements was notable, as was its emphasis on the South Vietnamese settling their own problems. In line with its position that Vietnam was one nation, the North Vietnam Government had nevertheless been sending supplies and cadres into the south since at least 1959. (Source: The New York *Times,* April 14, 1965.)

Pham Van Dong, Premier of the Democratic Republic of Viet-Nam, elucidated the unswerving stand of the government of the D.R.V. [Democratic Republic of Viet-Nam] on the Viet-Nam question in his report on government work at the second session of the United National Assembly. . . .

Premier Pham Van Dong said that it is the unswerving policy of the government of the D.R.V. to strictly respect the 1954 Geneva Agreements on Viet-Nam and to correctly implement their basic provisions as embodied in the following points:

1. Recognition of the basic national rights of the Vietnamese people— peace, independence, sovereignty, unity and territorial integrity. According to the Geneva Agreements, the United States government must withdraw from South Viet-Nam United States troops, military personnel, and weapons of all kinds, dismantle all United States military bases there, cancel its "military alliance" with South Viet-Nam. It must end its policy of intervention and aggression in South Viet-Nam. According to the Geneva Agreements, the United States government must stop its acts of war against North Viet-Nam, completely cease all encroachments on the territory and sovereignty of the D.R.V.

2. Pending the peaceful reunification of Viet-Nam, while Viet-Nam is still temporarily divided into two zones, the military provisions of the 1954 Geneva Agreements on Viet-Nam must be strictly respected. The two zones must refrain from joining any military alliance with foreign countries. There must be no foreign military bases, troops, or military personnel in their respective territory.

3. The internal affairs of South Viet-Nam must be settled by the South Vietnamese people themselves, in accordance with the program of the NFLSV [the Viet-Cong] without any foreign interference.

4. The peaceful reunification of Viet-Nam is to be settled by the Vietnamese people in both zones, without any foreign interference. . . .

If this basis is recognized, favorable conditions will be created for the peaceful settlement of the Viet-Nam problem, and it will be possible to consider the reconvening of an international conference along the pattern of the 1954 Geneva Conference on Viet-Nam.

The government of the D.R.V. declares that any approach contrary to the above-mentioned stand is inappropriate. Any approach tending to secure a United Nations intervention in the Viet-Nam situation is also inappropriate because such approaches are basically at variance with the 1954 Geneva Agreements on Viet-Nam.

65. MCNAMARA PRIVATELY EXPLAINS U.S. POLICY IN APRIL 1965

Secretary of Defense Robert McNamara revealed key assumptions about U.S. policy in a private interview on April 22, 1965. Particularly notable were his remarks about possible use of nuclear weapons and his fixation on the threat of China—a fixation that mirrored Johnson's concern as expressed in the President's Johns Hopkins speech. (Source: Off-the-record interview with Secretary of Defense McNamara by the New York *Times,* April 22, 1965. Papers of Arthur Krock, Princeton University Library.)

SUMMARY

Mr. McNamara's summary of the war situation now was as follows:

First, he insists strongly that the guerrilla war is NOT merely an indigenous rebellion, that in fact the Viet Cong do depend on outside power for weapons, strategy, tactical doctrine, daily operational control. . . . In two engagements this month, on April 5–6, SVN [South Vietnam] troops captured hundreds of weapons. 90% of small-bore arms were of [Communist] Bloc origin, mostly Chinese, some Czech. 100% of the large-bore were of Bloc origin. This outside assistance has dramatically increased in men and equipment in past 18 months—approximately the period of extreme SVN political instability following fall of Diem. To oppose the 150,000-odd regular and irregular VCs [Vietcong], 525,000 SVN forces of all kinds are in hand. This is a ratio of 4–5 to 1, compared to the accepted ratio of 10–1 needed in Greece, Philippines, Malaysia, elsewhere, to overcome well-led guerrillas.

So our strategy must be to improve the ratio. . . .

In general period of [U.S.] air bombings, [U.S.] Marine landings, and Quat [new South Vietnam President] takeover, he considers war situation to have improved.

ALTERNATIVE

The alternative to fighting the war as outlined, McN says, is not to negotiate a neutral, non-Communist SVN because that is not possible. The alternative is a Chinese-dominated Southeast Asia which he thinks means

246

a "Red Asia." Concedes possibility of Titoist tendencies in NVN [North Vietnam], but thinks China would inevitably dominate once we pull out. He further believes most of our allies share this view . . . and that their public statements are dictated by internal politics; he expects . . . "allies" generally to be with us when the chips are really down.

Bomb China?

McN says our "clear objective" is to maintain an independent, non-Communist SVN. Our policy is to reach this objective at lowest possible cost in casualties and risk. To attack Red China substantially increases the risks and costs, probably would bring Soviet Union to assistance of China. Such assistance not necessarily nuclear retaliation on us but perhaps Soviet pressures on Western Europe or to the South on Greece and Turkey. Doesn't believe China and Russia pushed together yet, division probably widened, but conceivable could be closed in near future and might well be by attack on China now.

Nuclear Weapons

We are NOT following a strategy that recognizes any sanctuary or *any weapons restriction*. But we would use nuclear weapons only after fully applying non-nuclear arsenal. In other words, if 100 planes couldn't take out a target, we wouldn't necessarily go to nuclear weapons; we would try 200 planes, and so on. But "inhibitions" on using nuclear are NOT "overwhelming." Conceded that would be a "gigantic step." Quote: "We'd use whatever weapons we felt necessary to achieve our objective, recognizing that one must offset against the price"—and the price includes all psychological, propaganda factors, etc. Also fallout on innocent. "Inconceivable" under current circumstances that nuclear would provide a net gain against the terrific price that would be paid. NOT inconceivable that the price would be paid in some future circumstances McN refuses to predict.

Withdrawal

If the U.S. withdrew from SVN, there would be a complete shift in the world balance of power. Asia goes Red, our prestige and integrity damaged, allies everywhere shaken (even those who publicly ask us to quit bombing, etc.). At home, he foresees as a result of these calamities a bad effect on economy and a disastrous political fight that could further freeze American political debate and even affect political freedom.

On the Other Hand

If U.S. achieved in SVN the objectives stated by LBJ in Baltimore [speech of April 7, 1965], there would be substantial political and economic and security gains. Way then open (McN sez) to combine birth control and economic expansion techniques in gigantic arc from SVN to Iran and the Middle East, bringing unimaginable developments to this region, proving worth of moderate, democratic way of growth for societies.

A Settlement

The U.S. must insist on a non-Communist, independent SVN. . . .

Off Record (cannot be used at all)

We have had no success in numerous attempts at infiltrating NVN with guerrillas of our own. About 50 per cent of SVN guerrillas sent north by various means wiped out. Now considered fruitless. . . . McN attributes this failure to tight police state controls in NVN. . . .

China

China will increase its military power substantially in coming decades. Not likely to be able to threaten US within a decade. Ties between Soviet Union and satellites have weakened, Soviet Union has matured and mellowed in period since 1918. Assumes some sort of evolution for China outlook and attitudes but will take much longer because they started from farther back than Soviet Union in industrializing process. Soviet Union was contained by a military alliance in expansionist period. So possible to contain China in her expansionist phase by similar alliances. . . .

66. OFF THE DIVING BOARD: THE DEBATES OF JULY 1965

For more than a year, Johnson had been pressured by the military authorities in the Pentagon and some of his closest civilian advisers to make a quick, major commitment to Vietnam before the South Vietnamese Government collapsed. By April 1965 he had decided to do so, but two months later the specifics were decided when McNamara asked for 200,000 American men to be sent. This request led to meetings on July 21 and 22 that are among the most important—and revealing—in the history of the war. The most fundamental questions, such as the threat of China and whether the United States could wage and win a long war 10,000 miles away in Asia, were debated secretly in the White House. (Source: Drawn from an account of the July 21 and 22 meetings by Jack Valenti, *A Very Human President* [New York, 1975], pp. 322–40, 340–53. Printed by permission of Mr. Valenti.)

Initially at the meeting of July 21 were Robert McNamara, secretary of defense; Dean Rusk, secretary of state; Cyrus Vance, deputy secretary of defense; McGeorge Bundy, special assistant to the president for national security affairs; General Earle Wheeler, chairman of the joint chiefs of staff; George Ball, under secretary of state; William Bundy, assistant secretary of state and brother of McGeorge Bundy; Henry Cabot Lodge, ambassador to Vietnam, and Jack Valenti, special assistant to the president, among others.

McNAMARA: They [the GVN, or government of South Vietnam] are trying to increase [their own forces] by 10,000 per month. Our country team is optimistic. But I am not. The desertion rate is high. . . . We did not find any threat of discontent among our own troops. U.S. morale is of the highest order. . . . [The enemy] are suffering heavy losses. They are well supplied with ammunition. I suspect much of the inflow of supplies is water-borne. . . . But even if we did have tight control, it would make little difference in the next six to nine months.

[The President entered the room]

JOHNSON: Would you please begin, Bob.

[McNamara summarized the Pentagon recommendation to plan to support 200,000 troops in Vietnam by the first of 1966 by calling up the same number of reserves. By mid-1966 approximately 600,000 additional men would be available.]

BALL: Isn't it possible that the VC will do what they did against the French—stay away from confrontation and not accommodate us?

WHEELER: Yes, that is possible, but by constantly harassing them, they will have to fight somewhere. . . .

BALL: Mr. President, I can foresee a perilous voyage, very dangerous. I have great and grave apprehensions that we can win under these conditions. But let me be clear. If the decision is to go ahead, I am committed.

JOHNSON: But, George, is there another course in the national interest, some course that is better than the one McNamara proposes? We know it is dangerous and perilous, but the big question is, can it be avoided? . . .

BALL: Take what precautions we can, Mr. President. Take our losses, let their government fall apart, negotiate, discuss, knowing full well there will be a probable take-over by the Communists. This is disagreeable, I know.

JOHNSON: I can take disagreeable decisions. But I want to know can we make a case for your thoughts? Can you discuss it fully? . . .

RUSK: What we have done since 1954 to 1961 has not been good enough. We should have probably committed ourselves heavier in 1961. . . .

LODGE: There is not a tradition of a national government in Saigon. There are no roots in the country. Not until there is tranquility can you have any stability. I don't think we ought to take this government seriously. There is simply no one who can do anything. We have to do what we think we ought to do regardless of what the Saigon government does. . . . [McNamara and Wheeler then returned to the Pentagon recommendation for more men to be sent to Vietnam. These men would give the South Vietnamese army a breathing space. No more than 100,000 would be sent at this time.]

JOHNSON: It seems to me that you will lose a greater number of men. I don't like that.

WHEELER: Not precisely true, Mr. President. The more men we have there the greater the likelihood of smaller losses.

JOHNSON: Tell me this. What will happen if we put in 100,000 more men and then two, three years later you tell me you need 500,000 more? How would you expect me to respond to that? And what makes you think if we put in 100,000 men, Ho Chi Minh won't put in another 100,000, and match us every bit of the way.

WHEELER (smiling): This means greater bodies of men from North Vietnam, which will allow us to cream them.

JOHNSON: But what are the chances of more North Vietnamese soldiers coming in?

WHEELER: About a fifty-fifty chance. The North would be foolhardy to put one-quarter of their forces in SVN. It would expose them too greatly in the North. . . .

[The meeting reconvened at 2:30 P.M.]

BALL: We cannot win, Mr. President. This war will be long and protracted. The most we can hope for is a messy conclusion. There remains a great danger of intrusion by the Chinese. But the biggest problem is the problem of the long war. . . . As casualties increase, the pressure to strike at the very jugular of North Vietnam will become very great. I am concerned about world opinion. . . . If the war is long and protracted, as I believe it will be, then we will suffer because the world's greatest power cannot defeat guerrillas. Then there is the problem of national politics. Every great captain in history was not afraid to make a tactical withdrawal if conditions were unfavorable to him. The enemy cannot even be seen in Vietnam. He is indigenous to the country. I truly have serious doubt that an army of westerners can successfully fight orientals in an Asian jungle. . . . The least harmful way to cut losses in SVN is to let the government decide it doesn't want us to stay there. Therefore, we should put such proposals to the SVN that they can't accept. Then, it would move to a neutralist position. I have no illusions that after we were asked to leave South Vietnam, that country would soon come under Hanoi control. . . . If we wanted to make a stand in Thailand, we might be able to make it. . . . Between a long war and cutting our losses, the Japanese would go for the latter. . . .

JOHNSON: But George, wouldn't all these countries say that Uncle Sam was a paper tiger, wouldn't we lose credibility breaking the word of three presidents. . . .

BALL: The worse blow would be that the mightiest power on earth is unable to defeat a handful of guerrillas. . . .

JOHNSON: There are two basic troublings within me. First, that western-ers can ever win a war in Asia. Second, I don't see how you can fight a war under direction of other people whose government changes every month. . . .

RUSK: If the Communist world finds out we will not pursue our commit-ment to the end, I don't know where they will stay their hand. I have to say I am more optimistic than some of my colleagues. I don't believe the VC have made large advances among the Vietnamese people. It is difficult to worry about massive casualties when we say we can't find the enemy. I feel strongly that one man dead is a massive casualty, but in the sense that we are talking, I don't see large casualties unless the Chinese come in.

LODGE: I feel there is a greater threat to start World War III if we don't go. Can't we see the similarity to our own indolence at Munich [the Munich conference of 1938 when Hitler, with the acquiescence of the West, seized part of Czechoslovakia]. I simply can't be as pessimistic as Ball. We have great seaports in Vietnam. We don't need to fight on roads. We have the sea. Let us visualize meeting the VC on our own terms. We don't have to spend all our time in the jungles. If we can secure our bases, the Vietnamese can secure, in time, a political movement to, one, appre-hend the terrorist, and two, give intelligence to the government. . . . The Vietnamese have been dealt more casualties than, per capita, we suffered in the Civil War. The Vietnamese soldier is an uncomplaining soldier. He has ideas he will die for.

CONFERENCE OF JULY 22 WITH PENTAGON OFFICIALS ON COMMITTING LARGE NUMBERS OF TROOPS TO VIETNAM

At the meeting were the President; McNamara; Vance; General Wheeler; General Harold K. Johnson, chief of staff of the Army; General

John P. McConnell, Air Force chief of staff; Admiral D. L. McDonald, chief of Naval Operations; General Wallace M. Greene, Jr., commandant of the Marine Corps; Secretary of the Air Force Harold Brown; Secretary of the Navy Paul Nitze; Bundy; and Valenti, among others.

JOHNSON: The options open to us are: one, leave the country, with as little loss as possible; two, maintain present force and lose slowly; three, add 100,000 men, recognizing that may not be enough and adding more next year. The disadvantages of number three option are the risk of escalation, casualties high, and the prospect of a long war without victory. . . .

McDONALD: I agree with McNamara that we are committed to the extent that we can't move out. If we continue the way we are now, it will be a slow, sure victory for the other side. By putting more men in it will turn the tide and let us know what further we need to do. I wish we had done this long before.

JOHNSON: But you don't know if 100,000 men will be enough. What makes you conclude that if you don't know where we are going—and what will happen—we shouldn't pause and find this out?

McDONALD: Sooner or later we will force them to the conference table.

JOHNSON: But if we put in 100,000 men won't they put in an equal number, and then where will we be?

McDONALD: No, if we step up our bombing. . . .

JOHNSON: Is this a chance we want to take?

McDONALD: Yes, sir, when I view the alternatives. Get out now or pour in more men. . . . I think our allies will lose faith in us.

JOHNSON: We have few allies really helping us now.

McNAMARA: The current plan is to introduce 100,000 men with the possibility of a second 100,000 by the first of the year. . . .

JOHNSON: Why wouldn't North Vietnam pour in more men? Also, why wouldn't they call on volunteers from China and Russia?

WHEELER: First, they may decide they can't win by putting in force they can't afford. At most they would put in two more divisions. Beyond that, they strip their country and invite a countermove on our part. Second, on volunteers—the one thing all North Vietnam fears is the Chinese. For them to invite Chinese volunteers is to invite China taking over North Vietnam. The weight of judgment is that North Vietnam may reinforce their troops, but they can't match us on a buildup. From a military viewpoint, we can handle, if we are determined to do so, China and North Vietnam.

McDONALD: . . . First, supply the forces Westmoreland has asked for. Second, prepare to furnish more men, 100,000, in 1966. Third, commence building in air and naval forces, and step up air attacks on North Vietnam. Fourth, bring in needed reserves and draft calls.

JOHNSON: Do you have any ideas of what this will cost?

MCNAMARA: Yes, sir, twelve billion dollars in 1966. . . . It would not require wage and price controls in my judgment.

MCCONNELL: If you put in these requested forces and increase air and sea effort, we can at least turn the tide to where we are not losing anymore. We need to be sure we get the best we can out of the South Vietnamese. We need to bomb all military targets available to us in North Vietnam. As to whether we can come to a satisfactory solution with these forces, I don't know. . . .

JOHNSON: Doesn't it really mean that if we follow Westmoreland's requests we are in a new war? Isn't this going off the diving board?

MCNAMARA: If we carry forward all these recommendations, it would be a change in our policy. We have relied on the South to carry the brunt. Now we would be responsible for satisfactory military outcome. . . .

JOHNSON: But I don't know how we are going to get the job done. There are millions of Chinese. I think they are going to put their stack in. Is this the best place to do it? We don't have the allies we had in Korea. Can we get our allies to cut off supplying the North?

MCNAMARA: No, sir, we can't prevent Japan, Britain, and the others from chartering ships to Haiphong [the North Vietnamese port].

JOHNSON: Are we starting something that in two or three years we simply can't finish?

BROWN: It is costly to us to strangle slowly. But the chances of losing are less if we move in. . . .

67. THE GREAT DEBATE OF 1966

The growing, divisive debate over the war occurred largely in "teach-ins" held on college campuses. But in early 1966 the Senate Foreign Relations Committee held hearings in which it examined top administration officials on Vietnam policy. Millions of Americans watched on television and many learned for the first time why and how the President was taking them further into the Indochina war. The debates ranged from the role of China to the nature of the American Revolution to the proper uses of history—indeed, the debates were largely over how history was to be read and interpreted. The Committee Chairman,

Senator J. William Fulbright (Dem.-Ark.) and Secretary of State Dean Rusk staged the main encounter, but they were joined by (among others) Senator Eugene McCarthy (Dem.-Minn.), Senator George Aiken (Rep.-Vt.), Senator Frank Church (Dem.-Idaho), and David Bell, Director of the Budget. (Source: United States Senate, Committee on Foreign Relations, *Supplemental Foreign Assistance, Fiscal Year 1966—Vietnam. Hearings . . . January 28, February 4, 8, 10, 17, 18, 1966* [Washington, 1966].)

SECRETARY RUSK. To put it in its simplest terms, Mr. Chairman, we believe that the South Vietnamese are entitled to a chance to make their own decisions about their own affairs and their own future course of policy: that they are entitled to make these decisions without having them imposed on them by force from North Vietnam or elsewhere from the outside. We are perfectly prepared to rely upon the South Vietnamese themselves to make that judgment by elections, through their own Government, by whatever way is suitable for them to make that decision.

Now, we have indicated a good many points which have a bearing on this matter. We are not, for example, trying to acquire a new ally. If South Vietnam and the South Vietnamese people wish to pursue a nonalined course by their own option, that is an option which is open to them.

If they wish to join in the regional activities in the area, such as Mekong River development and projects of that sort, that is open to them. But we do believe they are entitled not to have these answers decided for them on the basis of military force organized from Hanoi through an aggression initiated from Hanoi, in the leadership of a front which was organized in Hanoi in 1960 for the purpose of taking over South Vietnam by force.

THE CHAIRMAN. Do you think they can be a completely free agent with our occupation of the land with 200,000 or 400,000 men?

SECRETARY RUSK. If the infiltration of men and arms from the north were not in the picture, these troops of ours could come home. We have said that repeatedly. They went in there, the combat troops went in there, because of infiltration of men and arms from the north. That is the simple and elementary basis for the presence of American combat forces.

THE CHAIRMAN. May I ask what is the explanation of why in 1956, contrary to the terms of the Geneva accords, elections were not held? You have stated several times that the aggression started in 1960. But the events between 1954 when the agreement was signed and 1960 were not without significance.

We backed Diem, did we not? Didn't we have much to do with putting him in power?

254

SECRETARY RUSK. Well, we supported him.

THE CHAIRMAN. That is what I mean.

SECRETARY RUSK. That is correct.

THE CHAIRMAN. And he was, to an extent had, a certain dependence upon us, did he not?

SECRETARY RUSK: We were giving him very considerable aid, Mr. Chairman.

THE CHAIRMAN. I am informed that in 1955, in accordance with the treaty provisions, he was requested by the north to consult about elections, and that he refused to do so. Is that correct?

SECRETARY RUSK. Well, neither his government nor the Government of the United States signed that agreement. . . .

THE CHAIRMAN. Not having signed it, what business was it of ours for intervening and encouraging one of the participants not to follow it, specifically Diem?

SECRETARY RUSK. Well, the prospect of free elections in North and South Vietnam was very poor at that time.

THE CHAIRMAN. Now, they have always been poor, and will be for a hundred years, won't they? That was not news to you. I mean, this was a device to get around the settlement, was it not?

SECRETARY RUSK. No, no, Mr. Chairman. I do not believe the prospects of free elections, in South Vietnam anyhow, are all that dim.

THE CHAIRMAN. Have they ever had them in 2,000 years of history?

SECRETARY RUSK. They have had some free elections in the provinces and municipalities in May of last year.

THE CHAIRMAN. Under our control and direction.

SECRETARY RUSK. Not under our control and direction; no, sir.

THE CHAIRMAN. Who supervised them?

SECRETARY RUSK. Multiple candidates, with 70 percent of the registered voters voting, and with results which indicate that people in these local communities elected the people that you would expect them to elect in terms of the natural leaders of the community. . . .

SENATOR AIKEN. Are the successful candidates all living?

SECRETARY RUSK. I beg your pardon?

SENATOR AIKEN. Are the successful candidates still living now?

SECRETARY RUSK. Well, they are as far as the Government is concerned. The Vietcong continue to kill them, assassinate, kidnap them.

SENATOR AIKEN. Knock them off.

SECRETARY RUSK. I am sure that not all those who were elected are still in office.

SENATOR AIKEN. That discourages candidacies.

SECRETARY RUSK. Yes, it does.

255

THE CHAIRMAN. Well, there are a lot of things here that discourage candidacies, too. It is not a very easy life any way you take it.

But all I am really trying to say is I do not think that this dispute is worthy of an escalation that would result in a confrontation with China in a world war. I do not believe that there is much evidence that this is the kind of a test in which it would follow that, if we should make a compromise, then all the world will collapse because we have been defeated.

This country is much too strong, in my opinion, that it would suffer any great setback. We are much stronger than the Russians were when they withdrew from Cuba. For a week maybe people said they had had a rebuff and within a month everyone was complimenting them for having contributed to the maintenance of peace. . . .

SECRETARY RUSK. Yes. I do not understand though, Mr. Chairman, just what the substance of the compromise would be.

THE CHAIRMAN. Well, it strikes me that the essence—

SECRETARY RUSK. I mean some of the things you said suggested that we should abandon the effort in South Vietnam.

THE CHAIRMAN. No. I am not suggesting that we should abandon it, but that we should have a conference. I do not think you will get it until you propose reasonable terms that would allow the Vietnamese, even the liberation front, to have an opportunity to participate in an election.

After all, Vietnam is their country. It is not our country. We do not even have the right that the French did. We have no historical right. We are obviously intruders from their point of view. We represent the old Western imperialism in their eyes. I am not questioning our motives. I think our motives are very good, as has been testified on numerous occasions.

But I still think from their point of view it is their country, however bad the people have acted. Other countries have had civil wars; we had one. In my part of the country we resented it for a long time. So did yours. You can remember the feelings that were there. . . .

SENATOR MCCARTHY. Mr. Secretary, I have one question. I think we accepted for 5 or 6 years the ideas expressed by General [Douglas] MacArthur, General Eisenhower, General [James] Gavin, General [Matthew] Ridgway, and others that a land war in Asia was unthinkable.

Is that theoretical position still held or do we have among the military figures in America today a changed point of view?

SECRETARY RUSK. Senator, the nature of a struggle of this sort, where the initiative is not ours, where we did not start it, and where we didn't want it to begin with, and where the aggression comes from the other side is, of course, substantially determined by the other side.

At the present time the situation in South Vietnam does not take the form of armies, land armies, locked in combat with each other. It continues to be basically a guerrilla operation. The overwhelming part of the problem is terror and sabotage. The fixed units that the other side has— battalions or regiments—occasionally engage in combat. . . .

SENATOR MCCARTHY. I know that to be the case.

SECRETARY RUSK. The fire power that is available to the government and allied forces out there is very large indeed, and the other side has found it very difficult to sustain battalions or regiments in action for any protracted period.

SENATOR MCCARTHY. Well, I don't think that quite answers my question.

SECRETARY RUSK. I know it didn't, sir. . . .

SENATOR AIKEN. I have a couple for Mr. Bell to answer.

Are we insuring any type of private enterprise in South Vietnam?

MR. BELL. There is an agreement between the Vietnamese Government and ours which authorizes the normal kind of investments guarantees for American investments. But none have been issued over the past 12 months. There were some previously. . . .

SENATOR AIKEN. Has any private investment from the United States been made in the last 12 months?. . . .

MR. BELL. I would be glad to check the point for the record.

U.S. PRIVATE INVESTMENT IN VIETNAM DURING 1965

During calendar year 1965, the United States issued two specific risk guarantees to Caltex for investments totaling $722,000. In addition, there is underway an expansion of a paper and pulp manufacturing company in which Parsons & Whittmore are equity participants. The value of the equipment required for the expansion is estimated at $2 million.

Discussions are being held between the Government of Vietnam and a number of banking institutions regarding the possible establishment of an American branch bank in Saigon. . . .

SENATOR CHURCH. It seems to me that there is a difference between guerrilla war or revolution and the kind of aggression that we faced in Korea and in Europe, and, further, that the underdeveloped world is going to be beset with guerrilla wars, regardless of the outcome in Vietnam, and that we will have to live in a world afflicted with such revolutions for a long time to come.

That is why it is so important to try to determine what our basic foreign policy attitude is going to be in dealing with these revolutionary wars in many parts of the underdeveloped world in the future; and, as I have listened to your explanations this morning, I gather that wherever a revolution occurs against an established government, and that revolution, as most will doubtlessly be, is infiltrated by Communists, that the United States will intervene, if necessary, to prevent a Communist success.

This, at least, has been the policy we followed in the Dominican Republic and in Vietnam. I wonder whether this is going to continue to be the policy as we face new guerrilla wars in the future?

SECRETARY RUSK. Senator, I think it is very important that the different kinds of revolutions be distinguished. We are in no sense committed against change. As a matter of fact, we are stimulating, ourselves, very sweeping revolutions in a good many places. The whole weight and effort of the Alliance for Progress is to bring about far-reaching social, economic changes.

SENATOR CHURCH. That is change sought, Mr. Secretary, without violence. History shows that the most significant change has been accompanied by violence.

Do you think that with our foreign aid program we are going to be able, with our money, to avert serious uprisings in all of these destitute countries in future years?

SECRETARY RUSK. Not necessarily avert all of them, but I do believe there is a fundamental difference between the kind of revolution which the Communists call their wars of national liberation, and the kind of revolution which is congenial to our own experience, and fits into the aspirations of ordinary men and women right around the world.

There is nothing liberal about that revolution that they are trying to push from Peiping. This is a harsh, totalitarian regime. It has nothing in common with the great American revolutionary tradition, nothing in common with it.

SENATOR CHURCH. The objectives of Communist revolution are clearly very different indeed from the earlier objectives of our own. But objectives of revolutions have varied through the centuries.

The question that I think faces this country is how we can best cope with the likelihood of revolt in the underdeveloped world in the years ahead, and I have very serious doubts that American military intervention will often be the proper decision. I think too much intervention on our part may well spread communism throughout the ex-colonial world rather than thwart it.

Now, the distinction you draw between the Communist type of guerrilla war and other kinds of revolution, if I have understood it correctly, has been based upon the premise that in Vietnam the North Vietnamese have been meddling in the revolution in the south and, therefore, it is a form of aggression on the part of the north against the south.

But I cannot remember many revolutions that have been fought in splendid isolation. There were as many Frenchmen at Yorktown when Cornwallis surrendered as there were American Continentals.

Senator Pell tells me more. I accept the correction.

In any case, it seems to me that the Communists have not changed the rules of revolution by meddling in them, regardless of how much we disapprove of their goals.

When we were an infant nation we stood up for the right of revolution, and I am afraid—

SECRETARY RUSK. Senator, I just cannot—

SENATOR CHURCH. I am afraid, what I am worried about, Mr. Secretary, is this: That if we intervene too much in wars of this type, our policy may well turn out to be self-defeating. . . .

68. PRESIDENTS JOHNSON AND HO EXCHANGE VIEWS IN FEBRUARY 1967

By early 1967 the war was becoming more costly than either side had imagined twenty-four months before when U.S. escalation began. But both sides remained inflexible in their ultimate demands: the United States insisted that the Communists leave and allow South Vietnam to become a sovereign nation, while North Vietnam would accept only a U.S. evacuation and the unification of the country. The details of these two positions—and the high emotion accompanying them—vividly appeared in an exchange of letters between Johnson and Ho in February 1967. (Source: *President Ho Chi Minh Answers President L. B. Johnson* [Hanoi, 1967], pp. 9–12, 27–29.)

His Excellency Ho Chi Minh
President, Democratic Republic of Vietnam

Dear Mr. President,

I am writing to you in the hope that the conflict in Vietnam can be brought to an end. The conflict has already taken a heavy toll—in lives lost, in wounds inflicted, in property destroyed, and in simple human misery. If we fail to find a just and peaceful solution, history will judge us harshly.

Therefore, I believe that we both have a heavy obligation to seek earnestly the path to peace. It is in response to that obligation that I am writing directly to you. We have tried over the past several years, in a variety of ways and through a number of channels, to convey to you and your colleagues our desire to achieve a peaceful settlement. For whatever reasons, these efforts have not achieved any results.

It may be that our thoughts and yours, our attitudes and yours, have been distorted or misinterpreted as they passed through these various channels. Certainly that is always a danger in indirect communication.

There is one good way to overcome this problem and to move forward in the search for a peaceful settlement. That is for us to arrange for direct talks between trusted representatives in a secure setting and away from the glare of publicity. Such talks should not be used as a propaganda exercise but should be a serious effort to find a workable and mutually acceptable solution.

In the past two weeks, I have noted public statements by representatives of your government suggesting that you would be prepared to enter into direct bilateral talks with representatives of the U.S. Government, provided that we ceased "unconditionally" and permanently our bombing operations against your country and all military actions against it. In the last days, serious and responsible parties have assured us indirectly that this is in fact your proposal.

Let me frankly state that I see two great difficulties with this proposal. In view of your public position, such action on our part would inevitably produce worldwide speculation that discussions were under way and would impair the privacy and secrecy of those discussions. Secondly, there would inevitably be grave concern on our part whether your government would make use of such action by us to improve its military position.

With these problems in mind, I am prepared to move even further toward an ending of the hostilities than your government has proposed in either public statements or through private diplomatic channels. I am prepared to order a cessation of bombing against your country and the stopping of further augmentation of U.S. forces in South Vietnam as soon as I am assured that infiltration into South Vietnam by land and by sea has stopped. These acts of restraint on both sides would, I believe, make it possible for us to conduct serious and private discussions leading toward an early peace.

I make this proposal to you now with a specific sense of urgency arising from the imminent New Year holidays in Vietnam. If you are able to accept this proposal I see no reason why it could not take effect at the end of the New Year, or Tết, holidays. The proposal I have made would be greatly strengthened if your military authorities and those of the government of South Vietnam could promptly negotiate an extension of the Tết truce.

As to the site of the bilateral discussions I propose, there are several possibilities. We could, for example, have our representatives meet in Moscow where contacts have already occurred. They could meet in some other country such as Burma. You may have other arrangements or sites in mind, and I would try to meet your suggestions. . . .

Sincerely,

LYNDON B. JOHNSON

PRESIDENT HO CHI MINH'S REPLY TO U.S. PRESIDENT LYNDON B. JOHNSON

TO HIS EXCELLENCY MR LYNDON B. JOHNSON,
PRESIDENT
UNITED STATES OF AMERICA

Your Excellency,
On February 10, 1967, I received your message. This is my reply.

Vietnam is thousands of miles away from the United States. The Vietnamese people have never done any harm to the United States. But contrary to the pledges made by its representative at the 1954 Geneva Conference, the U.S. Government has ceaselessly intervened in Vietnam, it has unleashed and intensified the war of aggression in South Vietnam with a view to prolonging the partition of Vietnam and turning South Vietnam into a neo-colony and a military base of the United States. For over two years now, the U.S. Government has, with its air and naval forces, carried the war to the Democratic Republic of Vietnam, an independent and sovereign country.

The U.S. Government has committed war crimes, crimes against peace and against mankind. In South Vietnam, half a million U.S. and satellite troops have resorted to the most inhuman weapons and the most barbarous methods of warfare, such as napalm, toxic chemicals and gases, to massacre our compatriots, destroy crops, and raze villages to the ground. In North Vietnam, thousands of U.S. aircraft have dropped hundreds of thousands of tons of bombs, destroying towns, villages, factories, roads, bridges, dykes, dams, and even churches, pagodas, hospitals, schools. In your message, you apparently deplored the sufferings and destructions in Vietnam. May I ask you: Who has perpetrated these monstrous crimes? It is the U.S. and satellite troops. The U.S. Government is entirely responsible for the extremely serious situation in Vietnam.

261

The U.S. war of aggression against the Vietnamese people constitutes a challenge to the countries of the socialist camp, a threat to the national independence movement, and a serious danger to peace in Asia and the world.

The Vietnamese people deeply love independence, freedom and peace. But in the face of the U.S. aggression, they have risen up, united as one man, fearless of sacrifices and hardships; they are determined to carry on their Resistance until they have won genuine independence and freedom and true peace. Our just cause enjoys strong sympathy and support from the peoples of the whole world including broad sections of the American people.

The U.S. Government has unleashed the war of aggression in Vietnam. It must cease this aggression. That is the only way to the restoration of peace. The U.S. Government must stop definitively and unconditionally its bombing raids and all other acts of war against the Democratic Republic of Vietnam, withdraw from South Vietnam all U.S. and satellite troops, recognize the South Vietnam National Front for Liberation, and let the Vietnamese people settle themselves their own affairs. Such is the basic content of the four-point stand of the Government of the Democratic Republic of Vietnam, which embodies the essential principles and provisions of the 1954 Geneva Agreements on Vietnam. It is the basis of a correct political solution to the Vietnam problem.

In your message, you suggested direct talks between the Democratic Republic of Vietnam and the United States. If the U.S. Government really wants these talks, it must first of all stop unconditionally its bombing raids and all other acts of war against the Democratic Republic of Vietnam. It is only after the unconditional cessation of the U.S. bombing raids and all other acts of war against the Democratic Republic of Vietnam that the Democratic Republic of Vietnam and the United States could enter into talks and discuss questions concerning the two sides.

The Vietnamese people will never submit to force; they will never accept talks under the threat of bombs.

Our cause is absolutely just. It is to be hoped that the U.S. Government will act in accordance with reason.

Sincerely,

HO CHI MINH

69. VIETNAM AND THE IMPERIAL PRESIDENCY

By 1967 not only the costs of the war were escalating, but they occurred in areas that were surprising to most Americans. One of those areas was the power of the presidency, and no one was more surprised at the "imperial presidency" that had developed than Senator Fulbright. Throughout his career in the Senate, and particularly when he had led the Gulf of Tonkin Resolution through the Senate, he had worked for more presidential power. By 1967 he was stunned and saddened by how his former friend, President Johnson, was using those powers. And he—along with many others in the Senate and outside—was amazed when a top State Department official explained in a public hearing how the Constitution's provisions were being interpreted by the Executive, whether the Congress liked it or not. (Source: Under Secretary of State Nicholas Katzenbach before the Senate Foreign Relations Committee, August 17, 1967, *Congressional Record,* August 21, 1967, pp. 23390–91.)

[Sen. J. William Fulbright (Dem.-Ark.), Chairman of the Senate Foreign Relations Committee.] You say: "his"—that is the President—"his is a responsibility born of the need for speed and decisiveness in an emergency. His is the responsibility of controlling and directing all the external aspects of the nation's power." How do you fit this in with the constitutional provision as to the declaration of war by the Congress? . . .

MR. KATZENBACH. . . . The Constitution makes it very clear that on a declaration of war that it is the function of Congress to declare. I believe our history has been that the wars that we have declared have been declared at the initiative and instance of the Executive. The function of the Congress is one to declare. It is not one to wage, not one to conduct, but one simply to declare. That is the function of Congress as expressed in the Constitution.

The use of the phrase "to declare war" as it was used in the Constitution of the United States had a particular meaning in terms of those events, in terms of the practices which existed at that time, and which existed really until the United Nations organization, but it existed for a long time after that, to build on the structure that war was recognized to be an instrument of that policy, not in the climate today, which rejects that, which rejects the idea of aggression, which rejects the idea of conquest. . . .

Now, it came for a function. As you rightly say, it was recognized by the Founding Fathers that the President might have to take emergency action to protect the security of the United States, but that if there was going to be a use of the armed forces of the United States, that was a decision which Congress should check the Executive on, which Congress should support. . . . It would not, I think, correctly reflect the very limited objectives of the United States with respect to Vietnam. It would not correctly reflect our efforts there, what we are trying to do, the reasons why we are there. To use an outmoded phraseology, to declare war.

THE CHAIRMAN. You think it is outmoded to declare war?

MR. KATZENBACH. In this kind of a context I think the expression of declaring a war is one that has become outmoded in the international arena, that is not correctly reflected. But I think there is, Mr. Chairman, an obligation on the part of the Executive to give Congress the opportunity, which that language was meant to reflect in the Constitution of the United States, to give the Congress of the United States an opportunity to express its views with respect to this. In this instance . . . of Vietnam, Congress had an opportunity to participate in these decisions. Congress ratified the SEATO treaty [of 1954] by an overwhelming vote, which expressed the security concerns, the general obligation of the United States in accordance with its constitutional process to attempt to preserve order and peace and defense against aggression in Southeast Asia. . . .

THE CHAIRMAN. You mentioned that as a basis for the Tonkin Gulf resolution?

MR. KATZENBACH. Congress participated in that. As the situation there deteriorated, as American ships were attacked in the Tonkin Gulf, the President of the United States came back to Congress to seek the views of Congress with respect to what should be done in that area and with respect to the use of the military of the United States in that area, and on those resolutions Congress had the opportunity to participate and did participate. The combination of the two, it seems to me, fully fulfills the obligation of the Executive in a situation of this kind to participate with the Congress, to give the Congress a full and effective voice, the functional equivalent, the constitutional obligation expressed in the provision of the Constitution with respect to declaring war. . . .

THE CHAIRMAN. It seems to me . . . that you are now in a way of saying that this resolution [Tonkin Gulf Resolution] authorized a war with China.

MR. KATZENBACH. No, I think the resolution is quite precise in what it authorized. . . . Now in the course of that authorization, there can be risks, there can be risks taken. Other people could be involved. . . .

70. PRESIDENT JOHNSON'S "SAN ANTONIO FORMULA" OF SEPTEMBER 29, 1967

As U.S.-South Vietnamese troops seemed to be gaining the upper hand at last, President Johnson traveled to San Antonio, Texas, to give an upbeat account of the war. He again discussed why the United States had become involved, although note the lack of references by this time to China. Near the end of the address, he made a peace offer that became known as the "San Antonio Formula." Although it created much debate in the United States, the North Vietnamese rejected the formula because it did not include a united Vietnam and an immediate withdrawal of U.S. troops. (Source: United States Government, *Public Papers of the Presidents of the United States: Lyndon B. Johnson, 1967* [Washington, 1969], pp. 876–81.)

This evening I came here to speak to you about Vietnam. . . .

Doubt and debate are enlarged because the problems of Vietnam are quite complex. They are a mixture of political turmoil—of poverty—of religious and factional strife—of ancient servitude and modern longing for freedom. Vietnam is all of these things.

Vietnam is also the scene of a powerful aggression that is spurred by an appetite for conquest. . . .

I want to turn now to the struggle in Vietnam itself.

There are questions about this difficult war that must trouble every really thoughtful person. . . .

First, are the Vietnamese—with our help, and that of their other allies —really making any progress? Is there a forward movement? The reports I see make it clear that there is. Certainly there is a positive movement toward constitutional government. Thus far the Vietnamese have met the political schedule that they laid down in January 1966.

The people wanted an elected, responsive government. They wanted it strongly enough to brave a vicious campaign of Communist terror and assassination to vote for it. It has been said that they killed more civilians in 4 weeks trying to keep them from voting before the election than our

American bombers have killed in the big cities of North Vietnam in bombing military targets.

On November 1, subject to the action, of course, of the Constituent Assembly, an elected government will be inaugurated and an elected Senate and Legislature will be installed. . . .

There is progress in the war itself, steady progress considering the war that we are fighting; rather dramatic progress considering the situation that actually prevailed when we sent our troops there in 1965; when we intervened to prevent the dismemberment of the country by the Vietcong and the North Vietnamese.

The campaigns of the last year drove the enemy from many of their major interior bases. The military victory almost within Hanoi's grasp in 1965 has now been denied them. The grip of the Vietcong on the people is being broken.

Since our commitment of major forces in July 1965 the proportion of the population living under Communist control has been reduced to well under 20 percent. Tonight the secure proportion of the population has grown from about 45 percent to 65 percent—and in the contested areas, the tide continues to run with us.

But the struggle remains hard. The South Vietnamese have suffered severely, as have we—particularly in the First Corps area in the north, where the enemy has mounted his heaviest attacks, and where his lines of communication to North Vietnam are shortest. Our casualties in the war have reached about 13,500 killed in action, and about 85,000 wounded. Of those 85,000 wounded, we thank God that 79,000 of the 85,000 have been returned, or will return to duty shortly. Thanks to our great American medical science and the helicopter. . . .

As we have told Hanoi time and time and time again, the heart of the matter is really this: The United States is willing to stop all aerial and naval bombardment of North Vietnam when this will lead promptly to productive discussions. We, of course, assume that while discussions proceed, North Vietnam would not take advantage of the bombing cessation or limitation.

But Hanoi has not accepted any of these proposals. . . .

Why, in the face of military and political progress in the South, and the burden of our bombing in the North, do they insist and persist with the war?

From many sources the answer is the same. They still hope that the people of the United States will not see this struggle through to the very end. As one Western diplomat reported to me only this week—he had just been in Hanoi—"They believe their staying power is greater than ours and that they can't lose." A visitor from a Communist capital had this to say: "They expect the war to be long, and that the Americans in the end will be defeated by a breakdown in morale, fatigue, and psychological factors." The Premier of North Vietnam said as far back as 1962: "Americans do not like long, inconclusive war. . . . Thus we are sure to win in the end."

Are the North Vietnamese right about us?

I think not. No. I think they are wrong. . . .

71. THE AFTERMATH OF THE TET OFFENSIVE

In late January 1968 the Communist forces suddenly launched an offensive that delivered a severe psychological and political, as well as military, blow. The Communists suffered huge casualties, but as General Earle G. Wheeler (Chairman, Joint Chiefs of Staff) told President Johnson in this report of February 27, 1968, the war had taken a new —and perhaps extraordinarily costly—turn. It had been, Wheeler wrote, "a very near thing." His talks in Vietnam with MACV (U.S. Military Assistance Command in Vietnam), GVN (Government of Vietnam), and RVNAF (South Vietnam Armed Forces) now led to conclusions quite different from those offered by Westmoreland in his speeches three months before. (Source: Memorandum of February 27, 1968, from Wheeler to Johnson, reprinted in the New York *Times* Edition, Neil Sheehan et al., eds., *The Pentagon Papers* [New York, 1971], pp. 615–21.)

1. The Chairman, JCS and party visited SVN on 23, 24 and 25 February. This report summarizes the impressions and facts developed through conversations and briefings at MACV and with senior commanders throughout the country.

SUMMARY

—The current situation in Vietnam is still developing and fraught with opportunities as well as dangers.

—There is no question in the mind of MACV that the enemy went all out for a general offensive and general uprising and apparently believed that he would succeed in bringing the war to an early successful conclusion.

—The enemy failed to achieve his initial objective but is continuing his effort. Although many of his units were badly hurt, the judgement is that he has the will and the capability to continue.

—Enemy losses have been heavy; he has failed to achieve his prime objectives of mass uprisings and capture of a large number of the capital cities and towns. Morale in enemy units which were badly mauled or where the men were oversold the idea of a decisive victory at TET probably has suffered severely. However, with replacements, his indoctrination system would seem capable of maintaining morale at a generally adequate level. His determination appears to be unshaken.

—The enemy is operating with relative freedom in the countryside, probably recruiting heavily and no doubt infiltrating NVA units and personnel. His recovery is likely to be rapid; his supplies are adequate; and he is trying to maintain the momentum of his winter-spring offensive.

—The structure of the GVN held up but its effectiveness has suffered.

—The RVNAF held up against the initial assault with gratifying, and in a way, surprising strength and fortitude. However, RVNAF is now in a defensive posture around towns and cities and there is concern about how well they will bear up under sustained pressure.

—The initial attack nearly succeeded in a dozen places, and defeat in those places was only averted by the timely reaction of U.S. forces. In short, it was a very near thing.

—There is no doubt that the RD [Rural Development] Program has suffered a severe set back.

—RVNAF was not badly hurt physically—they should recover strength and equipment rather quickly (equipment in 2–3 months—strength in 3–6 months). Their problems are more psychological than physical.

—U.S. forces have lost none of their pre-TET capability. . . .

THE SITUATION AS IT STANDS TODAY:

a. Enemy capabilities.

(1) The enemy has been hurt badly in the populated lowlands, is practically intact elsewhere. He committed over 67,000 combat maneuver forces plus perhaps 25% or 17,000 more impressed men and boys, for a total of about 84,000. He lost 40,000 killed, at least 3,000 captured, and perhaps 5,000 disabled or died of wounds. He had peaked his force total to about 240,000 just before TET, by hard recruiting, infiltration, civilian impressment, and drawdowns on service and guerrilla personnel. So he has lost about one fifth of his total strength. About two-thirds of his trained, organized unit strength can continue offensive action. He is probably infiltrating and recruiting heavily in the countryside while allied forces are securing the urban areas. . . . The enemy has adequate muni-

tions, stockpiled in-country and available through the DMZ, Laos, and Cambodia, to support major attacks and countrywide pressure; food procurement may be a problem. . . . Besides strength losses, the enemy now has morale and training problems which currently limit combat effectiveness of VC guerrilla, main and local forces. . . .

d. GVN Strength and Effectiveness:

(1) Psychological—the people in South Vietnam were handed a psychological blow, particularly in the urban areas where the feeling of security had been strong. There is a fear of further attacks.

(2) The structure of the Government was not shattered and continues to function but at greatly reduced effectiveness.

(3) In many places, the RD program has been set back badly. In other places the program was untouched in the initial stage of the offensive. MACV reports that of the 555 RD cadre groups, 278 remain in hamlets, 245 are in district and province towns on security duty, while 32 are unaccounted for. It is not clear as to when, or even whether, it will be possible to return to the RD program in its earlier form. As long as the VC prowl the countryside it will be impossible, in many places, even to tell exactly what has happened to the program.

(4) Refugees—An additional 470,000 refugees were generated during the offensive. . . . It is anticipated that the care and reestablishment of the 250,000 persons or 50,000 family units who have lost their homes will require from GVN sources the expenditure of 500 million piasters for their temporary care and resettlement plus an estimated 30,000 metric tons of rice. . . .

What Does the Future Hold

a. Probable enemy strategy. We see the enemy pursuing a reinforced offensive to enlarge his control throughout the country and keep pressures on the government and allies. We expect him to maintain strong threats in the DMZ area, at Khe Sanh, in the highlands, and at Saigon, and to attack in force when conditions seem favorable. He is likely to try to gain control of the country's northern provinces. He will continue efforts to encircle cities and province capitals to isolate and disrupt normal activities, and infiltrate them to create chaos. He will seek maximum attrition of RVNAF elements. Against U.S. forces, he will emphasize attacks by fire on airfields and installations, using assaults and ambushes selectively. His central objective continues to be the destruction of the Government of SVN and its armed forces. As a minimum he hopes to seize sufficient territory and gain control of enough people to support establishment of the groups and committees he proposes for participation in an NLF dominated government.

72. LBJ AND THE WISEMEN: THE MARCH 26 MEETING

As part of his evaluation of the post-Tet situation, President Johnson summoned a group of so-called Wisemen for extensive talks at the White House. The group included such distinguished former government officials as McGeorge Bundy (John Kennedy's and Johnson's National Security Adviser until 1966); Arthur Dean (who negotiated an end to the Korean War in 1953); Cyrus Vance (former Under Secretary of Defense under Johnson); Douglas Dillon (former Secretary of the Treasury); General Omar Bradley (Harry Truman's Chairman of the Joint Chiefs); General Maxwell Taylor (formerly U.S. Ambassador to Vietnam); Robert Murphy (a top State Department troubleshooter since the 1930s); General Matthew Ridgway (perhaps President Eisenhower's most trusted military adviser, especially on Asian affairs); Henry Cabot Lodge (former U.S. Ambassador to both the United Nations and South Vietnam); and George Ball (formerly Kennedy's and Johnson's Under Secretary of State). But the crucial participant was crusty Dean Acheson, once Truman's Secretary of State and renowned as a tough "cold warrior." Acheson now closely examined the cable traffic between Washington and Saigon, then turned against continuing the war. His turn, and his powers as a debater (demonstrated briefly in the document when he responds to Abe Fortas, a close friend and adviser of Johnson's) strongly shaped the President's final decisions. The notes are cryptic but revealing summaries of these crucial discussions on March 26. (Source: "Meeting with Special Advisory Group," March 26, 1968, Meeting Notes File, Box 2, Lyndon B. Johnson Library, Austin, Texas.)

March 26, 1968

SUMMARY OF NOTES

McGEORGE BUNDY: There is a very significant shift in our position. When we last met we saw reasons for hope.

We hoped then there would be slow but steady progress. Last night and today the picture is not so hopeful particularly in the countryside.

Dean Acheson summed up the majority feeling when he said that we can no longer do the job we set out to do in the time we have left and we must begin to take steps to disengage.

That view was shared by:

George Ball
Arthur Dean
Cy Vance
Douglas Dillon
and myself (McGeorge Bundy)

We do think we should do everything possible to strengthen in a real and visible way the performance of the Government of South Vietnam.

There were three of us who took a different position:

General Bradley
General Taylor
Bob Murphy

They all feel that we should not act to weaken our position and we should do what our military commanders suggest.

General Ridgway has a special point of view. He wanted to so strengthen the Army of South Vietnam that we could complete the job in two years.

On negotiations, Ball, Goldberg and Vance strongly urged a cessation of the bombing now. Others wanted a halt at some point but not now while the situation is still unresolved in the I Corps area.

On troop reenforcements the dominant sentiment was that the burden of proof rests with those who are urging the increase. Most of us think there should be a substantial escalation. We all felt there should not be an extension of the conflict. This would be against our national interest.

The use of atomic weapons is unthinkable.

SUMMARY

RIDGWAY: I agree with the summary as presented by McGeorge Bundy.

DEAN: I agree. All of us got the impression that there is no military conclusion in sight. We felt time is running out.

DEAN ACHESON: Agree with Bundy's presentation. Neither the effort of the Government of Vietnam or the effort of the U.S. government can succeed in the time we have left. Time is limited by reactions in this country. We cannot build an independent South Vietnam; therefore, we should do something by no later than late summer to establish something different.

271

HENRY CABOT LODGE: We should shift from search-and-destroy strategy to a strategy of using our military power as a shield to permit the South Vietnamese society to develop as well as North Vietnamese society has been able to do. We need to organize South Vietnam on a block-by-block, precinct-by-precinct basis.

DOUGLAS DILLON: We should change the emphasis. I agree with Acheson. The briefing last night led me to conclude we cannot achieve a military victory. I would agree with Lodge that we should cease search-and-destroy tactics and head toward an eventual disengagement. I would send only the troops necessary to support those there now.

GEORGE BALL: I share Acheson's view. I have felt that way since 1961 —that our objectives are not attainable. In the U.S. there is a sharp division of opinion. In the world, we look very badly because of the bombing. That is the central defect in our position. The disadvantages of bombing outweigh the advantages. We need to stop the bombing in the next six weeks to test the will of the North Vietnamese. As long as we continue to bomb, we alienate ourselves from the civilized world. I would have the Pope or U Thant [Secretary-General of the United Nations] suggest the bombing halt. It cannot come from the President.

A bombing halt would quieten [sic] the situation here at home.

CY VANCE: McGeorge Bundy stated my views. I agree with George Ball.

Unless we do something quick, the mood in this country may lead us to withdrawal. On troops, we should send no more than the 13,000 support troops. . . .

GENERAL TAYLOR: I am dismayed. The picture I get is a very different one from that you have. Let's not concede the home front; let's do something about it.

FORTAS: The U.S. has never had in mind winning a military victory out there; we always have wanted to reach an agreement or settle for the status quo between North Vietnam and South Vietnam. I agree with General Taylor. . . . This is not the time for an overture on our part. I do not think a cessation of the bombing would do any good at this time. I do not believe in drama for the sake of drama.

ACHESON: The issue is not that stated by Fortas. The issue is can we do what we are trying to do in Vietnam. I do not think we can. Fortas said we are not trying to win a military victory. The issue is can we by military means keep the North Vietnamese off the South Vietnamese. I do not think we can. They can slip around and end-run them and crack them up.

73. PRESIDENT JOHNSON'S TELEVISED SPEECH OF MARCH 31, 1968

General Westmoreland in South Vietnam had asked for as many as 206,000 more U.S. troops to launch a new offensive. In the aftermath of the Tet offensive, however, Johnson's advisers, led by Clark Clifford and Dean Acheson, concluded that not even that number could win necessary military victories. The President's policies had hit a dead end. To save them, he appeared on nationwide television to announce new peace plans and military campaigns. Note especially his emphasis on the effect of the war on the U.S. economy. The fighting was claiming casualties at home as well as abroad. He concluded with a dramatic statement about his own political future. (Source: United States Government, *Public Papers of the Presidents of the United States: Lyndon B. Johnson, 1968* [Washington, 1970], pp. 469–76.)

Tonight I want to speak to you of peace in Vietnam and Southeast Asia.

No other question so preoccupies our people. No other dream so absorbs the 250 million human beings who live in that part of the world. No other goal motivates American policy in Southeast Asia.

For years, representatives of our Government and others have traveled the world—seeking to find a basis for peace talks.

Since last September, they have carried the offer that I made public at San Antonio.

That offer was this:

That the United States would stop its bombardment of North Vietnam when that would lead promptly to productive discussions—and that we would assume that North Vietnam would not take military advantage of our restraint.

Hanoi denounced this offer, both privately and publicly. Even while the search for peace was going on, North Vietnam rushed their preparations for a savage assault on the people, the government, and the allies of South Vietnam.

Their attack—during the Tet holidays—failed to achieve its principal objectives. . . . Tonight, I renew the offer I made last August—to stop the bombardment of North Vietnam. We ask that talks begin promptly,

273

that they be serious talks on the substance of peace. We assume that during those talks Hanoi will not take advantage of our restraint.

We are prepared to move immediately toward peace through negotiations.

So, tonight, in the hope that this action will lead to early talks, I am taking the first step to deescalate the conflict. We are reducing—substantially reducing—the present level of hostilities.

And we are doing so unilaterally, and at once.

Tonight, I have ordered our aircraft and our naval vessels to make no attacks on North Vietnam, except in the area north of the demilitarized zone where the continuing enemy buildup directly threatens allied forward positions and where the movements of their troops and supplies are clearly related to that threat.

The area in which we are stopping our attacks includes almost 90 percent of North Vietnam's population, and most of its territory. Thus there will be no attacks around the principal populated areas, or in the food-producing areas of North Vietnam.

Even this very limited bombing of the North could come to an early end—if our restraint is matched by restraint in Hanoi. But I cannot in good conscience stop all bombing so long as to do so would immediately and directly endanger the lives of our men and our allies. Whether a complete bombing halt becomes possible in the future will be determined by events. . . .

Now, as in the past, the United States is ready to send its representatives to any forum, at any time, to discuss the means of bringing this ugly war to an end.

I am designating one of our most distinguished Americans, Ambassador Averell Harriman, as my personal representative for such talks. In addition, I have asked Ambassador Llewellyn Thompson, who returned from Moscow for consultation, to be available to join Ambassador Harriman at Geneva or any other suitable place—just as soon as Hanoi agrees to a conference.

I call upon President Ho Chi Minh to respond positively, and favorably, to this new step toward peace. . . .

Some weeks ago—to help meet the enemy's new offensive—we sent to Vietnam about 11,000 additional Marine and airborne troops. They were deployed by air in 48 hours, on an emergency basis. But the artillery, tank, aircraft, medical, and other units that were needed to work with and to support these infantry troops in combat could not then accompany them by air on that short notice.

In order that these forces may reach maximum combat effectiveness, the Joint Chiefs of Staff have recommended to me that we should prepare to send—during the next 5 months—support troops totaling approximately 13,500 men. . . .

The tentative estimate of those additional expenditures is $2.5 billion in this fiscal year, and $2.6 billion in the next fiscal year.

These projected increases in expenditures for our national security will bring into sharper focus the Nation's need for immediate action: action to protect the prosperity of the American people and to protect the strength and the stability of our American dollar. . . .

Yet Congress has not acted. And tonight we face the sharpest financial threat in the postwar era—a threat to the dollar's role as the keystone of international trade and finance in the world. . . .

What is at stake is 7 years of unparalleled prosperity. In those 7 years, the real income of the average American, after taxes, rose by almost 30 percent—a gain as large as that of the entire preceding 19 years.

So the steps that we must take to convince the world are exactly the steps we must take to sustain our own economic strength here at home. In the past 8 months, prices and interest rates have risen because of our inaction. . . .

Our reward will come in the life of freedom, peace, and hope that our children will enjoy through ages ahead.

What we won when all of our people united just must not now be lost in suspicion, distrust, selfishness, and politics among any of our people.

Believing this as I do, I have concluded that I should not permit the Presidency to become involved in the partisan divisions that are developing in this political year.

With America's sons in the fields far away, with America's future under challenge right here at home, with our hopes and the world's hopes for peace in the balance every day, I do not believe that I should devote an hour or a day of my time to any personal partisan causes or to any duties other than the awesome duties of this office—the Presidency of your country.

Accordingly, I shall not seek, and I will not accept, the nomination of my party for another term as your President.

But let men everywhere know, however, that a strong, a confident, and a vigilant America stands ready tonight to seek an honorable peace—and stands ready tonight to defend an honored cause—whatever the price, whatever the burden, whatever the sacrifice that duty may require.

Thank you for listening.

Good night and God bless all of you.

74. THE CHICAGO RIOTS OF 1968

Johnson's appeal for unity and peace at home turned into orders for U.S. troops and the National Guard to clear streets of antiwar and civil rights protesters. In the summer, the protests—which had been growing since 1965—reached massive proportions after the assassinations of Martin Luther King and Robert Kennedy, and with the continued fighting in Vietnam. One outbreak occurred in late August when the Democrats met in Chicago to nominate Vice-President Hubert Humphrey as their presidential candidate. A special National Commission examined the riot. The excerpt of the commission's report given below describes the police brutality and some of its causes. Public opinion polls continued to show many Americans supporting the President's Vietnam policies, but the question was becoming whether the society could hold together, especially in urban areas and on college campuses, under the growing stress of the war. (Source: *Rights in Conflict: Convention Week in Chicago, August 25–29, 1966.* A report submitted by Daniel Walker, Director of the Chicago Study Team, to the National Commission on the Causes and Prevention of Violence, pp. 29–33.)

A SUMMARY
[OF THE RIOTS]

During the week of the Democratic National Convention, the Chicago police were the targets of mounting provocation by both word and act. It took the form of obscene epithets, and of rocks, sticks, bathroom tiles and even human feces hurled at police by demonstrators. Some of these acts had been planned; others were spontaneous or were themselves provoked by police action. Furthermore, the police had been put on edge by widely published threats of attempts to disrupt both the city and the Convention.

That was the nature of the provocation. The nature of the response was unrestrained and indiscriminate police violence on many occasions, particularly at night.

That violence was made all the more shocking by the fact that it was often inflicted upon persons who had broken no law, disobeyed no order, made no threat. These included peaceful demonstrators, onlookers, and large numbers of residents who were simply passing through, or happened to live in, the areas where confrontations were occurring.

Newsmen and photographers were singled out for assault, and their equipment deliberately damaged. Fundamental police training was ignored; and officers, when on the scene, were often unable to control their men. As one police officer put it: "What happened didn't have anything to do with police work." . . .

How did it start? With the emergence long before convention week of three factors which figured significantly in the outbreak of violence. These were: threats to the city; the city's response; and the conditioning of Chicago police to expect that violence against demonstrators, as against rioters, would be condoned by city officials.

The threats to the City were varied. Provocative and inflammatory statements, made in connection with activities planned for convention week, were published and widely disseminated. There were also intelligence reports from informants.

Some of this information was absurd, like the reported plan to contaminate the city's water supply with LSD. But some were serious; and both were strengthened by the authorities' lack of any mechanism for distinguishing one from the other.

The second factor—the city's response—matched, in numbers and logistics at least, the demonstrators' threats.

The city, fearful that the "leaders" would not be able to control their followers, attempted to discourage an inundation of demonstrators by not granting permits for marches and rallies and by making it quite clear that the "law" would be enforced.

Government—federal, state and local—moved to defend itself from the threats, both imaginary and real. The preparations were detailed and far ranging: from stationing firemen at each alarm box within a six block radius of the Amphitheatre to staging U.S. Army armored personnel carriers in Soldier Field under Secret Service control. Six thousand Regular Army troops in full field gear, equipped with rifles, flame throwers, and bazookas were airlifted to Chicago on Monday, August 26. About 6,000 Illinois National Guard troops had already been activated to assist the 12,000 member Chicago Police Force.

Of course, the Secret Service could never afford to ignore threats of assassination of Presidential candidates. Neither could the city, against the background of riots in 1967 and 1968, ignore the ever-present threat of ghetto riots, possibly sparked by large numbers of demonstrators, during convention week.

277

The third factor emerged in the city's position regarding the riots following the death of Dr. Martin Luther King and the April 27th peace march to the Civic Center in Chicago.

The police were generally credited with restraint in handling the first riots—but Mayor Daley rebuked the Superintendent of Police. While it was later modified, his widely disseminated "shoot to kill arsonists and shoot to maim looters" order undoubtedly had an effect.

The effect on police became apparent several weeks later, when they attacked demonstrators, bystanders and media representatives at a Civic Center peace march. There were published criticisms—but the city's response was to ignore the police violence.

That was the background. On August 18, 1968, the advance contingent of demonstrators arrived in Chicago and established their base, as planned, in Lincoln Park on the city's Near North Side. Throughout the week, they were joined by others—some from the Chicago area, some from states as far away as New York and California. On the weekend before the convention began, there were about 2,000 demonstrators in Lincoln Park; the crowd grew to about 10,000 by Wednesday.

There were, of course, the hippies—the long hair and love beads, the calculated unwashedness, the flagrant banners, the open lovemaking and disdain for the constraints of conventional society. In dramatic effect, both visual and vocal, these dominated a crowd whose members actually differed widely in physical appearance, in motivation, in political affiliation, in philosophy. The crowd included Yippies come to "do their thing," youngsters working for a political candidate, professional people with dissenting political views, anarchists and determined revolutionaries, motorcycle gangs, black activists, young thugs, police and secret service undercover agents. There were demonstrators waving the Viet Cong flag and the red flag of revolution and there were the simply curious who came to watch and, in many cases, became willing or unwilling participants.

To characterize the crowd, then, as entirely hippy-Yippie, entirely "New Left," entirely anarchist, or entirely youthful political dissenters is both wrong and dangerous. The stereotyping that did occur helps to explain the emotional reaction of both police and public during and after the violence that occurred.

Despite the presence of some revolutionaries, the vast majority of the demonstrators were intent on expressing by peaceful means their dissent either from society generally or from the administration's policies in Vietnam. . . .

278

Much of the violence witnessed in Old Town that night seems malicious or mindless:

> There were pedestrians. People who were not part of the demonstration were coming out of a tavern to see what the demonstration was . . . and the officers indiscriminately started beating everybody on the street who was not a policeman. . . .

A federal legal official relates an experience of Tuesday evening.

> I then walked one block north where I met a group of 12–15 policemen. I showed them my identification and they permitted me to walk with them. The police walked one block west. Numerous people were watching us from their windows and balconies. The police yelled profanities at them, taunting them to come down where the police would beat them up. The police stopped a number of people on the street demanding identification. They verbally abused each pedestrian and pushed one or two without hurting them. We walked back to Clark Street and began to walk north where the police stopped a number of people who appeared to be protesters, and ordered them out of the area in a very abusive way. One protester who was walking in the opposite direction was kneed in the groin by a policeman who was walking towards him. The boy fell to the ground and swore at the policeman who picked him up and threw him to the ground. We continued to walk toward the command post. A derelict who appeared to be very intoxicated, walked up to the policeman and mumbled something that was incoherent. The policeman pulled from his belt a tin container and sprayed its contents into the eyes of the derelict, who stumbled around and fell on his face.

It was on these nights that the police violence against media representatives reached its peak. Much of it was plainly deliberate. A newsman was pulled aside on Monday by a detective acquaintance of his who said: "The word is being passed to get newsmen." Individual newsmen were warned, "You take my picture tonight and I'm going to get you." Cries of "get the camera" preceded individual attacks on photographers.

75. NIXON APPEALS TO THE "SILENT MAJORITY"

President Nixon planned to bomb the North Vietnamese to the negotiating table while building up a self-sufficient South Vietnamese Army. To accomplish those two objectives, however, he needed time and also had to neutralize the growing antiwar sentiment in the United States. His speech of November 3, 1969, was written with all this in mind, and in the address he defined the cornerstone of his policy, the Guam (or as Nixon preferred, the Nixon) Doctrine. (Source, United States Government, *Public Papers of the Presidents of the United States: Richard M. Nixon, 1969* [Washington, 1971], pp. 901–9.)

ADDRESS TO THE NATION ON THE WAR IN VIETNAM. NOVEMBER 3, 1969

Good evening, my fellow Americans:

Tonight I want to talk to you on a subject of deep concern to all Americans and to many people in all parts of the world—the war in Vietnam.

I believe that one of the reasons for the deep division about Vietnam is that many Americans have lost confidence in what their Government has told them about our policy. The American people cannot and should not be asked to support a policy which involves the overriding issues of war and peace unless they know the truth about that policy. . . .

What are the prospects for peace?

Now, let me begin by describing the situation I found when I was inaugurated on January 20.

—The war had been going on for 4 years.

—31,000 Americans had been killed in action.

—The training program for the South Vietnamese was behind schedule.

—540,000 Americans were in Vietnam with no plans to reduce the number.

—No progress had been made at the negotiations in Paris and the United States had not put forth a comprehensive peace proposal.

—The war was causing deep division at home and criticism from many of our friends as well as our enemies abroad. . . .

But the question facing us today is: Now that we are in the war, what is the best way to end it?

In January I could only conclude that the precipitate withdrawal of American forces from Vietnam would be a disaster not only for South Vietnam but for the United States and for the cause of peace.

For the South Vietnamese, our precipitate withdrawal would inevitably allow the Communists to repeat the massacres which followed their take-over in the North 15 years before.

—They then murdered more than 50,000 people and hundreds of thousands more died in slave labor camps.

—We saw a prelude of what would happen in South Vietnam when the Communists entered the city of Hue last year. During their brief rule there, there was a bloody reign of terror in which 3,000 civilians were clubbed, shot to death, and buried in mass graves. . . .

For the United States, this first defeat in our Nation's history would result in a collapse of confidence in American leadership, not only in Asia but throughout the world. . . .

For the future of peace, precipitate withdrawal would thus be a disaster of immense magnitude.

—A nation cannot remain great if it betrays its allies and lets down its friends.

—Our defeat and humiliation in South Vietnam without question would promote recklessness in the councils of those great powers who have not yet abandoned their goals of world conquest.

—This would spark violence wherever our commitments help maintain the peace—in the Middle East, in Berlin, eventually even in the Western Hemisphere.

Ultimately, this would cost more lives.

It would not bring peace; it would bring more war.

For these reasons, I rejected the recommendation that I should end the war by immediately withdrawing all of our forces. I chose instead to change American policy on both the negotiating front and battlefront.

In a television speech on May 14, in a speech before the United Nations, and on a number of other occasions I set forth our peace proposals in great detail.

—We have offered the complete withdrawal of all outside forces within 1 year.

—We have proposed a cease-fire under international supervision.

—We have offered free elections under international supervision with the Communists participating in the organization and conduct of the elections as an organized political force. And the Saigon Government has pledged to accept the result of the elections.

We have not put forth our proposals on a take-it-or-leave-it basis. We have indicated that we are willing to discuss the proposals that have been put forth by the other side. We have declared that anything is negotiable except the right of the people of South Vietnam to determine their own future. . . .

Hanoi has refused even to discuss our proposals. They demand our unconditional acceptance of their terms, which are that we withdraw all American forces immediately and unconditionally and that we overthrow the Government of South Vietnam as we leave. . . .

It is in line with a major shift in U.S. foreign policy which I described in my press conference at Guam on July 25. Let me briefly explain what has been described as the Nixon Doctrine—a policy which not only will help end the war in Vietnam, but which is an essential element of our program to prevent future Vietnams. . . .

I laid down in Guam three principles as guidelines for future American policy toward Asia:

—First, the United States will keep all of its treaty commitments.

—Second, we shall provide a shield if a nuclear power threatens the freedom of a nation allied with us or of a nation whose survival we consider vital to our security.

—Third, in cases involving other types of aggression, we shall furnish military and economic assistance when requested in accordance with our treaty commitments. But we shall serve the cause of peace—not just in Vietnam but in the Pacific and in the world.

In speaking of the consequences of a precipitate withdrawal, I mentioned that our allies would lose confidence in America.

Far more dangerous, we would lose confidence in ourselves. Oh, the immediate reaction would be a sense of relief that our men were coming home. But as we saw the consequences of what we had done, inevitable remorse and divisive recrimination would scar our spirit. . . .

I know it may not be fashionable to speak of patriotism or national destiny these days. But I feel it is appropriate to do so on this occasion.

Two hundred years ago this Nation was weak and poor. But even then, America was the hope of millions in the world. Today we have become the strongest and richest nation in the world. And the wheel of destiny has turned so that any hope the world has for the survival of peace and freedom will be determined by whether the American people have the moral stamina and the courage to meet the challenge of free world leadership.

Let historians not record that when America was the most powerful nation in the world we passed on the other side of the road and allowed the last hopes for peace and freedom of millions of people to be suffocated by the forces of totalitarianism.

And so tonight—to you, the great silent majority of my fellow Americans—I ask for your support. . . .

Let us be united for peace. Let us also be united against defeat. Because let us understand: North Vietnam cannot defeat or humiliate the United States. Only Americans can do that.

76. THE INVASION OF CAMBODIA: THE DEBATE

On April 30, 1970, Nixon suddenly announced that U.S. and South Vietnamese troops were invading Cambodia to clean out the North Vietnamese camps in the eastern part of the country, and perhaps even capture a key Communist headquarters (which was never found). The President had been secretly bombing Cambodia—a declared neutral country—for a year; now he believed he had to invade to protect the flank of the departing U.S. troops. The United States erupted in protest and debate. A group of five U.S. senators asked Professor George Kahin of Cornell University to respond to Nixon's claims point by point. Kahin, a most distinguished scholar of modern Southeast Asia, released the following paper in mid-May 1970. (Source: George McT. Kahin, *Cambodia: The Administration's Version and the Historical Record* [Washington, 1970].)

This paper contains replies to prepared question and answer materials distributed by the Administration on May 1 in regard to the Cambodian invasion—as well as to certain statements made by the President in his April 30 speech.

THE ADMINISTRATION'S CLAIM OF U.S. RESPECT FOR CAMBODIA'S NEUTRALITY

Central to President Nixon's argument is the following statement in the introductory part of his April 30 speech. Going back to the Geneva Agreements of 1954 he stated: "American policy since then has been to scrupulously respect the neutrality of the Cambodian people." In the White

283

House's subsequently released (May 1) "Background Information on Cambodia" among the various hypothetical questions raised was one which reads: "Why do we have to support the Lon Nol government? Wasn't Sihanouk the legal ruler and wasn't he pushed out by a coup?" The answer provided by the White House states: "The question of who rules in Cambodia is a matter for the Cambodians to decide. We had absolutely nothing to do with the change."

THE HISTORICAL RECORD

It is to be hoped that the U.S. was not party to the overthrow of Sihanouk, but it is understandable why the many years of American clandestine activity in Cambodia makes Sihanouk think otherwise and may raise some doubt in the minds of anyone familiar with the pertinent historical record. There is a great deal in that record that departs radically from the President's assertion that it has been American policy to "scrupulously respect the neutrality of the Cambodian people."

In fact for the most of the last 15 years the U.S. has opposed Cambodian neutrality and applied various kinds of pressure to get it to assume an anti-Communist stance in alignment with American policy objectives. Following Cambodia's refusal to accept the security mantle incorporated in the SEATO protocol, American aid was halted. The Saigon and Bangkok governments imposed an economic blockade, and border violations were visited upon Cambodia from two of the United States' SEATO allies, Thailand and South Vietnam. (It was just after this that the Cambodians responded by opening diplomatic relations with the Soviet Union and agreed to accept aid from China.) . . .

By 1966 a campaign supported by CIA to pressure Sihanouk through support of the opposition Khmer Serei tied down a substantial part of the Cambodian army. Khmer Krom (members of South Vietnam's Cambodian minority) were recruited at high rates of pay and provided with extensive U.S. Special Forces training to carry out attacks into Cambodia from bases in both South Vietnam and Southeast Thailand. Border incursions by these forces in 1967 reached at least 12 miles into Cambodia.

THE ADMINISTRATION'S CLAIM OF NON-VIOLATION OF CAMBODIAN TERRITORY

Referring to Vietnamese communist sanctuaries in Cambodia, President Nixon stated on April 30: "For five years neither the U.S. nor South Vietnam moved against those enemy sanctuaries because we did not wish to violate the territory of a neutral nation."

THE HISTORICAL RECORD

In July 1965 the International Control Commission (I.C.C.) reported on evidence of border crossings into Cambodia by South Vietnamese forces, stating that there were 375 such incidents in 1964 and 385 in the first five months of 1965 alone. The commission unanimously concluded that "None of those incidents were provoked by the Royal Government of Cambodia." From that time on there were repeated reports of border incursions and air attacks against border areas inside Cambodia chiefly by South Vietnamese but also by American forces. . . .

On January 22, 1968, the U.S. acknowledged that a U.S.-South Vietnamese patrol had made a limited intrusion into Cambodia following fire from Vietnamese communist units on the Cambodian side. (NYT *[New York Times]* January 23, 1968)

In April 1969, U.S. air and artillery attacks were launched against communist bases inside Cambodia. (NYT April 26, 1969)

On May 8, 1969, U.S. B-52 bombers raided communist supply dumps and camps within Cambodia. (NYT May 9, 1969)

October–December, 1969, Sihanouk protested continuing U.S. bombing of Cambodian border areas.

THE ADMINISTRATION'S QUESTION:

Will this action (the American intervention in Cambodia) affect pacification and Vietnamization adversely by pulling ARVN and U.S. forces out of South Vietnam?

THE ADMINISTRATION'S ANSWER

One cannot assume that the enemy will be able to take advantage of the situation in this fashion since we have some indications that they are also giving priority attention to protecting base areas in Cambodia.

We believe that in any case we will gain, because in the long run damage to the bases will be greater and hurt the Communist effort in South Vietnam more than whatever limited gains in South Vietnam they might be able to make during this action.

This is the unanimous judgment of our responsible military leaders.

ANOTHER ANSWER

If it is true, as both Saigon and Washington now assert, that Vietnamization cannot succeed without denial of eastern Cambodian districts to the enemy, then the Administration has no alternative except to occupy these areas with South Vietnamese and/or American troops, and to make a

285

major and continuing commitment to shore up the Lon Nol government. This means that the scope of the war has been greatly expanded without any significant change in the balance of forces.

The South Vietnamese army, whose capacity to defend even South Vietnam is still critically dependent upon American military forces, is now called upon to spread its resources ever more thinly in longterm ground operations over half of Cambodia. It is clear that the number of Vietnamese soldiers available to relieve American manpower in Vietnam is now drastically reduced. To extend assignment of Saigon's forces to wide areas of Cambodia makes a travesty of whatever prospects for success Vietnamization might have enjoyed had the role of Saigon's troops been confined to Vietnam. Since Vietnamization means substitution of Vietnamese soldiers for Americans, it is clear that the process set in motion by the Cambodian invasion works directly against prospects for achievement of that policy and bringing American soldiers home. . . .

THE ADMINISTRATION'S QUESTION:

Do we not think that operations by U.S. forces inside Cambodia will jeopardize the prospects for negotiations?

THE ADMINISTRATION'S ANSWER

Recent North Vietnamese actions and statements give no indications that they are ready to negotiate. In fact, they may be postponing any serious negotiations which they might have contemplated until they can see what happens in Cambodia. . . .

ANOTHER ANSWER

It is already evident that the invasion of Cambodia has made President Thieu even more outspoken in his refusal to accept a negotiated settlement, and in his insistence upon a solution by military means. If, as the Administration has repeatedly stated, the Vietnamization program was designed to reduce American commitments in Southeast Asia and to facilitate the achievement of a negotiated settlement of the war, the Cambodian adventure is impossible to justify. By enlarging the area of conflict and the scope of American commitments and by increasing the number of disputing parties, it adds enormously to the length and complexity of any agenda for negotiations. With the U.S. and the Vietnamese now enmeshed in a Cambodian civil war a virtually insoluble Cambodian problem is added to the already intractable Vietnamese problem. It is no longer enough to settle the war in Vietnam and Laos; we are assuming a responsibility for settling a Cambodian war as well.

President Nixon's precipitate invasion of Cambodia has not only further polarized internal political forces in Cambodia; but by aligning Sihanouk (who for so long had managed to remain unaligned and genuinely neutral) with Moscow and Peking, it has increased polarization within the concerned international community. The President's action has seriously reduced the confidence of Japan and our most important European allies in America's foreign policy; and it has drastically undercut the possibilities for any Soviet offices in getting a negotiated solution of the Vietnam war underway.

THE ADMINISTRATION'S QUESTION:

What was the legal basis for the President's actions?

THE ADMINISTRATION'S ANSWER

The President was acting under his Constitutional authority as Commander-in-Chief of the Armed Forces to assure the security of the troops under his command, and also under his Constitutional authority as Chief Executive for the conduct of foreign affairs.

ANOTHER ANSWER

It is appalling for the Administration to define the legitimacy of President Nixon's act strictly in terms of American law and precedent.

Cambodia is a sovereign state. Since the U.S. acted without consulting its government, our invasion is a violation of international law.

It must be noted that Cambodia renounced the SEATO protocol providing protection for the former Indochina states. . . . If it is argued that the President made his decision in the context of American constitutional practice, it must be noted that his invasion of what he has referred to as a "neutral" country, has been taken in the absence of a declaration of war without the advice and consent of Congress.

77. THE INVASION OF CAMBODIA: THE WAR AT HOME

One of the worst outbreaks of violence and protest in twentieth-century American history erupted immediately after Nixon announced the invasion of Cambodia. The two worst incidents occurred at Kent State

University in Ohio and Jackson State in Mississippi. A special President's Commission investigated the murders, and its description of the killings at Kent State by the Ohio National Guard is given below. The primary cause of the Kent State protest was the war. Jackson State students rioted because of severe racial problems. Particularly noteworthy is the commission's view of student public opinion. Following the commission's report is a special series of memoranda written to Nixon, at his request, by two noted educators: Dr. Alexander Heard, Chancellor of Vanderbilt University, and Dr. James E. Cheek, President of Howard University, during June and July 1970. The memoranda must not have been pleasant reading for the President. (Source: *The Report of the President's Commission on Campus Unrest* [Washington, 1970], pp. 17–47, 233–73.)

THE RIOTS OF SPRING, 1970: A DESCRIPTION

On April 30, 1970, President Nixon announced that American and South Vietnamese forces were moving against enemy sanctuaries in Cambodia. Minutes after this announcement, student-organized protest demonstrations were under way at Princeton and Oberlin College. Within a few days, strikes and other protests had taken place at scores of colleges and universities throughout the country.

The expanding wave of strikes brought with it some serious disturbances. One of these was at Kent State University in Ohio, and approximately 750 Ohio National Guardsmen were sent to quell the disorders there.

On May 2, the ROTC building at Kent State was set afire. On May 4, Kent State students congregated on the university Commons and defied an order by the Guard to disperse. Guardsmen proceeded to disperse the crowd. The students then began to taunt Guard units and to throw rocks. . . .

Near the crest of Blanket Hill [on the Kent State campus] stands the Pagoda, a square bench made of 4-by-4 wooden beams and shaded by a concrete umbrella. The events which occurred as the Guard reached the Pagoda, turned, and fired on the students, are in bitter dispute.

Many guardsmen said they had hard going as they withdrew up the hill. Fassinger [a ranking National Guard officer] said he was hit six times by stones [thrown by the students], once on the shoulder so hard that he stumbled.

Fassinger had removed his gas mask to see more clearly. He said the guardsmen had reached a point between the Pagoda and Taylor Hall, and he was attempting to maintain them in a reasonably orderly formation, when he heard a sound like a shot, which was immediately followed by a volley of shots. He saw the troops on the Taylor Hall end of the line shooting. He yelled, "Cease fire!" and ran along the line repeating the command.

Major Jones [another ranking Guard officer] said he first heard an explosion which he thought was a firecracker. As he turned to his left, he heard another explosion which he knew to be an M-1 rifle shot. As he turned to his right, toward Taylor Hall, he said he saw guardsmen kneeling (photographs show some crouching) and bringing their rifles to their shoulders. He heard another M-1 shot, and then a volley of them. He yelled, "Cease fire!" several times, and rushed down the line shoving rifle barrels up and away from the crowd. He hit several guardsmen on their helmets with his swagger stick to stop them from firing.

General Canterbury [the ranking Guard officer] stated that he first heard a single shot, which he thought was fired from some distance away on his left and which in his opinion did not come from a military weapon. Immediately afterward, he heard a volley of M-1 fire from his right, the Taylor Hall end of the line. The Guard's fire was directed away from the direction from which Canterbury thought the initial, nonmilitary shot came. His first reaction . . . was to stop the firing.

Canterbury, Fassinger, and Jones—the three ranking officers on the hill —all said no order to fire was given.

Twenty-eight guardsmen have acknowledged firing from Blanket Hill. Of these, 25 fired 55 shots from rifles, two fired five shots from .45 caliber pistols, and one fired a single blast from a shotgun. Sound tracks indicate that the firing of these 61 shots lasted approximately 13 seconds. The time of the shooting was approximately 12:25 P.M. Four persons were killed and nine were wounded. . . .

Of the casualties, two were shot in the front, seven from the side, and four from the rear. All 13 were students at Kent State University. . . .

During the six days after the President's announcement of the Cambodian incursion, but prior to the deaths at Kent State, some twenty new student strikes had begun each day. During the four days that followed the Kent killings, there were a hundred or more strikes each day. A student strike center located at Brandeis University reported that, by the 10th of May, 448 campuses were either still affected by some sort of strike or completely closed down.

Ten days after the events at Kent State there were disturbances at Jackson State College, a black school in Jackson, Mississippi. On the night of May 14, students threw bricks and bottles at passing white motorists, a truck was set ablaze, and city and state police, called to protect firemen, were harassed by the crowd. Some policemen fired a fusillade into a girls' dormitory. Two Blacks were killed, and at least twelve were wounded.

Other schools joined the student strike, and many temporarily suspended classes in memory of those killed at Jackson State. By the end of May . . . nearly one third of the approximately 2,500 colleges and universities in America had experienced some kind of protest activity. The high point of the strikes was during the week following the deaths at Kent State. . . .

On the whole, American students are not as politically radical as some press reports might suggest. Only three years ago, in the spring of 1967, a Gallup poll of college students found that 49 percent classified themselves as "hawks" on the war in Vietnam. Since that time, there has been a dramatic shift of students' attitudes toward the war. A Gallup poll published in December 1969 found that only 20 percent of the students classified themselves as "hawks" while 69 percent classified themselves as "doves." At the same time, 50 percent—as compared to 64 percent of the adult public—approved of the way President Nixon was handling the situation in Vietnam. In 1965, one poll reported that only 6 percent of American students favored immediate withdrawal from Vietnam. In May 1970, a special Harris survey . . . conducted after the Cambodian incursion and the events at Kent State and Jackson State, found that 54 percent favored an end to the fighting in Vietnam and bringing American troops home as soon as possible.

THE RIOTS OF SPRING, 1970: THE CAUSES

Memorandum of June 19, 1970. We do not believe that our National Government really understands that a *national* crisis confronts us. The condition cannot be conceived as a temporary, aberrational outburst by the young, or simply as a "campus crisis" or a "student crisis." . . .

The Cambodian action—followed by the Jackson State and Kent State killings—sharply intensified feelings among students already protesting the war and showing disaffection with society generally. More important, Cambodia provoked and exposed antiwar and societal discontents among large numbers of students of normally moderate and conservative political viewpoints. . . .

Memorandum of July 6. Why do the President and disaffected college youth have trouble "communicating" about Vietnam? At least four factors are at work.

First, the President uses words that mean one thing to him but something different to many students. For example, he has emphasized that he and students both want "peace." By "peace," students mean an end to the killing immediately. To them the President seems to mean not that, but a "just peace" and "self-determination for South Vietnam," which they see as probably meaning maintenance of a pro-American regime in Saigon, continued U.S. military presence in Southeast Asia, and whatever military action is necessary to produce these ends.

Exacerbating this difficulty is the belief of many students—shared, it is fair to say, by many nonstudents—that the course we are on has no real chance of success. . . .

Second, what the President regards as successes, students often regard very differently. Reducing the troop level in Vietnam by sometime in 1971 to something over 200,000 men seems to many in Government a formidable achievement. The President so proclaims it. Yet to the young, who face the draft and think on the time scale of youth, these withdrawals seem wholly inadequate. Their attitude should not be mistaken for that of a draft dodger in World War II. They are not seeking to avoid personal danger. Rather they abhor personal involvement in a war they perceive as "immoral."

Third, to some students, the President appears not to understand the nature of the crisis that has come over the country. He speaks of "deep divisions" in the country. But "deep divisions" suggests a serious disagreement in a stable society, a matter of different groups holding different opinions. . . . [Students] see not just differences of opinion, but rather the whole social order as being in a state of erosion. . . .

Fourth, and this really underlies the other points, the President and some students proceed from vastly different assumptions. The President says, "America has never lost a war," as if "winning" or "losing" were the important consideration. He seems to them to hold attitudes derived from the "cold war," such as the domino theory, and to view Communism in Southeast Asia as a source of danger to America. Wrongly or rightly, many of our best-informed students do not share these assumptions. The President speaks of maintaining "national honor" and implies that this can be done through military power. . . . [Students] see the Vietnam war and its effects at home as obstructing fulfillment of their concept of national honor. Just as an earlier generation fought in World War II to preserve the nation's ideals, they want to end the war to help attain the nation's ideals. . . .

Why are the students not impressed by Soviet atrocities such as the invasion of Czechoslovakia [in 1968]? . . . First, they feel that by the wrongness of our own policies, such as the war in Vietnam, we have lost our moral standing to condemn other countries. Second, there is an obsession with our own problems, a feeling that our own crises should occupy all our attention. Third, the fear of Communism is less than existed a decade ago. . . .

How do they compare the United States with other countries generally? The students we speak of tend to be suspicious of all national powers, including the United States. . . . A generational loyalty appears to develop, a loyalty to young people internationally, that transcends national loyalties. . . .

Rather than emphasize what is good about America, most students emphasize what could be better about America. . . . Therefore, any form of injustice and inequality, such as is evident in our racial problems, is taken as an indictment of the entire social system, regardless of its improvements over the past, or its relative superiority over other societies.

78. U.S. MILITARY VETERANS QUESTION THE WAR, APRIL 1971

Antiwar protest soon assumed strange forms. In April 1971 a group of one thousand veterans of the Vietnam conflict marched on Washington to announce publicly their hatred for the war. Their spokesman, John Kerry, made eloquent, shocking statements about U.S. acts in Vietnam. But another veteran, Melville L. Stephens, also made a compelling argument that Americans now had a great responsibility to those Vietnamese who had risked everything to help the United States. The moral and political dilemmas were becoming more haunting and complex than most Americans—with their simple views about fighting communism—had ever imagined. (Source: United States Senate, Committee on Foreign Relations, *Legislative Proposals Relating to the War in Southeast Asia. Hearings . . . April 20, 21, 22, and 28 . . .* [Washington, 1971], pp. 180–210, 251–62.)

STATEMENT OF JOHN KERRY, VIETNAM VETERANS AGAINST THE WAR

MR. KERRY . . . I would like to say for the record, and also for the men behind me who are also wearing the uniforms and their medals, that my sitting here is really symbolic. I am not here as John Kerry. I am here

292

as one member of the group of 1,000, which is a small representation of a very much larger group of veterans in this country, and were it possible for all of them to sit at this table they would be here and have the same kind of testimony. . . .

I would like to talk, representing all those veterans, and say that several months ago in Detroit, we had an investigation at which over 150 honorably discharged and many very highly decorated veterans testified to war crimes committed in Southeast Asia, not isolated incidents but crimes committed on a day-to-day basis with the full awareness of officers at all levels of command.

It is impossible to describe to you exactly what did happen in Detroit, the emotions in the room, the feelings of the men who were reliving their experiences in Vietnam, but they did. They relived the absolute horror of what this country, in a sense, made them do.

They told the stories at times they had personally raped, cut off ears, cut off heads, taped wires from portable telephones to human genitals and turned up the power, cut off limbs, blown up bodies, randomly shot at civilians, razed villages in fashion reminiscent of Genghis Khan, shot cattle and dogs for fun, poisoned food stocks, and generally ravaged the countryside of South Vietnam in addition to the normal ravage of war, and the normal and very particular ravaging which is done by the applied bombing power of this country.

We call this investigation the "Winter Soldier Investigation." The term "Winter Soldier" is a play on words of Thomas Paine in 1776 when he spoke of the Sunshine Patriot and summertime soldiers who deserted at Valley Forge because the going was rough.

We who have come here to Washington have come here because we feel we have to be winter soldiers now. We could come back to this country; we could be quiet; we could hold our silence; we could not tell what went on in Vietnam, but we feel because of what threatens this country, the fact that the crimes threaten it, not reds, and not redcoats but the crimes which we are committing that threaten it, that we have to speak out.

I would like to talk to you a little bit about what the result is of the feelings these men carry with them after coming back from Vietnam. The country doesn't know it yet, but it has created a monster, a monster in the form of millions of men who have been taught to deal and to trade in violence, and who are given the chance to die for the biggest nothing in history; men who have returned with a sense of anger and a sense of betrayal which no one has yet grasped.

As a veteran and one who feels this anger, I would like to talk about it.

We are angry because we feel we have been used in the worst fashion by the administration of this country.

In 1970 at West Point, Vice President Agnew said "some glamorize the criminal misfits of society while our best men die in Asian rice paddies to preserve the freedom which most of those misfits abuse," and this was used as a rallying point for our effort in Vietnam.

But for us, as boys in Asia whom the country was supposed to support, his statement is a terrible distortion from which we can only draw a very deep sense of revulsion. Hence the anger of some of the men who are here in Washington today. It is a distortion because we in no way consider ourselves the best men of this country, because those he calls misfits were standing up for us in a way that nobody else in this country dared to, because so many who have died would have returned to this country to join the misfits in their efforts to ask for an immediate withdrawal from South Vietnam, because so many of those best men have returned as quadriplegics and amputees, and they lie forgotten in Veterans' Administration hospitals in this country which fly the flag which so many have chosen as their own personal symbol. And we cannot consider ourselves America's best men when we are ashamed of and hated what we were called on to do in Southeast Asia.

In our opinion, and from our experience, there is nothing in South Vietnam, nothing which could happen that realistically threatens the United States of America. And to attempt to justify the loss of one American life in Vietnam, Cambodia, or Laos by linking such loss to the preservation of freedom, which those misfits supposedly abuse, is to us the height of criminal hypocrisy, and it is that kind of hypocrisy which we feel has torn this country apart. . . .

What Was Found and Learned in Vietnam

We found that not only was it a civil war, an effort by a people who had for years been seeking their liberation from any colonial influence whatsoever, but also we found that the Vietnamese whom we had enthusiastically molded after our own image were hard put to take up the fight against the threat we were supposedly saving them from.

We found most people didn't even know the difference between communism and democracy. They only wanted to work in rice paddies without helicopters strafing them and bombs with napalm burning their villages and tearing their country apart. They wanted everything to do with the war, particularly with this foreign presence of the United States of America, to leave them alone in peace, and they practiced the art of survival by siding with whichever military force was present at a particular time, be it Vietcong, North Vietnamese, or American.

We found also that all too often American men were dying in those rice paddies for want of support from their allies. We saw first hand how money from American taxes was used for a corrupt dictatorial regime. We saw that many people in this country had a one-sided idea of who was kept free by our flag, as blacks provided the highest percentage of casualties. We saw Vietnam ravaged equally by American bombs as well as by search and destroy missions, as well as by Vietcong terrorism, and yet we listened while this country tried to blame all of the havoc on the Vietcong.

We rationalized destroying villages in order to save them. We saw America lose her sense of morality as she accepted very coolly a My Lai and refused to give up the image of American soldiers who hand out chocolate bars and chewing gum.

We learned the meaning of free fire zones, shooting anything that moves, and we watched while America placed a cheapness on the lives of orientals.

We watched the U.S. falsification of body counts, in fact the glorification of body counts. We listened while month after month we were told the back of the enemy was about to break. We fought using weapons against "oriental human beings," with quotation marks around that. We fought using weapons against those people which I do not believe this country would dream of using were we fighting in the European theater or let us say a non-third-world people theater, and so we watched while men charged up hills because a general said that hill has to be taken, and after losing one platoon or two platoons they marched away to leave the high for the reoccupation by the North Vietnamese because we watched pride allow the most unimportant of battles to be blown into extravaganzas, because we couldn't lose, and we couldn't retreat, and because it didn't matter how many American bodies were lost to prove that point. And so there were Hamburger Hills and Khe Sanhs and Hill 881's and Fire Base 6's and so many others.

Now we are told that the men who fought there must watch quietly while American lives are lost so that we can exercise the incredible arrogance of Vietnamizing the Vietnamese. . . . Each day to facilitate the process by which the United States washes her hands of Vietnam someone has to give up his life so that the United States doesn't have to admit something that the entire world already knows, so that we can't say that we have made a mistake. Someone has to die so that President Nixon won't be, and these are his words, "the first President to lose a war."

We are asking Americans to think about that because how do you ask a man to be the last man to die in Vietnam? How do you ask a man to be the last man to die for a mistake? But we are trying to do that, and we are doing it with thousands of rationalizations, and if you read carefully the President's last speech to the people of this country, you can see that he says, and says clearly:

> But the issue, gentlemen, the issue is communism, and the question is whether or not we will leave that country to the Communists or whether or not we will try to give it hope to be a free people.

But the point is they are not a free people now under us. They are not a free people, and we cannot fight communism all over the world, and I think we should have learned that lesson by now.

RETURNING VETERANS ARE NOT REALLY WANTED

But the problem of veterans goes beyond this personal problem, because you think about a poster in this country with a picture of Uncle Sam and the picture says "I want you." And a young man comes out of high school and says, "That is fine. I am going to serve my country." And he goes to Vietnam and he shoots and he kills and he does his job or maybe he doesn't kill, maybe he just goes and he comes back, and when he gets back to this country he finds that he isn't really wanted, because the largest unemployment figure in the country—it varies depending on who you get it from, the VA Administration 15 percent, various other sources 22 percent. But the largest corps of unemployed in this country are veterans of this war, and of those veterans 33 percent of the unemployed are black. That means 1 out of every 10 of the Nation's unemployed is a veteran of Vietnam.

The hospitals across the country won't, or can't meet their demands. It is not a question of not trying. They don't have the appropriations. A man recently died after he had a tracheotomy in California, not because of the operation but because there weren't enough personnel to clean the mucus out of his tube and he suffocated to death.

Another young man just died in a New York VA hospital the other day. A friend of mine was lying in a bed two beds away and tried to help him, but he couldn't. He rang a bell and there was nobody there to service that man and so he died of convulsions.

I understand 57 percent of all those entering the VA hospitals talk about suicide. Some 27 percent have tried, and they try because they come back to this country and they have to face what they did in Vietnam, and then they come back and find the indifference of a country that doesn't really care, that doesn't really care.

LACK OF MORAL INDIGNATION IN UNITED STATES

Suddenly we are faced with a very sickening situation in this country, because there is no moral indignation and, if there is, it comes from people who are almost exhausted by their past indignations, and I know that many of them are sitting in front of me. . . .

But we are here as veterans to say we think we are in the midst of the greatest disaster of all times now because they are still dying over there, and not just Americans, Vietnamese, and we are rationalizing leaving that country so that those people can go on killing each other for years to come. . . .

We are here in Washington also to say that the problem of this war is not just a question of war and diplomacy. It is part and parcel of everything that we are trying as human beings to communicate to people in this country, the question of racism, which is rampant in the military, and so many other questions also, the use of weapons, the hypocrisy in our taking umbrage in the Geneva Conventions and using that as justification for a continuation of this war, when we are more guilty than any other body of violations of those Geneva Conventions, in the use of free fire zones, harassment interdiction fire, search and destroy missions, the bombings, the torture of prisoners, the killing of prisoners, accepted policy by many units in South Vietnam. That is what we are trying to say. It is part and parcel of everything.

An American Indian friend of mine . . . put it to me very succinctly. He told me how as a boy on an Indian reservation he had watched television and he used to cheer the cowboys when they came in and shot the Indians, and then suddenly one day he stopped in Vietnam and he said "My God, I am doing to these people the very same thing that was done to my people." And he stopped. And that is what we are trying to say, that we think this thing has to end. . . .

THE CHAIRMAN. As I have stated, Mr. Melville L. Stephens who is a former, I am informed, lieutenant in the Navy, has been invited at the request of Senator Beall of Maryland and Senator Aiken. Mr. Stephens, will you proceed.

MR. STEPHENS. Mr. Chairman, I will be very brief because I know it is late. I would like to thank you and the other members of the committee for the opportunity to be here. I particularly appreciate the opportunity to speak because I know that my views are not very popular these days. . . .

I was in the Navy from June of 1967 until September of last year and spent nearly 34 months in the Southeast Asia combat zone. . . .

During this time I feel very fortunate to have made a great many friends among the Vietnamese people. I cannot speak more highly of my personal regard and affection for these people, both as friends and as comrades. My concern and the reason that I asked to speak today, is to ask you to consider carefully your course, so that peace for Americans does not come at the cost of additional sacrifice for these people.

It seems, that since I returned to the States last spring, that the cries for unconditional withdrawal and the setting of an immediate date for ending American support have become very loud, and I know that you on the committee have listened very carefully.

I believe that these arguments have two principal weaknesses. First, they are based on questions which certainly should have been asked in the early 1960's, but which were not. We are there; we have been there for a long time. The questions of legality and specific strategy which were valid 10 years ago are no longer the relevant ones.

Second, the very truth that all war is terrible and brutal is especially true of this one in which the civilian population is so intimately involved. Only those of us who have been there and fought and lived with the Vietnamese people can know how very true this is. I certainly agree that this war has gone on too long and must come to an end. But I ask you to consider carefully the manner in which you intend to end it.

U.S. RESPONSIBILITY TO SOUTH VIETNAMESE PEOPLE

I want to assure you, that after my nearly 3 years in Vietnam I am convinced that the overwhelming majority of the Vietnamese people are opposed to the Communists. A great many of them have taken their stand because of the American commitment to the Government of Vietnam. I would like to think that you and I and the American people have a responsibility to these Vietnamese [who] have had faith in us in the past, and have risked their lives for something they believe in. Peace for us must not come at the cost of their lives.

As I look around Washington today, and last week, I am very offended to see Americans carrying the flag of the VC. I fear that some Americans, in their passion for peace, have made heroes of the Vietcong. Let me assure you, Mr. Fulbright, that in South Vietnam, the Vietcong are not heroes.

I heard a great deal about atrocities last week, particularly from my fellow Vietnam veterans who were here. I certainly do not deny that some of them took place. But there is also another side which should be heard more often. I would like to tell you about two particular incidents, which I am personally aware of.

In the spring of 1969 near Can Tho in the southern part of the delta I was unfortunate enough to be a witness to the grenading of a Vietnamese school bus, which was clearly marked as a school bus, by the Vietcong. Two of the children were killed outright; several were wounded so severely that I doubt that they could possibly have survived; and three others were maimed in the most grotesque manner that you could imagine.

Earlier in my tour I became very close friends with a young Vietnamese boy of 11 named Tran who had been orphaned by the Vietcong. Tran told me that in the fall of 1967 his father had been elected to a local village office and Tran had been seized by the Vietcong in the area and had had his left arm cut off with a machete as an example to his father. His father had refused to resign even at this, but he, along with his mother, were killed in the Tet offensive of 1968.

Senator, as I say, I speak from personal experience. I speak of only a few incidents like this, but anyone who has spent any time in Vietnam will assure you of the brutality and the terror of the Communists. They, the Communists themselves, have been quite blunt in stating that terror and mass execution are their principal strategy. The South Vietnamese I lived with know this. They know that they take their lives in their hands when they support the Government of Vietnam and so they depend upon us for the support which we have promised.

I think I understand as well as any the passion of all of us in this country for an end to the war, but it is my firm conviction that peace at the price of these Vietnamese people is too expensive, and it is a peace that I could not live with.

I want to tell you from my own sense, from my own personal experience from nearly 3 years in Vietnam, that the setting of an arbitrary date for American withdrawal can only hurt the cause of the South Vietnamese people, and that I am firmly convinced that the current program, which I was a part of, and which I have watched since I left, is as progressive and ambitious as I believe the situation could permit.

When I speak of my fear for the Vietnamese people, I certainly don't speak of the generals and the admirals, of the high ranking officials. Frankly, I am quite sure that in a situation they can handle themselves. I do refer to the junior officers and the troops who I knew, to the merchants and to the farmers and to the local officials, those who we would call the average citizens of the country.

I think, sir, that the issue of ending this war is not the issue of our saving face; but the issue of our responsibility, as a nation and as individuals, to these citizens of South Vietnam. Many of them have committed themselves, because we very literally asked them to. I hope and urge that in our urgency for peace that we do not abandon them.

79. THE COSTS OF THE VIETNAM WAR

As the violence of 1968 and 1970 demonstrated, the costs of the war could be measured in many ways. In 1971 the Senate Foreign Relations Committee and its chairman, J. William Fulbright, asked the Library of Congress to measure the quantitative costs of the war. Particularly noteworthy was the section on the use of herbicides, especially Agent Orange, which many believed continued to claim victims among former U.S. soldiers in Vietnam a decade later. Agent Orange had high cancer-causing properties. As horrible as these costs were, however, Fulbright's introduction indicates that some of the greatest costs of the war could not be measured quantitatively. (Source: United States Senate, Committee on Foreign Relations, *Impact of the Vietnam War* [Washington, 1971].)

INTRODUCTION

. . . Although this report documents many of the measurable consequences of the war, it cannot reveal the intangible costs which in the long run may be of far greater significance. The survey spells out the casualty figures—827,000 U.S., South Vietnamese, and allied military personnel, over a million civilian casualties in South Vietnam, and countless thousands in Laos and Cambodia, and it is estimated that a third of the population of South Vietnam have become refugees in the course of the past 7 years. But those figures merely hint at the vast destruction of the social fabric and economies of Indochina wrought as a consequence of this tragic war. There is no way of measuring the true cost of a shattered social structure, lost opportunities for development, persistent inflation, black marketeering, corruption, and prostitution.

The survey recalls our attention to the 296,000 wounded Americans, but it cannot document the psychological effects of war on the two million who have returned physically intact. Nor can it quantify the effects of this experience on U.S. society—not only the direct economic costs realized through our own inflation, high interest rates and balance-of-payments deficits, but also the intangible costs in terms of erosion of respect for the law, further disruption of the constitutional system of checks and balances, increased distrust of Government, and the growing use of violence as a political tool. These indirect and intangible consequences of the war will have an enduring effect on our future.

It is ironic that the war which started, ostensibly, as one to defend freedom and democracy in South Vietnam may have the effect instead of seriously undermining democracy in the United States. In retrospect it is tragically clear that the almost $200 billion estimated by this study to be the cost of the war accrued so far would have been better devoted to solving the problems of our own society, rather than in pursuit of a futile military adventure which has served only to exacerbate them.

J. W. FULBRIGHT, CHAIRMAN.
[U.S. SENATE FOREIGN RELATIONS COMMITTEE]

[THE REPORT:]
MILITARY CASUALTIES AND LOSSES
A. CASUALTIES

By the beginning of March 1971, total U.S. military casualties in Indochina were just under 350,000, which is more than the U.S. sustained in World War I and more than twice the number of casualties during the Korean conflict. However, the Indochina casualties are still only about one-third as great as the total of American dead and wounded in World War II. The figure is also less than that for the South Vietnamese forces (approximately 470,000). Figures for total casualties of the North Vietnamese/Vietcong forces are not available, but the Department of Defense does maintain statistics on enemy forces killed in action. For this category, the Defense Department total is approximately 715,000. If noncombat deaths and wounded could be added, North Vietnamese/Vietcong casualties would exceed U.S. and South Vietnamese casualties by an even greater margin. . . .

The figure for total military casualties since 1960 for South Vietnam and North Vietnam is higher than that for the United States. The accompanying table shows the number of casualties for the forces of the Government of South Vietnam from the beginning of 1960 through February 1971. The cumulative figure of 472,013 killed and seriously wounded represents 2.6 percent of the population (17,867,000). If the South Vietnamese Government could provide the number of military killed in noncombat situations, the ratio of South Vietnamese casualties to total population would be even higher.

In regard to enemy military casualties, the Department of Defense issues figures only for those killed in action, when they can be verified by actual body count. On this basis, the Department of Defense maintains that 714,984 North Vietnamese and Vietcong have been killed in action in the period from 1960 to the end of February 1971 . . . , or about 3.45 percent of the population of North Vietnam. . . .

MILITARY USE OF HERBICIDES
A. EXTENT OF USE

In the early 1960's U.S. Armed Forces began to use herbicides in South Vietnam. In 1962, the earliest year for which statistics are available, aerial spraying of herbicides covered about 5,681 acres or 23 square kilometers of land. . . . In successive years, the use of herbicides increased rapidly in rough proportion to the overall U.S. military buildup in Vietnam, reaching a peak in 1967, when approximately 7,000 square kilometers (1.7 million acres) of forest and cropland were treated. . . .

Between 1962 and 1970, the most recent year for which full data are available, approximately 23,360 square kilometers (5,767,410 acres), or nearly one-seventh of the total land area of South Vietnam was treated with chemical herbicides in order to reduce vegetation and to destroy crops. To accomplish this task, it is estimated that more than 100-million pounds of herbicide, or about 6 pounds for every inhabitant, were sprayed on Vietnam.

1. Defoliation of forests

The greatest use of herbicides in South Vietnam has been on fairly mature tropical hardwood forests, which comprise about nine-tenths of the forested land in the country. Of these forests, covering about 100,000 square kilometers, some 20,000 square kilometers are estimated to have been sprayed, including many of the most valuable forests. One-quarter to one-third of these have been sprayed more than once. Some estimates indicate that one out of every eight or 10 trees is killed by a single spraying and that 50 to 80 percent are killed in areas where more than one spraying has occurred. Arthur H. Westing, forestry specialist and Director of the AAAS [American Association for the Advancement of Science] Commission, believes that about 35 percent of South Vietnam's 14 million acres of dense forest have been sprayed one or more times, resulting in the destruction of 6.2 billion board feet of merchantable timber. He contends that this figure represents the country's entire domestic timber needs, based on current demand, for the next 31 years. Moreover, the lost timber represents about $500 million in taxes that would otherwise have accrued to the South Vietnamese Government. . . .

2. Crop destruction

While the bulk of the spraying has been directed against the forests and brush, a significant proportion has been used on croplands, especially in the food-scarce mountainous Central Highlands, an area populated by about 1 million Montagnards and other tribal peoples. About 2,200 square kilometers of cropland have been sprayed since the program began in 1962, representing about 6 percent of the country's 37,000 square kilometers of cropland. The AAAS estimated that the spraying caused the destruction of enough food to feed approximately 600,000 persons for a year.

B. PHASEOUT OF PROGRAM

One of the principal chemical compounds used in the herbicide program is known as agent Orange, which contains a substantial proportion of a chemical substance known as 2, 4, 5–T. However, certain discoveries regarding the effects of this element of agent Orange led to a reassessment in 1970 of the U.S. herbicide program.

A study conducted for the National Cancer Institute by the Bionetics Research Laboratories during the period 1965–66 on the teratogenic (fetus-damaging) effects of selected pesticides and industrial chemicals showed that a large dose of 2, 4, 5–T administered orally to specific strains of mice during the central portion of the gestation period produced abnormal fetuses.

These findings led the U.S. Office of Science and Technology to impose, late in 1969, a series of restrictions on the use of 2, 4, 5–T within the United States. At the same time, it was announced that the Defense Department would restrict the use of agent Orange, which contains 2, 4, 5–T, to remote areas in Vietnam. In April 1970, when further laboratory evidence indicated that 2, 4, 5–T caused birth defects in mice, the domestic use of this herbicide was severely restricted. Shortly thereafter, the Defense Department ordered a halt to the use of compound Orange. This agent had been used mainly for forest clearing and to a lesser extent in anticrop operations. . . .

80. THE 1972 COMMUNIST OFFENSIVE— AND AFTER

In the spring of 1972 the Communists launched a major offensive. Nixon responded with massive bombing of the North and—for the first time—mining of key North Vietnam harbors used by Soviet and Chinese ships to unload supplies. The offensive was driven back. Some observers later claimed that at this point the main military thrust of the North Vietnamese had been broken, and with more perseverance the United States could have won the war militarily. This claim is doubtful in any case, but a congressional staff report written in May 1972 by two experts on Vietnam concluded that—as always—the situation was more complicated and ominous than it seemed. There was still no light at the end of the tunnel. (Source: United States Senate, Committee on Foreign Relations, *Vietnam: May 1972. A Staff Report* [Washington, 1972], pp. 14–20.)

SECURITY IN THE COUNTRYSIDE

The overall effect of the North Vietnamese offensive, its "success or failure" and the relative strength of the South Vietnamese Government's position, cannot be calculated solely in terms of cities lost or successfully defended, casualty figures or sortie rates. The security situation in the countryside—or, to put it another way, the impact of the offensive on pacification—must also be taken into account in any overall assessment of the current situation.

Among other comments on the security situation made in the course of our briefings were these:

(a) Not since the Tet offensive of 1968 has there been such a large decline in security during a one-month period.

(b) The enemy offensive was accompanied by record levels of terrorism, particularly in Military Region I.

(c) A great number of young people were abducted by the enemy during March and April, particularly in Military Regions I and II, since the local Viet Cong need manpower.

(d) The effect of the offensive on refugee resettlement and return-to-village programs has been "disastrous" with virtually all regular refugee programs in the 23 provinces in which new refugees have been generated halted and all efforts concentrated on emergency relief.

While Hamlet Evaluation System (HES) statistics are no longer taken with any great seriousness by American officials in either Washington or Saigon—some give them less credence than heretofore because the reporting is now done by the Vietnamese—the HES statistics are said to be considered to be useful in gauging broad trends in the security picture. Following are some of the measurements of change which took place during the first full month of the offensive.

In February of this year, 83% of the population was considered to be in category A or B—that is, under government control. As of April 30, this percentage had declined to 70.6%.

In February, 14% of the population was in category C—that is, contested. As of April 30, that percentage had risen to 19.2%.

In February only 3% of the population was in categories D and E—that is, considered insecure. By April 30, that percentage had risen to 7.1%. . . .

In assessing these and other current statistics, most U.S. officials in Vietnam tend to compare recent communist gains with those which followed the 1968 Tet offensive. By means of comparisons with the security situation in 1968 they can demonstrate, at least to their own apparent satisfaction, that conditions are not nearly as bad now as they were in 1968. While not even the most skeptical observers question this comparison, some Americans with long experience in Vietnam pointed out to us that it was misleading because the struggle for the countryside had begun long before 1968. It was their view that the present situation most nearly resembled that which existed in 1961 and 1962, and they pointed out that in those years the administrative and security apparatus of the Diem regime had begun to lose its earlier momentum and that there followed a period of steadily rising Viet Cong strength.

In this connection, one Province Senior Advisor began his review of the security situation with a series of colored charts indicating changes in the security situation in the province since 1968. When asked what the corresponding situation had been in 1966 or earlier, he replied that he did not know. Another American present, whose knowledge of the province dated back to the early 1960's, then noted that the districts which the advisor had described as the most insecure today, and in which government search and destroy operations were then being planned, were the very districts that had constituted the province's most serious security problems 10 years ago. The advisor replied: "All I know is that there has been progress, and progress as I can see it is tractors and Hondas."

Whether or not the Viet Cong strength in the rural areas will continue to grow apparently depends on several factors: the current strength of the Viet Cong local and main forces and the Viet Cong infrastructure; the ability of the ARVN to contain Viet Cong initiatives; and the potential of the South Vietnamese Government to reverse the inroads made by the Viet Cong in recent months. [ARVN is the U.S.-trained army of South Vietnam.]

Most American officials believed that as a result of the Tet offensive of 1968 and intensive efforts during the last 4 years, the Viet Cong infrastructure had been seriously damaged, although no official was willing or able to support this view with precise statistics. Some officials, both civilian and military, believed that the most convincing evidence of the Viet Cong's ineffectiveness was what they regarded as the absence of any significant Viet Cong participation in the current offensive. To support this view, they referred to various North Vietnamese directives and captured documents calling upon the Viet Cong to "rise" and to take various specific actions, few of which they have done. Their overall conclusion was that the Viet Cong had not "risen" because it no longer existed as a significant force.

Some Americans with long experience in Vietnam, the CIA officers who specialize in this subject and most Vietnamese to whom we talked disagreed. They said that, unlike the situation in the Tet offensive of 1968, there had been no call for a "general offensive, general uprising," the term used at that time. They pointed out that COSVN Directive 43 of March 1972 (COSVN is the Central Office for South Vietnam which is the Viet Cong field headquarters believed to be located at Kratie in Cambodia) stressed that the Viet Cong should lay the groundwork for "spontaneous uprisings" in South Vietnam in 1972, that there has been no call for a "general offensive, general uprising" in the course of this offensive and that they did not expect one because the Viet Cong were badly hurt in 1968 and would not surface again unless they were certain that the areas in which they did rise would not be recaptured by government forces. (COSVN Directive 43 and other COSVN directives and resolutions have, however, complained of a failure on the part of the Viet Cong cadre to establish a close relationship with the people in order to motivate them to rise up when the call does come and have also complained of the failure on the part of the Viet Cong to coordinate their activities with the successes achieved by main force elements.) According to these officials, the COSVN directives showed that the current offensive was regarded as an attempt to redress the balance of forces by inflicting heavy casualties on South Vietnamese army units, seizing base areas and weakening the government's pacification efforts.

One official American's view was that the North Vietnamese offensive had been motivated in part by Hanoi's recognition of how badly Viet Cong strength had deteriorated over the past 4 years. According to this view, the North Vietnamese had been compelled to employ their own main forces in order to disrupt the government's security program sufficiently to enable the Viet Cong to regain sufficient freedom of action in the countryside.

Whether by North Vietnamese design or not, this result has occurred. In many areas of Vietnam the Viet Cong had a freedom of movement which they had not enjoyed for years. . . .

Over the long term it is not only the question of new areas brought under communist control, but also the overall psychological shock that has resulted from the impact of the North Vietnamese offensive, that is significant in considering the security situation in the countryside. In many of the areas we visited we were told that the people had again become fearful that the government was incapable of protecting them. In some areas, particularly along the coastal area of Military Regions I and II, many Vietnamese apparently believed that the United States had deliberately allowed the North Vietnamese to advance as part of a deal involving the cession of territory.

Such an emotionally fragile environment affords obvious opportunities for exploitation by the Viet Cong. . . .

Almost every advisor with whom we spoke identified "the question of leadership" as South Vietnam's greatest single problem. In the course of our two week stay, the quality of ARVN leadership, in both civil and military capacities and at every level from President Thieu on down, was criticized or at least questioned by everyone with whom we spoke—both Vietnamese and Americans. It is an important aspect of the problem of security in the countryside because all Regional Commanders, Province Chiefs and District Chiefs are ARVN officers.

Most observers believe that the problem begins at the top of the government. It is said that President Thieu has picked his key commanders and provincial officials primarily on the basis of their loyalty to him, rather than on the basis of integrity or military ability. Despite the present serious situation, there are apparently no indications that Thieu intends to make the sweeping changes which many American and Vietnamese observers believe are needed to transform the ARVN into a well led army and to enhance the effectiveness of the government's control over the countryside.

It took almost a complete disaster to bring about the dismissal of General Lam as commander of Military Region I. In that extreme circumstance, Thieu did select one of the most respected ARVN generals as Lam's replacement, but in the same week he also selected General Toan as Military Region II Commander to succeed General Dzu. Military Region II had long been considered a "Siberia" to which less well qualified and out-of-favor officers were sent. Despite the fact that the major North Vietnamese offensive had long been expected in the region, Dzu, whose reputation was none too good, had been left in command. His successor, Toan, is openly referred to in Saigon as the "cinnamon king," an allusion to his illicit business dealings, and we were told that he had been charged with sexually assaulting a 15-year-old girl. . . .

Closely related to the question of leadership is the question of ARVN morale. American military men acknowledged that the morale of ARVN troops was good when they were well led and had confidence in their leaders. . . .

81. THE SECRET NIXON-THIEU DEAL OF JANUARY 5, 1973

South Vietnam President Nguyen Van Thieu refused to accept the U.S.–North Vietnam peace agreement because it allowed the North's troops to remain in the South. Thieu, moreover, did not believe that if he got into trouble the United States would reenter the war to help. Nixon tried to show his good faith and willingness to use immense force by launching a massive bombing attack on North Vietnam during Christmas of 1972. He then wrote Thieu the following secret letter assuring the South Vietnamese leader that the United States could be depended on in a crisis. Unfortunately for Thieu, Nixon and Kissinger never asked Congress to ratify this policy to make it a national commitment, and when the crisis did arrive in 1975 Nixon had been driven from the White House. But this letter helped make possible the peace that allowed the last large detachments of U.S. combat troops to leave Vietnam in 1973. (Source: The New York *Times,* May 1, 1975, p. 16.)

This will acknowledge your letter of December 20, 1972.

There is nothing substantial that I can add to my many previous messages, including my December 17 letter, which clearly stated my opinions and intentions. With respect to the question of North Vietnamese troops, we will again present your views to the Communists as we have done vigorously at every other opportunity in the negotiations. The result is certain to be once more the rejection of our position. We have explained to you repeatedly why we believe the problem of North Vietnamese troops is manageable under the agreement, and I see no reason to repeat all the arguments.

We will proceed next week in Paris along the lines that General Haig explained to you. Accordingly, if the North Vietnamese meet our concerns on the two outstanding substantive issues in the agreement, concerning the DMZ and the method of signing, and if we can arrange acceptable supervisory machinery, we will proceed to conclude the settlement. The gravest consequences would then ensue if your government chose to reject the agreement and split off from the United States. As I said in my December 17 letter, "I am convinced that your refusal to join us would be an invitation to disaster—to the loss of all that we together have fought for over the past decade. It would be inexcusable above all because we will have lost a just and honorable alternative."

As we enter this new round of talks, I hope that our countries will now show a united front. It is imperative for our common objectives that your government take no further actions that complicate our task and would make more difficult the acceptance of the settlement by all parties. We will keep you informed of the negotiations in Paris through daily briefings of Ambassador Lam.

I can only repeat what I have so often said: The best guarantee for the survival of South Vietnam is the unity of our two countries which would be gravely jeopardized if you persist in your present course. The actions of our Congress since its return have clearly borne out the many warnings we have made.

Should you decide, as I trust you will, to go with us, you have my assurance of continued assistance in the post-settlement period and that we will respond with full force should the settlement be violated by North Vietnam. So once more I conclude with an appeal to you to close ranks with us.

82. A DEBATE OVER HELPING SOUTH VIETNAM, 1974

As U.S. combat troops left Vietnam, attention switched to Congress. It would have to be that body which appropriated money and supplies to keep the South Vietnamese military in readiness. The United States did pour arms and munitions into the country in 1973 and 1974, but by the latter year the American economy was entering a crisis of its own. Senator William Proxmire (Dem.-Wisc.) believed the time had arrived to reevaluate aid to South Vietnam. His view was countered by Senator Barry Goldwater (Rep.-Ariz.). (Source: *Congressional Record,* August 21, 1974, pp. 29176–79.)

MR. PROXMIRE. Mr. President, why should the Senate increase the amount of funds it approved last year for the South Vietnamese Armed

Forces by 27 percent? That is precisely what the bill before us will do. . . .

My amendment would allow the same appropriations for Vietnam as accepted by the Senate last year—$550 million. . . .

Congress and the President now face the fact that even with all of our hard efforts, fiscal year 1975 spending will be a mammoth $40 billion or 15 percent over last year at a time when we face the worst inflation in our peacetime history. . . . Of all the areas in the Federal budget, there is less need for sending hundreds of millions in military aid to Vietnam than any other single item. . . .

What about the strategic situation in South Vietnam? By not increasing our military commitment to that nation will we be handing it over to the Communists? Well, the Vietnamese war has been going on for over 20 years. We have acted in the history of that conflict only in the last 10- or 12-year period. The war was going on before we got there. It is going on even though we left.

No one can say that our contribution has been inadequate. According to the Defense Intelligence Agency—DIA—U.S. military aid to South Vietnam was eight times greater—think of that, Mr. President, our aid to South Vietnam was eight times greater than that given by the two Communist powers to North Vietnam in 1973. Since 1966 the DIA estimates show the United States spent 29 times as much in Indochina as the Soviets and Peoples Republic of China combined. . . . While Chinese and Russian arms shipments were reduced by more than half from 1972 to 1973, the United States increased its shipments by $286 million in the same 1-year period. . . .

It has become more and more evident in the past few months that South Vietnam does not need increases in military aid in order to survive. Within the last 2 months, both Defense Secretary Schlesinger and Admiral Moorer have declared that the military situation in South Vietnam is far from critical. On June 5, 1974, Secretary Schlesinger told the House Foreign Affairs Committee that the United States no longer expects a major Communist offensive in South Vietnam. . . .

Unfortunately much of our assistance has gone to line the pockets of corrupt officers and bureaucrats. Talk to anyone who has served in Vietnam at any level. They will tell you of the black market operations, the U.S. military assistance goods being sold on the same street as the U.S. warehouses, the bribery and corruption that is expected at every level of Government. . . . South Vietnam's 92 generals have only recently been ordered to cut their personal staffs of chauffeurs, bodyguards, and servants from 36 to 11 each. . . . Think of it. Only 11 chauffeurs and servants each.

Evidence has also been uncovered recently that a number of new American A-37s worth $500,000 each—are being dismantled and sold for scrap on the black market in Saigon. A police raid on an illegal scrap operation yielded the wings of 15 planes as well as substantial amounts of other U.S.-made military equipment which were being readied for foreign export. We ship it to them. They tear it down and export it out of the country for a profit. Not a bad deal some would say. . . .

MR. GOLDWATER. Mr. President, I rise in opposition to the pending measure. . . .

What the Senator does not realize is that the North Vietnamese have been preparing for this massive offensive for a long time. That offensive is underway.

Contrary to what he may have been told, the offensive is underway and the North Vietnamese are in better shape to pursue a successful campaign at this time than they have been at any time in the 20 years that this long war has gone on.

Even though the figure that he uses, that we give eight times the aid that the Soviets in Red China give to North Vietnam, I think if one reduces it to cost, one will find that they probably give a little more than we do in actual equipment. They have not only rebuilt the air bases that were used in the area just south of the DMZ; they have built new paved runways north of the DMZ and south of the DMZ [De-Militarized Zone].

They have a petroleum pipeline that now can service air units and reservice ground units to the very close proximity of Saigon. They have railroads built toward the south that they did not have before and, as I have mentioned, some greatly improved roads.

So far, Mr. President, I feel that if we renege on giving South Vietnam what we told her we would give, South Vietnam is going to be in a very bad way. It is true that there has been graft over there. It is true that they have misused our equipment. I have been in that part of the world. In fact, in World War II I served in that part of the world. Misusing equipment and having dishonesty among the military seems to be a way of life for them. It has always been.

But the important thing, I believe, is that—and we cannot laugh this off —with the present ability of the North Vietnamese to wage a successful war, the whole of Vietnam can become a Communist part of this world. Then I have to remind my colleagues that when this happens, Laos undoubtedly will fall, Cambodia will fall. Then we are going to be confronted with a question of what we do about our very valued allies, the Thais.

Just to the south of Thailand, in fact, on the Thai peninsula, is the opportunity to build a canal or a pipeline across the isthmus that will make the delivery of oil to our own shores and to our ally, Japan, that much easier. If we lose all of Southeast Asia, Mr. President, because we want to renege on the money that we have promised them, then I think the United States is going to wind up suffering far, far more than the $150 million that is involved in the Senator's amendment. . . .

MR. PROXMIRE. I hope we can come to some kind of conclusion on this, because for so many years, as I say, this has been going on, year after year. We say, "We shall just continue it another year, take a harder look at it next time."

In the midst of tremendous inflation, it is a great burden on the American people, and with the enormous contribution we have made to South Vietnam, compared to anything from the outside, it seems to me that this is a limited, modest request which I make of the Senator.

83. KISSINGER, CONGRESS, AND THE FALL OF SOUTH VIETNAM

In early 1975 the Communists launched a major offensive and, much to their surprise, the South Vietnamese Army began to disintegrate rapidly. Secretary of State Henry Kissinger and President Gerald Ford tried to put the best face on the tragedy by asking Congress for $722 million to bolster the fast-disappearing South Vietnam force. When Kissinger appeared before the Senate Appropriations Committee to request the funds, a most revealing discussion analyzed the terrible course of the war and why the U.S. ally was going down. (Source, United States Senate, Committee on Appropriations, *Emergency Military Assistance . . . Fiscal Year 1975. Hearings . . . April 15, 1975* [Washington, 1975], pp. 36–39, 49, 67.)

SECRETARY KISSINGER. At the time of the Paris accords it was my belief that the South Vietnamese with the existing balance in South Vietnam would be able to maintain their security, and if the North Vietnamese had lived up to the Paris accords which prohibited the infiltration of additional personnel or materiel, the military situation in South Vietnam could have been maintained indefinitely.

SENATOR MONTOYA. [Joseph M. Montoya, Dem.-N. Mex.] Now, on April 5 in your press conference at Palm Springs, you stated that at that time there had been infiltration by North Vietnam into South Vietnam with approximately 18 divisions. Now why did that happen, if you say that we had military parity or perhaps you can tell us when that military parity started to disintegrate.

SECRETARY KISSINGER. The military parity began to disintegrate during the course of last year, when the accumulated cuts in American aid, some of which were due to inflationary pressures and to the rise in oil prices, began to force the South Vietnamese into a static defensive position while the North Vietnamese continued their infiltration. During the last year, for example . . . casualties began to mount drastically, and the South Vietnamese Army had 30,000 killed last year, which is at least one answer to the question of whether they were fighting. . . .

Then early this year, as a result of many factors, the North Vietnamese changed what in our judgment was their original plan. [We expected only local offensives this year, but] some time in January the North Vietnamese changed their approach and began a massive infiltration of all of their reserve divisions, including some recruits that had only one month of training.

SENATOR MONTOYA. How many men did they come down with?

SECRETARY KISSINGER. About 270,000.

SENATOR MONTOYA. And what was the strength of the South Vietnamese army at that point? . . .

SECRETARY KISSINGER. I think the South Vietnamese Army was numerically larger than the North Vietnamese Army, but I think that is a deceptive figure because the South Vietnamese Army had to be strung along 500 miles of frontier while the North Vietnamese could always concentrate all of their divisions at whichever point they wanted to attack, and they were free of any danger of attack themselves. I think the South Vietnam Army was something like 350,000 to 400,000 men. . . .

SENATOR MONTOYA. And you made a statement in your presentation that the United States had no legal obligation to aid South Vietnam. Am I correct in that statement?

SECRETARY KISSINGER. I said it had no legal obligation that was not submitted to the Congress, but it is correct that we had no legal obligation.

SENATOR MONTOYA. And that the only premise for a moral obligation was, and I will read it to you as you stated it, "But we do have a deep moral obligation rooted in the history of our involvement and sustained by the continuing effort of our friends." Now, how long are we to sustain this moral obligation, assuming that we had it since our initial involvement in South Vietnam?

SECRETARY KISSINGER. Senator, I have said . . . that it would be extremely tempting to give a terminal date, but the fact is there are many

313

situations in the world where the threat is constant and where a terminal date cannot be given unless the possible aggressor decides to give up his aggression. We have had a commitment to Europe, in the entire postwar period, and we cannot give that a terminal date. We have a commitment to Israel and we cannot give that a terminal date. . . .

SENATOR MONTOYA. In your statement you tell us that you want $396 million to sustain South Vietnam for 60 days and of course the other $326 million of the $722 million is for the purpose of organizing ranger units and training more manpower for self-defense. Now, in the light of this budgetary request, what happens after the 60 days? Are you going to come in and ask for more millions of dollars to sustain them? . . .

SECRETARY KISSINGER. Senator, after the 60 days, depending of course upon the military situation and assuming there has been no negotiation, we would be requesting from the Congress the sum that we have already submitted, which is $1.3 billion. . . .

SENATOR MONTOYA. Can you tell us of any other country in the world that has a moral obligation, or is doing something about a moral obligation to South Vietnam?

SECRETARY KISSINGER. There are few other countries; the tragedy of our situation is that there are few countries that feel any sense of moral obligation to South Vietnam. . . .

SENATOR MONTOYA. . . . In all seriousness, do you think that the expenditure of the money contained in this budget request will help the situation in South Vietnam and create an atmosphere whereby a political settlement can be made?

SECRETARY KISSINGER. In all seriousness, Senator, I recall no set of discussions between the President and his senior advisers that were more prayerfully conducted than these. . . . [It] was his judgment—with which I fully concurred—that whatever prediction you make about the future, we will be better off with this sum than without this sum. . . .

SENATOR BELLMON [Henry Bellmon, Dem.-Okla.]. . . . You sometimes have been called a "modern miracle worker" in diplomacy, and you brought about more normal relations with China and—

SECRETARY KISSINGER. If I may say so, not by me, but I may sometimes not have protested sufficiently loudly when it was applied.

SENATOR BELLMON. Also you helped bring about the agreement with Russia, but these are the same nations that have supplied the North Vietnamese. It is hard for us to understand if our relations with China and Russia are being improved, or being used here.

SECRETARY KISSINGER. When people say we have been used, one has to ask the question of what have we given them. The second is we have never said that detente means that these will be cooperative relationships. Detente is composed of many elements in which ideological hostility and a certain amount of competitiveness continue. The primary purpose of detente with the Soviet Union has been to try to minimize the danger of nuclear war and to ease tensions generally. What happened is that the level of military supplies from the Soviet Union has remained roughly constant over the years. The level of military supplies from the United States has declined. The Soviet Union has not seemed to ask the question of a terminal date as consistently as we have. . . .

SENATOR HOLLINGS [Ernest Hollings, Dem.-S.C.]. General Westmoreland and others advocated the resumption of bombing. You don't advocate that, do you?

SECRETARY KISSINGER. No, I do not advocate it, and I repeat, I have based our case on a moral obligation and not on a legal obligation that is unknown to the Congress. . . .

SENATOR HUDDLESTON [Walter Huddleston, Dem.-Ky.]. So the American people want to know whether or not after all of these years this additional funding will actually lead toward any conclusion that is any better than what is going to happen whenever we do stop. Is there an answer to that?

SECRETARY KISSINGER. There is no certain answer to that question. I wish there were.

84. A SUMMING UP

The fall of South Vietnam and the end of the thirty-year war in Indochina led to a number of attempts to put the tragedy in perspective. One of the best was published two days before crammed U.S. helicopters rescued the last American officials from Saigon and the oncoming Communist army. This essay reached back two hundred years to gain the best perspective, and to gently warn about the lessons of America's past for America's future. (Source: "An Irony of History," *Newsweek,* April 28, 1975, pp. 16–17.)

On a muddy field in Lexington, Mass., Gerald Ford reviewed a troop of Americans dressed up in Colonial Army uniforms. In the rubble of Xuan Loc and a dozen other outposts surrounding Saigon, South Vietnamese soldiers girded for what seemed their country's last battle. In the belfry of Boston's Old North Church, Ford hung up a lantern symbolic of Paul

Revere's ride. In the streets of Phnom Penh, war-weary Cambodians hung out the white flags of surrender.

History dealt America one of its ironies last week. At the very moment that the nation began celebrating the Bicentennial of its own war for independence, two countries that the U.S. had struggled mightily to help were in the process of losing theirs. What should have been a moment of cheer was in consequence one of consternation, and the President, instead of inviting his fellow countrymen to join a party, asked them to bind up their wounds. "It is time," he told the crowds at Concord, "to place the hand of healing over the heart of America."

The Ford Administration seemed at last to have reached the painful realization that the Indochina cause was lost. The State Department's Vietnam task force was dubbed "the death watch," and a high-ranking White House official admitted that it would be "impossible" to obtain the requested $722 million for military aid from Congress. . . .

It was clear that the White House had resigned itself to salvaging what it could from the Vietnam debacle, and top priority was the evacuation of the 4,000 Americans still in Saigon. After weeks of resisting a pullout from Saigon, the Administration hastily marshaled an armada of ships and squadrons of helicopters to begin the evacuation—an operation that could turn into a nightmare if vengeful Communist troops or embittered South Vietnamese soldiers turned their guns on fleeing Americans.

There was little that the U.S. or South Vietnam seemed able to do to hold back the Communist onslaught. Fully one-third of the forces that had been assembled to defend Xuan Loc were destroyed in the carnage. . . . For a few days, Cambodia's last non-Communist government talked as if it might fight to the end. Then Khmer Rouge rockets began to scream into the heart of Phnom Penh, and the government gave up. . . . The first of the conquering bands of Khmer Rouge guerrillas marched in to take possession of Phnom Penh. They were welcomed by thousands of cheering Cambodians. . . . But within hours of the Communist take-over, there were reports that "many" officials of the fallen government had been beheaded, and U.S. officials predicted further brutal reprisals. There will be "great human suffering," Kissinger forecast. "They will try to eliminate all political opponents."

When the maneuvering over Ford's Vietnam aid requests began, it seemed that the President and the Congress might come to terms. But after a rare meeting between Ford and the full Senate Foreign Relations Committee, some White House aides were bitter. "There was little if any sense of obligation or compassion for the Vietnamese," one complained. "It did not make me proud to be an American." Ford himself later blamed Congress once again for Vietnam's plight. "The United States did not carry out its commitment in the supplying of military hardware and economic aid," he told the American Society of Newspaper Editors. "If we had, this present tragic situation in South Vietnam would not have occurred."

. . . Senate Majority Leader Mike Mansfield [Dem.-Mont.] snapped that such an accusation was "a distortion so immense that it borders on the irrational." . . . There was a growing feeling on Capitol Hill that the Administration was using the Americans in Vietnam as hostages to extort the aid appropriation from Congress. Initial statistics on the number of Americans who had left Saigon turned out to be inflated. . . . Congress was also fearful that the evacuation might embroil U.S. troops in Indochina once again. Congress insisted that GI's could be used only to protect the withdrawal. "To find any pretext to the contrary," declared Mansfield, "is to raise once again the specter of Watergate—the specter of gross illegal behavior on the part of officials of the United States." . . .

The high hopes and wishful idealism with which the American nation had been born had not been destroyed, but they had been chastened by the failure of America to work its will in Indochina. In the second century of its independence, the United States gradually—but indisputably—emerged as the most powerful nation in the world. Now, the world and the ability of the United States to influence it have changed. It was still far too soon to tell what the third century of America's independence would bring, but there was no question that it was dawning in a spirit of doubt and contrition.

NOTES FOR PART II

1. The authors wish to thank Professor George Kahin for his generosity in sharing parts of his forthcoming book on the Indochina conflict. The chapter on the post-war French phase was very useful.

2. George W. Perkins to Acheson, Oct. 22, 1949, *FRUS, 1949,* IV, p. 495.

3. U.S. Delegation/Tripartite Meeting to Secretary of State, Apr. 20, 1950, *FRUS, 1950,* III, p. 897.

4. Merchant to Mr. Lacy, July 19, 1950, Lot Files, PSA, Box 8, Folder, "Mutual Defense Assistance."

5. U.S. Delegation/Tripartite Meeting to Secretary of State, loc. cit.

6. Department of State, *Bulletin,* Sept. 5, 1949, pp. 323–24.

7. Acheson to Truman, Feb. 16, 1950, *FRUS, 1950,* I, pp. 834–40. Memorandum for Discussion, "Foreign Economic Policy," Jan. 14, 1950, George M. Elsey papers. Ibid., Memorandum for the President, "Development of Policy for Adjusting the Balance of Payments of the U.S.," Jan. 26, 1950, p. 1–20.

8. Memorandum (Attachment), Secretary of State to the President, Feb. 16, 1950, *FRUS, 1950,* I, p. 839. Ibid., III, Bonestell to Ohly, March 20, 1950, pp. 36–40.

9. Tracy Voorhees, "Proposal for Strengthening Defense Without Increasing Appropriations," Apr. 5, 1950, Tracy S. Voorhees papers.

10. Stanley Andrews to Tracy Voorhees, "A Proposal to Correlate Economic Aid to Europe with Military Defense," May 29, 1950, Stanley Andrews papers. Ibid., Voorhees to Andrews, "Commentary," June 2, 1950.

11. Butterworth to Acting Secretary of State, Oct. 27, 1948, NARS—890.50/10-2748.

12. NSC 64, Feb. 27, 1950, *FRUS, 1950,* VI, p. 747.

13. NSC 124/2, June 25, 1952 [PPS Draft, March 27, 1952], *FRUS, 1952–1954,* XIII, p. 84. As the date indicates, NSC 124 (and the quote from it) was formulated in 1952. Its concerns for SEA raw materials—especially Malayan rubber exports as a British dollar-earner—was already part of the conventional wisdom by 1950. NSC 124 is used here because it is published and more readily accessible and verifiable to the readers. For more elaborate and developed analysis and documentation, see Andrew Rotter, "The Big Canvas," dss., Stanford University, 1981, Chs. 4 and 8.

14. Rotter, "The Big Canvas." The authors wish to thank Professor Rotter for his scholarly kindness and work in sharing copies of documents unearthed in his dissertation. That dissertation, when published, will be a major contribution to the growing historiography on the roots of American involvement in Southeast Asia.

15. Acting Political Adviser in Japan (Sebald) to Secretary of State, Sept. 16, 1947, *FRUS, 1947,* VI, p. 290.

16. Ibid., p. 292.

Throughout the Notes section the abbreviation *FRUS* is used for *Foreign Relations of the United States.* PSA is used for Philippines and South Asia desk.

17. "U.S. Post-Treaty Policy Toward Japan," Apr. 23, 1952, PSA, Box 13. Acheson to "Certain Diplomatic Offices," May 8, 1949, *FRUS, 1949*, VII, pp. 736–37.

18. General Headquarters, Supreme Command for Allied Powers (SCAP), to Tracy Voorhees, Mar. 22, 1950, Record Group-9: DA CX MacArthur Archives.

19. For a highly sophisticated treatment of postwar Japan, the dollar gap, and the Southeast Asia region, see William Borden, *Pacific Alliance* (Madison, Wisc., 1984). The authors owe much to Mr. Borden, by way of a heavy intellectual debt as well as gratitude for his great labor and openness in making many of his documents available to us. His excellent book has relevance not only to America's early commitment in SEA, but to the global and regional framework in which it occurs.

20. Sherwood Fine to SCAP, Economic and Scientific Section, Nov. 9, 1949, Box 4, SEA, Tracy Voorhees papers.

21. Consul Max W. Bishop to Secretary of State, Nov. 21, 1944, 740.0011 P.W./11–1044.

22. PSA to Assistant Secretary of State for Far Eastern Affairs, Mar. 16, 1950, *FRUS, 1950*, VI, p. 62.

23. Ambassador in Thailand (Stanton) to Secretary of State, Jan. 19, 1950, *FRUS, 1950*, VI, p. 697.

24. Acheson to Consulate at Hanoi, May 20, 1949, *FRUS, 1949*, VII, pp. 29–30.

25. Secretary of State to Consulate at Hanoi, May 20, 1949, *FRUS, 1949*, VII, p. 29.

26. Public release, Secretary Acheson, Feb. 1, 1950, *FRUS, 1950*, VI, p. 711.

27. PPS 51, "Paper on United States Policy Toward Southeast Asia," Mar. 29, 1949, *FRUS, 1949*, VII, pp. 1129, 1132.

28. Chargé in France (Bohlen) to Secretary of State, Feb. 16, 1950, *FRUS, 1950*, VI, p. 734. Ibid., p. 745.

29. George C. Herring, *America's Longest War*, pp. 14–23. Good, short summary of 1951–52 period.

30. Ambassador in France (Bruce) to Secretary of State, Nov. 21, 1950, *FRUS, 1950*, VI, p. 930.

31. NSC 48/5, "U.S. Objectives, Policies and Courses of Action in Asia," May 17, 1951, *FRUS, 1951*, VI, p. 61.

32. Memo for Record, Ridgway Conference with Dulles and Sebald, Apr. 22, 1951, Matthew B. Ridgway papers.

33. Economic and Scientific Bureau, June 3, 1952, John Dower collection.

34. ESB, Feb. 2, 1952, Dower collection.

35. Loc. cit.

36. Draft Statement of Policy Proposed by NSC on "U.S. Objectives and Courses of Action with Respect to S.E. Asia," June 19, 1952, National Archives, unnumbered.

NOTES FOR PART III

1. Dwight D. Eisenhower, *Mandate for Change: 1953–1956* (New York, 1963), pp. 95–96.

2. J. Lawton Collins, *War in Peacetime* (Boston, 1969), p. 324. General Mark Clark, when commander of Army Field Forces, had prepared an "estimate of forces

required to obtain military victory." Eisenhower did not even give him an opportunity to present his proposals. Later, of course, the Korean War seemed to some a Cold War triumph, instead of what the *Helena* conferees considered it: a steady worsening stalemate. And, ironically, some Vietnam post-mortems blamed American defeat on ignoring the positive lessons of Korea, i.e., that the Communist advance could be halted by conventional warfare tactics. In Korea, it is argued, "internal" security was left to the government in power, while United Nations forces concentrated on stopping "external" aggression. See, for example, Colonel Harry Summers, *On Strategy: The Vietnam War in Context* (Washington, 1981), especially p. 47.

3. "Midway in the Geneva Conference," speech by Secretary Dulles, May 7, 1954, in Department of State, *American Foreign Policy, 1950–1955,* 2 vols. (Washington, 1957), II, p. 2386; "Summary of Remarks . . . December 11, 1952," *The Papers of John Foster Dulles,* Mudd Library, Princeton University, Princeton, N.J. (Hereafter, *Dulles MSS.)*

4. The most speculated-about alternative, naturally, was the possibility of using atomic weapons. Recently declassified documents reveal that Eisenhower and Dulles came to believe that atomic threats, however hedged, had played a key role in breaking the impasse on the prisoners-of-war issue that held up a Korean armistice. Air Force Chief of Staff General Nathan Twining thought atomic bombs could have rescued the French, and perhaps won the Indochinese War, during the Dienbienphu crisis in 1954. The difference was that in 1953 Eisenhower used the threat to secure an honorable exit; he never believed that one could employ the bomb successfully as a substitute for troops. If no one could figure out how atomic bombs could be used in situations like Indochina, Dulles continued to seek a way to make such a threat credible. For a discussion see John Lewis Gaddis, *Strategies of Containment* (New York, 1982), pp. 169–70.

5. Eisenhower, *Mandate for Change,* p. 372.

6. Department of State, *American Foreign Policy, 1950–1955,* II, p. 2390.

7. Conversation with Eisenhower, Mar. 24, 1953, *Dulles MSS.*

8. Undated background memorandum, [Sept. 1950,] ibid.; speech to the French National Political Science Institute, May 5, 1952, ibid.

9. Dulles to Jackson, Aug. 24, 1954, ibid.

10. "The Chance for Peace," Apr. 16, 1953. The speech was designed to allow Eisenhower to show the initiative in an American "peace offensive" in the wake of Joseph Stalin's death. Dulles frequently cited it later as justification for American intervention in Indochina.

11. "Substance of Discussions . . . at the Pentagon Building," Sept. 4, 1953, *FRUS, 1952–1954,* XIII, *Indochina* (2 parts), I, p. 756.

12. "Outline of Major U.S. Statements and Actions Reflecting Recent U.S. Policies towards Indochina," July 27, 1954, *Dulles MSS.*

13. Bernard B. Fall, *Hell in a Very Small Place: The Siege of Dien Bien Phu* (Philadelphia, 1966), p. 51. As American policy-makers feared, moreover, the end of the war in Korea did permit the Communist Chinese to supply artillery to the Vietminh. With these weapons, and their ability to transport them to the hills around Dienbienphu, the Vietminh won their gamble.

14. On Russian and Chinese signals, see Philippe Devillers and Jean Lacouture, *End of a War: Indochina, 1954* (New York, 1969), pp. 40–41.

15. United States Government, *Public Papers of the Presidents of the United States: Dwight D. Eisenhower, 1954* (Washington, 1958), pp. 245–55.

16. "Memorandum by the Secretary of State to the President," Mar. 23, 1954, *FRUS, 1952–1954,* XIII, Part 1, pp. 1141–42.

17. Speech to Overseas Press Club, Mar. 29, 1954, in Department of State, *American Foreign Policy, 1950–1955,* (Washington, 1957), II, p. 2376.

18. "Memorandum for the Secretary's File," Apr. 5, 1954, *Dulles MSS;* "Memorandum of a Conversation with the President," Apr. 2, 1954, ibid.

19. Apr. 10, 1954, draft in ibid.

20. Devillers and Lacouture, *End of a War,* pp. 82–83.

21. "Memorandum of Discussion . . . ," Apr. 6, 1954, *FRUS, 1952–1954,* XIII, Part 1, pp. 1250–65.

22. "Proposed 'Talking Paper' . . . ," ca. Apr. 23, 1954, *Dulles MSS.*

23. Foreign Secretary Anthony Eden received a personal visit from the American Ambassador Winthrop Aldrich during which the latter explained why Washington was so concerned about China's participation at Geneva. Then came a proposal that before Geneva the three powers, Britain, France, and the United States, should join in a warning, "which would carry with it the threat of naval and air action against the Chinese coast and of active intervention in Indo-China itself." See Anthony Eden, *Full Circle* (Boston, 1960), p. 103. Aside from the war scares, the constant, to the point of obsessive, imprecations against China suggested that Washington would do practically anything to prevent Peking's achieving the status of "great power," including blocking progress at Geneva. Among those who felt concern about Indochina as a back door to war with China was Army Chief of Staff General Matthew B. Ridgway, who saw a drift toward the "thesis" that a preventative war against Communist China was necessary. "To my way of thinking the desire to intervene in Indo-China, the willingness to use force in dealing with Quemoy and Matsu reflects a thinking which trends dangerously toward acceptance of the doctrine of 'preventative war.' " *Memoirs* (New York, 1956), pp. 279–80.

24. "Memorandum of Discussion . . . ," *FRUS, 1952–1954,* XIII, Part 2, pp. 1431–45.

25. Townsend Hoopes, *The Devil and John Foster Dulles* (Boston, 1973), p. 222.

26. Fall, *Hell in a Very Small Place,* pp. 424–25.

27. Jean Lacouture, *Vietnam: Between Two Truces* (New York, 1966), p. 10.

28. Ibid., p. 11.

29. Final Draft of Manila Speech, Sept. 15, 1954, *Dulles MSS.* The key sentences read: "The Indochina Armistice created obstacles to these three *countries* becoming parties to the Treaty at the present time. The Treaty will, however, to the extent practicable, throw a mantle of protection over these young nations." (Emphasis added.) A recent account, Guenter Lewy, *America in Vietnam* (New York, 1978), argues that nobody at Geneva, including the delegates from the North, took the idea of early elections "seriously." Nor, under international law, could the newly independent Indochinese states be bound by anything the French had conceded. Lewy also points to the vagueness of the provisions about elections. It was merely a device, the elections, to hide the fact that as in other Cold War situations a military demarcation line was bound to become a political one as well (pp. 8–9). The point is well made, but not really convincing given the nature of the Geneva

Conference, which, unlike those other Cold War instances, included delegates from both sides, and the demands from Hanoi that the agreement be fulfilled.

30. Lacouture, *Vietnam: Between Two Truces,* pp. 12–13.

31. Edward Geary Lansdale, *In the Midst of Wars* (New York, 1972), p. 159.

32. Interview with Lawton Collins, Dulles Oral History Project, *Dulles MSS.*

33. Lacouture, *Vietnam: Between Two Truces,* p. 63.

34. transcript, May 12, 1955, *Dulles MSS.*

35. Marvin Kalb and Elie Abel, *Roots of Involvement: The U.S. in Asia, 1784–1971* (New York, 1971), p. 102.

36. Ibid., p. 103.

37. See Guenter Lewy, *America in Vietnam,* pp. 16–18; Gareth Porter, ed., *Vietnam: A History in Documents* (New York, 1981), p. xxx.

38. See United States Senate, Subcommittee of the Committee on Foreign Relations, *Hearings: The Situation in Vietnam,* 86th Cong., 1st Sess. (Washington, 1959).

39. Kalb and Abel, *Roots of Involvement,* pp. 103–4.

40. George W. Ball, *The Past Has Another Pattern: Memoirs* (New York, 1982), p. 183.

41. Ibid.

42. Arthur M. Schlesinger, Jr., *A Thousand Days* (Boston, 1965), pp. 546–47.

43. Kalb and Abel, *Roots of Involvement,* p. 118. The quotation refers to a troop decision about Laos, but the authors make the point that the 1962 "neutralization" of that country increased determination to see it through in Vietnam.

44. Figures from Lewy, *America in Vietnam,* p. 24, and United States Senate, Committee on Foreign Relations, *Background Information Relating to Southeast Asia and Vietnam,* 90th Cong., 1st Sess. (Washington, 1967), pp. 267–68.

45. Maxwell D. Taylor, *Swords and Plowshares* (New York, 1972), p. 340.

46. United States Senate, Committee on Foreign Relations, Staff Study, *U.S. Involvement in the Overthrow of Diem, 1963,* 92d Cong., 2d Sess. (Washington, 1972), p. 2.

47. Taylor, *Swords and Plowshares,* p. 407.

48. Tom Wicker, *JFK and LBJ: The Influence of Personality Upon Politics* (New York, 1968), p. 205.

NOTES FOR PART IV

1. Tom Wicker, "The Wrong Rubicon," in Robert Manning and Michael Janeway, eds., *Who We Are: An Atlantic Chronicle of the United States and Vietnam* (Boston, 1969), p. 216.

2. George Reedy, *Lyndon B. Johnson: A Memoir* (New York, 1982), p. 158.

3. George C. Herring, "The War in Vietnam," in Robert A. Divine, ed., *Exploring the Johnson Years* (Austin, Texas, 1981), p. 41.

4. James C. Thomson, Jr., "How Could Vietnam Happen?" in Manning and Janeway, eds., *Who We Are,* pp. 198–99.

5. Reedy, *Johnson,* p. 2.

6. Ronnie Dugger, *The Politician: The Life and Times of Lyndon Johnson* (New York, 1982), pp. 131–32, 140, 144. Dugger also has the Patman quote.

7. This is drawn from the discussion in William Appleman Williams, "Thoughts on Rereading Henry Adams," *Journal of American History,* LXXVIII (June 1981), pp. 7–15.

8. Thomson, "How Could Vietnam Happen?" p. 204.

9. Reedy, *Johnson,* p. 16.

10. United States Government, *Public Papers of the Presidents of the United States: Lyndon B. Johnson, 1964* (Washington, 1965), p. 1391.

11. Ibid., p. 928; United States Senate, Foreign Relations Committee, 90th Cong., 2d Sess., *The Gulf of Tonkin: The 1964 Incidents* (Washington, 1968); George W. Ball, *The Past Has Another Pattern: Memoirs* (New York, 1982), p. 379.

12. Bundy is quoted in George C. Herring, *America's Longest War: The U.S. and Vietnam, 1950–1975* (New York, 1979), p. 130.

13. Gareth Porter, *Vietnam: A History in Documents* (New York, 1981), pp. 292–93; Dugger, *The Politician,* p. 43.

14. Roger Hilsman, *To Move a Nation* (New York, 1967), p. 531.

15. Thomson, "How Could Vietnam Happen?" pp. 204–5.

16. The best account is Larry Berman, *Planning a Tragedy: The Americanization of the War in Vietnam* (New York, 1982), especially Chaps. 3 and 4.

17. "Bill Moyers Talks About the War and LBJ," in Manning and Janeway, eds., *Who We Are,* p. 262.

18. Interview of Chester Cooper, July 9, 1969, Oral History, Lyndon B. Johnson Library, Austin, Texas, pp. 22–23.

19. New York *Times,* Aug. 30, 1966, p. 3.

20. The text of the speech is in Ibid., July 13, 1966, p. 2.

21. Ibid., May 15, 1967, p. 1.

22. Ibid., Sept. 11, 1966, p. E2.

23. "Bill Moyers Talks About the War and LBJ," pp. 269–70.

24. United States Government, *Public Papers of the Presidents of the United States: Lyndon B. Johnson, 1966* (Washington, 1967), pp. 4, 1406–10.

25. Herring, "The War in Vietnam," p. 27.

26. New York *Times,* Feb. 13, 1966, F2:5–6; ibid., Nov. 26, 1967, p. F14.

27. Ibid., Feb. 16, 1966, p. 1.

28. "Notes of Meeting, Feb. 27, 1968," Meeting Notes File, Lyndon B. Johnson Library; Neil Sheehan, et al., eds., *The Pentagon Papers* (New York, 1971), pp. 592–94.

29. Interview of Benjamin Read, Oral History, Lyndon B. Johnson Library, pp. 29–30.

30. Peter Braestrup, *Big Story,* 2 vols. (Westview, Colo., 1977); also Westmoreland quote in Herring, "The War in Vietnam," p. 49: "It was like two boxers in a ring, one having the other on the ropes, close to a knockout, when the apparent winner's second inexplicably throws in a towel."

31. Herring, "The War in Vietnam," p. 52.

32. Porter, *Vietnam: A History in Documents,* pp. 354–57.

33. "Notes of the President's Tuesday Luncheon Meeting," Feb. 6, 1968, Meeting

Notes File, Lyndon B. Johnson Library; Sheehan, et al., eds., *The Pentagon Papers,* p. 612.

34. Interview of Harry McPherson, Oral History, Lyndon B. Johnson Library, Tape #5, pp. 16–17.

35. Henry Kissinger, *The White House Years* (Boston, 1979), p. 236.

36. Richard J. Whalen, *Catch the Falling Flag* (Boston, 1972), p. 137.

37. Seymour Hersh, *The Price of Power: Kissinger in the Nixon White House* (New York, 1983), pp. 50–51; Kissinger, *The White House Years,* p. 235.

38. Hersh, *The Price of Power,* pp. 77–79, 82, 119, 120–30.

39. Kissinger, *The White House Years,* pp. 292–93.

40. Washington *Post,* July 22, 1973, p. A22; Hersh, *The Price of Power,* p. 61.

41. Anthony Lewis' review of Theodore White's *Breach of Faith* in *The New Yorker,* Aug. 11, 1975, p. 81.

42. Robert Shaplen, "Letter from Indo-China," ibid., May 16, 1970, pp. 138–40.

43. Kissinger, *The White House Years,* pp. 266, 268–69.

44. Hersh, *The Price of Power,* pp. 582, 597.

45. Ibid., pp. 615–17.

46. Ibid., p. 629.

47. Henry Kissinger, *Years of Upheaval* (Boston, 1982), p. 338, also p. 302.

48. New York *Times,* Jan. 18, 1975, p. 3.

49. Richard Rovere, "Reflections . . . ," *The New Yorker,* Oct. 28, 1967, p. 90.

50. Thomson and Cooper to McGeorge Bundy, Oct. 22, 1965, Cooper Memos, NSC Name File, Lyndon B. Johnson Library.

51. New York *Times,* July 6, 1971, p. 14.

52. Lawrence S. Kaplan, "The Treaties of Paris and Washington, 1778 and 1949: Reflections on Entangling Alliances," in Ronald Hoffman and Peter J. Albert, eds., *Diplomacy and Revolution: The Franco-American Alliance of 1778* (Charlottesville, Va., 1981), p. 179.

53. Quoted, with an analysis, in Theodore Draper, *Present History* (New York, 1983), p. 239.

54. Various statements of this idea can be found in "Vietnam Retrospective," Smithsonian Institution, *The Wilson Center/Reports, Spring 1983* (Washington, 1983); also Harry G. Summers, Jr., *On Strategy: The Vietnam War in Context* (Carlisle Barracks, Pa., 1981).

55. Michael Herr, *Dispatches* (New York, 1977), p. 44.

56. A superb discussion is in John E. Mueller, "The Search for the 'Breaking Point' in Vietnam," *International Studies Quarterly,* XXIV (Dec. 1980), 497–531; Rusk is quoted on p. 497.

57. New York *Times,* May 6, 1966, p. 2.

SELECTED BIBLIOGRAPHY

Reference and General Works.   The first volume to consult for further reading (at least works published until 1981) should be the superb guide to U.S. diplomatic history, Richard Dean Burns, editor, *Guide to American Foreign Relations Since 1700* (1983). A more specialized and highly useful reference is Milton Leitenberg and Richard Dean Burns, *The Vietnam Conflict* (1973), especially good for periodical essays. There are several standard narrative volumes: George C. Herring, *America's Longest War: The U.S. and Vietnam, 1950–1975* (1979), a superb account with an excellent bibliography; Stanley Karnow, *Vietnam: A History* (1983), based on first-hand experiences as well as extensive research; George M. Kahin and John W. Lewis, *The United States in Vietnam* (1969), excellent and written by top authorities on Southeast Asia and China; and Chester Cooper, *Lost Crusade* (1970), a balanced, well-written insider's account. On the Vietnamese side, see several important volumes by Joseph Buttinger, especially, *A Dragon Defiant: A Short History of Vietnam (1972);* the seminal work by the noted journalist Bernard Fall (who died in Vietnam), particularly *The Two Vietnams: A Political and Military Analysis* (1964); Frances Fitzgerald's prize-winning *Fire in the Lake: The Vietnamese and the Americans in Vietnam* (1972); Jean Lacouture's standard biography, *Ho Chi Minh;* and Douglas Pike, *History of Vietnamese Communism* (1978).

Documents.   The obvious place to begin is the twelve books of the Department of Defense's original *The Pentagon Papers* (1971) covering 1945 to 1968; the one-volume paperback edition of those *Papers* edited by Neil Sheehan, et al., *The Pentagon Papers* (1971), published by the New York *Times;* U.S. Congress, Senate, Subcommittee on Building and Grounds, *The Pentagon Papers* (The Senator Gravel Edition) (1971) an easy-to-use paperback, four-volume set; The U.S. Department of State, *Foreign Relations of the United States* (1861–), now only up through 1954 but for those years a crucial source for the entire range of U.S. policy; and two volumes edited by Gareth Porter, *Vietnam: The Definitive Documentation of Human Decisions,* 2 vols. (1979), and *Vietnam: A History in Documents,* (1981), a paperback volume that is especially valuable for North Vietnamese material and Porter's introductions. For a superb analysis of the Pentagon documents, be certain to consult George M. Kahin, "The Pentagon Papers: A Critical Evaluation," *American Political Science Review,* LXIX (June 1975), pp. 675–84.

Origins–1945. The basic source is now Ronald H. Spector, *U.S. Army in Vietnam. Volume I: Advice and Support, The Early Years, 1941–1960* (1983), the official U.S. Army history, based on newly opened sources; Ellen Hammer, *The Struggle for Indochina, 1940–1955* (1966), older but still good; Russell H. Fifield, *Americans in Southeast Asia* (1973), a general overview; Christopher Thorne, *Allies of a Kind* (1978), superb on Franklin Roosevelt's dilemmas between 1941 and 1945; and Archimedes L. A. Patti, *Why Viet Nam?: Prelude to America's Albatross* (1980), a first-hand account by the OSS agent who dealt with Ho in 1945; the standard interpretation of Open Door diplomacy is William Appleman Williams, *The Tragedy of American Diplomacy* (1971).

1945–54. Dean Acheson's biography, *Present at the Creation* (1969), should be checked against Gaddis Smith, *Dean Acheson* (1970); and Robert Blum, *Drawing the Line* (1982), fine on 1949–50. In addition to Spector and Hammer listed above, see also Herbert Parmet, *Eisenhower and the American Crusades* (1972), to be used with Eisenhower's own *Mandate for Change, 1953–1956* (1963) and Robert F. Randle, *Geneva 1954* (1969). The classic account is Bernard B. Fall, *Hell in a Very Small Place* (1966) on Dienbienphu. Robert Divine, *Eisenhower and the Cold War* (1981) and David Carlton's most important *Anthony Eden* (1981) open up new perspectives. Key is William S. Borden, *The Pacific Alliance . . . 1947–1955* (1984).

1954–63. A place to start is Gary Wills' iconoclastic *Nixon Agonistes* (1970), provocative on both Eisenhower and Kennedy; the standard favorable biography is Arthur Schlesinger, *1000 Days: John F. Kennedy in the White House* (1965), but also see Henry Fairlie, *The Kennedy Promise* (1973); David Halberstam, *The Making of a Quagmire* (1964), a prize-winning corrective; Edward G. Lansdale, *In the*

Midst of Wars (1972), an American James Bond in the Vietnamese revolution; and Robert Scigliano, *South Vietnam* (1964), still useful. David Calleo, *Imperious America* (1982) may be the best framework yet constructed for understanding Kennedy (and the next four presidents as well). Warren Cohen, *Dean Rusk,* is the standard biography; and see also Richard Walton, *Cold War and Counterrevolution* (1972).

1964–75. Start with Lyndon Johnson's own *The Vantage Point* (1971), but check it closely against George W. Ball, *The Past Has Another Pattern: Memoirs* (1982), a dissenter; Ronnie Dugger's *The Politician: The Life and Times of Lyndon Johnson* (1982); Larry Berman, *Planning a Tragedy* (1982), on the critical 1965 decisions; James C. Thompson, *Rolling Thunder* (1980); Daniel Ellsberg, *Papers on the War* (1972); United States Senate, Committee on Foreign Relations, *The Gulf of Tonkin* (1968); and the George Herring essay in Robert Divine, ed., *Exploring the Johnson Years* (1981). The military view is in Dave Richard Palmer, *Summons of the Trumpet* (1978), important; General William C. Westmoreland's angry *A Soldier Reports* (1976); Raphael Littauer and Norman Uphoff, eds., *The Air War in Indochina* (1972); and the most influential book defending the U.S. conduct of the war, Guenter Lewy, *America in Vietnam* (1978). On North Vietnam, in addition to Lacouture see Jon M. Van Dyke, *North Vietnam's Strategy for Survival* (1972) and documents from the Porter volumes mentioned above. On Nixon's policies, the standard defenses are in Richard Nixon, *RN: Memoirs of Richard Nixon* (1978); Henry Kissinger's *The White House Years* (1979), and *Years of Upheaval* (1982); but these can now be closely checked against Seymour Hersh's astonishing analysis of Kissinger, *The Price of Power* (1983); William Shawcross, *Sideshow: Kissinger, Nixon and the Destruction of Cambodia* (1979); Paul Kattenburg, *The Vietnam Trauma in American Foreign Policy, 1945–1975* (1980), by an old Vietnam hand; Allan E. Goodman, *The Lost Peace* (1978); Gareth Porter's superb analysis of the 1973 pact, *A Peace Denied* (1975); Frank Snepp, *Decent Interval: An Insider's Account of Saigon's Indecent End* (1977); and Jonathan Schell's linking of Vietnam and Watergate and the fall of the Imperial Presidency, *The Time of Illusion* (1975).

For the post-1975 debate, see especially *Vietnam Reconsidered,* edited by Harrison E. Salisbury (1984), 67 short, fine essays representing many points of view; Harry G. Summers, Jr., *On Strategy* (1981), a seminal volume greatly influencing later U.S. military and political thinking about the war; Anthony Lake, ed., *The Legacy of Vietnam* (1976); Myra MacPherson, *Long Time Passing: Vietnam and the Haunted Generation* (1984), based on some five hundred interviews of people who endured the war in Vietnam and the United States; and Ole Holsti and James Roseneau, *American Leadership in World Affairs: Vietnam and the Breakdown of Consensus* (1984). The debate has been shaped by first-hand and sometimes fictional accounts. Two of the best are Michael Herr, *Dispatches* (1977), a journalist's supercharged memoir; and Frederick Downs, *The Killing Zone* (1978), by a former infantryman.

INDEX

and economy of South Vietnam, 142–43

elimination of, 144, 145, 205–7

and Franco-Japanese, 35

installed as president, 140–41, 185

Johnson on, 193, 194, 241

and Lodge, 207–8

and Nixon, 142

Rusk on, 202, 203

U.S. support of, 142–43, 183, 184, 185

and Viet Cong strength in the countryside, 305

Dienbienphu battle, 135, 136–37, 152

Dieu, Hoang, 18

Dillon, Douglas, 271, 272

Dinh, Truong, 15, 16

DMZ, 269, 308, 311

Dollar Gap, 47, 49, 51

"Domino theory," 134, 156–57, 231

Don, Tran Van, 144, 205

Dong, Pham Van, 244–45

Drake, Francis, 3

Draper, William H., Jr., 79

DRV (Democratic Republic of Vietnam), 93, 94, 96, 197–98, 245

Dugger, Ronnie, 216

Dulles, John Foster

on British commitment, 157–59

on Diem, 141

and A. Eden, 159–60, 182

and Eisenhower, 132–34, 165–66

on French in Indochina, 161–63

and Geneva conference, 137–39

on problems facing United States in foreign relations, 59

on SEATO, 165–66, 172–74, 180–82

on Soviet "program," 131–32

on Vietnam (1955), 178–79

on Vietnamese elections, 163–65, 185–86

warning to China, 150–51

Dung, Van Tien, 36

Dzu (General), 307

E

EDC (European Defense Community), 136

Eden, Anthony

and Dulles, 159–60, 182

Plan on elections, 164

Eden Plan, 164

Eisenhower, Dwight D.

appeal to Churchill, 139, 153–55

and crisis at Dienbienphu, 136

and "domino theory," 134, 156–57, 231

and Dulles on Indochina, 132–34

and Dulles on SEATO, 165–66

on Ho Chi Minh, 96

on independence of Laos, 186–88